MATHEMATICS 901
VARIABLES AND NUMBERS

CONTENTS

I. **EXPRESSIONS** 2

Variables 2

Number Skills 12

The Distributive Property 16

II. **SIGNED NUMBERS** 28

Definition 28

Addition 31

Subtraction 35

Multiplication 40

Division 42

Author: **Robert L. Zenor, M.A., M.S.**

Editor: Richard W. Wheeler, M.A.Ed.

Consulting Editor: Rudolph Moore, Ph.D.

Revision Editor: Alan Christopherson, M.S.

Alpha Omega Publications®

804 N. 2nd Ave. E., Rock Rapids, IA 51246-1759
© MCMXCVI by Alpha Omega Publications, Inc.   All rights reserved.
LIFEPAC is a registered trademark of Alpha Omega Publications, Inc.

VARIABLES AND NUMBERS

This LIFEPAC® is your introduction to a system of mathematics unlike the arithmetic you learned in the elementary grades. In arithmetic you were taught the rules that govern the four operations of the system—addition, subtraction, multiplication, and division; and you were told which operation to perform on a given set of numbers to get the answer. Here are typical examples of exercises in arithmetic: $4 + 3 = 7$, $7 - 2 = 5$, $13 \times 4 = 52$, $12 \div 3 = 4$.

Algebra, like geometry, trigonometry, and calculus, is another of several mathematical *systems*. Like arithmetic, it has its own operating rules. Unlike arithmetic, algebra often requires you to find the value of one of the numbers—the *unknown*—in an exercise. Sometimes, you will have to decide for yourself what operation to use, and sometimes several operations will be used. Toward the end of this LIFEPAC, you will learn how to apply the arithmetic operations to numbers less than zero—the negative numbers.

OBJECTIVES

Read these objectives. The objectives tell you what you will be able to do when you have successfully completed this LIFEPAC.

When you have finished this LIFEPAC, you should be able to:

1. Identify bases, exponents, constants, variables, numerical coefficients, terms, sums, and products.

2. Simplify algebraic expressions when possible.

3. Evaluate algebraic expressions.

4. Translate algebraic expressions.

5. Perform operations with signed numbers.

Survey this LIFEPAC. Ask yourself some questions about this study. Write your questions here.

_____

_____

_____

_____

_____

_____

_____

I. EXPRESSIONS

OBJECTIVES

When you have completed this section, you should be able to:

1. Identify bases, exponents, constants, variables, numerical coefficients, terms, sums, and products.
2. Simplify algebraic expressions when possible.
3. Evaluate algebraic expressions.
4. Translate algebraic expressions.

The expression 8 + 3 is a *numerical expression*: *numerical* because it consists of numbers; *expression* because it expresses an operation, in this case addition.

In algebra letters of the alphabet are used to represent numbers. These letters are referred to either as *unknowns* or as *variables*. An expression that contains a variable, such as $n + 3$, is an *algebraic expression*. Learning to handle algebraic expressions is the first step in this new system of mathematics. You will have an opportunity in this section to review and practice basic number skills and then to apply those skills in simplifying expressions by the distributive property.

• • • • • • **VARIABLES** •

If expressions, whether numerical or algebraic, imply addition, they are called *sums*; if they imply subtraction, they are called *differences*; if multiplication, *products*; and if division, *quotients*. These four operations will now be used in evaluating expressions.

SUMS AND DIFFERENCES

In the expression $n + 3$, n and 3 are *addends*. Since we have inserted the plus sign between the letter n and the number 3, the expression is called an *indicated sum*. Its value cannot be determined until we know the value of n.

The expression $n - 3$ means that 3 is to be subtracted from n. Likewise, $3 - n$ means that n is to be subtracted from 3. $n - 3$ is called an *indicated difference*. The expressions $n - 3$ and $3 - n$ are not necessarily equal, because subtraction is an *ordered* operation. We see that $8 - 3$ cannot be $3 - 8$. The *differences* are different.

In an algebraic expression, the letter that represents a number is called a *variable*. In the expression $n + 8$, n is the variable and 8 is the *constant*.

Here are some other models of sums and differences.

$5 - y$ $\qquad$ $x + 6$ $\qquad$ $A + 10$ $\qquad$ $A + B$ $\qquad$ $x + y$ $\qquad$ $x - y$

 Simplify. Work from left to right and perform any operation in parentheses first.

Model: $9 + 12 - 3 = 21 - 3 = 18$

$(2 + 5) - 4 = 7 - 4 = 3$

1.1	$9 + 6$	_____	1.2	$8 + 13$	_____
1.3	$5 + 22$	_____	1.4	$17 + 16$	_____
1.5	$32 + 43$	_____	1.6	$9 + 5 + 4$	_____
1.7	$3 + 8 + 4$	_____	1.8	$10 + 15 + 4$	_____
1.9	$17 + 18 + 5$	_____	1.10	$14 + 13 + 7$	_____
1.11	$10 - 6 + 8$	_____	1.12	$15 - 4 + 1$	_____
1.13	$17 - 3 - 4$	_____	1.14	$13 - 8 + 10$	_____
1.15	$28 + 4 - 10$	_____	1.16	$5 + (6 - 4)$	_____
1.17	$10 + (3 - 2)$	_____	1.18	$29 - (7 + 2)$	_____
1.19	$(13 + 2) - 8$	_____	1.20	$(50 + 5) - 11$	_____

 Write the meaning of each of the following expressions.

Model: $x + 10$ $\qquad$ The sum of some number x and 10.

1.21 $n + 5$ _____

1.22 $n - 5$ _____

1.23 $x + 8$ _____

1.24 $x - 8$ _____

3

1.25 $8 - x$ _____

1.26 $5 - y$ _____

1.27 $x + (5 + 7)$ _____

1.28 $x - (8 + 2)$ _____

1.29 $x + (8 - 2)$ _____

1.30 $x + x$ _____

 Identify the variable and constant in each of the following expressions and tell if it is a sum, a difference, or neither.

		Variable	Constant	Operation
Model:	$x - 8$	a. __x__	b. __8__	c. difference
1.31	$6 + y$	a._____	b._____	c._____
1.32	$N - 8$	a._____	b._____	c._____
1.33	A	a._____	b._____	c._____
1.34	$B - 3$	a._____	b._____	c._____
1.35	$C + 10 + 12$	a._____	b._____	c._____

Write an algebraic expression of each of the following statements.

1.36   The sum of n and 6.   _____

1.37   The difference of 8 and n.   _____

1.38   The difference of n and 10.   _____

1.39   The sum of n and itself.   _____

1.40   The sum of n and the sum of 8 and 6.   _____

Sums like $8 + 3$ may be written as $3 + 8$. The sum 11 is the same in either case. The ability to interchange addends is called the *commutative property* of addition.

Also, sums like $4 + 2 + 7$ may be obtained from $(4 + 2) + 7$ or from $4 + (2 + 7)$. The sum 13 is the same in either case. The ability to change the grouping of the addends is called the *associative property* of addition. These two properties can be used to simplify expressions.

Model: Simplify $3 + x + 7$.

$$3 + x + 7 = x + 3 + 7$$
$$= x + (3 + 7)$$
$$= x + 10$$

Simplify.

1.41 $x + 7 + 8$ 1.42 $7 + x + 3$

_____   _____

1.43 $9 + 7 + n$ 1.44 $x + 15 - 4$

_____   _____

1.45 $(20 + 2) + r$ 1.46 $8 + r - 4$

_____   _____

1.47 $15 + x + 10 - 4$ 1.48 $(15 - 10) + n$

_____   _____

1.49 $5 + n + (15 - 2)$ 1.50 $1.5 + 3.82$

_____   _____

1.51 $17.25 + 3.9$ 1.52 $19.62 + 8.33 + 5.7$

_____   _____

1.53 $1.005 + 3.54$ 1.54 $73.05 + 8.006$

_____   _____

1.55 $15.63 + 7.956 + 82.735$ 1.56 $25.63 - 8.23$

_____   _____

1.57 $73.543 - 23.683$ 1.58 $28.543 - 14.26 - 3.65$

_____   _____

1.59 $x + 6.2 + 8.5$ 1.60 $7.5 + n + 9.63$

_____   _____

5

1.61	$81.56 + n - 2.55$		1.62	$7.95 - 3.86 + N$
	_____			_____
1.63	$22.6 + x - 11.3 + 1.2$		1.64	$77.65 - 15.56 + x + 1.2$
	_____			_____

PRODUCTS

The numerical expression $7 + 7$ can be renamed several ways, one of which is 2 times 7. We wish to omit the (x) as a times sign. In algebra we will use the dot, $2 \bullet 7$, or the parentheses, $(2)(7)$. Therefore, the product of 6 and 9 will be written as $6 \bullet 9$ or $(6)(9)$. Likewise, if one of the *factors is literal* — the n in 7 times n — we will write the product as $7n$. The dot or parentheses are not to be used when writing literal products.

Models: $6 \bullet 4$, $6x$, $5n$, $15r$, $r17$, $A15$

Product expressions such as $r \bullet 17$ and $A \bullet 15$ are to be written with the constant preceding the variable, $17r$ and $15A$. The constant preceding the variable in a product is called a *numerical coefficient*.

Find the product of each of the following expressions.

1.65	$6 \bullet 5$	_____	1.66	$8 \bullet 4$	_____
1.67	$7 \bullet 6$	_____	1.68	$9 \bullet 8$	_____
1.69	$4 \bullet 10$	_____	1.70	$(5)(10)$	_____
1.71	$(15)(12)$	_____	1.72	$(3)(50)$	_____
1.73	$(40)(5)$	_____	1.74	$(70)(20)$	_____
1.75	$6(15)$	_____	1.76	$7(22)$	_____
1.77	$8(15)$	_____	1.78	$16(30)$	_____
1.79	$10(23)$	_____	1.80	$5 \bullet 7 \bullet 8$	_____
1.81	$12 \bullet 5 \bullet 8$	_____	1.82	$3(4)(5)$	_____
1.83	$6(2)(5)$	_____	1.84	$15(2)(8)$	_____

6

Name the numerical coefficient of each of the following expressions.

1.85 $6x$ _____   1.86 $5n$ _____

1.87 $22r$ _____   1.88 $16p$ _____

1.89 $13q$ _____   1.90 $8 \bullet 2N$ _____

1.91 $3 \bullet 2x$ _____   1.92 $7.2r$ _____

1.93 $9(14)P$ _____   1.94 $2(3)(6)q$ _____

In the operation $5 \bullet 7$, the product is the same if the expression is changed to $7 \bullet 5$. That is, $5 \bullet 7 = 7 \bullet 5$. The ability to interchange factors is called the *commutative property* of multiplication. Also, the *associative property* of multiplication allows you to change the grouping of the factors.

These two properties can be used to simplify expressions. When more than one variable is used, the letters are to be written in alphabetical order.

Model 1:   Rewrite $B \bullet 5 \bullet A$
$$\begin{aligned} B \bullet 5 \bullet A &= 5 \bullet B \bullet A \\ &= 5 \bullet (B \bullet A) \\ &= 5 \bullet (A \bullet B) \\ &= 5AB \end{aligned}$$

Model 2:   Rewrite $7 \bullet K \bullet 5 \bullet H$

$7 \bullet K \bullet 5 \bullet H$ may be rewritten as $(7 \bullet 5)(H \bullet K)$ using the commutative and associative properties; thus, the simplified form is $35HK$.

Simplify. Remember: When more than one variable is used, the letters are to be written in alphabetical order. Also, no dots are to be shown in the final answers.

1.95 $6 \bullet x \bullet 7$ _____   1.96 $5 \bullet P \bullet 2$ _____

1.97 $3 \bullet S \bullet R$ _____   1.98 $8 \bullet x \bullet 2 \bullet y$ _____

1.99 $a \bullet c \bullet 2 \bullet 5$ _____   1.100 $C \bullet 5 \bullet 2 \bullet A$ _____

1.101 $4 \bullet Q \bullet 2 \bullet P$ _____   1.102 $10 \bullet K \bullet 2$ _____

7

Write the meaning of each of the following expressions.

Model: $4A$ The product of 4 and some number.

Model: $10N - 2$ The difference between ten times some number and 2.

1.103 $7n$ _____

1.104 $6P$ _____

1.105 $8N + 5$ _____

1.106 $7 + 2x$ _____

1.107 $12x - 10$ _____

1.108 $52 - 25x$ _____

EXPONENTS

The numerical expression 5 times 5 may be written as 5^2. The 2 is called an exponent. The exponent is a counter for the number of repeated factors. Thus $6 \bullet 6 = 6^2$ and $8 \bullet 8 \bullet 8 = 8^3$.

In the case of literal expressions, we have $x \bullet x = x^2$ and $A \bullet A \bullet A = A^3$. Conversely, x^3 means $x \bullet x \bullet x$, or three factors of x.

Models:
$$x^2 = x \bullet x \qquad P^2 = P \bullet P \qquad (ab)^2 = ab \bullet ab$$
$$x^3 = x \bullet x \bullet x \qquad P^3 = P \bullet P \bullet P \qquad (ab)^3 = ab \bullet ab \bullet ab$$
$$x^4 = x \bullet x \bullet x \bullet x \qquad P^4 = P \bullet P \bullet P \bullet P \qquad (ab)^4 = ab \bullet ab \bullet ab \bullet ab$$

x^2 is read, "The square of x" or "x squared."
x^3 is read, "The cube of x" or "x cubed."
x^4 is read, "The fourth power of x" or "x to the fourth."

x^n is an *indicated power*. x is called the base, and n is the *exponent* of the base.

In each case, identify the base and the exponent of the indicated power.

Model: 3^8 base = __3__   exponent = __8__

		Base	Exponent			Base	Exponent
1.109	2^6	_____	_____	1.110	3^9	_____	_____
1.111	5^{10}	_____	_____	1.112	8^3	_____	_____
1.113	x^6	_____	_____	1.114	y^5	_____	_____
1.115	7^n	_____	_____	1.116	9^P	_____	_____
1.117	15^{x+1}	_____	_____	1.118	10^{3x-1}	_____	_____

▶▶▷ **Write each of the following expressions in product form.**

Model: $A^3 = A \bullet A \bullet A$

1.119	6^3	= _____	1.120	7^4	= _____
1.121	x^2	= _____	1.122	y^5	= _____
1.123	3^3	= _____	1.124	1^4	= _____
1.125	2^5	= _____	1.125	$(\frac{1}{2})^3$	= _____
1.127	$(2.5)^2$	= _____	1.128	$(.01)^4$	= _____

 Simplify each of the following expressions.

Model: $3^2 = 3 \bullet 3 = 9$

1.129	2^3	_____	1.130	4^2	_____
1.131	5^3	_____	1.132	3^5	_____
1.133	10^3	_____	1.134	10^4	_____
1.135	17^2	_____	1.136	20^2	_____
1.137	7^3	_____			

✳✳✳ Circle the larger number in each pair.

Model: 1^2, $\boxed{2^2}$ since $1^2 = 1 \cdot 1 = 1$ and $2^2 = 2 \cdot 2 = 4$

1.138 2^5 or 5^2 1.139 5^2 or 5^3

1.140 3^2 or 2^3 1.141 3^3 or 2^5

1.142 $(\frac{1}{2})^3$ or $(\frac{1}{3})^2$ 1.143 $(.2)^2$ or $(.3)^2$

▲▲▸ Write the following products in exponential form.

Model: $A \bullet A \bullet A = A^3$

1.144 $x \bullet x \bullet x \bullet x$ _____   1.145 $B \bullet B \bullet B \bullet B \bullet B$ _____

1.146 $P \bullet P$ _____   1.147 $N \bullet N \bullet N$ _____

1.148 $A \bullet B \bullet A \bullet B$ _____   1.149 $C \bullet d \bullet C \bullet d \bullet C$ _____

1.150 $xyyx$ _____   1.151 $PPQQQ$ _____

1.152 $abcabcabc$ _____   1.153 $xyzxyz$ _____

EVALUATING EXPRESSIONS

Expressions containing variables can be *evaluated* when numerical values are given to the variables.

Model: In the expression $A + 4$
             If $A = 10$, then $10 + 4 = 14$.
             If $A = 75$, then $75 + 4 = 79$.

To evaluate expressions involving more than one operation, you are to use the following *order of operations*: working left-to-right, do any powers first, then do any multiplications or divisions, and finally do any additions or subtractions.

Model 1:   Evaluate $5x - 10$ for $x = 30$

Solution: Replace x with 30 and evaluate.

	$5x - 10$
Replace x with 30	$5 \bullet 30 - 10$
Multiply	$150 - 10$
Subtract	140

Model 2: Evaluate $A^2 + 2A + 5$ for $A = 4$.

Solution: $A^2 + 2A + 5$
$4^2 + 2 \cdot 4 + 5$
$16 + 8 + 5$
$24 + 5$
29

Evaluate.

1.154 $a + 6$ for $a = 10$ _____

1.155 $16 - B$ for $B = 2$ _____

1.156 B^2 for $B = 9$ _____

1.157 A^2 for $A = 2.3$ _____

1.158 $x^2 + 2$ for $x = 5.1$ _____

Evaluate for $a = 2$, $b = 3$, **and** $c = 4$.

1.159 $5a$ _____

1.160 $2b$ _____

1.161 $4c$ _____

1.162 a^2 _____

1.163 ab _____

1.164 $a + b$ _____

1.165 $a + b + c$ _____

1.166 $ab + c$ _____

1.167 $a + bc$ _____

1.168 abc _____

1.169 a^2b _____

1.170 $a^2 b^2 c^2$ _____

1.171 $2a - b$ _____

1.172 $c - a$ _____

1.173 $b - a$ _____

1.174 $3a^2$ _____

1.175 $3ab$ _____

1.176 $4ab^2$ _____

1.177 $(a + b)^2$ _____

1.178 $(b + c)^3$ _____

1.179 $a^2b^2 + b^2c^2$ _____

1.180 $a + b^2$ _____

1.181 $4(a + b)$ _____

1.182 $3(a + b)^2$ _____

1.183 $(b + c)^2$ _____

1.184 $(a + b + c)^2$ _____

1.185 $(b - a)^2$ _____

1.186 $3a^2 + 4b^2$ _____

1.187 $5a^3 + 2b$ _____

1.188 $3(a + b + c)^2$ _____

Write the algebraic expression for each of the following sentences. Use any letters you wish.

1.189   Seven added to some number.   _____

1.190   The square of some number.   _____

1.191   Two times the cube of some number.   _____

1.192   The difference between the square of a number and 10.   _____

1.193   The difference between the squares of two numbers.   _____

Write in words the meaning of each expression.

1.194 x^3 _____

1.195 $x^2 + 2$ _____

1.196 $3x^2 - 4$ _____

1.197 $A^2 - B^2$ _____

1.198 $3A + 4B^2$ _____

================================ **NUMBER SKILLS** ================================

Success with algebra is directly related to your understanding of basic skills in arithmetic. Included in this section is practice in adding, subtracting, multiplying, and dividing. Practice with fractions and percents is also included.

INTEGERS AND DECIMALS

Addition, subtraction, multiplication, and division of integers and decimals are building-blocks skills for working with fractions and percents.

Add.

1.199	65 84	1.200	73 58	1.201	96 82 45	1.202	57 29 78

1.203	65 43 92 75	1.204	623 532 481	1.205	962 853 451	1.206	7.26 5.38 62.73

1.207   5.06   1.208   52.631
          12.55   7.05
           1.075   9.006

▶▶▶ **Subtract**.

1.209	72 58	1.210	59 28	1.211	73 48	1.212	92 79
1.213	523 99	1.214	6521 438	1.215	5431 3413	1.216	5.83 2.96
1.217	93.056 43.685	1.218	1.2306 0.9615				

▦▣▫ **Multiply. Show your work.**

1.219	633 4	1.220	586 28	1.221	7.23 .02	1.222	52.63 1.54
1.223	0.056 .73	1.224	929 29	1.225	5263 251	1.226	4.356 27.3
1.227	66.28 5.84	1.228	10.05 1.06				

✳✴✴ **Divide. Show your work.**

1.229	$\frac{659}{8}$	1.230	$\frac{732}{2}$	1.231	$\frac{564}{4}$	1.232	$\frac{121}{11}$
1.233	$\frac{144}{6}$	1.234	$8\overline{)2563}$	1.235	$9\overline{)28.54}$	1.236	$7\overline{)5280}$
1.237	$63\overline{)596}$	1.238	$85\overline{)726.5}$	1.239	$9.2\overline{)52.063}$		

FRACTIONS

Remember that fractions must have common denominators to be added or subtracted. Products of fractions are found by multiplying numerator by numerator and denominator by denominator. Quotients of fractions are found by using the reciprocal of the divisor and then multiplying. All results are to be reduced to lowest terms.

Models:

$$\frac{1}{2} + \frac{1}{3} = \frac{3}{6} + \frac{2}{6} = \frac{5}{6}$$

$$\frac{3}{5} \cdot \frac{2}{6} = \frac{6}{30} = \frac{1}{5}$$

$$3\frac{1}{4} - 2\frac{1}{5} = 3\frac{5}{20} - 2\frac{4}{20} = 1\frac{1}{20}$$

$$2\frac{1}{2} \div 1\frac{3}{7} = \frac{5}{2} \div \frac{10}{7} = \frac{5}{2} \cdot \frac{7}{10} = \frac{35}{20} = \frac{7}{4} \text{ or } 1\frac{3}{4}$$

 Add. Show your work.

1.240 $\quad \frac{2}{3} + \frac{3}{8} =$

1.241 $\quad \frac{5}{4} + \frac{7}{9} =$

1.242 $\quad \frac{15}{7} + \frac{2}{3} + \frac{1}{6} =$

1.243 $\quad 1\frac{2}{3} + 5\frac{3}{8} =$

1.244 $\quad 10\frac{3}{7} + 19\frac{5}{9} =$

1.245 $\quad 1\frac{1}{2} + 5\frac{3}{4} =$

 Subtract. Show your work.

1.246 $\quad \frac{6}{11} - \frac{4}{11} =$

1.247 $\quad \frac{9}{32} - \frac{1}{16} =$

1.248 $\quad \frac{13}{16} - \frac{3}{8} =$

1.249 $\quad 5\frac{1}{6} - 2\frac{2}{3} =$

2.250 $\quad 7\frac{9}{16} - 5\frac{1}{5} =$

1.251 $\quad 2\frac{5}{8} - 1\frac{3}{8} =$

 Multiply. Show your work.

1.252 $\quad \frac{2}{3} \cdot \frac{5}{8} =$

1.253 $\quad \frac{5}{17} \cdot \frac{3}{8} =$

1.254 $\quad \frac{4}{11} \cdot \frac{10}{8} =$

1.255 $\quad 7\frac{1}{8} \cdot 5\frac{2}{3} =$

1.256 $\quad 15\frac{4}{9} \cdot 3\frac{1}{5} =$

 Divide. Show your work.

1.257 $\quad \frac{2}{3} \div \frac{4}{9} =$

1.258 $\quad \frac{1}{3} \div \frac{3}{8} =$

14

1.259 $\frac{4}{11} \div \frac{4}{9} =$ 1.260 $8\frac{1}{2} \div 2\frac{1}{4} =$

PERCENT

Skills with percent include converting percents to decimals, decimals to percents, and fractions to percent. To change percents to decimals, divide the percent by 100; to change decimals to percent, multiply the decimal by 100 and include the % sign. To change fractions to percent, multiply the fraction by 100, reduce the result, and include the % sign.

Models: Change 34% to a decimal number.
$34\% = 34 \div 100 = 0.34$

Change 0.19 to a percent.
$0.19 = 0.19 \cdot 100\% = 19\%$

Change $\frac{3}{4}$ to a percent.

$\frac{3}{4} = \frac{3}{4} \cdot 100\% = \frac{300}{4}\% = 75\%$

 Change each percent to a decimal.

1.261   16%   _____   1.262   22%   _____

1.263   0.5%   _____   1.264   302%   _____

1.265   1.6%   _____

 Change each decimal number to a percent.

1.266   0.15   _____   1.267   0.06   _____

1.268   1.05   _____   1.269   32   _____

1.270   0.0075   _____

 Change each fraction to a percent. Show your work.

1.271 $\frac{1}{2}$ _____   1.272 $\frac{3}{8}$ _____

1.273 $\frac{5}{20}$ _____   1.274 $\frac{4}{12}$ _____

1.275 $\frac{15}{50}$ _____

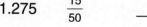 **Write the required quantities. Show your work.**

1.276   15% of 20   _____   1.277   13% of 50   _____

1.278	72% of 653	_____		1.279	35% of 70	_____
1.280	30 is what % of 60	_____		1.281	66 is what % of 150	_____
1.282	70 is 30% of what number	_____		1.283	90 is 50% of what number	_____

THE DISTRIBUTIVE PROPERTY

Algebraic expressions often use parentheses to group a sum or difference of two or more numbers. The *distributive property* is the rule that may be used to evaluate the product of a number and an expression in parentheses.

NUMBERS

The expression 7(4 + 5) means to multiply seven by the sum of 4 and 5. If we add the 4 and 5 first we have

$$7(4 + 5) = 7(9) = 63.$$

However, we may multiply another way:

$$7(4 + 5) = 7 \bullet 4 + 7 \bullet 5$$
$$= 28 + 35$$
$$= 63$$

Both methods lead to the same result. The latter method applies the *distributive property*.

Another model of the distributive property is

$$8(5 + 6) = 8 \bullet 5 + 8 \bullet 6$$
$$= 40 + 48$$
$$= 88$$

To verify that this method of multiplication is correct, add the 5 and 6 first, then multiply:

$$8(5 + 6) = 8(11) = 88.$$

The distributive property stated formally is

For numbers $a, b, c,$
$a(b + c) = ab + ac$ and $a(b - c) = ab - ac.$

16

Models:

$$6(3 + 2) = 6 \cdot 3 + 6 \cdot 2$$
$$= 18 + 12$$
$$= 30$$

$$7(5 - 2) = 7 \cdot 5 - 7 \cdot 2$$
$$= 35 - 14$$
$$= 21$$

$$3(20 + 2) = 3 \cdot 20 + 3 \cdot 2$$
$$= 60 + 6$$
$$= 66$$

$$12(100 - 1) = 12 \cdot 100 - 12 \cdot 1$$
$$= 1200 - 12$$
$$= 1188$$

 Use the distributive property and simplify. Show your work as in the preceding models.

1.284 $8(4 + 3)$ 1.285 $9(8 + 2)$ 1.286 $15(5 + 2)$

_____   _____   _____

1.287 $17(4 + 1)$ 1.288 $13(5 + 4)$ 1.289 $20(2 + 3)$

_____   _____   _____

1.290 $6.5(5 + 1)$ 1.291 $8.6(3.2 + 4.6)$ 1.292 $7(2 + 3 + 4)$

_____   _____   _____

1.293 $5(5 + 4 + 1)$ 1.294 $6(3 + 2 + 5)$ 1.295 $10(1 + 3 + 5)$

_____   _____   _____

$x + y$ is called an *indicated sum*, $x \cdot y$ is called an *indicated product*, and $x - y$ is called an *indicated difference*.

17

Models: Indicated sums

Indicated differences

$6 + 8$
$m + 2$
$d + (6 - 3)$
$(7 + m) + n$
$4 \cdot 5 + 4 \cdot 7$

$5 - 3$
$2 - s$
$y - (4 + 3)$
$5m - 4n$
$3 \cdot 7 - 3 \cdot 2$

Indicated products

$6 \cdot 8$
$2j$
$r(6 + 5)$
$3p \cdot 4q$
$4(5 + 7)$

Since the distributive property states that $a(b + c) = ab + ac$ and $a(b - c) = ab - ac$, we may also write $ab + ac = a(b + c)$ and $ab - ac = a(b - c)$.

$ab + ac$ is an indicated sum, and $a(b + c)$ an indicated product.

$ab - ac$ is an indicated difference, and $a(b - c)$ is an indicated product.

Model: Change $6 \cdot 2 + 6 \cdot 5$ to an indicated product.

Solution: Since $a \cdot b + a \cdot c = a(b + c)$
and in our problem $a = 6$, $b = 2$, and
$c = 5$, we have $6 \cdot 2 + 6 \cdot 5 = 6(2 + 5)$.

This is an example of using the distributive
property to change an indicated sum to
an indicated product.

Change the following indicated sums to indicated products as in the preceding model. (Do not find the answer.)

1.296	$5 \cdot 20 + 5 \cdot 3$	1.297	$8 \cdot 16 + 8 \cdot 4$	1.298	$9 \cdot 7 + 9 \cdot 8$
	_____		_____		_____
1.299	$6 \cdot 5 + 6 \cdot 8$	1.300	$15 \cdot 4 + 15 \cdot 10$	1.301	$9 \cdot 10 + 9 \cdot 5$
	_____		_____		_____
1.302	$5 \cdot 8 + 9 \cdot 5$	1.303	$4 \cdot 7 + 8 \cdot 7$	1.304	$3 \cdot 10 + 20 \cdot 3$
	_____		_____		_____

One numerical application of the distributive property is simplifying multiplication. Suppose you want to multiply 8 times 105. Using the distributive property:

$$8 \cdot 105 = 8(100 + 5) = 800 + 40 = 840$$

Model: $9 \cdot 99$
    Step 1   Think $99 = 100 - 1$
    Step 2   So $9 \cdot 99 = 9(100 - 1)$
    Step 3 $= 900 - 9$
    Step 4   Therefore, 891 is the product of $9 \cdot 99$.

■▯▪ Use the distributive property to perform the following multiplications.

1.305 $5 \cdot 23$ $= 5(20 + 3)$ $=$ __100__ $+$ __15__ $=$ _____

1.306 $4 \cdot 21$ $= 4(20 + 1)$ $=$ a._____ $+$ b._____ $=$ c._____

1.307 $7 \cdot 15$ $= 7(10 + 5)$ $=$ a._____ $+$ b._____ $=$ c._____

1.308 $6 \cdot 17$ $=$ a._____ $=$ b._____ $=$ c._____

1.309 $8 \cdot 14$ $=$ a._____ $=$ b._____ $=$ c._____

1.310 $8 \cdot 15$ $=$ a._____ $=$ b._____ $=$ c._____

1.311 $6 \cdot 12$ $=$ a._____ $=$ b._____ $=$ c._____

1.312 $9 \cdot 98$ $= 9(100 - 2)$ $=$ __900 - 18__ $=$ _____

1.313 $9 \cdot 9$ $= 9(10 - 1)$ $=$ a._____ $=$ b._____

1.314 $8 \cdot 97$ $=$ a._____ $=$ b._____ $=$ c._____

1.315 $9 \cdot 102$ $=$ a._____ $=$ b._____ $=$ c._____

1.316 $7 \cdot 19$ $=$ a._____ $=$ b._____ $=$ c._____

1.317 $5 \cdot 29$ $=$ a._____ $=$ b._____ $=$ c._____

1.318 $12 \cdot 102$ $=$ a._____ $=$ b._____ $=$ c._____

VARIABLES

Most applications of the distributive property involve one or more variables.

Models: Products Sums or Differences

$$6(x + 2) = 6x + 12$$
$$x(x + 4) = x^2 + 4x$$
$$A(B + C) = AB + AC$$
$$(x + 3)5 = 5x + 15$$
$$(R + 4)R = R^2 + 4R$$
$$5(x - 5) = 5x - 25$$
$$x(x - 5) = x^2 - 5x$$
$$A(B - C) = AB - AC$$
$$(A - 3)4 = 4A - 12$$
$$(N - 5)N = N^2 - 5N$$

Change the following products to sums or differences.

Models: $5(x + 3) = 5 \bullet x + 5 \bullet 3 = 5x + 15$
$2m(m - 4) = 2m \bullet m - 2m \bullet 4 = 2m^2 - 8m$

1.319 $6(x + 4)$ = _____

1.320 $7(A - 6)$ = _____

1.321 $12(A - B)$ = _____

1.322 $20(A + B)$ = _____

1.323 $10(N + 3)$ = _____

1.324 $(x + 2)3$ = _____

1.325 $(x - 6)5$ = _____

1.326 $N(N - 7)$ = _____

1.327 $p(3 + p)$ = _____

1.328 $p(5 - p)$ = _____

1.329 $x(4 - x)$ = _____

1.330 $5(x^2 + 6)$ = _____

1.331 $7(x^2 + 6x)$ = _____

1.332 $12(2x + 1)$ = _____

1.333 $3(5x - 4)$ = _____

1.334 $4(x^2 + x + 1)$ = _____

1.335 $5(N^2 + 2N - 1)$ = _____

1.336 $6(A^2 - A - 4)$ = _____

1.337 $8(p^2 + 3p - 4)$ = _____

1.338 $16(4 - 2K + k^2)$ = _____

1.339 $9(y^2 + 5y + 6)$ = _____

1.340 $x(x^2 + 2x)$ = _____

1.341 $p(p^2 - 3p)$ = _____

1.342 $N(N^2 + 2N + 1)$ = _____

1.343 $R(3R^2 - 2R - 1)$ = _____   1.344 $2x(x^2 + 3x + 5)$ = _____

1.345 $6x(2x^2 + 3x)$ = _____   1.346 $15x(5x^2 + 6x + 3)$ = _____

1.347 $x^2(x^2 + 2x + 1)$ = _____

Change the sums or differences to products.

Models: $5x + 5 = 5 \bullet x + 5 \bullet 1 = 5(x+1)$

$x^2 - 2x = x \bullet x - x \bullet 2 = x(x - 2)$

1.348 $6x + 12$ = _____   1.349 $7x + 14$ = _____

1.350 $8x - 16$ = _____   1.351 $12x + 36$ = _____

1.352 $13x - 26$ = _____   1.353 $10A - 20$ = _____

1.354 $A^2 + 5A$ = _____   1.355 $P^2 - 10P$ = _____

1.356 $B^2 + 6B$ = _____   1.357 $x^3 + x^2$ = _____

1.358 $6x^2 + 6y^2$ = _____   1.359 $6A + 6B + 6C$ = _____

SIMPLIFYING EXPRESSIONS

Algebraic expressions can be simplified by combining, through addition or subtraction, as many *variable terms* or *constant terms* as possible.

In the expression $6(x + 2) + 3$, before any addition can be done, the first term, the product of $6(x + 2)$, must be rewritten as a sum: $6(x + 2) + 3 = 6x + 12 + 3$. Now we may add the two constants 12 and 3, and we get $6(x + 2) + 3 = 6x + 15$. $6x$ and 15 cannot be added; therefore, the expression $6x + 15$ is an indicated sum in its simplest form.

Model 1:   Simplify, if possible, $7(A + 3) - 10$.

Solution: $7(A + 3) - 10 = 7A + 21 - 10$
$= 7A + 11$

Model 2:   Simplify $10 + 3(2x + 6) - 20$

        Solution: $10 + 6x + 18 - 20$
                            $6x + 10 + 18 - 20$
                            $6x + 28 - 20$
                            $6x + 8$

Simplify each of the following expressions. Show your work.

1.360 $7(x + 2) + 12$ 1.361 $8(x + 6) - 10$

_____   _____

1.362 $13(x + 2) + 13$ 1.363 $10(2x + 3) - 20$

_____   _____

1.364 $15(x + 1) + 5$ 1.365 $4(x + 1) - 4$

_____   _____

1.366 $12 + 3(4 + x)$ 1.367 $15 + 6(x + 1)$

_____   _____

1.368 $18(x + 1) - 9$ 1.369 $7(2x + 1) - 7$

_____   _____

1.370 $4(3x + 3) - 10$ 1.371 $(2x + 3)5 + 6$

_____   _____

1.372 $10 + 4(x + 1) + 5$ 1.373 $12 + 3(2x - 3) + 4$

_____   _____

1.374 $18 + 5(2x - 1) + 3$ 1.375 $14 + 2(3x + 8) - 22$

_____   _____

Some variable terms may be combined by using the distributive property. In the expression $3x + 4x$, the terms $3x$ and $4x$, both products, have a *common factor* x; that is, both numbers 3 and 4 multiplied by the number x.

Model 1: $3x + 4x = (3 + 4)x$
$$= 7x$$

Model 2: $7x + 2x = (7 + 2)x$
$$= 9x$$

Model 3: $7x - 2x = (7 - 2)x$
$$= 5x$$

The same distributive property also tells us that $6x + 4y$ cannot be combined. Why?

Terms with *like* variables (the same variables with the same respective exponents) may be combined by adding or subtracting their numerical coefficients.

Models:

$6x - 4x \quad = (6 - 4)x \quad = 2x$

$8y + 15y \quad = (8 + 15)y \quad = 23y$

$7AB - 3AB = (7 - 3)AB \quad = 4AB$

$5N^2 + 7N^2 = (5 + 7)N^2 = 12N^2$

$8p^2 + 7p \quad =$ (cannot be combined since the exponents are not the same)

Simplify by combining terms when possible.

1.376 $8x + 3x$

1.377 $2x + x$

1.378 $5x + 8x$

1.379 $12x + 3x$

1.380 $15x + 2x$

1.381 $7x - 5x$

1.382 $4x - x$

1.383 $10x - 3x$

1.384 $18x - 6x$

1.385 $22x - 10x$

_____

_____

1.386 $7.8x - 2.1x$

1.387 $9.6x - 4.3x$

_____

_____

1.388 $0.2x + 1.5x$

1.389 $0.05x + 1.02x$

_____

_____

1.390 $8x + 2x + 3x$

1.391 $5x + 2x + 7x$

_____

_____

1.392 $10x - 2x + 3x$

1.393 $15x - 4x + 11x - 2x$

_____

_____

1.394 $12A + 2 + A - 1$

1.395 $2A + 3A + B + 4B$

_____

_____

1.396 $7N - 2N + 3P + 2P$

_____

Model 1:   Simplify $5(x + 2) + 6x + 3$

                Solution: $5(x + 2) + 6x + 3$
                                        $5x + 10 + 6x + 3$
                                        $5x + 6x + 10 + 3$
                                        $11x + 13$

Model 2:   Simplify $5(x + 3) + 3(x + 2)$

                Solution: $5(x + 3) + 3(x + 2)$
                                          $5x + 15 + 3x + 6$
                                        $5x + 3x + 15 + 6$
                                        $8x + 21$

MATHEMATICS

901

LIFEPAC TEST

48 / 60

Name _____

Date _____

Score _____

MATHEMATICS 901: LIFEPAC TEST

Perform the indicated operations (each answer, 3 points).

1. $(-5) + (-4) + (7)$ _____

2. $6 - 2 + 5 - 8 - 10$ _____

3. $6 \cdot (-5)$ _____

4. $7 - (-4) + 3(-6)$ _____

5. $18 \div (-6)$ _____

6. $-72 \div (-4)$ _____

Evaluate each expression for $x = 10$**,** $y = -5$**, and** $z = -2$ (each answer, 3 points).

7. xyz _____

8. $x^2 + 2yz$ _____

9. $x^2 + y^2 + z^2$ _____

10. $\dfrac{x^2}{y} + \dfrac{x^2}{z}$ _____

Complete each sentence (each answer, 2 points).

11.   The exponent for the indicated power in $5^4 + 6$ is _____ .

12.   The numerical coefficient in $7 + (-3x^2)$ is _____ .

13.   The variable term in $5x^3 + 2$ is _____ .

14.   The constant term in $3p^2 - 2p + 5$ is _____ .

1

Follow the directions (each answer, 3 points).

15.   Change $7(x + 3)$ to a sum.   _____

16.   Change $10q - 20$ to a product.   _____

Follow the directions (each answer, 5 points).

17.   Write in words the meaning of $5x - 7$.

          _____

18.   Write in algebraic form "the difference between 5 times the square of a number and twice that number."

          _____

Simplify (each answer, 3 points).

19. $6x + 6 + 5x - 8$ _____

20. $3(x - 4) + 8(x + 2)$ _____

NOTES

▶▶▶ Simplify as in the preceding models. Show your work.

1.397 $6(A + 2) + 5A$

_____

1.398 $7(B + 3) + 2B$

_____

1.399 $8(C + 10) + 20$

_____

1.400 $5(R + 2) - 6$

_____

1.401 $8(R + 6) - 2R$

_____

1.402 $15(x + 3) + 2x$

_____

1.403 $8(x^2 + 2) + 20$

_____

1.404 $7(p^2 + 5) - 20$

_____

1.405 $13(y^2 + 2) - 13$

_____

1.406 $3(y^2 + y) + y$

_____

1.407 $4(x^2 + 2x) + 3x$

_____

1.408 $12(R^2 + 7R) - 20R$

_____

1.409 $8(xy + 8) + 1$

_____

1.410 $7(PQ + 2) + PQ$

_____

1.411 $5(MN + 1) - 5$

_____

1.412 $2(x + y) + 3(x + y)$

_____

1.413 $8(A + 2B) + 6(2A + B)$

_____

1.414 $9(x + y) + 2(x - y)$

_____

1.415 $15(x + y) + 12 (x - y)$

_____

Review the material in this section in preparation for the Self Test. The Self Test will check your mastery of this particular section. The items missed on this Self Test will indicate specific areas where restudy is needed for mastery.

SELF TEST 1

Multiply (each answer, 3 points).

1.01 $11(2x + 3)$

_____

1.02 $12(5x - 4)$

_____

1.03 $8(3 - 2x)$

_____

Simplify (each answer, 3 points).

1.04 $3x + 3 + 2$

_____

1.05 $5x + 4x + 1$

_____

1.06 $6(x + 2) + 7$

_____

Identify the numerical coefficient of the variable and the constant term (each answer, 2 points).

		Numerical Coefficient	Constant Term
1.07	$6x + 5$	a._____	b._____
1.08	$7x^3 + 2$	a._____	b._____

Identify the base and the exponent for the indicated power (each answer, 2 points).

		Base	Exponents
1.09	5^2	a._____	b._____
1.010	8^3	a._____	b._____
1.011	$(x^2 + 3)$	a._____	b._____

Evaluate (each answer, 3 points).

1.012 5^3 _____

1.013 $(3 + 4)^2$ _____

1.014 x^3 for $x = 2$ _____

1.015 $A^2 + B^2$ for $A = 2, B = 3$ _____

1.016 $N^2 + 2N + 1$ for $N = 5$ _____

Write in algebraic form (each answer, 5 points).

1.017   8 times the square of a number   _____

1.018   The difference of 3 squared and
        5 times a number   _____

Write in words (each answer, 5 points).

1.019 $x^3 + 4$ _____

1.020 $5x - 2$ _____

Write the required quantities (each answer, 5 points).

1.021   Find 15% of 63   _____

1.022   Find $\dfrac{5}{8} + \dfrac{7}{12}$ _____

1.023   Find $(0.56)(2.36)$ _____

1.024   Find $2\dfrac{3}{8} \cdot 5\dfrac{3}{4}$ _____

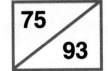

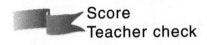

Score _____

Teacher check _____

Initial   Date

The study of *signed numbers* consists of defining the negative number and developing the rules for addition, subtraction, multiplication, and division. The term *number* here stands for all whole numbers *and* fractions, both positive *and* negative.

DEFINITION

This number line can be used to picture the whole numbers. The arrow denotes that the numbers continue to increase as the line continues to the right. Fractions and decimals can also be located on the number line. In fact all of the *positive numbers* (and zero) can be found on this number line.

If we continue the same line to the left of zero, we have all of the *negative numbers*.

The negative numbers are designated with the minus sign. Thus -5 means *negative five*.

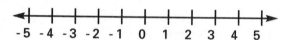

Notice that each number to the right of zero has a corresponding number to the left of zero. We call these numbers *opposites* of each other.

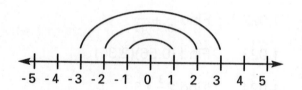

Models:	-3 is the opposite of 3
	-2 is the opposite of 2
	-1 is the opposite of 1

We may also say that 2 is the opposite of -2, 3 is the opposite of -3, and so on.

The words *opposite*, *negative*, and *minus* are often used in the same sense:

-5 may be read as: { negative five, minus five, or the opposite of five

The *order* of two numbers indicates their relative sizes; for example, 5 is less than 7. Order symbols are < (is less than), = (is equal to) and > (is greater than).

Between any two numbers, one and only one of the three order symbols must be true.

Model: If 6 > 3 is true, then 6 < 3 and
          6 = 3 are false.

On the number line, any number to the *right* of another number *is greater than* the number. On the number line, any number to the *left* of another number *is less than* the number.

Models: 6 is to the *right* of 3.
           Therefore, 6 > 3.

           3 is to the *right* of 0.
           Therefore, 3 > 0.

           5 is to the *left* of 7.
           Therefore, 5 < 7.

           -7 is to the *left* of -1.
           Therefore, -7 < -1.

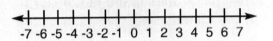

Write the opposite of each of the following numbers.

2.1   6   _____   2.2   5   _____

2.3   10   _____   2.4   3   _____

2.5   4   _____   2.6   -2   _____

2.7   -5   _____   2.8   -6   _____

2.9   -8   _____   2.10   -4   _____

2.11 $10   _____   2.12   -$50   _____

2.13   -8°   _____   2.14   15°   _____

2.15   -22 ft.   _____

Name these numbers on the number line.

2.16   2 units to the right of zero.   _____

2.17   5 units to the left of zero.   _____

2.18   7 units to the left of -1.   _____

2.19   5 units to the right of -6.   _____

2.20   2 units to the left of -3.   _____

2.21   5 units less than -4.   _____

2.22   7 units more than -5.   _____

2.23   12 units to the left of zero.   _____

Use <, >, or = to show each relationship.

2.24   6 _____ 7   2.25   8 _____ 8

2.26   4 _____ 10   2.27   10 _____ 5

2.28   -3 _____ 0   2.29   5 _____ 0

2.30   -2 _____ -3   2.31   -5 _____ -5

2.32   8 _____ -4   2.33   -6 _____ 6

2.34   -8 _____ -9   2.35   -12 _____ -15

2.36   -.3 _____ .4   2.37   4.2 _____ -1.6

2.38 $-\dfrac{2}{3}$ _____ $-\dfrac{3}{4}$

 Answer true or false.

2.39   _____   -4 < -6

2.40   _____   The opposite of 8 is -8.

2.41   _____   The opposite of the opposite of -10 is -10.

2.42   _____   0 > 6

 Complete the number pattern.

2.43   2, 1, 0   _____

2.44   6, 4, 2, 0,   a._____ ,   b._____ ,   c._____

2.45   -3, -2, -1,   a._____ ,   b._____ ,   c._____

2.46   15, 10, 5,   a._____ ,   b._____ ,   c._____

2.47   -20, -16, -12, a._____ ,   b._____ ,   c._____ ,   d._____

═══════ **ADDITION** ═══════════════════════

We will now look at addition of positive and negative numbers using the number line.

Study the following models of addition.

Models: To add two positive numbers

3 + 2

Locate the first addend (3). Then move to the *right* 2 spaces. For a positive second addend move *right*. Thus, 3 + 2 = 5.

To add one positive and one negative number.

3 + (-4)

Find positive 3. Then move *left* 4 spaces to (-1). For a negative second addend move *left*. Thus 3 + (-4) = -1.

To add two negatives numbers.

(-3) + (-2)

Locate first addend (-3). Then move left 2 spaces to (-5). Thus (-3) + (-2) = (-5).

To add: Positive numbers move right.
Negative numbers move left.

Study these models. Think of the number line.

6 + 5   = 11   -6 + 5   = -1

6 + (-5) = 1   (-6) + (-5) = -11

Model 1:   Simplify   -5N + 7N

Solution: -5N + 7N
(-5 + 7)N
2N

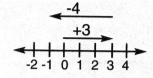

32

Model 2:   Simplify $-6x + (-10x)$

                Solution: $-6x + (-10x)$
                                $[-6 + (-10)]x$
                                $-16x$

▶ ▶ ▸ **Write the sum.**

2.48 $8 + 2$ = _____   2.49 $9 + 16$ = _____

2.50 $13 + 2$ = _____   2.51 $15 + 22$ = _____

2.52 $8 + 13$ = _____   2.53 $-9 + 5$ = _____

2.54 $-10 + 15$ = _____   2.55 $14 + (-3)$ = _____

2.56 $17 + (-5)$ = _____   2.57 $-9 + (-7)$ = _____

2.58 $-8 + (-4)$ = _____   2.59 $-20 + (-30)$ = _____

2.60 $-6 + 6$ = _____   2.61 $9 + (-9)$ = _____

2.62 $12 + (-12)$ = _____   2.63 $12 + 3 + (-1)$ = _____

2.64 $7 + 9 + (-4)$ = _____   2.65 $9 + 2 + (-3) + (-4)$ = _____

2.66 $(-6) + (-5) + 7$ = _____   2.67 $5x + 7x$ = _____

2.68 $8x + (-3x)$ = _____   2.69 $2x + (-5x)$ = _____

2.70 $10x - 3x + (-5x)$ = _____   2.71 $12x - 8x - 2x$ = _____

33

Model:

In the following squares, the sum of each row is written at the end of the row. The sum of each column is written below each column. Then sums of each row and column are added. The answers should agree.

If the sum of the column sums is not the same as the sum of the row sums, then you have made an error and must start over.

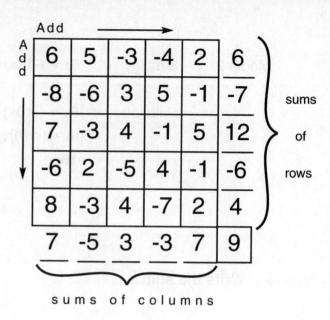

Add →

A d d ↓

6	5	-3	-4	2	6
-8	-6	3	5	-1	-7
7	-3	4	-1	5	12
-6	2	-5	4	-1	-6
8	-3	4	-7	2	4
7	-5	3	-3	7	9

} sums of rows

sums of columns

Complete the addition of squares.

2.72

5	-8	2	_____ a.
-7	6	-4	_____ b.
10	-9	2	_____ c.

g. ☐

____ d. ____ e. ____ f.

2.73

10	-6	2	-9	_____ a.
3	-3	7	-7	_____ b.
-8	4	-10	5	_____ c.
2	-9	3	-4	_____ d.

i. ☐

____ e. ____ f. ____ g. ____ h.

In the given space make an addition square of 6 rows and 6 columns. Fill in your own numbers, both positive and negative. Regardless of what numbers you use, the sum of the sums of rows and columns must agree. If the sums do not agree, start adding again.

2.74

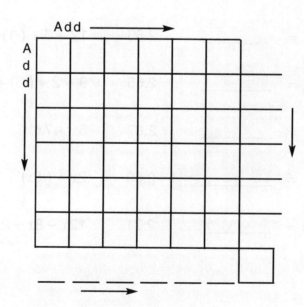

Add →

A d d ↓

Repeat exercise 2.74 by making a chart with ten rows and ten columns.

2.75

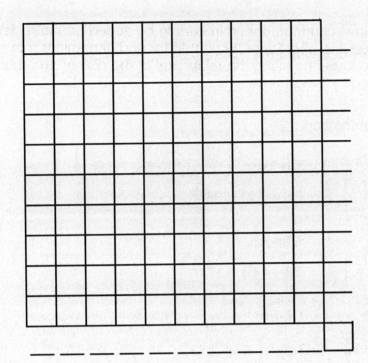

→ **Evaluate for** $x = 2$, $y = -3$, $z = -4$.

2.76 $x + y + z$ 2.77 $x - y - z$ 2.78 $2x + 2y + 2z$

_____   _____   _____

2.79 $y + y + y$ 2.80 $z + z + z$

_____   _____

========== **SUBTRACTION** ==========

In the subtraction problem $20 - 6$, we are asking, "What number, when added to 6, will equal 20?"

Model 1:   20
        Subtract   6
                      ___   } 6 + 14 = 20
                       14

$20 - 6 = 14$ because $14 + 6 = 20$

Model 2:   38
           −12
           ‾‾‾
            26   } 12 + 26 = 38

            38 − 12 = 26 because 26 + 12 = 38

We can use addition to check each subtraction.

Model 3:   Subtract   36   Check:
                         (−2)
                         ‾‾‾‾
                          38   }   38 + (−2) = 36

Model 4:   17   Check:
                       − (−5)
                       ‾‾‾‾‾
                         22   }   22 + (−5) = 17

Model 5:   Subtract (−20)   Check:
                          5
                       ‾‾‾‾
                        −25   }   (−25) + 5 = −20

Model 6:   (−30)   Check:
                       − (10)
                       ‾‾‾‾‾
                         −40   }   (−40) + (10) = −30

Model 7:   (−50)   Check:
                       −(−20)
                       ‾‾‾‾‾
                         −30   }   (−30) + (−20) = − 50

On the number line, when we seek the difference
between two numbers we find the distance and
direction from the second number to the first number.
As in addition, moving right indicates a positive
number and moving left indicates a negative number.

difference of 4
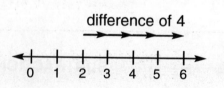

Model: In the case of (+6) − (+2),
             4 is the difference.

Thus, (+6) − (+2) = 4
Check: 4 + (+2) = (+6)

difference of −4
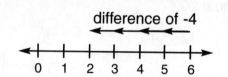

Model 2:   In the case of (+2) − (+ 6),
             −4 is the difference.

Thus, (+2) − (+6) = −4
Check: −4 + (+6) = (+2)

Model 3:   For

$$
\begin{array}{r}
6 \\
-\,(\,{-2}\,) \\
\hline
8
\end{array}
$$

Thus, 6 − (-2) = 8

Check: 8 + (-2) = 6

difference = 8

$$
\begin{array}{c}
\longrightarrow\!\!\!\longrightarrow\!\!\!\longrightarrow\!\!\!\longrightarrow \\
\longleftarrow\!\!|\!\!|\!\!|\!\!|\!\!|\!\!|\!\!|\!\!|\!\!|\!\!|\!\!|\!\!|\!\!|\!\!|\!\!|\!\!|\!\!\longrightarrow \\
\text{-7 -6 -5 -4 -3 -2 -1 0 1 2 3 4 5 6 7}
\end{array}
$$

Study these four models.

$$
\begin{array}{r}
8 \\
-\,(\,2\,) \\
\hline
6
\end{array}
$$

Check: 6 + 2 = 8

$$
\begin{array}{r}
8 \\
-\,(\,{-2}\,) \\
\hline
10
\end{array}
$$

Check: 10 + (-2) = 8

$$
\begin{array}{r}
(\,{-8}\,) \\
-\,(\,{+2}\,) \\
\hline
-10
\end{array}
$$

Check: (-10) + 2 = -8

$$
\begin{array}{r}
(\,{-8}\,) \\
-\,(\,{-2}\,) \\
\hline
-6
\end{array}
$$

Check: (-6) + (-2) = (-8)

To subtract a positive or negative number, add the opposite.
$A - B = A + (-B)$

Model 1:   5 − 2

Subtract   Add opposite

$$
\begin{array}{r}
5 \\
-\,(\,{+2}\,) \\
\end{array}
\quad\rightarrow\quad
\begin{array}{r}
5 \\
+\,(\,{-2}\,) \\
\hline
3
\end{array}
$$

Model 2:   5 − (−2).

           Subtract   Add opposite

                5   →   5
            − (-2)   →   + (+2)
                                   7

           5 − (−2) = 7   because   7 + (−2) = 5.

Subtract by adding the opposite.

	Subtract		Add		Subtract		Add
2.81	10	→	10	2.82	15	→	15
	(6)	→	(-6)		(-4)	→	4

	Subtract		Add		Subtract		Add
2.83	-12	→	-12	2.84	6	→	a. _____
	(8)	→	a. _____		(-6)	→	b. _____
			b. _____				c. _____

2.85	15	2.86	13	2.87	15
	(12)		(-4)		(-9)

| 2.88 | 20 | 2.89 | 2 | 2.90 | 5 |
| | (-22) | | (8) | | (-4) |

| 2.91 | 12 | 2.92 | 1 | 2.93 | (-18) |
| | (-13) | | (-1) | | (4) |

| 2.94 | (-20) | 2.95 | (-60) | 2.96 | (-25) |
| | (10) | | (30) | | (25) |

38

2.97	(-10)	2.98	(-16)	2.99	(-22)
	(-5)		(-4)		(-4)

2.100   (-33)
         (-11)

 Simplify.

2.101 $6 - (5)$ _____   2.102 $7 - (8)$

2.103 $(-10) - (4)$ _____   2.104 $(-15) - (-3)$ _____

2.105 $15 - (-15)$ _____   2.106 $12 - (-10)$ _____

2.107 $(-6) - (-4)$ _____   2.108 $1 - (-3)$ _____

2.109 $(3P) - (4P)$ _____   2.110 $(7x) - (-2x)$ _____

2.111 $(5x) - (-8x)$ _____   2.112 $(-4x) - (-8x)$ _____

Find the differences.

2.113   6 , 5   _____   2.114   10 , 12   _____

2.115   13 , 20   _____   2.116   6 , -1   _____

2.117   (-8) , 4   _____   2.118   (-6) , 5   _____

2.119 $6x$, $2x$ _____   2.120 $8a$, $4a$ _____

2.121   Tuesday the temperature was -12° and Wednesday it warmed up to 20°. What was the temperature change from Tuesday to Wednesday?

_____

_____

Since 4 • 2 means *four twos* or 2 + 2 + 2 + 2 = 8, and 3 • 6 means t*hree sixes* or 6 + 6 + 6 = 18, we may say that 3(-2) means *three negative twos* or (-2) + (-2) + (-2) = (-6). Also, we know that -2(3) = (3)(-2) since multiplication is a commutative operation. Now, since 2(3) = +6
$$\downarrow \qquad \downarrow$$
and -2(3) = -6,
we conclude that if you change the sign of one factor, then the sign of the product is changed.

By this same reasoning, we may conclude that

Since   +3(-2) = -6,
$$\downarrow \qquad \downarrow$$
then   (-3)(-2) = +6.

This process leads to the following rules for multiplication of positive and negative numbers.

The product of two numbers of *like signs* is positive.
The product of two numbers of *unlike signs* is negative.

Study these four models.

Like signs

(+12)(+6) = 72
(-12)(-6) = 72

Unlike signs

(+12)(-6) = (-72)
(-12)(+6) = (-72)

 Find the products.

2.122	6 • 5	_____	2.123	8 • 4	_____

2.124	9(6)	_____	2.125	4(20)	_____

2.126	7(32)	_____	2.127	8(-4)	_____
2.128	10(-2)	_____	2.129	3(-8)	_____
2.130	4(-7)	_____	2.131	5(-4)	_____
2.132	(-22)5	_____	2.133	(-33)(4)	_____
2.134	(-8)(7)	_____	2.135	(-9)(7)	_____
2.136	(-11)(4)	_____	2.137	(-3)(-4)	_____
2.138	(-8)(-5)	_____	2.139	(-6)(-8)	_____
2.140	(-10)(-10)	_____	2.141	(-5)(-6)	_____
2.142	(6)(5)(4)	_____	2.143	(-7)(2)(3)	_____
2.144	(-9)(-8)(2)	_____	2.145	(-3)(-4)(-5)	_____
2.146	(-8)(-4)(-3)	_____	2.147	(-5)(-6)(-2)(-1)	_____
2.148	(6)(-3)(-4)	_____	2.149	(3.2)(-5.6)	_____
2.150	(8.34)(-5.7)	_____	2.151	(-7.2)(3)	_____
2.152	$(\frac{1}{2})(\frac{3}{4})$	_____	2.153	$(\frac{6}{5})(\frac{5}{8})$	_____
2.154	$(-\frac{7}{8})(-\frac{3}{4})$	_____	2.155	$(-\frac{3}{10})(-\frac{5}{9})$	_____

Evaluate for $A = 5$, $B = -4$, and $C = 2$.

2.156	A^2	_____	2.157	B^2	_____
2.158	C^2	_____	2.159	AB	_____

41

2.160	BC	_____	2.161	AC	_____
2.162	$3AB$	_____	2.163	$A + B$	_____
2.164	$2A - B$	_____	2.165	$C - 3B$	_____
2.166	$B - C$	_____	2.167	$2B - 3C$	_____
2.168	$A^2 - B^2$	_____	2.169	$A^2 + B^2$	_____
2.170	$B^2 - C^2$	_____	2.171	$C^2 - B^2$	_____
2.172	$(-A)^2$	_____	2.173	$(-B)^2$	_____
2.174	$(-C)^2$	_____	2.175	B^3	_____

DIVISION

Division is the inverse operation of multiplication, and we can use multiplication to check division.

That is, $\frac{12}{2} = 6$ because $6 \cdot 2 = 12$,

$72 \div 12$ or $\frac{72}{12} = 6$ because $12 \cdot 6 = 72$.

Therefore, $(-72) \div 12$ or $\frac{-72}{12} = -6$ because $12(-6) = -72$;

and $(-72) \div (-12)$ or $\frac{-72}{-12} = 6$ because $(-12)(6) = -72$.

Therefore, the same rules apply to division as to multiplication.

> The quotient of two numbers of *like* signs is *positive*.
> The quotient of two numbers of *unlike* signs is *negative*.

Models:	Like signs	Unlike signs

Like signs:

$$\frac{50}{10} = 5$$

$$\frac{-50}{-10} = 5$$

Unlike signs:

$$\frac{+50}{-10} = -5$$

$$\frac{-50}{+10} = -5$$

 Divide.

2.176	$6 \div 3$	_____	2.177	$8 \div 4$
2.178	$10 \div 5$	_____	2.179	$12 \div 3$
2.180	$6 \div (-3)$	_____	2.181	$8 \div (-4)$
2.182	$10 \div (-5)$	_____	2.183	$12 \div (-3)$
2.184	$(-6) \div 3$	_____	2.185	$(-8) \div 4$
2.186	$(-10) \div 5$	_____	2.187	$(-12) \div (3)$
2.188	$(-6) \div (-3)$	_____	2.189	$(-8) \div (-4)$
2.190	$(-10) \div (-5)$	_____	2.191	$(-12) \div (-3)$
2.192	$\frac{72}{(-9)}$	_____	2.193	$\frac{-93}{3}$
2.194	$\frac{(-80)}{(-20)}$	_____	2.195	$\frac{(-100)}{(-5)}$
2.196	$\frac{4x}{-2}$	_____	2.197	$\frac{-8x}{4}$
2.198	$\frac{12x^2}{-4}$	_____	2.199	$\frac{-18y}{-3}$

Evaluate for $M = 10$, $N = -5$, $P = -2$.

2.200 $\dfrac{M}{N}$

2.201 $M \bullet N$

2.202 $\dfrac{M}{P}$

2.203 $M \bullet P$

2.204 $M \bullet N \bullet P$

2.205 $\dfrac{M}{N \bullet P}$

2.206 $\dfrac{N}{M}$

2.207 $\dfrac{P}{M}$

2.208 $\dfrac{M^2}{P^2}$

2.209 $\dfrac{N^2}{P}$

2.210 $\dfrac{P^3}{M}$

2.211 $\dfrac{M \bullet N}{N}$

Before you take this last Self Test, you may want to do one or more of these self checks.

1. _____ Read the objectives. Determine if you can do them.
2. _____ Restudy the material related to any objectives that you cannot do.
3. _____ Use the SQ3R study procedure to review the material:
   a. **S**can the sections.
   b. **Q**uestion yourself again (review the questions you wrote initially).
   c. **R**ead to answer your questions.
   d. **R**ecite the answers to yourself.
   e. **R**eview areas you didn't understand.
4. _____ Review all activities, and Self Tests, writing a correct answer for each wrong answer.

SELF TEST 2

Perform the indicated operations (each answer, 3 points).

2.01 $3 + (-4)$ _____   2.02 $5 - (-8)$ _____

2.03 $-4 + (-10)$ _____   2.04 $(-1) + (1)$ _____

2.05 $(-6)(4)$ _____   2.06 $(-4)(-5)$ _____

2.07 $(23)(5)$ _____   2.08 $(-43)(-3)$ _____

2.09 $27 \div (-3)$ _____   2.010 $(-50) \div (-2)$ _____

2.011 $(-10) \div (-20)$ _____   2.012 $15N \div (-3)$ _____

2.013 $(-8) + (-2) + 5$ _____   2.014 $(-2) + (-2) + (-2)$ _____

2.015 $5 - 3 + 3 - 5$ _____

2.016 $\begin{array}{r} 8 \\ -(-2) \\ \hline \end{array}$ 2.017 $\begin{array}{r} (-10) \\ -(-4) \\ \hline \end{array}$

2.018 $15 - (11)$ _____   2.019 $27 - (-9)$ _____

Evaluate each expression for $A = 5, B = -2, C = 4, D = -6$ (each answer, 3 points).

2.020 A^2 _____   2.021 $5B^2$ _____

2.022 C^3 _____   2.023 AB _____

2.024 DC _____   2.025 $A + B + C$ _____

2.026 $C + D - B$ _____   2.027 $\dfrac{ACD}{B}$ _____

2.028 $A^2 - B^2$ _____   2.029 A^3 _____

2.030	$6DC$	_____	2.031	$C^2 + 2C + 1$	_____
2.032	$\dfrac{AB}{CD}$	_____	2.033	B^C	_____

Identify the base and exponent for each indicated power (each answer, 2 points).

		base	exponent
		base	exponent

2.034	$6^4 + 3$	a. _____	b. _____
2.035	$5P^2$	a. _____	b. _____
2.036	$3x^5$	a. _____	b. _____
2.037	x^t	a. _____	b. _____

Identify the numerical coefficient and the constant term (each answer, 2 points).

		Numerical Coefficient	Constant Term

2.038	$3x + 6$	a. _____	b. _____
2.039	$5x - 8$	a. _____	b. _____
2.040	$5x^2$	a. _____	b. _____
2.041	$6p^2 + 10$	a. _____	b. _____

Change to sums or differences (each answer, 3 points).

2.042	$6(x + 8)$	_____	2.043	$3(x^2 - 1)$	_____
2.044	$-4(N + 9)$	_____	2.045	$5(-8 + P)$	_____

Change to products (each answer, 3 points).

2.046 $x + x$ _____

2.047 $3N + 4N$ _____

2.048 $5R - 2R$ _____

2.049 $3P + 5P$ _____

Write in words the meaning of each expression (each answer, 5 points).

2.050 $N^3 + 6$ _____

2.051 $2p + 3q$ _____

Write in algebraic form (each answer, 5 points).

2.052   2 times the cube of some number N _____

2.053   The sum of 5 squared and 7 times
some number P _____

2.054   The difference between x squared and
x cubed   _____

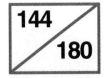

$\dfrac{144}{180}$

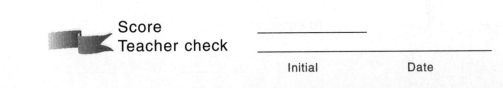

Score   _____

Teacher check   _____

Initial   Date

Before taking the LIFEPAC Test, you may want to do one or more of these self checks.
1. _____ Read the objectives. Check see if you can do them.
2. _____ Restudy the material related to any objectives that you cannot do.
3. _____ Use the SQ3R study procedure to review the material.
4. _____ Review activities, Self Tests, and LIFEPAC Glossary.
5. _____ Restudy areas of weakness indicated by the last Self Test.

GLOSSARY

associative property —	$(a + b) + c = a + (b + c)$ or $(ab)c = a(bc)$
base —	The x in x^n indicating the value to be used as a factor n times.
commutative property —	$a + b = b + a$ or $ab = ba$.
constant —	Any number of known value.
difference —	The result of subtraction.
distributive property —	$a(b + c) = ab + ac$ or $a(b - c) = ab - ac$
exponent —	The n in x^n indicating the number of factors or x.
numerical coefficient —	A numerical factor like 5 in $5x$.
opposite —	A number on one side of zero that has a corresponding number to other side of zero. (Example: The opposite of 3 is -3; the opposite of -10 is 10.)
product —	The result of multiplication.
quotient —	The result of division.
sum —	The result of addition.
variable —	A letter used to represent a number.
< —	Is less than.
> —	Is greater than.
= —	Is equal to.

MATHEMATICS 902
SOLVING EQUATIONS
AND INEQUALITIES

CONTENTS

I. SENTENCES AND FORMULAS 2
   Numerical Sentences 2
   Sentences with Variables 8
   Formulas 12
   Verbal Sentences 17

II. SOLVING EQUATIONS 25
   Addition Property 25
   Multiplication Property 31
   Multistep Equations 37
   Use of Parentheses 44
   Literal Equations 50

III. SOLVING INEQUALITIES 58
   The Line Graph 58
   Addition and Multiplication Properties 60
   Sentence with Absolute Value 67

Author:	**Robert L. Zenor, M.A., M.S.**
	Art Landrey
Editor:	Richard W. Wheeler, M.A.Ed.
Consulting Editor:	Rudolph Moore, Ph.D.
Revision Editor:	Alan Christopherson, M.S.

Alpha Omega Publications®

804 N. 2nd Ave. E., Rock Rapids, IA 51246-1759
© MCMXCVI by Alpha Omega Publications, Inc.   All rights reserved.
LIFEPAC is a registered trademark of Alpha Omega Publications, Inc.

SOLVING EQUATIONS AND INEQUALITIES

Algebra is one of several *systems* of mathematics; other systems are arithmetic, geometry, trigonometry, and calculus. Algebra expresses ideas in symbolic language—equations, inequalities, and formulas—with the use of positive and negative numbers and letters.

One of the most important and useful functions of algebra is to simplify the process of solving problems. Many mathematical problems are too complex to solve by arithmetic methods, and require translating the problem into *symbolic* language. When the translation into algebraic sentences has been done, we must solve the sentence to obtain the solution to the problem. In this LIFEPAC® we will learn how to solve many kinds of algebraic sentences.

OBJECTIVES

Read these objectives. The objectives tell you what you will be able to do when you have successfully completed this LIFEPAC.

When you have finished this LIFEPAC, you should be able to:

1. Evaluate expressions.
2. Interpret and evaluate formulas.
3. Translate a verbal statement into symbolic language.
4. Solve an equation.
5. Solve an inequality.
6. Graph the solutions of sentences involving absolute value.

Survey the LIFEPAC. Ask yourself some questions about this study. Write your questions here.

_____

_____

_____

_____

_____

_____

_____

_____

_____

I. SENTENCES AND FORMULAS

OBJECTIVES

When you have completed this section, you should be able to:

1. Evaluate expressions.
2. Interpret and evaluate formulas
3. Translate a verbal statement into symbolic language.

Equations and inequalities are mathematical sentences. A formula is a sentence which expresses a principle. Verbal sentences that express quantitative relationships may be translated into equations or inequalities.

⊙ ⊙ ⊙ NUMERICAL SENTENCES ⊙ ⊙ ⊙ ⊙ ⊙ ⊙ ⊙ ⊙ ⊙ ⊙ ⊙

Expressions such as "two times six equals twelve" and "six is greater than four" are verbal sentences. If we translate these sentences into numerical symbols, we have $2 \cdot 6 = 12$ and $6 > 4$, respectively. A numerical sentence must contain one of three symbols ($>$, $<$, or $=$) to make it complete. A numerical sentence may be either true or false.

$6 > 10$ is a numerical sentence; however, it is a false statement. Likewise, $8 = 5$ is also false. In our study of algebra and algebraic sentences, we will be concerned primarily with true sentences and merely be aware of sentences that are false.

Write *true* **or** *false*.

1.1	_____	$6 + 2 = 10 - 2$	1.6	_____ $-6 - 2 < 6 + 2$
1.2	_____	$3(5 + 3) = 5(3 + 3)$	1.7	_____ $10 - 15 < 15 - 10$
1.3	_____	$7 + 5 > 7 + 4$	1.8	_____ $3(5 + 2) = 3 \cdot 7$
1.4	_____	$8 - 6 > 8 - 5$	1.9	_____ $\frac{16}{4} = \frac{100}{25}$
1.5	_____	$6 \cdot 5 - 3 > 7 \cdot 5 + 2$	1.10	_____ $3(4 + 5) = 3 \cdot 4 + 3 \cdot 5$

2

1.11 _____ $5(7 - 3) = 5 \cdot 7 - 5 \cdot 3$ 1.14 _____ $\frac{15}{5} - 2 = 0$

1.12 _____ $6 \cdot 5 = 5 \cdot 6$ 1.15 _____ $\frac{8}{8} + 1 > 2$

1.13 _____ $5^2 + 7 > 7^2 - 5$

PROPERTIES OF ZERO

Mathematical sentences including zero are common. Several properties of zero are important in working with these sentences.

Properties of zero:

A.   Any number times zero equals zero.

B.   Zero divided by any nonzero number equals zero.

C.   Zero cannot be used as a divisor.

D.   Zero added to a number equals that number.

E.   A number added to its opposite equals zero.

A.   Models: $7 \cdot 0 = 0$ and $0 \cdot x = 0$

B.   Models: $\frac{0}{6} = 0$ and $\frac{0}{y} = 0$ if $y \neq 0$.

C.   Models: $\frac{3}{0}$ is impossible and $\frac{a}{0}$ is impossible

These quotients are *undefined*.

D.   Models: $8 + 0 = 8$ and $0 + b = b$

E.   Models: $3 + (-3) = 0$ and $-c + c = 0$

PROPERTIES OF ONE

Mathematical sentences including one are also common. These properties of one can be helpful in working with these sentences.

Properties of one:

    A.   One times any number equals the number.

    B.   Any nonzero number divided by itself equals one.

    C.   Any number divided by one equals the number.

A.   Models: $12 \cdot 1 = 12$ and $1 \cdot R = R$

B.   Models: $\frac{4}{4} = 1$ and $\frac{T}{T} = 1$ if $T \neq 0$

C.   Models: $\frac{9}{1} = 9$ and $\frac{N}{1} = N$

 Evaluate each of the following expressions. Work in space below problem, and circle your answer.

    Models: $4(1 - 0) = 4(1) = 4$

            $\frac{A}{1} - A \cdot 0 = A - 0 = A$

1.16 $6 \cdot 0$ 1.20 $0 \cdot 15 - 15$

1.17 $0 \cdot 5$ 1.21 $7 \cdot \frac{1}{7}$

1.18 $6(1 - 1)$ 1.22 $A - A + 1$

1.19 $\frac{10}{10} + 2$ 1.23 $3 \cdot 1 - 1 \cdot 3$

1.24 $\frac{8}{1} + \frac{8}{8}$ 1.28 $7 (B - B)$

1.25 $\frac{15}{0} + 6$ 1.29 $13 (8 - 8)$

1.26 $\frac{0}{15} + 6$ 1.30 $(7 + 3) 0$

1.27 $x \cdot 1 + \frac{x}{1}$

ABSOLUTE VALUE

Sentences including absolute values are less common than those with 1 or 0. Absolute value is, however, a very important concept in mathematics.

The absolute value of a number is the number without regard to sign.

The expression $|5| = 5$ is an *absolute value sentence*. The vertical bar on each side of a number is the symbol for absolute value.

Models: $|7| = 7$ $|-8| = 8$

$|12 - 9| = |3| = 3$

$|4 - 7| = |-3| = 3$

The more formal definition of absolute value is

$|x| = x$ if x is positive and

$|-x| = --x = x$ if x is negative

$|x| = 0$ if x is zero.

 Evaluate each problem. Show work in space below each problem, and circle your answer.

Models: $|6 - 9| = |-3| = 3$

$|6| - |9| = 6 - 9 = -3$

1.31 $|6|$

1.38 $- 4 |-4|$

1.32 $|6 - 1|$

1.39 $- 8 |2|$

1.33 $|8 - 9|$

1.40 $7 |8 - 8|$

1.34 $|5 - 15|$

1.41 $|5| - |-5|$

1.35 $|3 + 2|$

1.42 $|x| - |-x|$

1.36 $|2 - 10|$

1.43 $0 \cdot |- 6|$

1.37 $3 \cdot |-3|$

1.44 $2 |P| - |P|$

6

1.45 $|3 - 5 + 7|$

▶▶▶ **Evaluate.** Given $a = 5,$
$b = -3,$
$c = -2.$

$$|a - b| = |5 - (-3)| = |5 + 3| = |8| = 8$$
$$|a| - |b| = |5| - |-3| = 5 - 3 = 2$$
$$|a + c| = |5 + (-2)| = |3| = 3$$

1.46 $|a + b|$ _____

1.47 $|a - c|$ _____

1.48 $|b - c|$ _____

1.49 $|b + c|$ _____

1.50 $|a + b - c|$ _____

1.51 $|a| + |b| + |c|$ _____

1.52 $|a^2|$ _____

1.53 $|b^2|$ _____

1.54 $|c^2|$ _____

1.55 $|-a^2|$ _____

1.56 $|ab|$ _____

1.57 $|bc|$ _____

1.58 $|a^2 - b^2|$ _____

1.59 $|c^2 + b^2|$ _____

1.60 $|a^2 + b^2 + c^2|$ _____

The sentence $n + 8 = 10$ is an algebraic sentence. This sentence may be true or false, depending on the value used for the variable n. If n is replaced by 2, the sentence is true; however, if n is replaced by any other number, the sentence is false.

We call his type of sentence a *conditional* sentence or an *open* sentence.

Hereafter, we will refer to an open sentence having an equal sign (=) as an equation. We desire to find the value of the variable that will *satisfy* the equation; that is, a value that will make the sentence true.

Model: Solve $N - 10 = 30$

Solution: Find the number N such that when 10 is subtracted from it, the difference is 30.

The solution is $N = 40$.

The check is $40 - 10 = 30$

$30 = 30$ True

Model: Solve $5N = 30$

Solution: 5 times what number is 30?

The answer is $N = 6$

The check is $5 \cdot 6 = 30$

$30 = 30$ True.

Model: Solve $\frac{x}{12} = 8$

Solution: What number divided by 12 is 8?

The answer is $x = 96$

The check is $\frac{96}{12} = 8$

$8 = 8$ True.

Circle the number that makes the sentence true.

1.61	$N + 5 = 10$	5, -5, 0	1.66	$3A = -15$	-5, 5, -12
1.62	$x - 6 = 10$	6, 10, 16	1.67	$\frac{P}{5} = 20$	60, 100, 15
1.63	$A + 15 = 10$	5, -5, 10	1.68	$\frac{R}{2} + 5 = 10$	20, 10, -8
1.64	$x - 4 = -8$	4, -2, -4	1.69	$5B - 2 = 18$	8, 10, 4
1.65	$2x = 14$	8, 6, 7	1.70	$2x + 1 = 21$	10, 12, 14

At this time you are solving equations by inspection; that is, the value of the letter—called the *unknown*—is fairly evident because the equation is simple. Also, in activities 1.61 through 1.68, you merely had to try each of the choices until one of them fit.

But how would you approach the equation

$$\frac{4}{5}x - 13 - 2x = \frac{1}{5} ?$$

A systematic way must exist to solve such complicated equations. In fact there is, and it will be introduced in Section II.

See if you can figure out a system for solving equations as you work the next set of exercises.

 Write the solution to each sentence. Work in the space below the problem, and circle your answer, (Hint: Using the number line may be helpful in solving some of the following equations.)

Model: $-30 = N - 5$

Solution: Rewrite the subtraction $N - 5$ as the corresponding addition $N + (-5)$. Use the number line to determine what number must be added to -5 to obtain -30. Thus, $N = -25$.

1.71	$3x = 12$	1.73	$7x = 21$
1.72	$5p = 10$	1.74	$x - 5 = 10$

1.75	$A - 6 = -10$	1.84	$3x - 2 = 10$
1.76	$B + 5 = -8$	1.85	$5x - 5 = 5$
1.77	$7x = 49$	1.86	$\frac{x}{2} = 9$
1.78	$-8x = 24$	1.87	$\frac{a}{6} = 9$
1.79	$-5x = -25$	1.88	$\frac{n}{5} = 3$
1.80	$\frac{B}{5} = 10$	1.89	$\frac{x}{6} = 8$
1.81	$\frac{x}{3} = -10$	1.90	$9a = 81$
1.82	$\frac{P}{12} = 2$	1.91	$8x = 72$
1.83	$2x + 1 = 11$	1.92	$9x = 108$

1.93	$10a = 100$	1.103	$48 = 12x$
1.94	$n - 7 = 4$	1.104	$12 = a - 15$
1.95	$n + 8 = 17$	1.105	$52 = n + 26$
1.96	$x - 7 = 14$	1.106	$\frac{x}{3} = 8$
1.97	$y + 9 = 11$	1.107	$\frac{a}{3} = 7$
1.98	$8 + y = 13$	1.108	$\frac{x}{2} = 10$
1.99	$a - 6 = 18$	1.109	$\frac{a}{9} = 9$
1.100	$x + 12 = 26$	1.110	$\frac{x}{4} = -11$
1.101	$y + 17 = 30$	1.111	$\frac{n}{2} = -6$
1.102	$37 = m - 14$	1.112	$\frac{n}{7} = -8$

1.113 $\frac{a}{9} = -8$ 1.120 $-4a = -44$

1.114 $-4a = 32$ 1.121 $9b = 513$

1.115 $-4a = -32$ 1.122 $21 = b - 14$

1.116 $-7y = 28$ 1.123 $-21 = b - 14$

1.117 $-7y = -28$ 1.124 $43 = x - 21$

1.118 $4a = -36$ 1.125 $-43 = x - 21$

1.119 $-4a = 40$

FORMULAS

     Sentences that are used for specific applications are called *formulas*. A formula does not change from problem to problem. Each has been found to be a mathematical expression of a natural law.

For example, the *area of a square* is a measurement of a flat space bounded by sides of equal length.

The formula for area is $A = s^2$

where the number s stands
for the length of the side of the square. The area A
then depends on the size of the square.

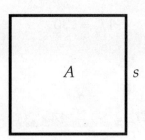

Hence,

if s = 10 cm
then A = 10^2 cm^2
and A = 100 cm^2

The perimeter of a rectangle means the *distance around* the rectangle. The formula is

$$P = 2l + 2w.$$

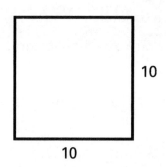

Here we need two measures, the length and width. Therefore,

if l = 20 cm and w = 15 cm
then P = $2l + 2w$
and P = 2 (20 cm) + 2(15 cm)
P = 40 cm + 30 cm
P = 70 cm

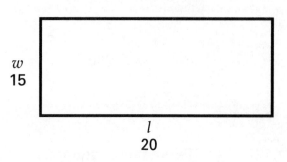

These formulas will be used in this section and throughout succeeding LIFEPACs.

$A = s^2$		Area of square
$A = lw$		Area of rectangle
$P = 4s$		Perimeter of square
$P = 2l + 2w$		Perimeter of rectangle
$I = prt$		interest, principal, rate, time
$d = rt$		distance, rate, time
$A = \dfrac{(a + b)\,h}{2}$		Area of trapezoid
$P = 3s$		Perimeter of an equilateral triangle
$A = \dfrac{bh}{2}$		Area of triangle
$V = lwh$		Volume of rectangular solid
$V = e^3$		Volume of cube
$A = \pi r^2$		Area of circle
$C = 2\pi r$		Circumference of circle
$V = \pi r^2 h$		Volume of cylinder

Write the correct formula and find the required quantities.
Circle your answer.

1.126   Area of square:

    a.   Formula is   _____

    b. $s = 2$ d. $s = 3.6$

    c. $s = 200$ e. $s = \frac{3}{8}$

1.127   Perimeter of square:

    a.   Formula is   _____

    b. $s = 5$ d. $s = 8.6$

    c. $s = 25$ e. $s = 3\frac{1}{2}$

1.128   Area of rectangle:

    a.   Formula is   _____

    b. $l = 10, w = 5$ d. $l = 10.2, w = 12.6$

    c. $l = 36, w = 10$ e. $l = 9\frac{1}{2}, w = 23\frac{1}{2}$

1.129   Distance:

    a.   Formula is   _____

    b. $r = 50$, $t = 6$ d. $r = 750$, $t = 3.5$

    c. $r = 360$, $t = 8$ e. $r = 200$, $t = 1\frac{1}{2}$

1.130   Area of triangle:

    a.   Formula is   _____

    b. $b = 10$, $h = 5$ d. $b = 9.62$, $h = 8.3$

    c. $b = 50$, $h = 20$ e. $b = 12\frac{1}{2}$, $h = 3\frac{2}{3}$

1.131   Volume of cube:

    a.   Formula is   _____

    b. $e = 5$ d. $e = 13.3$

    c. $e = 36$ e. $e = 7\frac{3}{5}$

1.132   Volume of rectangular solid:

    a.   Formula is   _____

    b. $l = 5, w = 6, h = 8$

    c. $l = 36, w = 42, h = 10$

    d. $l = 10.2, w = 8.6, h = 20.5$

    e. $l = 5\frac{3}{8}, w = 8\frac{1}{2}, h = 7\frac{8}{9}$

1.133   Area of circle:

    a.   Formula is   _____

    b. $r = 6, \pi = 3.14$ d. $r = 5\frac{1}{4}, \pi = 3\frac{1}{7}$

    c. $r = 9.2, \pi = 3.14$

Find the required information. Circle your answer.

1.134   If $P = 3x - 2y$, find P for

     a. $x = 10, y = 5$ c. $x = 26.8, \; y = 5.2$

     b. $x = 123, y = 100$

1.135   If $s = 16\,t^2$, find s for

     a. $t = 1$ c. $t = 3.4$

     b. $t = 5$ d. $t = 1\frac{1}{2}$

═ ▪ ═ ▪ ═══ **VERBAL SENTENCES** ═══ ▪ ═══ ▪ ═══ ▪ ═══ ▪ ═══ ▪ ═══

Each algebraic sentence may be translated into a verbal sentence; and conversely a verbal sentence may be translated into a symbolic or algebraic sentence.

A few definitions are necessary to translate words to symbols.

Study the following translations.

Word or Phrase	Translation
more than, increased by, sum	+
difference, less than, minus	−
times, product	x or · or ( ) ( )
quotient, per	÷ or ⟍ or —
equals, will be, is	=
is less than	<
is greater than	>

Model 1: A number increased by ten is fifty.

Translation:

A number	n
increased by	+
ten	10
is	=
fifty.	50

$$n + 10 = 50$$

Solution: $n = 40$

Check: $40 + 10 = 50$

$50 = 50$ True

Model 2: The difference between five times a number and twenty is seventy.

Translation:

Five times a number	$5n$
and the difference between	−
twenty	20
is	=
seventy.	70

$$5n - 20 = 70$$

Solution: $n = 18$

Check: $5(18) - 20 = 70$

$90 - 20 = 70$

$70 = 70$ True

Model 3:   Jan's age in 10 years will
          be 25; how old is Jan?

Translation: $J + 10 = 25$

Solution: $J = 15$

Check: $15 + 10 = 25$
              $25 = 25$ True

 Write the letter *and* the open sentence from COLUMN II on the line preceding COLUMN I.

COLUMN I

1.136 _____ A number increased by 10 is 33.

1.137 _____ The product of 9 and a number is 20.

1.138 _____ The sum of a number and 6 is 50.

1.139 _____ The difference of a number and 6 is 50.

1.140 _____ 6 less than a number is 25.

1.141 _____ Eight times a number is 32.

1.142 _____ One-ninth of a number is 40.

1.143 _____ Twice the sum of a number and 6 is 13.

1.144 _____ The quotient of a number and 10 is 70.

1.145 _____ 6 more than a number is greater than 72.

COLUMN II

a) $2(x + 6) = 13$ g) $x + 6 = 50$

b) $N - 6 = 50$ h) $9P = 40$

c) $8p = 32$ i) $9B = 20$

d) $A + 10 = 33$ j) $x - 6 = 25$

e) $x + 6 > 72$ k) $\frac{N}{9} = 40$

f) $6 - R = 25$ l) $\frac{N}{10} = 70$

Translate the verbal statement to an algebraic open sentence.

1.146   A number increased by 20 is 133.   _____

1.147   A number decreased by 13 is 57.   _____

1.148   The sum of a number and 52 is 73.   _____

1.149   The difference between a number
          and 8 is 22.   _____

1.150   6 less than a number is 30.   _____

1.151   A number less 10 is 22.   _____

1.152   8 more than twice a number is 50.   _____

1.153   9 less than three times a number is 40.   _____

1.154   The product of 6 and a number is 33.   _____

1.155   The product of 8 and the square of a
          number is 50.   _____

1.156   The sum of 6 and the square of x is 50.   _____

1.157   The sum of a number and 17 is greater
          than 68.   _____

1.158   The difference between 10 and a number
          is less than the sum of 8 and the number.   _____

1.159   Five times the sum of a number and 15
          is 50.   _____

1.160   Eight times the difference of a number
          and 17 is 30.   _____

 Translate each equation to a verbal statement.

1.161 $x + 5 = 18$ _____

1.162 $x - 8 = 70$ _____

1.163 $2N + 5 = 30$ _____

1.164 $3(2 + N) = 72$ _____

          _____

1.165 $5x^2 + 2 = 15$ _____

          _____

Review the material in this section in preparation for the Self Test. The Self Test will check your mastery of this particular section. The items missed on this Self Test will indicate specific areas where restudy is needed for mastery.

SELF TEST 1

Evaluate. Show work in space below each problem, and circle your answer (each answer, 4 points).

1.01 $|3|$ 1.09 $7 \cdot 0 \cdot 8 \cdot 5$

1.02 $|\text{-}3|$ 1.010 $9 \cdot 0 + 9 \cdot 1$

1.03 $|8 + 7|$ 1.011 $6 \cdot 1 - \dfrac{6}{1}$

1.04 $|7 - 8|$ 1.012 $7(x - x)$

1.05 $3|\text{-}4| + |2|$ 1.013 $(9 + 2)\,0$

1.06 $5|7 - 9| - 2$ 1.014 $\dfrac{8}{8} - 1$

1.07 $\text{-}3|\text{-}4| - |\text{-}5|$ 1.015 $\dfrac{10}{10} - \dfrac{10}{1}$

1.08 $8(5 - 5)$ 1.016 $|6| - |\text{-}6|$

Solve. Show work in space below each problem, and circle your answer (each answer, 4 points).

1.017 $x + 5 = 15$

1.018 $x - 6 = 12$

1.019 $x - 8 = -20$

1.020 $2x + 1 = 19$

1.021 $3x - 1 = 20$

1.022 $5x + 5 = 30$

1.023 $\frac{x}{2} = 10$

1.024 $\frac{x}{5} = 20$

1.025 $\frac{x}{12} = 3$

1.026 $\frac{2x}{5} = \frac{2}{5}$

1.027 $\frac{3x}{8} = \frac{3}{4}$

1.028 $\frac{1}{4}x + \frac{3}{4} = 1$

1.029 $5x = 30$

1.030 $8x = 72$

1.031 $10x = 120$

Evaluate the formula. Show work in space below each problem, and circle your answer (each answer, 3 points).

1.032 $A = s^2$

    a. $s = 12$ c. $s = 1.5$

    b. $s = 13$

1.033 $P = 2l + 2w$

    a. $l = 5, w = 3$ b. $l = 30, w = 6\frac{1}{2}$

1.034 $s = 16t^2$

    a. $t = 5$ c. $t = 3\frac{1}{2}$

    b. $t = 1.2$

1.035 $C = 2\pi r$

    a. $r = 3, \pi = 3.14$ c. $r = 42, \pi = 3\frac{1}{7}$

    b. $r = 6.2, \pi = 3.14$

1.036 $V = lwh$

      a. $l = 10, w = 8, h = 6$ c. $l = 18\frac{1}{2}, w = 10, h = 5\frac{1}{2}$

      b. $l = 5.1, w = 7.3, h = 12.5$

Write an open sentence for each statement (each answer, 5 points).

1.037   20 times a number is 73.   _____

1.038   The sum of 8 and a number is 100.   _____

1.039   The difference between a number
        and 50 is less than 200.   _____

1.040   8 less than a number is 75.   _____

1.041   6 times the sum of a number and
        12 is 40.   _____

153 / 191

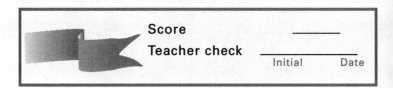

Score _____
Teacher check _____
            Initial   Date

24

II. SOLVING EQUATIONS

Equations soon become too complicated to solve mentally or by inspection. We need to develop a mathematical process that will solve the equation systematically.

○—○—○ **ADDITION PROPERTY** ○—○—○—○—○—○—○

The addition property states that you may add any number you choose to both sides (or members) of an equation without changing its status of equality.

> **THE ADDITION PROPERTY OF EQUALITY**
>
> For all real numbers a, b, c:
>
> If $\qquad\qquad a = b$
>
> then $\qquad a + c = b + c$

Model 1:   If $\qquad\qquad 6 = 6$
                  then $\qquad 6 + 9 = 6 + 9$

Model 2:   If $\qquad\qquad 12 = 12$
                  then $\qquad 12 - 5 = 12 - 5$

(Subtracting a *positive* number is the same as adding a *negative* number.)   **REMEMBER?**

Model 3: $\qquad\qquad x - 4 = 20$

Add 4 $\qquad x - 4 + 4 = 20 + 4$
we have $\qquad\quad x + 0 = 24$
and $\qquad\qquad\quad\; x = 24$

Check in the $\qquad 24 - 4 \overset{?}{=} 20$
original equation $\qquad\quad 20 = 20$ True

25

Model 4: $x + 7 = 30$

   Add -7 $x + 7 - 7 = 30 - 7$
                 $x + 0 = 23$
                 $x = 23$

   Check $23 + 7 \overset{?}{=} 30$
                 $30 = 30$ True

Model 5: $2x = x - 4$
   Add -x $2x - x = x - x - 4$
                 $x = 0 - 4$
                 $x = -4$

   Check $2(-4) \overset{?}{=} -4 - 4$
                 $-8 = -8$ True

 Solve and check. Show work in space below each problem, and circle your answer.

2.1 $N + 3 = 10$ 2.4 $x + 7 = -8$

   Ck. _____   Ck. _____
       _____   _____

2.2 $N + 6 = 12$ 2.5 $x - 9 = -10$

   Ck. _____   Ck. _____
       _____   _____

2.3 $N - 4 = 13$ 2.6 $x + 12 = -30$

   Ck. _____   Ck. _____
       _____   _____

2.7 $y - 8 = 10$

Ck. _____
_____

2.8 $y - 12 = -10$

Ck. _____
_____

2.9 $y + 13 = -13$

Ck. _____
_____

2.10 $x + 15 = 15$

Ck. _____
_____

2.11 $x + 30 = 29$

Ck. _____
_____

2.12 $x - 50 = 52$

Ck. _____
_____

2.13 $7 + N = 20$

Ck. _____
_____

2.14 $-7 + N = 20$

Ck. _____
_____

2.15 $-10 + N = 50$

Ck. _____
_____

2.16 $15 + x = 72$

Ck. _____
_____

2.17 $13 + x = 90$ 2.22 $83 = x + 5$

Ck. _____
_____

2.18 $52 + x = 132$ 2.23 $96 = x - 10$

Ck. _____
_____

2.19 $-72 + y = 90$ 2.24 $106 = x + 15$

Ck. _____
_____

2.20 $-80 + y = 80$ 2.25 $100 = x - 100$

Ck. _____
_____

2.21 $-80 + y = -80$ 2.26 $100 = x + 100$

Ck. _____
_____

2.27 $75 = 25 + x$

Ck. _____
    _____

2.28 $2x = 15 + x$

Ck. _____
    _____

2.29 $3x = 2x + 10$

Ck. _____
    _____

2.30 $5x = 4x - 8$

Ck. _____
    _____

2.31 $5x - 4x + 2 = 20$

Ck. _____
    _____

2.32 $7x - 6x - 10 = 13$

Ck. _____
    _____

2.33 $10x - 9x + 1 = 1$

Ck. _____
    _____

2.34 $x + 5 = 2x$

Ck. _____
    _____

2.35 $3x + 10 = 4x$

Ck. _____
    _____

2.36 $120 + 5x = 6x$

Ck. _____
    _____

2.37 $2x + 6 = x + 15$ 2.42 $N - 8.1 = 1.96$

        Ck. _____   Ck. _____
            _____   _____

2.38 $3x - 4 = 2x - 10$ 2.43 $x - .02 = 1.96$

        Ck. _____   Ck. _____
            _____   _____

2.39 $5x - 8 = 4x + 20$ 2.44 $x + 1.05 = 7.26$

        Ck. _____   Ck. _____
            _____   _____

2.40 $N + 3.2 = 9.6$ 2.45 $x + 0.001 = 1.222$

        Ck. _____   Ck. _____
            _____   _____

2.41 $N - 9 = 1.25$ 2.46 $x + \frac{1}{2} = \frac{3}{4}$

        Ck. _____   Ck. _____
            _____   _____

2.47 $\quad x - \dfrac{1}{8} = \dfrac{3}{8}$ 2.49 $\quad 2x + 1.05 = x - 3.56$

Ck. _____

_____

Ck. _____

_____

2.48 $\quad x + \dfrac{3}{7} = \dfrac{5}{8}$ 2.50 $\quad 7x - \dfrac{3}{8} = 6x - \dfrac{5}{8}$

Ck. _____

_____

Ck. _____

_____

 **MULTIPLICATION PROPERTY**

The multiplication property states that you may multiply *both* sides of an equation by any number you choose without changing the status of equality.

> **THE MULTIPLICATION PROPERTY OF EQUALITY**
>
> For all real numbers a, b, c:
>
> If $a = b$
>
> then $a \cdot c = b \cdot c$

Model 1:   If $15 = 15$

then $6 \cdot 15 = 6 \cdot 15$

Model 2:   If $16 = 16$,

then $\dfrac{1}{2} \cdot 16 = \dfrac{1}{2} \cdot 16$

The multiplying factor we will choose is the whole number or fraction that changes the numerical coefficient of our unknown to 1.

Model 3:

$$6x = 42$$

Multiply by $\frac{1}{6}$ $\quad \frac{1}{6} \cdot 6x = \frac{1}{6} \cdot 42$

$$x = \frac{42}{6} = 7$$

Check in the $\qquad 6 \cdot 7 \overset{?}{=} 42$

original equation $\quad 42 = 42$ True

$\left(\begin{array}{l} \text{Multiplying by } \frac{1}{6} \text{ is the same as} \\ \text{dividing by 6.} \end{array} \right)$ REMEMBER?

Model 4:

$$\frac{-x}{8} = 32$$

Multiply by -8 $\quad -8 \cdot \frac{-x}{8} = -8 \cdot 32$

$$x = -256$$

Check $\qquad \frac{-(-256)}{8} \overset{?}{=} 32$

$$32 = 32 \text{ True}$$

In Model 4, fraction $\frac{-x}{8}$ may also be written as $-\frac{1}{8}x$.

Model 5:

$$\frac{2}{3}x = 14$$

Multiply by $\frac{3}{2}$ $\quad \frac{3}{2} \cdot \frac{2}{3}x = \frac{3}{2} \cdot 14$

$$x = \frac{42}{2} = 21$$

Check $\qquad \frac{2}{3} \cdot 21 \overset{?}{=} 14$

$$14 = 14 \quad \text{True}$$

In Model 5, $\frac{2}{3}x$ may also be written as the fraction $\frac{2x}{3}$.

$\left(\begin{array}{l} \text{What you do to one side of an} \\ \text{equation, you must do to both} \\ \text{sides.} \\ \qquad \text{and} \\ \text{A number times its reciprocal} \\ \text{equals 1.} \end{array} \right)$ REMEMBER?

Model 6:

$$1.6x = 3.2$$

Multiply by $\frac{1}{1.6}$ $\frac{1}{1.6} \cdot 1.6x = \frac{1}{1.6} \cdot 3.2$

$$x = \frac{3.2}{1.6} = 2$$

Check $1.6 \cdot 2 \overset{?}{=} 3.2$

                         $3.2 = 3.2$ True.

 Solve and check. Circle your answer.

2.51 $6x = 18$

Ck. _____
_____

2.52 $5x = 25$

Ck. _____
_____

2.53 $7x = -49$

Ck. _____
_____

2.54 $3x = -39$

Ck. _____
_____

2.55 $8x = -72$

Ck. _____
_____

2.56 $10x = 100$

Ck. _____
_____

2.57 $\frac{x}{6} = 2$

Ck. _____
_____

2.58 $\frac{x}{7} = 20$

Ck. _____
_____

2.59 $\frac{1}{9}x = 1$

Ck. _____

_____

2.60 $\frac{1}{8}x = -2$

Ck. _____

_____

2.61 $\frac{x}{10} = -10$

Ck. _____

_____

2.62 $\frac{x}{12} = -15$

Ck. _____

_____

2.63 $-5x = -10$

Ck. _____

_____

2.64 $-8x = -24$

Ck. _____

_____

2.65 $-13x = -52$

Ck. _____

_____

2.66 $\frac{-x}{3} = 2$

Ck. _____

_____

2.67 $\frac{-1}{15}x = 13$

Ck. _____

_____

2.68 $\frac{-x}{20} = 10$

Ck. _____

_____

2.69 $\dfrac{-N}{5} = -5$

Ck. _____
_____

2.74 $15x = 63$

Ck. _____
_____

2.70 $\dfrac{-1}{6}y = -8$

Ck. _____
_____

2.75 $13x = -12$

Ck. _____
_____

2.71 $\dfrac{-x}{15} = -15$

Ck. _____
_____

2.76 $22x = -68$

Ck. _____
_____

2.72 $8x = 7$

Ck. _____
_____

2.77 $48x = -72$

Ck. _____
_____

2.73 $9x = 22$

Ck. _____
_____

2.78 $\dfrac{2}{3}x = 8$

Ck. _____
_____

2.79 $\frac{5}{2}x = 10$

Ck. _____
_____

2.80 $\frac{8x}{3} = 24$

Ck. _____
_____

2.81 $\frac{9x}{7} = 18$

Ck. _____
_____

2.82 $\frac{11x}{3} = 22$

Ck. _____
_____

2.83 $\frac{12x}{5} = 36$

Ck. _____
_____

2.84 $\frac{-2x}{5} = 8$

Ck. _____
_____

2.85 $\frac{1}{2}x = -9$

Ck. _____
_____

2.86 $\frac{2}{15}x = -30$

Ck. _____
_____

2.87 $18 = \frac{3x}{5}$

Ck. _____
_____

2.88 $22 = \frac{11}{3}x$

Ck. _____
_____

MATHEMATICS

9 0 2

LIFEPAC TEST

62 / 77

Name _____

Date _____

Score _____

MATHEMATICS 902: LIFEPAC TEST

Work these problems and circle your answers (each answer, 4 points).

1.   Evaluate: $|-6| + 3|4| + |-5| - 0 \cdot 6$

2.   Given $R = x(A + B)$, solve for B.

3.   Given $A = \frac{bh}{2}$, find A when $b = 12.6$, $h = 42$.

Write the answers (each answer, 5 points).

4.   Write an equation for "10 times the sum of a number and 14 is equal to 9 times the number".

_____

5.   Write a verbal statement for $2x - 3 = 6$.

_____

Graph the solution (each graph, 3 points).

6. $|x| = 7$

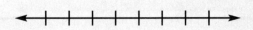

7. $|x| < 3$

8. $|x| + 1 > 2$

9. $3x + 1 < 7$

10. $2x - 1 > 5$

Solve. Show work in space below each problem, and circle your answer (each answer, 4 points).

11. $3x = 15$

12. $5x - 1 = 26$

13. $7x + 2 = 10$

14. $\frac{x}{2} = -5$

15. $\frac{3x}{6} + 1 = 7$

16. $\frac{5x}{2} - 3 = 17$

17. $5(2x - 1) = 6$

19. $4(x - 3) - 2(x - 1) > 0$

18. $7x + 1 < 4(x - 2)$

20. $3(3x - 1) + 2(3 - x) = 0$

NOTES

3

2.89 $\quad -16 = \frac{8x}{5}$

Ck. _____
_____

2.90 $\quad \frac{5x}{6} = 2$

Ck. _____
_____

2.91 $\quad \frac{-7}{8}x = -5$

Ck. _____
_____

2.92 $\quad \frac{9x}{7} = 10$

Ck. _____
_____

2.93 $\quad \frac{-13x}{2} = 5$

Ck. _____
_____

2.94 $\quad -\frac{16}{7}x = 3$

Ck. _____
_____

2.95 $\quad \frac{2x}{9} = -65$

Ck. _____
_____

(((((((((((((((((((((((**MULTISTEP EQUATIONS**)))

We will now use *both* the addition and the multiplication properties to solve an equation.

Model 1:

$$\frac{x}{5} + 7 = 22$$

Add -7

$$\frac{x}{5} + 7 - 7 = 22 - 7$$

$$\frac{x}{5} + 0 = 15$$

Multiply by 5:

$$5 \cdot \frac{x}{5} = 5 \cdot 15$$

$$x = 75$$

Check in the
original equation

$$\frac{75}{5} + 7 \overset{?}{=} 22$$

$$15 + 7 \overset{?}{=} 22$$

$$22 = 22 \quad \text{True}$$

Model 2:

$$13x - 9 = 73$$

Add 9

$$13x - 9 + 9 = 73 + 9$$

$$13x = 82$$

Multiply by $\frac{1}{13}$:

$$\frac{1}{13} \cdot 13x = \frac{1}{13} \cdot 82$$

$$x = \frac{82}{13}$$

Check

$$13 \cdot \frac{82}{13} - 9 \overset{?}{=} 73$$

$$82 - 9 \overset{?}{=} 73$$

$$73 = 73 \quad \text{True}$$

Model 3:

$$\frac{7x}{5} + 10 = 38$$

Add -10

$$\frac{7x}{5} + 10 - 10 = 38 - 10$$

$$\frac{7x}{5} = 28$$

Multiply by $\frac{5}{7}$:

$$\frac{5}{7} \cdot \frac{7}{5}x = \frac{5}{7} \cdot 28$$

$$x = 20$$

Check $\frac{7}{5} \cdot 20 + 10 = 38$

$28 + 10 = 38$

$38 = 38$ True

Note: In general to solve multistep equations, *add* first and then *multiply*.

 Solve and check. Circle your answer.

2.96 $6x + 2 = 14$

2.99 $7x - 2 = 12$

Ck. _____
_____
_____

Ck. _____
_____
_____

2.97 $3x + 5 = 17$

2.100 $10x - 5 = 15$

Ck. _____
_____
_____

Ck. _____
_____
_____

2.98 $4x + 5 = 25$

2.101 $12x - 8 = 16$

Ck. _____
_____
_____

Ck. _____
_____
_____

2.102 $\dfrac{x}{5} + 1 = 7$

2.106 $\dfrac{x}{13} - 5 = 5$

Ck. _____

_____

_____

Ck. _____

_____

_____

2.103 $\dfrac{x}{3} + 5 = 2$

2.107 $\dfrac{x}{15} - 8 = 20$

Ck. _____

_____

_____

Ck. _____

_____

_____

2.104 $\dfrac{x}{7} + 9 = 15$

2.108 $\dfrac{2x}{3} + 1 = 3$

Ck. _____

_____

_____

Ck. _____

_____

_____

2.105 $\dfrac{x}{12} - 3 = 2$

2.109 $\dfrac{3x}{5} + 4 = 19$

Ck. _____

_____

_____

Ck. _____

_____

_____

2.110 $\dfrac{5x}{7} + 5 = 30$

Ck. _____

_____

_____

2.111 $\dfrac{5x}{9} - 3 = 7$

Ck. _____

_____

_____

2.112 $\dfrac{8x}{13} - 2 = 14$

Ck. _____

_____

_____

2.113 $\dfrac{12x}{7} - 8 = 28$

Ck. _____

_____

_____

2.114 $9x + 1 = 11$

Ck. _____

_____

_____

2.115 $8x - 16 = 15$

Ck. _____

_____

_____

2.116 $3x - 4 = 13$

Ck. _____

_____

_____

2.117 $13x - 2 = 20$

Ck. _____

_____

_____

2.118 $20x - 20 = 90$

Ck. _____

_____

_____

2.119 $17x + 15 = 67$

Ck. _____

_____

_____

2.120 $\frac{7x}{2} + 5 = 8$

Ck. _____

_____

_____

2.121 $\frac{3x}{2} + 7 = 20$

Ck. _____

_____

_____

2.122 $\frac{8x}{7} + 9 = 30$

Ck. _____

_____

_____

2.123 $\frac{13x}{15} - 1 = 20$

Ck. _____

_____

_____

2.124 $\frac{18x}{5} - 5 = 5$

Ck. _____

_____

_____

2.125 $\frac{7x}{3} - 15 = 30$

Ck. _____

_____

_____

2.126 $16 = 2x - 1$

Ck. _____
_____
_____

2.127 $33 = 5x - 4$

Ck. _____
_____
_____

2.128 $15 = 22x + 7$

Ck. _____
_____
_____

2.129 $8x + 2 = 6x + 10$

Ck. _____
_____
_____

2.130 $9x - 4 = 7x - 10$

Ck. _____
_____
_____

2.131 $5x - 2 = 3x - 20$

Ck. _____
_____
_____

2.132 $15x + 6 = 10x + 21$

Ck. _____
_____
_____

2.133 $8x - 3 = 2x - 5$

Ck. _____
_____
_____

2.134 $13x + 7 = 5x - 20$ 2.136 $16x - 5 = 18x - 2$

Ck. _____   Ck. _____
    _____   _____
    _____   _____

2.135 $13x - 6 = 7 - 12x$ 2.137 $3x + 7 = 15 - 4x$

Ck. _____   Ck. _____
    _____   _____
    _____   _____

**************** **USE OF PARENTHESES** ***********************************

Parentheses in an algebraic equation require the use of the *distributive* property in conjunction with the *addition* and *multiplication* properties.

Model 1: $3(x + 2) = 24$

Distribute $3x + 6 = 24$
Add -6 $3x + 6 - 6 = 24 - 6$
                      $3x = 18$

Then
Multiply by $\frac{1}{3}$ $\frac{1}{3} \cdot x = \frac{1}{3} \cdot 18$

                      $x = 6$

Check in the original equation

$3(6 + 2) = 24$

$3(8) = 24$

$24 = 24$ True

NOTE: Always use the distributive property *first* to remove the parentheses; *add*, then *multiply* to isolate x on one side of the equation.

Model 2:

$$5(2x - 3) = 30$$

Distribute

$10x - 15 = 30$

add 15

$10x - 15 + 15 = 30 + 15$

$10x = 45$

Multiply by $\frac{1}{10}$

$\frac{1}{10} \cdot 10x = \frac{1}{10} \cdot 45$

$x = \frac{45}{10} = \frac{9}{2}$

Check

$5(2 \cdot \frac{9}{2} - 3) = 30$

$5(6) = 30$

$30 = 30$ True

Model 3:

$$5(2x + 3) = 2(x + 7)$$

Distribute

$10x + 15 = 2x + 14$

Add -15

$10x + 15 - 15 = 2x + 14 - 15$

$10x = 2x - 1$

Add -2x

$10x - 2x = 2x - 2x - 1$

$8x = -1$

Multiply by $\frac{1}{8}$

$\frac{1}{8} \cdot 8x = \frac{1}{8} \cdot (-1)$

$x = -\frac{1}{8}$

Check

$5(2(-\frac{1}{8}) + 3) \stackrel{?}{=} 2(-\frac{1}{8} + 7)$

$5(-\frac{1}{4} + \frac{12}{4}) \stackrel{?}{=} 2(-\frac{1}{8} + \frac{56}{8})$

$5(\frac{11}{4}) \stackrel{?}{=} 2(\frac{55}{8})$

$\frac{55}{4} = \frac{55}{4}$ True

Solve and check. Circle your answer.

2.138 $3(x + 2) = 12$

2.142 $9(x + 2) = 36$

2.139 $5(x - 2) = 50$

2.143 $10(x - 3) = 70$

2.140 $7(x + 1) = 21$

2.144 $4(x + 2) = 48$

2.141 $8(x - 1) = 24$

2.145 $11(x + 1) = 121$

2.146 $13(x - 3) = 39$ 2.150 $5(x + 1) = 4(x + 8)$

2.147 $-3(x - 4) = 15$ 2.151 $3(x - 1) = 2(x + 3)$
         [Hint: $-3(x - 4)$ is $-3x + 12$]

2.148 $-5(x + 4) = 40$ 2.152 $7(x + 2) = 6 (x + 5)$

2.149 $-7(x - 3) = -63$ 2.153 $6 (x - 2) = 4 (x + 10)$

2.154 $9(x-1) = 7(x-3)$

2.155 $5(x-3) = 3(x-7)$

2.156 $3(x+2) + 4(x-5) = 10$

2.157 $5(x-2) + 7(x-3) = 5$

2.158 $7(x-3) + 3(4-x) = -8$

2.159 $8(x-3) - 5(x+2) = 6$

2.160 $8(2x-3) - 5(3x-4) = 10$

2.161 $10(x-4) - 10(4-x) = 40$

2.162 $7(3 - x) = 8(4 - 2x)$

2.163 $13(3 - 2x) + 4(x + 1) = 7$

2.164 $5(x - 3) + 4(x + 3) = 3(x - 1)$

2.165 $7(x + 4) - 8(x + 3) = 5(2x - 1)$

2.166 $8(x + 4) - 3(x + 1) = 7(2 - x)$

2.167 $9(x - 3) + 8(x + 6) = 4(8 - 7x)$

2.168 $7(x + 2) - 3(x + 1) = 5(x - 6) - 8(2x - 6)$

LITERAL EQUATIONS

The formula $d = rt$ is the expression relating the measures of distance, rate (or speed), and time. Since the variable d is in the left member of the equation alone, we say either that d is the *subject* of the sentence, or that *the equation is solved for* d.

The relationship between d, r, and t may be expressed two other ways: solved for r or solved for t.

To solve $d = rt$ for r, we use the multiplication property.

Model 1:

$$d = rt$$

Multiply by $\frac{1}{t}$

$$\frac{1}{t} \cdot d = \frac{1}{t} \cdot rt$$

$$\frac{d}{t} = r \quad \text{or} \quad r = \frac{d}{t}$$

Likewise, to solve for t, we multiply by $\frac{1}{r}$.

Model 2:

$$d = rt$$

$$\frac{1}{r} \cdot d = \frac{1}{r} \cdot rt$$

$$\frac{d}{r} = t \text{ or } t = \frac{d}{r}$$

We now have all three forms of the formula.

$$d = rt, \ r = \frac{d}{t}, \ t = \frac{d}{r}$$

Model 3:

Solve

$$P = 2l + 2w \text{ for } w,$$

$$P = 2l + 2w$$

Add - $2l$

$$P - 2l = 2l + 2w - 2l$$

$$P - 2l = 2w$$

Multiply by $\frac{1}{2}$

$$\frac{1}{2}(P - 2l) = \frac{1}{2} \cdot 2w$$

$$\frac{P - 2l}{2} = w \quad \text{or} \quad w = \frac{P - 2l}{2}$$

Model 4:

Solve

$$A = \frac{h}{2}(a + b) \text{ for } b.$$

$$A = \frac{h}{2}(a + b)$$

Multiply by 2 $\qquad 2A = 2 \cdot \frac{h}{2}(a + b)$

$$2A = h(a + b)$$

Distribute $\qquad 2A = ha + hb$

add -ha $\qquad 2A - ha = ha + hb - ha$

$$2A - ha = hb$$

Multiply by $\frac{1}{h}$ $\qquad \frac{1}{h}(2A - ha) = \frac{1}{h} \cdot hb$

$$\frac{2A - ha}{h} = b \quad \text{or} \quad b = \frac{2A - ha}{h}$$

NOTE: To solve a literal equation, use the addition, multiplication, and distributive properties to get the desired variable on one side alone.

 Solve for the variable indicated. Circle your answer.

2.169 $\qquad x + a = yb \qquad$ for y $\qquad\qquad$ 2.172 $\qquad xy + p = 5 \qquad$ for y

2.170 $\qquad x - a = y - 6 \qquad$ for a $\qquad\qquad$ 2.173 $\qquad ab - c = 10 \qquad$ for b

2.171 $\qquad ab + c = 5 \qquad$ for c $\qquad\qquad$ 2.174 $\qquad ab + c = d \qquad$ for b

2.175	$ab + c = d$	for a		2.181	$P = 2l + 2w$	for l
2.176	$ab + cd = 5$	for c		2.182	$P = 2l + 2w$	for w
2.177	$3a + 2b = c$	for b		2.183	$ax + by = c$	for y
2.178	$3abc + b = 5$	for c		2.184	$ax - by = c$	for x
2.179	$i = prt$	for r		2.185	$A = lw$	for w
2.180	$i = prt$	for p		2.186	$A = lw$	for l

2.187 $\qquad A = \frac{h}{2}(b+c) \qquad$ for c $\qquad$ 2.188 $\qquad A = \frac{h}{2}(b+c) \qquad$ for h

 Review the material in this section in preparation for the Self Test. This Self Test will check your mastery of this particular section as well as your knowledge of the previous section.

SELF TEST 2

Evaluate. Show work in space below each problem, and circle your answer (each answer, 4 points).

2.01 $\qquad 5|{-3}| - 2$ $\qquad\qquad$ 2.04 $\qquad 7(A - A)$

2.02 $\qquad |{-6}| - |{-6}|$ $\qquad\qquad$ 2.05 $\qquad 8 \cdot 0 \cdot 7$

2.03 $\qquad 5|{-10}| + 6|{-10}|$ $\qquad\qquad$ 2.06 $\qquad 7 \cdot 1 - \frac{7}{1}$

Solve. Show work in space below each problem, and circle your answer (each answer, 4 points).

2.07 $\qquad x - 8 = 10$ $\qquad\qquad$ 2.09 $\qquad x + 4 = 32$

2.08 $\qquad x - 8 = -10$ $\qquad\qquad$ 2.010 $\qquad 2x = 32$

54

2.011 $5x = -25$

2.014 $\frac{x}{7} = -3$

2.012 $-8x = -48$

2.015 $\frac{-x}{8} = -5$

2.013 $\frac{x}{6} = 10$

Evaluate the formula. Show work in space below each problem, and circle your answer (each answer, 3 points).

2.016 $V = e^3$ for

    a. $e = 2$ b. $e = 1.3$ c. $e = \frac{1}{2}$

2.017 $I = prt$ for

    a. $p = 200, r = .05, t = 1$

    b. $p = 3{,}000, r = .07, t = 3$

2.018 $A = \frac{bh}{2}$ for

        a. $b = 8, h = 10$ b. $b = 20.8, h = 6.2$

Write an open sentence (each answer, 5 points).

2.019   8 times the cube of a number is 64. _____

2.020   7 times the sum of a number and 6
            is greater than 63. _____

Solve each equation. Show work in space below each problem, and circle your answer (each answer, 4 points).

2.021 $x + 8 = 17$ 2.025 $5x = 35$

2.022 $x - 10 = -30$ 2.026 $7x = 78$

2.023 $5x - 6 = 4x + 8$ 2.027 $-10x = -210$

2.024 $7x + 9 = 6x - 5$ 2.028 $5x = -123$

2.029 $\dfrac{3x}{2} = 15$

2.030 $\dfrac{5x}{7} = -20$

2.031 $5x - 3 = 12$

2.032 $7x + 8 = 43$

2.033 $\dfrac{3x}{4} + 3 = 27$

2.034 $\dfrac{5x}{7} - 5 = 50$

2.035 $4(x + 2) = 12$

2.036 $6(2x - 1) = 18$

2.037 $7(x - 2) = 4(x - 3)$

2.038 $5(2x - 6) + 3(2x - 8) = 0$

2.039   Solve for c in $ac - D = R$

2.040   Solve for l in $P = 2l + 2w$

$\dfrac{137}{171}$

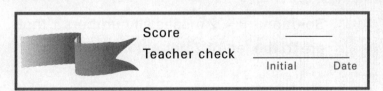

Score   _____

Teacher check   _____
                 Initial   Date

Sentences that use the *equal* symbol are called equations. Sentences that use either the *less than* symbol (<) or the *greater than* symbol (>) are called *inequalities*.

THE LINE GRAPH

The following sentences are inequalities:

$$x > 5 \qquad 6x - 3 < 4 \qquad 7(x - 3) > 5(x + 2)$$

In the sentence $x > 5$, we are asking for all numbers that are greater than 5. There are infinitely many numbers that make this sentence true. We may show this solution by means of the line graph.

The solution to $x > 5$ is all numbers to the right of 5 but *not including* 5. The open circle on 5 means is not included in the solution.

Model 1:

Graph the solution of $x < 2$.

Solution: $x < 2$ means all numbers x that are to the left of 2 but *not including* 2.

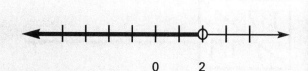

Model 2:
Graph $x > -2$.

Solution:

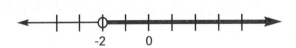

Model 3:
Graph $x + 3 < 5$.

Solution: Since 2 + 3 is equal to 5,
then a number less than
2 when added to 3 will be
less than five. Thus,
graph $x < 2$

 Solve each inequality mentally; then graph the solution.

3.1 $x < 3$

3.6 $x < -2$

3.2 $x > -3$

3.7 $x < 0$

3.3 $x > 0$

3.8 $x < -3$

3.4 $x > -4$

3.9 $x < 1$

3.5 $x > 4$

3.10 $x + 1 > 2$

3.11 $x - 1 > 2$

←—+—+—+—+—+—+—+—+—+—→

3.17 $3x < -6$

←—+—+—+—+—+—+—+—+—+—→

3.12 $x + 2 < 5$

←—+—+—+—+—+—+—+—+—+—→

3.18 $5x > -10$

←—+—+—+—+—+—+—+—+—+—→

3.13 $x - 2 < 2$

←—+—+—+—+—+—+—+—+—+—→

3.19 $2x < 5$

←—+—+—+—+—+—+—+—+—+—→

3.14 $2x > 4$

←—+—+—+—+—+—+—+—+—+—→

3.20 $3x > 4$

←—+—+—+—+—+—+—+—+—+—→

3.15 $3x < 3$

←—+—+—+—+—+—+—+—+—+—→

3.21 $2x < -3$

←—+—+—+—+—+—+—+—+—+—→

3.16 $2x < -2$

←—+—+—+—+—+—+—+—+—+—→

///////////// **ADDITION AND MULTIPLICATION PROPERTIES** /////////

The Addition Property of Inequalities states that you may add any number you choose to both sides of an inequality without changing the order of inequality.

THE ADDITION PROPERTY OF INEQUALITY
For numbers a, b, c: If $\quad\quad a < b$ $\quad\quad$ If $\quad\quad a > b,$ $\quad\quad\quad\quad$ and Then $\quad a + c < b + c$ $\quad\quad$ Then $\quad a + c > b + c$

We can test the addition property by looking at some numerical examples. Since $6 < 10$, any number added to both sides of this sentence will not change the *order* of the sentence.

Model 1:   6 < 10

           6 + 7 < 10 + 7

              13 < 17   True

Model 2:   10 > 4

           10 + 20 > 4 + 20

              30 > 24   True

Model 3:   -6 < 7

           -6 − 5 < 7 − 5

              -11 < 2   True

The multiplication property of inequality states that multiplying both sides of an inequality by the same number may or may not change the status of the inequality.

MULTIPLICATION PROPERTY OF INEQUALITY

A.   If both sides of an inequality are multiplied by a *positive* number, the order of the inequality remains *unchanged*.

B.   If both sides of an in equality are multiplied by a *negative* number, the order of the inequality is *reversed*.

A. Models   For $c > 0$

If	$a < b$	If	$a > b$
	and		
then	$ac < bc$	then	$ac > bc$
	$-1 < 5$		$6 > 5$
	$-1(8) < 5(8)$		$6 \cdot 5 > 5 \cdot 5$
	$-8 < 40$ True		$30 > 25$ True

B. Models   For $c < 0$

If	$a < b$		If	$a > b$
		and		
then	$ac > bc$		then	$ac < bc$

$$8 < 10 \qquad\qquad\qquad 6 > -9$$

$$8(-3) > 10(-3) \qquad\qquad 6\,(-4) < (-9)\,(-4)$$

$$-24 > -30 \quad \text{True} \qquad\qquad -24 < 36 \quad \text{True}$$

Model 1:   Solve $x + 5 < 20$

Solution: $x + 5 < 20$

Add -5 $x + 5 - 5 < 20 - 5$

$$x + 0 < 15$$

$$x < 15$$

Model 2:   Solve $3x - 7 > 20$

Solution: $3x - 7 > 20$

Add 7 $3x - 7 + 7 > 20 + 7$

$$3x + 0 > 27$$

$$3x > 27$$

Multiply by $\frac{1}{3}$ $\frac{1}{3} \cdot 3x > \frac{1}{3} \cdot 27$

$$x > 9$$

Model 3:   Solve $10 - 4x < 30$

Solution $10 - 4x < 30$

Add -10 $10 - 10 - 4x < 30 - 10$

$-4x < 20$

Multiply by $-\frac{1}{4}$ $(-\frac{1}{4})(-4x) > (-\frac{1}{4})(20)$

$x > -5$

➡ **Solve each inequality using the addition and multiplication properties.** Circle your answer.

3.22 $x + 5 > 10$ 3.25 $x + 5 > -10$

3.23 $x - 5 > 10$ 3.26 $x + 3 < 10$

3.24 $x - 5 > -10$ 3.27 $x - 3 < -10$

3.28	$x + 3 > -10$	3.36	$9x > -36$
3.29	$x - 5 < -8$	3.37	$-5x > 10$
3.30	$x - 6 < 4$	3.38	$-6x < 36$
3.31	$2x > 16$	3.39	$-10x > -40$
3.32	$3x < 9$	3.40	$-7x < -21$
3.33	$5x > 25$	3.41	$-9x > -45$
3.34	$7x < -14$	3.42	$15x < -45$
3.35	$9x < -27$	3.43	$2x + 6 > 4$

3.44 $3x - 5 < 4$

3.45 $7x - 10 > 18$

3.46 $2x - 7 < 5$

3.47 $3x + 9 > 27$

3.48 $5x - 8 < 2$

3.49 $5x < 16 + x$

3.50 $3x > 10 - 2x$

3.51 $12x < 22 + x$

3.52 $12x + 2 < 11x + 5$

3.53 $8x - 10 > 7x + 20$

3.54 $15x - 9 > 10x + 1$

3.55 $13x - 4 < 12x - 1$

3.56 $5(2x + 1) < 10$

3.57 $3(x - 1) > 4$

3.58 $7(x - 2) < -5$

3.59 $8(x + 1) > 7(x + 2)$

3.60 $9(x - 3) < 4(x + 10)$

3.61 $3(x + 2) > 0$

3.62 $7(x - 3) < 0$

3.63 $7(x + 4) > 0$

3.64 $5(2x - 6) < 0$

3.65 $3(x + 1) + 2(x + 2) > 0$

3.66 $7(x - 1) + 6 (x + 2) < 0$

3.67 $\frac{7x}{2} < 5$

3.68 $\frac{3x}{7} > 4$

3.69 $\frac{5x}{11} < 2$

3.70 $\frac{-4x}{7} > 10$

3.71 $\frac{-8x}{13} + 5 > 2$

3.72 $-\dfrac{9x}{11} - 7 < -5$

◆◆◆◆◆◆◆◆◆ **SENTENCES WITH ABSOLUTE VALUE** ◆◆◆◆◆◆◆◆◆◆◆◆◆◆◆◆◆

The equation $|x| = 2$ is read "the absolute value of some number is equal to 2," and two values of x will make this open sentence true. Either $x = 2$ since $|2| = 2$, or $x = -2$ since $|-2| = 2$. The solution for this equation is graphed as

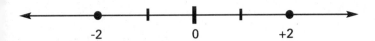

When using a number line, the absolute value of any number can be thought of as the distance from zero to that number, without regard to direction. The number 2 is 2 units from 0, so $|2| = 2$; the number -2 is also 2 units from 0, so $|-2| = 2$.

Absolute value can be used in inequality expressions, such as $|x| > 2$. The numbers to the right of 2 and the numbers to the left of -2 are all more than 2 units from 0. Therefore the absolute value of any such number is also more than 2, or $|x| > 2$. The solution for this inequality is graphed as

For inequality $|x| < 2$, the absolute value of any such number is less than 2. Because the numbers between -2 and 2 are all less than 2 units from 0, the solution for this inequality is graphed as

You may need to use the addition and multiplication properties to simplify open sentences involving absolute value.

Model 1:   Graph the solution of $|x| - 1 = 3$

Solution: $|x| - 1 = 3$

Add 1 $|x| - 1 + 1 = 3 + 1$

                    $|x| = 4$

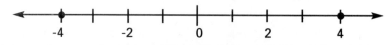

Model 2:   Graph the solution of $2|x| + 4 < 10$.

Solution: $2|x| + 4 < 10$

              $2|x| + 4 - 4 < 10 - 4$

                  $2|x| < 6$

Multiply $\frac{1}{2}$ $\frac{1}{2} \cdot 2|x| < \frac{1}{2} \cdot 6$

                  $|x| < 3$

Model 3:   Graph the solution of $|x| > 1\frac{1}{2}$

Solution:

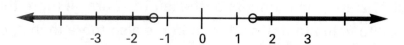

Model 4:   Graph the solution of $|x + 2| = 4$.

Solution: If $x = 2$, then $x + 2 = 2 + 2 = 4$, and $|4| = 4$.

If $x = -6$ then $x + 2 = -6 + 2 = -4$, and $|-4| = 4$.

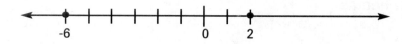

Model 5:   Graph the solution of $|x - 1| > 0$.

Solution: There is only one number having an absolute value of zero, and that is zero itself.

If $x = 1$, then $x - 1 = 1 - 1 = 0$, and $0 = 0$.

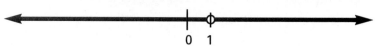

Model 6:　Graph the solution of $|x| + 4 = 1$.
Solution:
$$|x| + 4 = 1$$
$$|x| + 4 - 4 = 1 - 4$$
$$|x| = -3, \text{ which has no solution}$$
since the absolute value
of a number cannot be
negative.

(no solution)

Graph the solution of each open sentence.

3.73　　$|x| = 10$

3.77　　$|x| = -2$

3.74　　$|x| < 3$

3.78　　$|x| > 1$

3.75　　$|x| > 4$

3.79　　$|x| + 1 < 3$

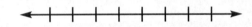

3.76　　$|x| = 5$

3.80　　$|x| - 1 > 2$

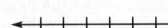

3.81 $|x| - 3 > 3$

<----+---+---+---+---+---+---+---+---->

3.87 $4|x| - 1 < -4$

<----+---+---+---+---+---+---+---+---->

3.82 $2|x| < 4$

<----+---+---+---+---+---+---+---+---->

3.88 $|x| < \frac{1}{2}$

<----+---+---+---+---+---+---+---+---->

3.83 $3|x| > 6$

<----+---+---+---+---+---+---+---+---->

3.89 $|x| > \frac{3}{2}$

<----+---+---+---+---+---+---+---+---->

3.84 $2|x| = 10$

<----+---+---+---+---+---+---+---+---->

3.90 $|x| + 1 > \frac{7}{2}$

<----+---+---+---+---+---+---+---+---->

3.85 $2|x| + 1 < 5$

<----+---+---+---+---+---+---+---+---->

3.91 $|x - 1| < 4$

<----+---+---+---+---+---+---+---+---->

3.86 $5|x| + 3 < 18$

<----+---+---+---+---+---+---+---+---->

3.92 $|x + 1| < 5$

<----+---+---+---+---+---+---+---+---->

Before you take this last Self Test, you may want to do one or more of these self checks.

1. _____ Read the objectives. See if you can do them.
2. _____ Restudy the material related to any objectives that you cannot do.
3. _____ Use the SQ3R study procedure to review the material:
   a. **S**can the sections.
   b. **Q**uestion yourself (Review the questions you wrote initially).
   c. **R**ead to answer your questions.
   d. **R**ecite the answers to yourself.
   e. **R**eview areas you did not understand.
4. _____ Review all vocabulary, activities, and Self Tests, writing a correct answer for every wrong answer.

SELF TEST 3

Evaluate. Show work in space below each problem, and circle your answer (each answer, 4 points).

3.01 $-3\,|4|\,+7\cdot0$

3.04 $a = \dfrac{h}{2}\,(b + c)$, for

       a. $b = 8, c = 6, h = 5$

3.02 $|\text{-}5|\;-\;|\text{-}5|$

       b. $b = 15, c = 12, h = 9$

3.03 $|\text{-}6|\;+\;|6|$

Translate (each answer, 5 points).

3.05   Write an equation for " the sum of 8 times a number and 7 is twice the number."

_____

3.06   Write a verbal statement for $3(x + 2) = 6$.

_____

Solve. Show work in space below each problem, and circle your answer (each answer, 4 points).

3.07 $3x + 6 = 12$

3.08 $5x - 8 = 63$

3.09 $9(x - 2) = 18$ 3.012 $\frac{5x}{7} - 8 = 14$

3.010 $7(x - 3) = 4(x + 5)$ 3.013   Solve for A in $BA + C = D$

3.011 $\frac{7x}{3} + 2 = \text{-}15$

Graph the solution. Show any work in space below each problem (each answer, 5 points).

3.014 $x < 4$

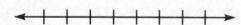

3.015 $x > \text{-}3$

3.016 $x < \text{-}1$

3.017 $2x < 7$

3.018 $3x > 6$

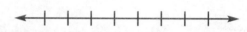

3.019 $x - 1 < 2$

Solve. Show work in space below each problem, and circle your answer (each answer, 4 points).

3.020 $3x + 1 < 7$ 3.021 $5x + 7 > 17$

3.022	$2x - 8 < 17$		3.025	$3(x + 2) > x$

3.023	$3(x - 2) < 18$		3.026	$\frac{11x}{5} > 11$

3.024	$9(x - 3) > 27$		3.027	$-\frac{7x}{3} < 2$

3.028 $\frac{3x}{5} > -6$

Graph the solution. Show any work in space below each problem (each answer, 5 points).

3.029 $|x| = 2$

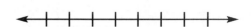

3.034 $|x| > 5$

3.030 $|x| = 1$

3.035 $|x| + 3 > 7$

3.031 $|x| = -5$

3.036 $|x| < \frac{1}{2}$

3.032 $|x| < 2$

3.037 $|x| + 1 < 3$

3.033 $|x| < 4$

3.038   Given $A = 3(B + C)$, solve for B (5 points).

_____

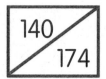

140 / 174

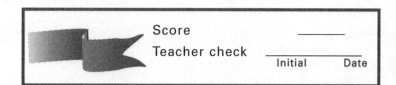

Score _____

Teacher check _____

Initial   Date

     Before taking the LIFEPAC Test, you may want to do one or more of these self checks.

1. _____ Read the objectives. See if you can do them.
2. _____ Restudy the material related to any objectives that you cannot do.
3. _____ Use the SQ3R study procedure to review the material.
4. _____ Review activities, Self Tests, and LIFEPAC vocabulary words.
5. _____ Restudy areas of weakness indicated by the last Self Test.

GLOSSARY

absolute value — A number without regard to sign.

equation — A mathematical sentence whose verb is equal (=).

formula — A mathematical expression of a natural law.

inequality — A mathematical sentence whose verb is either "is greater than" (>) or "is less than" (<).

perimeter — The distance around a geometric figure.

MATHEMATICS 903
PROBLEM ANALYSIS AND SOLUTION

CONTENTS

I. WORDS AND SYMBOLS 2
Translating Words to Symbols 2
Solving Verbal Problems 6

II. SIMPLE VERBAL PROBLEMS 13
Simple Number Problems 13
Number Problems with More Unknowns 20
Geometry Problems 23
Problems Involving Money 31

III. MEDIUM VERBAL PROBLEMS 41
Age Problems 41
Motion Problems 45
Lever Problems 50
Integer Problems 54

IV. CHALLENGING VERBAL PROBLEMS 63
Number Problems and Geometry Problems 63
Age, Motion, and Lever Problems 66
Integer, Investment, and Mixture Problems 68
GLOSSARY 74

Author: James Coe, M.A.
Editor-In-Chief: Richard W. Wheeler, M.A.Ed.
Editor: Robin Hintze Kreutzberg, M.B.A.
Consulting Editor: Robert L. Zenor, M.A., M.S.
Revision Editor: Alan Christopherson, M.S.

Alpha Omega Publications®

804 N. 2nd Ave. E., Rock Rapids, IA 51246-1759
© MCMXCVI by Alpha Omega Publications, Inc.   All rights reserved.
LIFEPAC is a registered trademark of Alpha Omega Publications, Inc.

MATHEMATICS 905
PROBLEM ANALYSIS AND SOLUTION

CONTENTS

I. WORDS AND SYMBOLS 2
Translating Words into Symbols 2
Solving Verbal Problems 8

II. SIMPLE VERBAL PROBLEMS 13
Simple Number Problems 13
Number Problems with More Unknowns 20
Geometry Problems 23
Problems Involving Money 37

III. MIXTURE AND RATE PROBLEMS 41
Age Problems 41
Mixture Problems 45
Work Problems 50
Motion Problems 54

IV. CHALLENGING VERBAL PROBLEMS 63
Number Problems and Geometry Problems 63
Mixture and Rate Problems 69

GLOSSARY 74

Author: James Cox, M.A.
Editor-in-Chief: Richard W. Wheeler, M.A.Ed.
Editor: Robin Hintze Kreutzberg, M.B.A.
Consulting Editor: Robert Zenor, M.A., M.S.
Revision Editor: Alan Christopherson, M.S.

PROBLEM ANALYSIS AND SOLUTION

A typical and normal question asked by students about algebra is "What good will this subject do me?" or "How will I ever use this course?" This LIFEPAC® contains many good answers to those questions.

We study numbers and their behavior properties and we learn to solve equations all for a major purpose: to solve application problems. Many practical problems are just too complicated to figure out by arithmetic.

Certain words and phrases can easily be translated into symbols and equations. Other word problems involve careful reading and rereading before they can be translated into equations. A four-step procedure can be used for all word problems. Word problems can be problems that deal with certain numbers or they can be about geometry, money, ages, motion, levers, integers, or mixtures.

Although at times textbook problems may not seem realistic, they serve two purposes. They give students an opportunity to learn problem-solving techniques; and they allow perceptive students to see the practical potential in using algebra to solve live problems, whether architectural, engineering, medical, or other science-related problems.

OBJECTIVES

Read these objectives. The objectives tell you what you will be able to do when you have successfully completed this LIFEPAC.

When you have finished this LIFEPAC, you should be able to:

1. Change word problems to symbols.
2. Write equations to solve word problems effectively.
3. Solve problems involving two or more numbers, problems involving geometric concepts, and problems involving money.
4. Solve age problems, motion problems, lever problems, and integer problems.
5. Solve problems with complications beyond the very easy level.

Survey the LIFEPAC. Ask yourself some questions about this study. Write your questions here.

_____

_____

_____

_____

_____

_____

_____

_____

I.   WORDS AND SYMBOLS

OBJECTIVES

When you have completed this section, you should be able to:

1. Change word problems to symbols.
2. Write equations to solve word problems effectively.

Before we learn to solve word problems using algebra, we should look at some general procedures. We must be able to translate certain words and phrases and we must have an identifiable procedure to solve each problem.

TRANSLATING WORDS TO SYMBOLS

Too many words are used in word problems to discuss in one lesson, but we can identify some of them. Some words you must be able to identify and use for solving word problems are these: *sum, difference, product, quotient, exceeds, by, excess, diminished by, more than, greater than, fewer than, less than, less, twice, doubled, tripled, consecutive, divided by, divided into, quotient of, increased by, decreased by, times, plus, minus, subtracted from, multiplied by, square of, square root of, cube of, is equal to, is less than, is greater than, numerator,* and *denominator.* These words indicate which operation or operations will be used to solve the word problem. In most cases, addition, subtraction, multiplication, or division will be involved in the translation from words into symbols.

The concept used most often is the sum of two numbers. Many times, seemingly, the idea is cleverly disguised, but you should look for it when solving a word problem.

Models: Two angles are complementary.

Joe and Mary have 48 books on animals.

Traveling in opposite directions, Tom and Jerry leave Auburn.

Exceeds by and *excess* are used to show subtraction or addition.

Models: If Laura exceeds the 55 mph speed limit by x, then her speed will be 55 + x.

If Don's weight, x, exceeds 175 pounds, the amount of excess could be written as $x - 175$.

If you can identify words that describe certain mathematical symbols, you can improve your reading of word problems.

Model: Frank has some money. George has $7 more than Frank. How much money do George and Frank have together?

Let x represent Frank's money. Then $x + 7$ means George has $7 more than Frank. $x + (x + 7)$ represents the amount of money George and Frank have together.

Complete these activities.

1.1 List the operation words given on page 2 into the five groups.

a. words that involve addition

_____   _____

_____   _____

_____   _____

_____   _____

b. words that involve subtraction

_____   _____

_____   _____

_____   _____

_____   _____

c. words that involve multiplication

_____   _____

_____   _____

_____   _____

_____   _____

3

d. words that involve division

_____   _____

_____   _____

e. words that are not involved with +, −, x, ÷

_____   _____

_____   _____

_____   _____

_____   _____

Write examples of sentences using one word or a phrase from each of the five groups.

Model: Subtraction: George has $19 less than Tom.

1.2   Addition: _____

1.3   Subtraction: _____

1.4   Multiplication: _____

1.5   Division: _____

1.6   Other: _____

Write each of the word expressions in mathematical symbols. Use symbols of grouping when necessary. Do not combine the numbers or simplify the expressions.

1.7   The sum of 8 and 4   _____

1.8   The difference between six and three _____

1.9   The product of 9 and 8   _____

1.10   Twelve divided by six   _____

1.11   4 minus x _____

1.12   The square of 6   _____

1.13   The excess when five exceeds x _____

4

1.14 x exceeded by 3   _____

1.15   Twice x decreased by 4   _____

1.16   Fourteen decreased by three times a number   _____

1.17   Four more than the quotient of x and 3   _____

1.18   2 increased by the cube of n _____

1.19   12 diminished by 6 times a number   _____

1.20   Three times the difference between t and y _____

1.21   The quotient of 12 and 5 times a number   _____

1.22   Nine times a number diminished by 7   _____

1.23   The consecutive integer after the integer n _____

1.24   The triple of x _____

1.25   12 less than 3 times a number   _____

1.26   Two times the sum of 4 and y _____

1.27   Jeri is three years younger than Laura, whose age is x. How old is Jeri?   _____

1.28   In a softball diamond, the distance from first base to third base is 1.4 times the distance from first base to home plate. If x represents the distance from first base to home plate, how would you represent the distance from first base to third base?   _____

1.29   One side of a square is $a + 3$ inches. What is the perimeter of the square?   _____

1.30   How many cents are in x quarters and 25 dimes?   _____

1.31   The width of a rectangle is y feet long, and it is 4 feet longer than it is wide. What is the area of the rectangle?   _____

1.32   A boy is 6 years older than his sister, whose age is x. What is the boy's age?   _____

1.33   A room is 15 feet long and y feet wide. How many square yards are in the floor area?   _____

1.34   What is the average of 171 and x?   _____

1.35   A house costs $600 more than 12 times the

       lot on which it was built. If the lot cost

       x dollars, what did the house cost?   _____

1.36   A man walks 10 miles in x hours. How far

       does he walk in one hour?   _____

1.37   How many minutes are in m hours?   _____

1.38   A plane flies x mph. How far can it go

       in y hours?   _____

1.39   If a pipe can fill a tank in x hours, what

       fractional part of the tank will be filled

       in one hour?   _____

1.40   Four years ago, Tammy's age was x. How old

       is she now?   _____

=========================== **SOLVING VERBAL PROBLEMS** ===========================

Word problems, sometimes called verbal problems, can be very frustrating. If an organized approach to their solution is used, much of the frustration will be avoided. A very simple four-step system can help you organize your problem solving:

1.   Identify the number(s) that you are looking
    for and choose a variable for the unknown
    number. If you are looking for more than one
    number make a careful choice for your variable
    and define the other significant numbers of the
    problem in terms of that variable.

2.   Write an equation (or inequality if the
    problem doesn't give an equality relationship).
    This step requires careful examination
    of the variables from Step 1 and their
    relationship to each other or other numbers
    in the problem. You may need to reread the
    problem several times.

3.   Solve the equation using the techniques
    learned in the preceding LIFEPAC. Be sure
    to check your equation.

4. Identify your answer(s) and check the conditions of the problem. Answers should be labeled as age of son, age of father; first number, second number; rate of motor boat, rate of canoe; and so on.

The check you did in Step 3 has very little to do with this check. If your equation is correct, however, you may be doing the same arithmetic to check the problem. The best approach in checking your word problem is to forget Steps 1, 2, and 3 and to check the answer independently of your steps.

Many word problems can be categorized as one type or another. When reading a word problem for the first time, learn to think of it as a geometry problem, an integer problem, a coin problem, an age problem, or whatever kind of problem it is.

DEFINITIONS

Age problem: a word problem that involves the ages of people.

Coin problem: a word problem that involves nickels, dimes, quarters, or half dollars. Sometimes different denominations of bills are used also ($1 bill, $5 bill).

Geometry problem: a word problem that involves geometric figures. Usually a sketch is drawn to help with the solution.

Integer problem: a word problem that involves integers. The integers are the counting numbers, their opposites, and zero.

Mixture problem: a word problem that involves mixing of ingredients, sometimes in liquid form.

In the problems that follow, pay strict attention to the suggested approach and the models that are given for each type of problem. Remember the four steps:

1. Identify each unknown number; choose a variable expression for each number.
2. Write an equation or inequality.
3. Solve the equation or inequality.
4. Identify and label answer(s), and check the conditions stated in the problem.

Read these word problems carefully. They will be the basis for the next set of activities.

Problem 1. A chess team won 4 times as many matches as it lost. If 16 matches were won, how many games did the team lose?

Problem 2. The length of a rectangle is 12 inches more than its width. What is the width of the rectangle if the perimeter is 42 inches? (Remember that the perimeter of a rectangle equals length + length + width + width.)

Problem 3. A man traveled a certain number of miles by automobile and then nine times as far by airplane. His total trip was 600 miles in length. How far did he travel by plane?

Problem 4. If Sarah is 24 years younger than her mother and if the sum of their ages is 68, how old is Sarah?

Problem 5. Jane is 8 years older than Tom. Five years ago Jane was 3 times as old as Tom. How old is Tom now?

Problem 6. Mark had 3 times as many quarters as nickels. He had $1.60 in all. How many nickels and how many quarters did Mark have?

Problem 7. How many quarts of water must be added to 4 quarts of a 20% water mixture to obtain a 50% mixture?

Problem 8. Joe can wash and wax his car in 4 hours. Susan can wash and wax her car in 3 hours. If they worked together to wash their sick friend's car how long would it take them?

Problem 9. The tens' digit of a number is twice the ones' digit. The sum of the digits in the number is 12. What is the number?

Problem 10. A triangle has a perimeter of 48. If 2 sides are equal and the third side is 6 less than the equal sides, what is its length?

The first step in solving a word problem is to identify the variable. Let x be a variable used in each of the ten problems. Tell what the variable expressions represent in the problems.

Model: Problem 1 x represents the number of games the chess team lost

                                   $4x$ represents the number of games the chess team won

1.41   Problem 2 x represents   _____

                                   $x + 12$ represents   _____

1.42   Problem 3 x represents   _____

                                   $9x$ represents   _____

1.43	Problem 4	x represents	_____
		$x - 24$ represents	_____
Model:	Problem 5	x represents Tom's age	
		$x + 8$ represents Jane's age	
1.44	Problem 6	x represents	_____
		$3x$ represents	_____
1.45	Problem 7	x represents	_____
		$x + 4$ represents	_____
Model:	Problem 8	t represents the time it takes to wash and wax a car together	
		1 car/ 4 hours represents Joe's rate	
		1 car/ 3 hours represents Susan's rate	
1.46	Problem 9	x represents	_____
		$2x$ represents	_____
1.47	Problem 10	x represents	_____
		$x - 6$ represents	_____

 The second solution step is to write an equation for the problem. Write an equation for each of the word problems.

Model:	Problem 1	$4x = 16$
1.48	Problem 2	_____
1.49	Problem 3	_____
1.50	Problem 4	_____
1.51	Problem 5	_____
1.52	Problem 6	_____
1.53	Problem 7	_____
Model:	Problem 8	$1/4(t) + 1/3(t) = 1$ car (rate x time = work)
1.54	Problem 9	_____
1.55	Problem 10	_____

 Write the problem numbers beside the correct description.

| 1.56 | geometry problem(s) | _____ |
| 1.57 | age problem(s) | _____ |

1.58	digit problem(s)	_____
1.59	work problem(s)	_____
1.60	coin problem(s)	_____
1.61	mixture problem(s)	_____

 Write each of these statements as an equation. Choose your own variable if one is not given.

1.62	Three pounds of butter at $\$n$ per pound cost $3.85.	_____
1.63	One-half of a certain number is 95.	_____
1.64	The perimeter of a rectangle is 68 in. The perimeter equals twice the length of l in., plus twice the width of 9 in.	_____
1.65	Mary Lou has 2 more nickels than pennies, and she has 30 coins all together.	_____
1.66	Jim weighs 30 lb. less than Tom, and together they weigh 210 lb.	_____
1.67	A class of 19 pupils has 5 more girls than boys.	_____
1.68	One side of a triangle is x in., another side is $2x$ in., a third side is $2x$ in., and the perimeter is 36 in.	_____
1.69	John has three times as many marbles as Bill, and together they have 100 marbles.	_____
1.70	Mr. Randall is three times as old as his son John. Nine years ago he was nine times as old as John.	_____

- ■ - ■ - ■ - ■ - ■ - ■ - ■ - ■ - ■ - ■ - ■ - ■ - ■ - ■ - ■ -

 Review the material in this section in preparation for the Self Test. This Self Test will check your mastery of this particular section. The items missed on this Self Test will indicate specific areas where restudy is needed for mastery.

SELF TEST 1

Choose the correct letter to identify the right multiple choice answer (each answer, 2 points).

1.01 John's weight exceeds 100 lbs. by x. John's weight would be represented by

_____ .

    a. $100 + x$ b. $x - 100$ c. $100 - x$ d. none of these

1.02 The sum of two numbers is x. If one of the numbers is 12, what is the other?

_____

    a. $12 - x$ b. $x - 12$ c. $12 + x$ d. $12 \cdot x$

1.03   The difference of two numbers is 6. The smaller number is x. Represent the other

number. _____

   a. $6 - x$ b. $x \div 6$ c. $6 - (x - 6)$ d. $6 + x$

1.04   A certain number is decreased by 28. Represent the second number if x is the

original number. _____

   a. $28 - x$ b. $x - 28$ c. $x + 28$ d. none of these

1.05   Twice a certain number is tripled. The resulting number is _____.

   a. $2x + 3$ b. $2x - 3$ c. $(2x)3$ d. $\frac{1}{3}(2x)$

1.06   After John worked at a job for 10 years, his salary doubled. What is his salary

after 10 years if he started at x? _____

   a. $\frac{1}{2}x$ b. $x + 2$ c. $x - 2$ d. $2x$

1.07   12 is divided by x. Which does not represent the quotient? _____

   a. $\frac{12}{x}$ b. $12 \div x$ c. $x \div 12$ d. x divided into 12

1.08   The quotient of a number $x + 4$ and 12 is _____.

   a. $\frac{x}{12} + 4$ b. $x + \frac{1}{3}$ c. $\frac{x + 4}{12}$ d. $\frac{x}{4} + 12$

1.09   The square root of 144 is best described as _____.

   a. 144^2 b. $\sqrt{144}$ c. $16 \cdot 9$ d. $12 \cdot 12$

1.010   If the numerator of the fraction $\frac{x}{6}$ is increased by 10, the result will be

_____.

   a. $\frac{x}{16}$ b. $\frac{x - 10}{16}$ c. $x + \frac{5}{3}$ d. $\frac{x + 10}{6}$

Write each word expression in mathematical symbols (each answer, 3 points).

1.011   The difference of 6 and x _____

1.012   The quotient of y and 6 increased by 4   _____

1.013   One side of a square is $3x + 2$. What is the perimeter? _____

1.014   How many hours are in x days?   _____

1.015 How old will Bill be in 10 years if he is $x + 2$

   years old now?   _____

1.016 17 decreased by the square of x _____

1.017 If Susie is 14, what was her age x years ago?   _____

1.018 4 more than x tripled   _____

1.019 The value in cents of 4 quarters and x dimes   _____

1.020 Joe can paint x houses in a five-day work week.

   How many can he paint in one day?   _____

Complete these items (each answer, 3 points).

1.021 Name the four steps for solving a word problem.

   1. _____

   2. _____

   3. _____

   4. _____

1.022 Dwayne's garden is triangle-shaped with two equal sides and a third side that is 4

   ft. more than the length of an equal side. If the perimeter is 49 ft., how long is

   each side? This problem is _____ .

   a. an age problem   c. a geometry problem

   b. a distance problem   d. a coin problem

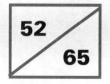

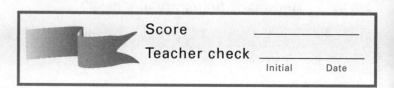

II. SIMPLE VERBAL PROBLEMS

OBJECTIVE
When you have completed this section, you should be able to:

3. Solve problems involving two or more numbers, problems involving geometry, and problems involving money.

Many number tricks could be carefully analyzed as word problems. Suppose I ask you to double your age and multiply the result by 10. Then add the number of eggs in 30 dozen and divide that result by 2. Subtract the number of cents in seven quarters plus one nickel, divide by 10, and the result will reveal your age. Are you overwhelmed by the magic? Look at the following expression. Let x be your age. Then by following the instructions, you can write the algebraic expression $(\frac{2x\,(10) + 360}{2} - 180) \div 10$, which equals the mystery number. By simplifying the expression, you will see that x is your age.

Many other verbal problems can be solved algebraically. This section will deal with number (integer) problems, geometry problems, and money (coin) problems.

SIMPLE NUMBER PROBLEMS

Some problems have variables that must be added or subtracted to form the equation for the solution.

The problem should be stated in these three models. The complete step-by-step solution is fine, but *must* be preceded by a statement of the problems.

Model 1: George has $12, which is $7 more than Tom has. How much money does Tom have?

Step 1 { Let x be the amount of money Tom has, and $x + 7$ be the amount of money George has.

Step 2 {
$$x + 7 = 12$$
$$x = 5$$

Step 3
$$5 + 7 \overset{?}{=} 12$$
$$12 = 12$$
Tom has $5.

Step 4 Check:
$$\$ \ 7$$
$$+ \ 5$$
$$\overline{\$ \ 12}$$

Some problems involve multiplication or division in Steps 1 and 3 of our problem solving procedure.

Model 2:   The width of a rectangle is 9 ft. The length of the rectangle is a multiple of 9. The area is 324 sq. ft. Find the length.

Step 1   Let $9x$ be the length of the rectangle.

Step 2
$$9(9x) = 324$$
$$81x = 324$$
$$x = 4$$

Step 3
$$9(9 \cdot 4) \stackrel{?}{=} 324$$
$$9 \cdot 36 \stackrel{?}{=} 324$$
$$324 = 324$$

Step 4   The length of the rectangle is 36 ft.; 36 is a multiple of 9.

Check: 36 ft.
         x 9 ft.
         —————
         324 sq. ft.

Some problems combine operations in the first two steps. Look for words that tell you to add, subtract, multiply, or divide.

Model 3:   Joe is 5 years older than twice Theresa's age. The sum of their ages is 23. What are their ages?

Step 1   Let x be Theresa's age and

$2x + 5$ be Joe's age.

Step 2
$$x + 2x + 5 = 23$$

Step 3
$$3x + 5 = 23$$
$$3x = 18$$
$$x = 6$$
$$6 + 5 + 12 \stackrel{?}{=} 23$$
$$23 = 23$$

Step 4   Joe is 17 years old. Theresa is 6 years old.

Check: 6   12   17
         x 2   + 5   + 6
         ———   ———   ———
         12   17   23

These problems (2.1 – 2.25) can be done after a thorough study of the models. Even though the models deal with money, geometry, and age, they are considered examples of number problems.

Solve these problems using all four steps.

2.1   A number increased by 13 is 30. Find the number.

Variable:

Equation:

Solution to equation:

Check the problem:

2.2   Three-sevenths of a number is 21. Find the number. (Continue showing all steps as in problem 2.1.)

2.3   If 3 times a certain number increased by 4 is equal to 28, what is the number?

2.4   The larger of two numbers is 5 times the smaller number. The sum of the numbers is 54. Find the numbers.

2.5   One positive number is 8 times another number. Their difference is 70. Find the numbers.

2.6 Harvey is 3 times as old as Jane. The sum of their ages is 48 years. Find the age of each.

2.7 Twice a number plus 4 is -54. Find the number.

2.8 The difference between 7 times a number and 5 is 51. Find the number.

2.9 A board 60 in. long is cut into two parts so that the longer piece is 5 times the shorter. What are the lengths of the two pieces?

2.10 Twice a number is 16 more than 42. What is the number?

2.11   If six times a certain number is added to 8, the result is 32. Find the number.

2.12   Two consecutive numbers have a sum of 23. Find the numbers. (Hint: Add 1 to find the next number $x + 1$.)

2.13   17 is equal to a certain number increased by twice 3. What is the number?

2.14   A number plus 7 more than the number is 29. What is the number?

2.15   Of two numbers, one exceeds the other by 32. Their sum is 46. Find the numbers.

2.16   Twice a certain number less 17 equals 37. Find the number.

2.17   If 9 is subtracted from two-thirds of a number, the result is 7. Find the number.

2.18   Seven times a number minus the number is -48. Find the number.

2.19   The product of a number and 8 is 81. Find the number.

2.20   Ten less than twice a number is the same as 7 times the number. Find the number.

2.21   Five times a number is the same as 30 more than 8 times the number. Find the number.

2.22   Two fewer than a number doubled is the same as the number decreased by 38. Find the number.

2.23   If a number is tripled, it equals the product of four and the number diminished by two. Find the number.

2.24   Three multiplied by the sum of 4 and a number is the same as 18 more than the number. Find the number.

2.25   The quotient of a number and 2 is the same as the difference of the number doubled and 3. Find the number.

Some problems seem more complicated because they have more than two unknowns to be determined. These problems are naturally longer, but not always more difficult.

Model: The sum of three numbers is 76. If the second number is twice the first and the third number is one more than the second, what are the three numbers?

Let x be the first number and
$2x$ be the second number and
$2x + 1$ be the third number.

$$x + 2x + 2x + 1 \ = \ 76$$
$$5x + 1 \ = \ 76$$
$$5x \ = \ 75$$
$$x \ = \ 15$$
$$15 + 2(15) + 2(15) + 1 \ \overset{?}{=} \ 76$$
$$75 + 1 \ \overset{?}{=} \ 76$$
$$76 \ = \ 76$$

15 is the first number.

30 is the second number.

31 is the third number.

Check: 15   30   15
            x 2   + 1   30
            ‾‾‾   ‾‾‾   + 31
             30   31   ‾‾‾
                                     76

Show all four steps in each of these word problem solutions.

2.26   The sum of three numbers is 62. The second number is equal to the first number diminished by 4. The third number is four times the first. What are the numbers?

2.27   The sum of three numbers is 26. The second number is twice the first and the third number is 6 more than the second. Find the numbers.

2.28   Separate 846 into 3 parts so that the second part is twice the first part and the third part is triple the second part.

2.29   A Girl Scout troop sold cookies. If they sold 5 more boxes the second week than they did the first, and if they doubled the sales of the second week for the third week to sell a total of 431 boxes of cookies, how many did they sell each week?

2.30   A man divided $9,000 among his wife, son, and daughter. The wife received twice as much as the daughter, and the son received $1,000 more than the daughter. How much did each receive?

2.31   Ted weighs twice as much as Julie. Mike weighs three times as much as Julie. Together they weigh 210 lbs. What is the weight of each person?

2.32   The four oldest people in Golden City have lived 384 years. The difference in ages for the youngest and the next oldest is 14. The next youngest is 3 years older than the youngest. The oldest is 20 years older than the average of the next oldest and youngest. How old is each?

2.33   Four numbers have a total of 92. The first number is twice the second number and the third number is 4 more than the sum of the first two. The fourth number is 3 less than the difference of the first two numbers. What are the numbers?

2.34   Nine pounds of sweet potatoes cost the same as 6 pounds of apples. One pound of sweet potatoes costs twice as much as a pound of onions, while a pound of apples costs 24 cents more than a pound of onions. Find the cost of each.

2.35   "I am 3 times as old as Sue is," said Frank to Ann. "On the other hand, I am 15 years older than John, while Sue is 1 year younger than John. How old am I?"

GEOMETRY PROBLEMS

Many problems involve simple geometric figures. A sketch is often helpful with this type of problem and may replace Step 1 of the solution process. You should also be familiar with certain formulas you have studied in previous LIFEPACs.

Perimeter Formulas

Rectangle	p =	$2l + 2w$
Square	p =	$4s$
Triangle	p =	$a + b + c$
Circle	c =	$2\pi r$

REMEMBER?

Area Formulas

Rectangle	A =	lw
Square	A =	s^2
Triangle	A =	$\frac{1}{2}bh$
Circle	A =	πr^2
Trapezoid	A =	$\frac{1}{2}h(b_1 + b_2)$

REMEMBER?

Model: The length of a rectangle is twice its width. The perimeter is 60 ft. Find the length and the width of the rectangle.

$$2x + 2(2x) = 60$$
$$6x = 60$$
$$x = 10$$
$$20 + 40 \overset{?}{=} 60$$
$$60 = 60$$

10 is the width
20 is the length

x

(This diagram replaces the "Let . . ." statement.)

$2x$

Check:

10	20	20
x 2	x 2	+ 40
20	40	60

Geometry problems can involve use of the words *complementary* or *supplementary*. Two angles are complementary if the sum of their measures is 90°. Two angles are supplementary if the sum of their measures is 180°.

DEFINITIONS

Complementary angles: two angles whose sum is 90°. Each angle is the complement of the other.
Supplementary angles: two angles whose sum is 180°. Each angle is the supplement of the other.

Model: Two angles are supplementary. One contains 30° more than the other. Find the angles.

Let x be the measure of the first angle and $180 - x$ be the measure of the second angle.

$$180 - x = x + 30$$
$$150 = 2x$$
$$x = 75$$
$$180 - 75 \overset{?}{=} 75 + 30$$
$$105 = 105$$

The measures of the angles are 75 and 105.

Check:

75	75
+ 105	+ 30
180	105

Two properties of geometric figures will be helpful when dealing with the angles of a triangle or the angles of a quadrilateral.

PROPERTIES

A. The sum of the measures of the angles of a triangle is 180°.
B. The sum of the measures of the angles of a quadrilateral is 360°.

Model: In a trapezoid, the second angle is twice the first. The third angle has a measure that is 40° less than the measure of the second angle. The third and fourth angles are supplementary. What are the measures of the angles?

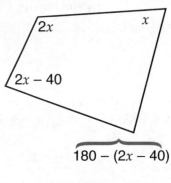

$$x + 2x + 2x - 40 + 180 - (2x - 40) = 360$$
$$5x - 40 + 180 - 2x + 40 = 360$$
$$3x + 180 = 360$$
$$3x = 180$$
$$x = 60$$

$$180 - (2x - 40)$$

The angle measures are 60°, 120°, 80°, and 100°.

Check:

60	120	100	100
x 2	-40	+80	60
120	80	180	80
			100
			360

$$60 + 120 + 120 - 40 + 180 - 80 \stackrel{?}{=} 360$$
$$480 - 120 \stackrel{?}{=} 360$$
$$360 = 360$$

Solve these problems using the four steps. Step 1 may be replaced by a labeled sketch.

2.36   Find the length of the side of a square with a perimeter of 60 cm.

2.37   If the area of a rectangle is 144 sq. in. and the length of one side is 18 in., what is the length of the other side?

2.38   The sides of a triangle are represented by x, $3x$, and $3x + 2$. Find each side if the perimeter is 37.

2.39   The circumference of a circle is 132 yds. Find the radius using $\pi = \dfrac{22}{7}$.

2.40   One side of a rectangle is 3 less than the other side and the perimeter is 54 inches long. What are the dimensions of the rectangle?

2.41   In a trapezoid the sum of the bases is 28 and the area is 84. What is the altitude or height of the trapezoid?

2.42   In a triangle the area is 16 more than the base. If the height is 6, what is the length of the base?

2.43   The first side of a triangle is 2 cm. longer than the second side. The third side is 5 cm. shorter than twice the second side. The perimeter is 49 cm. Find the length of each side.

2.44   A square and an equilateral triangle have the same perimeter. Each side of the triangle is 16 m. Find the length of each side of the square.

2.45   The perimeter of the rectangular top of a bookcase is 54 in. Find the length if the width is 7 in.

2.46   The length of a rectangle is twice its width. The perimeter is 60 ft. Find its area.

2.47   Each of the equal sides if an isosceles triangle exceeds the base by 5 in. If the perimeter is 100 in., what are the lengths of the three sides?

2.48   In an isosceles triangle the base is a whole number and is 4 ft. less than the sum of the two equal sides. The perimeter is a whole number between 0 and 75 feet. Find the possible lengths of the equal sides.

2.49   The length of the first side of a triangular piece of wood is twice the length of the second side and the length of the third side is one inch less than the first side. If the perimeter is 79 what are the lengths of the sides?

2.50   A rectangular field is 4 times as long as it is wide. If the length is decreased by 10 in. and the width is increased by 2 in. the perimeter will be 80 inches. Find the dimensions of the original field.

2.51   In a triangle the measure of the first angle is one-half the measure of the second angle. The third angle's measure is 20° less than the measure of the second angle. What are the measures of the angles?

2.52   Two angles of a triangle have equal measures, but the third angle's measure is 36° less than the sum of the other two. Find the measure of each angle of the triangle.

2.53   Find two supplementary angles if the measure of the first is four times the measure of the second.

2.54   An angle is 25° less than the measure of its complement. What is the measure of the smaller angle?

2.55   An angle is 14° more than the measure of its complement. Find the number of degrees in each angle.

2.56   An angle measures 15° more than twice its supplement. Find the measure of the supplement.

2.57   If the three angles of a triangle have equal measures, find that measure.

2.58   In a quadrilateral each angle is double another angle. What are the measures of the angles?

2.59   If a quadrilateral is inscribed in a circle, its opposite angles will be supplementary. Find the measure of angle A if the measure of angle $C = 40°$.

2.60   Two angles are complementary. One contains 30° more than the other. Find both angles.

2.61   How large is an angle whose supplement contains 12° less than three times its complement?

2.62   One angle of a triangle measures 6° more than the second. The third angle measures 4° less than 3 times of the sum of the measures of the first two angles. Find the measures of the three angles.

2.63   In a quadrilateral two angles are equal. The third angle has a measure that is equal to the sum of the equal angles. The fourth angle is 75° less than twice the sum of the other three angles. What are the measures of the angles?

=========== **PROBLEMS INVOLVING MONEY** ===========

Interest problems are based on the formula for simple interest and the formula for amount.

FORMULAS

$$i = prt$$
$$A = p + i$$

The interest earned is represented by i, and p represents the principal, or the number of dollars invested. The time the money is invested is represented by t and is generally stated in years or fractions of a year. The rate at which interest is paid is represented by r.

The amount is simply what your investment is worth if you consider the total amount of the original investment and the interest earned. A more complicated formula is used to determine the value of your investment over a period of years, if you let the interest accumulate.

DEFINITIONS

Amount formula: $A = p + i$ is a formula used to determine the value an investment after the interest has been credited.

Interest: a payment for the use of money borrowed or invested.

Interest formula: $i = prt$ is the formula used to compute the interest for a specific principal, interest rate, and time period.

Principal: the amount of money invested or borrowed at a certain rate of interest.

Model 1: Find the interest on $1,400 invested at 7% for 1 year. (Use either $\frac{7}{100}$ or 0.07 for 7%.)

$i = 1,400 \left(\frac{7}{100}\right) 1$

$i = 98$

Model 2: Mr. Jones needs interest income of $5,000. How much money must he invest for one year at 7%? (Give answer to nearest dollar.)

$$5,000 \quad = \quad p \left(\frac{7}{100}\right)1$$
$$500,000 \quad = \quad 7p$$
$$p \quad = \quad 71,428\tfrac{4}{7}$$

$71,429 must be invested.

Check: $\qquad 5,000 \quad = \quad \frac{50,000}{7} \left(\frac{7}{100}\right) 1$

$$
\begin{array}{r}
\$71,429 \\
\times \quad .07 \\
\hline
\$5,000.03
\end{array}
$$

Coin problems involve a certain number of pennies, nickels, dimes, quarters, half-dollars and silver dollars. You should distinguish between the number of coins and the value of the coins. The value of the coins must be added, not the number of coins, to get the total value of the coins.

When a word problem involves money, be careful with the decimal point. In some cases, you may want to change dollar amounts to cents.

Model: $18.48 = 1848¢

32

Model: George has $31.15 from paper route collections. He has 5 more nickels than quarters and 7 fewer dimes than quarters. How many of each coin does George have?

Let x = the number of quarters and
$x + 5$ = the number of nickels and
$x - 7$ = the number of dimes.

Value of quarters		Value of nickels		Value of dimes		Total value
$25x$	+	$5(x + 5)$	+	$10(x - 7)$	=	3,115
$25x$	+	$5x + 25$	+	$10x - 70$	=	3,115
				$40x$	=	3,160
				x	=	79
$25(79)$	+	$5(79 + 5)$	+	$10(79 - 7)$	=	3,115
1,975	+	420	+	720	=	3,115
		2,395	+	720	=	3,115

George has 79 quarters, 84 nickels, and 72 dimes.

Check:
$19.75	$0.25	$0.05	$0.10
4.20	x 79	x 84	x 72
+ 7.20	$19.75	$4.20	$7.20
$31.15			

 Use the interest formulas to find the following values.

2.64 p = $300 r = 7% t = 2   Find i.   _____

2.65 p = $14,300 $r = 7\frac{1}{2}\%$ t = 4   Find i.   _____

2.66 i = $125 r = 6% t = 1   Find p.   _____

2.67   George invests some money at 4% per year. After half a year he receives $20 interest. Find the principal.

2.68   A man earns $112 interest in one year on an investment of $1,400. What was his rate of interest?

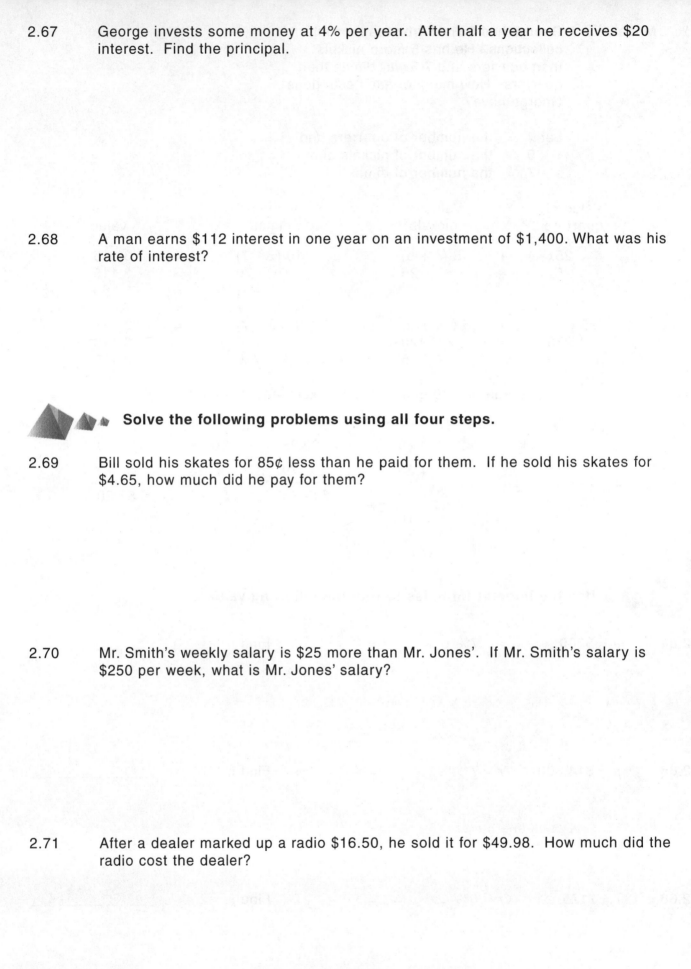 **Solve the following problems using all four steps.**

2.69   Bill sold his skates for 85¢ less than he paid for them. If he sold his skates for $4.65, how much did he pay for them?

2.70   Mr. Smith's weekly salary is $25 more than Mr. Jones'. If Mr. Smith's salary is $250 per week, what is Mr. Jones' salary?

2.71   After a dealer marked up a radio $16.50, he sold it for $49.98. How much did the radio cost the dealer?

2.72   A boy earned $10 more than twice as much as his sister. Together they earned $60. How much did each earn?

2.73   George drew half of his money out of the bank to go shopping. After spending $9, he had $3 left. How much did he have in the bank originally?

2.74   A boy has 11 coins in dimes and quarters. Their value is $1.70. How many of each does he have? (Hint: Let x be the number of quarters and $11 - x$ be the number of dimes.)

2.75   John has 83¢ in pennies and quarters. He has 5 more pennies than quarters. How many coins of each kind does he have?

2.76   Sally has seven times as many dimes as nickels. Their value is $3.00. How many nickels does she have?

2.77   A clerk was asked to change a $10 bill. She returned 9 more dimes than nickels and twenty-one more quarters than dimes. How many coins of each did she return?

2.78   A club treasurer has $28.45 consisting of nickels, dimes, and quarters. She has 9 more nickels than dimes and three times as many dimes as quarters. How many does she have of each coin?

2.79   For a school play, 739 tickets valued at $857 were sold. Some cost $1 and others cost $1.50. How many $1 tickets were sold?

2.80   A bank teller was asked to cash a check for $260 with three times as many one-dollar bills as fives and half as many tens as fives. What denominations of cash should the teller have given?

2.81   Bob has in his pocket a number of pennies, five times as many nickels as pennies, and 6 more quarters than pennies. The coins amount to a value of $2.52. Find the number of pennies.

MATHEMATICS

9 0 3

LIFEPAC TEST

$\dfrac{38}{47}$

Name _____

Date _____

Score _____

MATHEMATICS 903: LIFEPAC TEST

Match the items on the left with the letter of the best description on the right (each answer, 2 points).

1. _____ sum   a. result of multiplying numbers

2. _____ area of a square   b. result of dividing numbers

3. _____ lever problem formula   c. $c = 2\pi r$

4. _____ product   d. $A = lw$

5. _____ interest formula   e. $i = prt$

6. _____ area of a circle   f. $A = p + i$

7. _____ difference   g. $w_1 d_1 = w_2 d_2$

8. _____ rate formula   h. $r = \dfrac{d}{t}$

9. _____ consecutive even integers   i. $n, n + 2$

10. _____ quotient   j. result of adding numbers

       k. $A = s^2$

       l. $d = rt$

       m. result of subtracting numbers

       n. $x, x + 1$

       o. $A = \pi r^2$

In the following items, read the problem involved and choose the best answer in each multiple choice question (each answer, 2 points).

11. If six times a certain number is added to 8, the result is 32.

    The number in this problem would be represented as _____ .

    a. $x + 8$ b. x c. $32 - x$ d. $6x$

12. The equation for the problem is _____ .

    a. $6x = 32$ c. $6x = 8 + 32$

    b. $x + 8 = 32$ d. $6x + 8 = 32$

13. The number we are looking for in this problem is _____.

    a. 4   b. $6\frac{2}{3}$ c. 40   d. 12

Use the following information for problems 14-16.
Peggy had three times as many quarters as nickels. She had $1.60 in all.
How many nickels and how many quarters did she have?

14. The variable n would be used to represent _____.

    a. number of nickels   c. the value of the nickels

    b. number of quarters   d. the value of the quarters

15. The equation for the problem is _____.

    a. $n + 3n = 1.60$ c. $5n + 75n = 1.60$

    b. $n + 3n = 160$ d. $5n + 75n = 160$

16. The solution to the problem is _____.

    a. 2 nickels   c. 4 nickels and 12 quarters

    b. 40 nickels   d. 2 nickels and 6 quarters

Use the following information for problems 17-19.
Ralph is 3 times as old as Sara. In 6 years, Ralph will be only twice as old as Sara will be then. Find Ralph's age now.

17. Ralph's age now would be represented as _____.

    a. x b. $3x$ c. $x + 6$ d. $3x + 6$

18. The equation for solving this problem is _____.

    a. $3x + 2x$ c. $3x + 6 = 2 (x + 6)$

    b. $x + 6 = 2 (3x + 6)$ d. $3x + 6 = 2x + 6$

19. Ralph's age is _____.

    a. 6   b. 12   c. 18   d. 24

20. Find two consecutive integers whose sum is 67.
    The larger integer should be represented as _____.

    a. x b. $x + 1$ c. $x + 2$ d. $x - 1$

21. The integers are _____.

    a. 32 and 35   c. 34 and 35

    b. 33 and 35   d. 33 and 34

2

22.   The first side of a triangle measures 5 in. less than the second side. The third side is 3 in. more than the first side, and the perimeter is 17 in. How long is each side? Show all work. (5 points).

2.82   Thomas has $6.35 in dimes and quarters. The number of dimes is three more than three times the number of quarters. How many quarters does he have?

2.83   In changing a $5 bill on her paper route, Jeri gave her customer 9 more dimes than nickels and seven fewer quarters than dimes. How many coins of each type did the customer receive?

Review the material in this section in preparation for the Self Test. This Self Test will check your mastery of this particular section as well as your knowledge of the previous section.

SELF TEST 2

Complete these items (each answer, 3 points).

2.01   What variable expressions would you use to represent a number and another number which is 8 more than the original?

a. the original number _____   b. the other number _____

2.02   If the sum of the numbers in the previous item (2.01) is 42, what equation could be used to find the numbers? _____

2.03   The formula for finding the area of a rectangle is $A =$ _____ .

2.04   The formula for finding the circumference of a circle is $C =$ _____ .

2.05   The sum of the measures of two complementary angles is _____ .

2.06   The formula for finding interest is $i =$ _____ .

2.07   Represent the value of 5 nickels and x dimes. _____

2.08   If $400 is invested at the rate of 6% for one year, what will be the total value of the investment (the amount)? _____

Use the four steps to solve each of the following problems (each problem, 5 points).

2.09   If 4 times a certain number increased by 6 is equal to 94, what is the number?

2.010   The product of 8 and the sum of 4 and a number is 112. What is the number?

2.011   The quotient of a number and 3 is the same as the difference of the number doubled and 5. What is the number?

2.012   The sum of three numbers is 69. If the second number is equal to the first diminished by 8, and the third number is 5 times the first, what are the numbers?

2.013　　Greg weighs twice as much as Theresa. John weighs three times as much as Theresa. Together they weigh 480 lbs. How much does Greg weigh?

2.014　　Dad's age is equal to the sum of Laura's, Jeri's and Theresa's ages. If Jeri is 4 years older than Theresa and 3 years younger than Laura, and Dad's age is 38, how old is each daughter?

2.015　　If the area of a rectangle is 296 square inches and its width is 8 inches, what is its length?

2.016　　A triangle has an area of 144 sq. inches and its base is 2 ft. long. What is the altitude of the triangle?

2.017　　In a triangle, the measure of one angle is twice the measure of another angle. The third angle is equal to the sum of the other two angles. What are the measures of the angles?

2.018   A boy has 93¢ in pennies, nickels, dimes, and quarters. He has two more quarters than dimes. If he has as many nickels as dimes and as many pennies as quarters, how many of each coin does he have?

2.019   Mr. Gonzales' weekly salary is $40 more than Mr. Williams' salary. If Mr. Gonzales' salary is $280 per week, what is Mr. Williams' salary?

2.020   If a man earns $420 interest in one year at 7%, what was the amount of money invested?

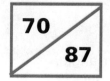

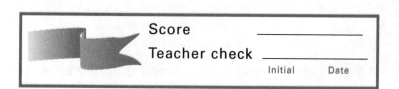

III. MEDIUM VERBAL PROBLEMS

OBJECTIVE

When you have completed this section, you should be able to:

4. Solve age problems, motion problems, lever problems, and integer problems.

Age problems, problems dealing with rate of travel and time, lever problems, and integer problems require special techniques for their solutions. They may involve a table, a sketch, or use of a certain type of formula. In this section pay particular attention to the special solution techniques of each problem type.

AGE PROBLEMS

The simple idea of subtracting or adding a number to determine one's age in the past or in the future is often a helpful technique to use for solving age problems.

Model: Joe's age is 5 less than twice his age 10 years ago. How old is Joe?

$$\text{Let } x = \text{Joe's age and}$$
$$x - 10 = \text{Joe's age ten years ago.}$$

Joe's age is 5 less than twice his age 10 years ago

$$x = 2(x - 10) - 5$$
$$x = 2x - 20 - 5$$
$$x = 2x - 25$$
$$25 = x$$

Joe is 25 years old.

Check:
$$25 \overset{?}{=} 2(25 - 10) - 5$$
$$25 \overset{?}{=} 2(15) - 5$$
$$25 \overset{?}{=} 30 - 5$$
$$25 = 25$$

You should draw a chart when working problems that involve ages of two or more people. A chart helps you organize the basic information and allows the equation to be written with the least amount of thinking.

41

Model: George is 3 times as old as his sister Kate. Kate is 5 years younger than their sister Sue. In 5 years, George will be twice as old as Kate. How old is each now?

	age now	age in 5 years
George	3x	3x + 5
Kate	x	x + 5
Sue	x + 5	x + 10

The table should be filled in by simply adding 5. Leave the new relationship for the equation.

George will be twice Kate.

$$3x + 5 = 2(x + 5)$$
$$3x + 5 = 2x + 10$$
$$x = 5$$
$$3(5) + 5 \stackrel{?}{=} 2(5 + 5)$$
$$15 + 5 \stackrel{?}{=} 2(10)$$
$$20 = 20$$

George is 15 years old.
Kate is 5 years old.
Sue is 10 years old.

Check:

5	5	10
x 3	+ 5	x 2
15	10	20

 **Represent these answers in terms of x.**

3.1   If Tammy is x years old now, how old will she be in 10 years?   _____

3.2   How old was Tammy 11 years ago?   _____

3.3   If Tom is 5 more than twice Dick's age, how old is he?   _____

3.4   If Harry's age is $3x - 12$, how old will he be 15 years from now?   _____

3.5   How old was Lisa x years ago if she is now 13?   _____

Solve these word problems using the four-step approach.

3.6   If Joy's age now is 3 times her age 14 years ago, how old is she?

3.7   John's age increased by 11 is 5 less than 5 times his age. How old is he?

3.8   If Doris lives to be 100, her age will be 8 less than 4 times her wedding day age. How old was she when she was married?

3.9   In 28 years a man will be twice as old as he will be in 2 years. How old is he now?

3.10   Four years ago, Tom's age was $\frac{3}{4}$ of the age he will be in 6 years. How old is he now?

3.11 Tom's age is three less than twice the age of his brother Dick. The sum of their ages is twenty-seven. Find the age of each brother.

3.12 Laura is 6 years older than Theresa. In two years Laura will be twice as old as Theresa. Find their ages.

3.13 Dick is now seven times as old as Harry. In six years Dick will be five times as old as Harry. How old will Harry be in 5 years?

3.14 Tom's age is 17 and his father's age is 50. How many years ago was the father four times as old as Tom?

3.15 Susan is three times as old as Nancy, and Carrie is 5 years younger than Susan. Three years ago the sum of their ages was 56. What was Nancy's age four years ago?

Motion problems deal with distance traveled. The formula for finding the distance traveled when you know the rate of travel and the time of travel is: $d = rt$.

DEFINITIONS

Motion problem: a word problem that involves the distance a moving object will travel at a certain average rate for a given period of time.

Rate: the distance an object will travel divided by the time it will travel: $r = \dfrac{d}{t}$.

Model: A car is traveling 50 miles per hour. How far will it travel in 4 hours?

$$d \ = \ rt$$
$$d \ = \ 50 \cdot 4$$
$$d \ = \ 200$$

In using this formula, if the rate is in miles per hour and the time is in minutes, be sure that you change the units appropriately.

In many distance problems, a sketch can be very helpful to aid in analyzing the problem.

Model: A motorist and a bicyclist leave the same place and proceed in opposite directions. If the bicycle is traveling 15 mph and the auto is traveling 55 mph, in how many hours will they be 140 miles apart?

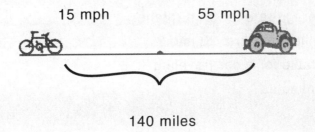

140 miles

Let t = the number of hours

$$15t + 55t = 140$$
$$70t = 140$$
$$t = 2$$
$$15(2) + 55(2) \overset{?}{=} 140$$
$$30 + 110 \overset{?}{=} 140$$
$$140 = 140$$

They will be 140 miles apart in 2 hours.

Check:

15	55	110
x 2	x 2	+30
30	110	140

Motion problems can generally be organized with tables.

Model: In the previous model, the information could have been organized in a table.

	r	t	d
automobile	55	t	$55t$
bicyclist	15	t	$15t$

$$70t = 140$$
$$t = 2 \text{ hrs}$$

Total distance $70t$ The time is 2 hours.

 **Write the required information.**

3.16   How far does a bus travel in 4 hrs. at 55 mph?

3.17   What is the time required to travel 100 miles on a bicycle at 20 miles per hour?

3.18   What is the average rate for an airplane that flies 480 miles in 2 hrs. 30 min.?

3.19   Complete this table for a car traveling 50 mph for 30 minutes.

r	t	d

3.20   Fifty-six minutes is what part of an hour?   _____

 Show the four steps in the following word problems.

3.21   If an airplane goes 420 miles in 2 hrs., what is the average rate in miles per hour?

3.22   Two boys who live 14 miles apart start at noon to walk toward each other at rates of 3 mph and 4 mph respectively. In how many hours will they meet?

3.23   A troop of scouts hike to the scout cabin at the rate of 2 miles per hour. They ride back to headquarters at 18 miles per hour. If the round trip takes 10 hours, how far is headquarters from the cabin?

3.24   Harry's motorboat can make an average of 8 miles per hour. One day he sets out for a trip, only to have the motor break down. Harry rows back at two miles an hour. When he reaches his dock, he finds that he has been gone 5 hours. How far has he rowed?

3.25   To reach a vacation spot, the Jones family first traveled by plane and then drove the remaining distance in a rented car. The distance by car was 125 kilometers less than the distance by plane. The total distance was 500 kilometers less than three times the distance traveled by car. Find the distance flown in the airplane.

3.26   Mr. Black leaves Chicago at 8:00 A.M. and drives north on the highway at an average speed of 50 miles per hour. Mr. Smith leaves Chicago at 8:30 A.M. and drives along the same highway at an average speed of 60 mph. At what time will Mr. Smith overtake Mr. Black? (Hint: Let t be Mr. Smith's time in hours; then $t + \frac{1}{2}$ will be Mr. Black's time since he left 30 minutes earlier.)

3.27   The average speed of a train is 20 miles per hour faster than that of a car. In 8 hours and 40 minutes, the train covers the same distance that the car covers in 13 hours. Find the average speed of each.

3.28   Two trucks started toward each other at the same time from towns 500 km apart. One truck traveled at a rate of 65 km per hour, while the other traveled at 60 km per hour. After how many hours did they meet?

3.29 Dick sets out on a hike. After walking for a while at 5 miles per hour, he discovers he has forgotten his lunch. A passing truck takes him home at 20 miles an hour. When he gets home he finds that he has lost exactly one hour. How far had he walked?

3.30 Tom took a trip of 1,020 miles. He traveled by train at 55 miles an hour and the same number of hours by plane at 285 mph. How many hours did the trip take?

3.31 In a race, Mary is 50 ft. in front of Susie after 10 seconds. How fast can Mary run if Susie runs 20 ft. per second?

3.32 A train travels 90 miles in $1\frac{1}{2}$ hours. How many miles will the train go, traveling at the same rate in 6 hours?

3.33 Tim and Galen were walking toward town at 3 km per hour. Half an hour later, Liz and Tammy left from the same point and walked in the same direction at 4 km per hour. For how many hours had the boys walked when the girls caught up with them?

3.34   A freight train averaging 45 mph and an express train averaging 60 mph leave the station at the same time. How long will the express train take to get 100 miles ahead of the freight train?

3.35   A man drives out in the country at an average rate of 40 mph. In the evening traffic he drives back at 30 mph. If the total traveling time is 7 hours, what is the distance traveled?

LEVER PROBLEMS

In a *lever problem* the formula $w_1 d_1 = w_2 d_2$ gives the relationship of the weight and distances from the *fulcrum*.

DEFINITION

Lever problem: a word problem that deals with the lever principle which involves a fulcrum and balance. Seesaws are good examples of levers.

Fulcrum: the pivot or support point of a lever.

Model 1:   George and Susan are on the seesaw. If George weighs 114 lbs. and his sister Sue weighs 57 lbs., while the length of the board is 12 ft., how far should each be from the resting point (fulcrum) of the board to balance?

Let x = the distance George sits from the fulcrum, and

$$12 - x = \text{the distance Susan sits from the fulcrum.}$$
$$114(x) = 57(12 - x)$$
$$114x = 684 - 57x$$
$$171x = 684$$
$$x = 4$$
$$114(4) = 57(8)$$
$$456 = 456$$

The distance for George is 4 ft.
The distance for Susan is 8 ft.

Check:
```
        8        114        57
      + 4        x  4       x 8
      ———        ———        ———
       12        456        456
```

The problem we just worked would have been just as easy if we had drawn a sketch.

George: x Susan: $12 - x$

Model 2: $114x = 57(12 - x)$
The remainder of
this solution is the
same as in Model 1.

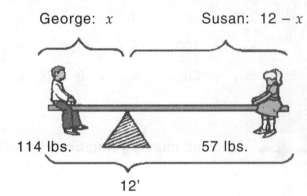

114 lbs.   57 lbs.

12'

Sometimes in a lever problem, the fulcrum is hard to find and a sketch of the situation can be very helpful. The sketch may take the place of Step 1 in the four steps for solving problems.

Model: How much weight needs to be applied to the end of a pry bar to move a rock? The rock weighs 640 lbs. and the pry bar is 6 ft. long. The fulcrum is located 1 ft. from the rock.

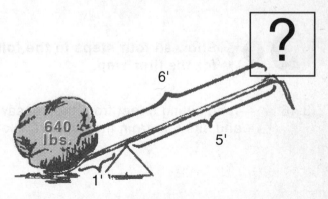

6'

5'

640 lbs.

1'

$$640(1) = 5(x)$$
$$640 = 5x$$
$$x = 128$$
$$640(1) = 5(128)$$
$$640 = 640$$

To move the rock, 128 lbs. of weight are needed.

Check:

128	640	5
x 5	x 1	+ 1
640	640	6

 Will the following levers balance? Write *yes* or *no*.

3.36 $w_1 = 40,$ $d_1 = 4;$ $w_2 = 80,$ $d_2 = 2$ _____

3.37 $w_1 = 60,$ $d_1 = 3;$ $w_2 = 75,$ $d_2 = 2$ _____

3.38 $w_1 = 50,$ $d_1 = 8;$ $w_2 = 80,$ $d_2 = 5$ _____

3.39 $w_1 = 100,$ $d_1 = 4;$ $w_2 = 50,$ $d_2 = 8$ _____

3.40 $w_1 = 30,$ $d_1 = 8;$ $w_2 = 60,$ $d_2 = 5$ _____

 Find the missing number that will make these levers balance.

3.41 $w_1 = 12,$ $d_1 = 5;$ $w_2 = ?,$ $d_2 = 6$ _____

3.42 $w_1 = ?,$ $d_1 = 8;$ $w_2 = 10,$ $d_2 = 4$ _____

3.43 $w_1 = 10,$ $d_1 = ?;$ $w_2 = 8,$ $d_2 = 5$ _____

3.44 $w_1 = 10,$ $d_1 = 2;$ $w_2 = 5,$ $d_2 = ?$ _____

3.45 $w_1 = 150,$ $d_1 = 3;$ $w_2 = 75,$ $d_2 = ?$ _____

Show all four steps in the following word problems. A sketch may be drawn for the first step.

3.46   Tom, sitting 5 feet from the seesaw support, balances a friend who weighs 110 lbs. and sits 6 ft. from the support. How heavy is Tom?

3.47   A weight of 200 grams is 40 cm from the center support of a stick. Where would a weight of 400 grams balance the stick?

3.48   Jack weighs 148 lbs. and Jill weighs 116 lbs. How far from Jack on a seesaw 13.2 ft. long is the support balancing them?

3.49   Kim weighs 72 kg and Eddie weighs 60 kg. Kim is sitting 2 m from the fulcrum of a seesaw. How far from Kim should Eddie sit to balance the seesaw?

3.50   A girl wishes to raise a 400 lb. rock with a crowbar 6 ft. in length. She places it so that the stone is 1 ft. from the fulcrum. How much force must she use to move the rock?

3.51   Weights of 40 lbs. and 50 lbs. are placed on opposite sides of the fulcrum and they balance. If one weight is a foot nearer the fulcrum than the other, where is each weight placed?

3.52   A worker, tearing down a barn, uses a pinch bar 4 ft. long with the shorter end 2 in. from the fulcrum. If the worker can exert a force of 150 lbs. at one end of the pinch bar, how great a force can he exert at the other end? (Note the differences in units, 2 in. and 4 ft. Units must be the same when using the lever formula.)

3.53   Two boys weighing 100 and 150 lbs. respectively use a 15 ft. plank for a teeter-totter. Where should the fulcrum be placed for balance?

3.54   A weight of 200 grams is 40 centimeters from the center support of a meter stick. Where would a weight of 300 grams balance the stick?

=== **INTEGER PROBLEMS** ===

You know what integers are. Counting by one gives consecutive integers.

Model 1:   Some consecutive integers are 4, 5, 6, and 7.

Model 2:   If n is an integer, then n, $n + 1$, $n + 2$, and $n + 3$ are consecutive integers.

To solve a problem with consecutive integers you represent them as in Model 2.

Model: Find three consecutive integers such that the smallest integer increased by seven is equal to half the largest integer.

Let x, $x + 1$, and $x + 2$ be the integers.

smallest	increased by 7	is	half	the largest

$$x \qquad\qquad +7 \qquad\qquad = \quad \tfrac{1}{2}(x + 2)$$

$$x + 7 \quad = \quad \tfrac{1}{2}x + 1$$

$$x \quad = \quad \tfrac{1}{2}x - 6$$

$$\tfrac{1}{2}x \quad = \quad -6$$

$$x \quad = \quad -12$$

$$-12 + 7 \quad = \quad \tfrac{1}{2}(-12 + 2)$$

$$-5 \quad = \quad \tfrac{1}{2}(-10)$$

The integers are -12, -11, and -10.

Check:
$$\begin{array}{r} -12 \\ +\ 7 \\ \hline -5 \end{array} \qquad \tfrac{1}{2}(-10) = -\tfrac{10}{2} = -5$$

Consecutive odd and even numbers are found when we count by two's. If we start with an odd number and count by two's, we will say consecutive odd numbers.

Model 1:   Some consecutive odd numbers are 17, 19, 21, and 23.

If we start with an even number and count by two's, we will say consecutive even numbers.

Model 2:   Some consecutive even integers are 22, 24, 26, 28, 30, and 32.

Read integer problems carefully as the odd or even adjective is easy to miss.

Model: The lengths of the sides of a triangle are consecutive even integers. Find the lengths of the sides if the perimeter is 42.

Let x, $x + 2$, and $x + 4$ be the even integers.

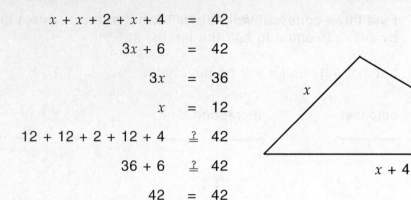

$$x + x + 2 + x + 4 = 42$$
$$3x + 6 = 42$$
$$3x = 36$$
$$x = 12$$
$$12 + 12 + 2 + 12 + 4 \overset{?}{=} 42$$
$$36 + 6 \overset{?}{=} 42$$
$$42 = 42$$

The sides have lengths of 12, 14, and 16.

Check:

	12	12	14
	14	+ 2	+ 2
	+ 16	14	16
	42		

 Answer these questions.

3.55   If $48 = k$, what numbers are represented

by $k - 1$ and $k - 2$?   _____

3.56   If k is an even integer, how would you

represent the next 6 even integers?   _____

 **Use the four steps to solve each of the following word problems dealing with integers.**

3.57   The sum of two consecutive integers is 71. Find the integers.

3.58   Find four consecutive integers whose sum is 114.

3.59   Find four consecutive integers if the sum of the first and second is 63.

3.60   Harvey plans to use 5 ft. of shelving for four shelves whose lengths are to be a series of consecutive even numbers. How many inches long should each shelf be?

3.61   Find 4 consecutive even integers whose sum is 140.

3.62   The sum of three consecutive integers is -21. Name the integers.

3.63   The sum of the least and greatest of three consecutive integers is 50. What is the middle integer?

3.64   The larger of two consecutive odd integers is 7 greater than twice the smaller. Find the integers.

3.65   The sum of three consecutive odd integers is 1,509. What are the integers?

3.66   Find three consecutive odd integers such that the sum of the largest and twice the smallest is 25.

3.67   Twice the second of two consecutive integers Increased by the first is 26. Find the integers.

3.68   Three times the second of two consecutive even integers increased by twice the first is 46.

3.69   Three numbers each have a difference of 3. If their sum is 3,648, what are the numbers?

   Review the material in this section in preparation for the Self Test. This Self Test will check your mastery of this particular section as well as your knowledge of the previous section.

SELF TEST 3

Complete these items (each answer, 3 points).

3.01   Terry is x years old. Represent his age

12 years from now.   _____

3.02   Six years ago, Paul's age was $2x$. Represent

his age 3 years from now.   _____

3.03   A car traveled 35 miles per hour. In how

many hours did it travel 280 miles?   _____

3.04   State the formula used in motion problems.   _____

3.05   State the formula used in lever problems.   _____

3.06   If x represents the distance to the fulcrum

from one end of a 16 ft. plank, what represents

the distance from the other end?   _____

3.07   If $2x + 6$ is an even integer, write the next

two odd integers.   _____

3.08   Is the sum of an odd number of consecutive

odd integers even or odd?   _____

Show all four steps in the solutions of the following problems (each problem, 5 points).

3.09   In 30 years, a man will be twice as old as he will be in 2 years. How old is he now?

3.010   Joe's age is 4 less than twice the age of his brother Tom. The sum of their ages is 41. Find the age of each.

3.011   John is twice as old as Bill. Greg is 7 years older than Bill. Four years ago, the sum of their ages was 55. How old is Greg?

3.012   Sharon and Ken drove to the service station at 60 km per hour. They returned home by bicycle at 15 km per hour. The entire trip took 4 hours. How far was the round trip?

3.013   Two cars start from the same town at the same time and travel in opposite directions. One car averages 50 miles per hour and the other 60 miles per hour. In how many hours will they be 550 miles apart?

3.014   John sets out for camp at 9:00 A.M. and walks 4 miles an hour. Ted leaves camp at 9:30 A.M. and walks at 5 miles per hour. At what time will Ted overtake John?

3.015   Tammy and Theresa are at the park. If Tammy weighs 120 lbs. and Theresa weighs 60 lbs., where should the fulcrum be located on a 12 ft. teeter-totter?

3.016   Robert weighs 180 lbs. and Gene weighs 120 lbs. How far from the fulcrum must Robert sit to balance Gene, who is sitting 6 ft. from the fulcrum?

3.017   Marvin can exert a force of 180 lbs. How heavy a rock can he lift if he uses a crowbar that is 5 ft. long and if he places the fulcrum so that it is 6 in. from the rock?

3.018   Find two consecutive integers whose sum is 125.

3.019   Find four consecutive odd integers whose sum is 112.

3.020   Find three consecutive integers such that the sum of the second and third exceeds
one-half of the first by 33.

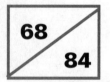

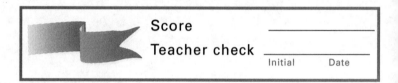

IV. CHALLENGING VERBAL PROBLEMS

OBJECTIVE

When you have completed this section, you should be able to:

5. Solve problems with complications beyond the very easy level.

Problems in a textbook tend to be oversimplified and are designed to help you learn how to use the algebraic method for finding solutions.

Out of textbook problems or real life situation problems require more organizational ability not only because they can be more complicated, but because they sometimes involve too much information or not enough information. The problems included in this section have the right amount of information but should present you with a challenge for organizing their complications.

══════ NUMBER PROBLEMS AND GEOMETRY PROBLEMS ══════

The following problems are presented as "challenge" problems in the subject of numbers and geometry.

They may require a few more readings and a little more patience, but the procedures covered in the first sections of this LIFEPAC should be followed. You might want to reread the first three sections before you start the problems.

 Use the four–step procedure to solve each problem.

4.1 Farmer Brown needs 0.03 acre of land to grow 1 bushel of corn and 0.06 acre to grow 1 bushel of wheat. He has at most 480 acres of land for planting and wants to use at least half of that acreage. If he decides to grow twice as much corn as wheat, find a. the maximum and b. the minimum number of bushels of corn he can grow.

4.2 A man bought two lots for the same price. He sold one at a profit of $3,000 and the other at a loss of $1,500, receiving twice as much for the first lot as for the second. What did each lot cost?

4.3   In a den are three lamps of equal size, a radio that uses one-third the number of watts used by a lamp, and a heater that uses fifteen times as many watts as a lamp. When all are in use, the total electrical power is 1.1 kilowatts. How many watts does the radio use? (1 kilowatt = 1,000 watts)

4.4   If 15 is decreased by 7 times the sum of 5 and 3 times a number, the result is 12 more than twice the sum of the number and 7. Find the number.

4.5   The Marble Club has six members. Each member contributes his marbles and holds office on the basis of the number of marbles he contributes. The president has contributed 104 more marbles than the vice-president, who in turn has contributed 203 more than the treasurer. The secretary donated $\frac{1}{2}$ the amount of the vice-president. The marble counter contributed 3 more than the sergeant of arms, and they have contributed 485 marbles together. If the total number of marbles is 3,886, how many did each contribute?

4.6   The length of a picture is 4 feet less than twice its width. To frame it, 76 feet of framing are needed. Find the dimensions of the picture.

4.7   The sides of a triangle can be represented by three consecutive odd integers. If the first side is doubled and the third side is increased by 3, the triangle will be isosceles. Find the perimeter of the isosceles triangle.

4.8   The base of a triangle has the same length as a side of a square. The second side of the triangle is 2 inches longer than the base, and the third side is 6 inches longer than the base. If the perimeter of the triangle equals that of the square, find the longest side of the triangle.

4.9   From Hanover, New Hampshire to Albany, New York is 5 miles farther than from Albany to Burlington, Vermont. From Burlington to Hanover is 45 miles less than from Burlington to Albany. What are the distances between the three places if a round trip from any one of the places is 392 miles?

4.10   The length of a rectangle is 1.2 meters more than the width. If the length were decreased by 1.5 meters, and the width were increased by 0.6 meter, the perimeter would be 6.2 meters. Find the length and the width of the original rectangle.

These problems will require careful reading and organization using the table and sketch techniques used in earlier lessons.

  Use the four-step procedure to solve each problem.

4.11   Allen is three times as old as Bettie, and Catherine is five years younger than Allen. Three years ago the sum of their ages was 56. What are their present ages?

4.12   William is $\frac{1}{6}$ as old as his father but 5 years older than his sister Mary. If the sum of all their ages is 51, how old is William?

4.13   A man has five sons, each three years older than the next younger. The age of the oldest in three years will be three times the present age of the next to the youngest. How old is each son?

4.14   The Cape Cod canal is eleven miles long. A passenger boat goes from New York to Boston, via the canal and ocean, in $15\frac{1}{3}$ hrs., while a freighter makes the same trip in 30 hrs. On the ocean the passenger boat averages 18 mph while the freighter averages half that rate. Inside the canal the freighter's rate was two-thirds that of the passenger boat. How far is New York from Boston via the canal and ocean. (Hint: Use a table for the canal to obtain information used in second table for the ocean.)

4.15   After flying for 5 hrs., a pilot increased his speed 10 mph. He flew at this speed for 2 hrs., and then decreased the speed to what it had been at first. The entire flying time was 8 hrs., and the distance was 1,532 mi. What was the rate of flying after the speed was increased?

4.16   A ship must average 22 miles per hour to make its ten-hour run on schedule. During the first four hours, bad weather caused it to reduce its speed to 16 miles per hour. What should its speed be for the rest of the trip to keep the ship to its schedule?

4.17   George weighs 60 lbs. more than $\frac{1}{2}$ his younger brother Galen's weight. If their weights balance when George is 4 ft. from the fulcrum on a 10 ft. long teeterboard, what are their weights?

4.18   Joe, Jane, and Bill weigh 40, 70, and 90 lbs. respectively and use a plank 15 ft. long for a teeterboard. Bill sits 3 ft., Jane 5 ft., and Joe 8 ft. from the fulcrum, on the same side. How far must their father, who weighs 188 lbs., sit from the fulcrum to balance his children?

4.19   Two men lift a weight of 216 lbs., suspended from a pole 6 ft. long carried between them. If the weight is $2 \frac{1}{2}$ ft. from one man and $3 \frac{1}{2}$ ft. From the other, how much does each lift?

INTEGER, INVESTMENT, AND MIXTURE PROBLEMS

Investment problems are similar to the coin problems in a previous lesson, since you are concerned with the value of each investment. The decimal fractions occur constantly, so be careful with your computations.

Model: Mr. Thompson invested a sum at 4% and $1,000 more at 6%. His return totals $140 a year. Find how much he invested at each rate.

Let x = the number of dollars
invested at 4%, and

x + $1,000 = the amount invested at 6%

interest on x at 4%		interest on $(x + 1,000)$ at 6%		total interest
0.04x	+	0.06(x + 1,000)	=	140
0.04x	+	0.06x + 60	=	140
		0.10x + 60	=	140
		0.10x	=	80
		x	=	800
		0.04(800) + 0.06(1,800)	$\overset{?}{=}$	140
		32.00 + 108.00	$\overset{?}{=}$	140
	140		=	140

$800 was invested at 4% and
$1,800 was invested at 6%.

Check: $800 $1,800 $32
          x .04   x   .06   +108
          ———   ———   ———
          $32.00 $108.00 $140

Mixture problems are similar to investment problems, but they involve a percentage content of each type of mixture quantity.

Mixture problems: a word problem that involves mixing items or quantities of different values.

Model: How much alcohol must be added to a pint of tincture of arnica, containing 20% arnica and 80% alcohol, to reduce it to a 10% arnica solution?

0% arnica   20% arnica   10% arnica

x 1 pt. $x + 1$
(amount of   (amount of   (total
alcohol to   20% arnica)   amount of
be added)   10% arnica)

0.00 (x) $+$ 0.20 (1) $=$ 0.10 $(x + 1)$

$$0.20 = 0.1x + 0.1$$

$$0.1 = 0.1x$$

$$x = 1$$

$$0.00(1) + 0.20(1) \quad \overset{?}{=} \quad 0.10(1 + 1)$$

$$0 + 0.2 \quad \overset{?}{=} \quad 0.1 \, (2)$$

$$0.2 = 0.2$$

1 pint of alcohol must be added.

Check: 1   2
            x 0.20   x 0.10
            ——————   ——————
             0.20   0.20

Use the four–step procedure to solve each problem.

4.20   Find three consecutive numbers such that if twice the second number is added to 7 times the first number, the sum exceeds 4 times the last by 74.

4.21   Find four consecutive odd integers such that the sum of the first three exceeds the fourth by 18.

4.22   Find three consecutive integers such that the sum of the second and third exceeds $\frac{1}{2}$ of the first by 33.

4.23   Mr. Turner invested a sum of money at 7% and twice that sum at 3%. His yearly return was $390. How much did Mr. Turner invest at each rate?

4.24   One sum is invested at 5% and three times as much at 8%. The total annual interest is $580. How large is each sum?

4.25   A mixture of 30 lb. of candy sells for $1.10 a pound. The mixture consists of chocolates worth $1.50 a pound and chocolates worth 90¢ a pound. How many pounds of each kind were used to make the mixture?

4.26   Brine is a solution of salt and water. If a tub contains 50 pounds of a 5% solution of brine, how much water must evaporate to change it to an 8% solution?

4.27   To reduce 16 ounces of a 25% solution of antiseptic to a 10% solution, how much distilled water should a nurse add?

4.28   The capacity of an automobile cooling system is 16 quarts. If it is full of a 15% antifreeze solution, how many quarts must be replaced by a 90% solution to give 16 quarts of a 65% solution?

Before you take this last Self Test, you may want to do one or more of these self checks.

1. _____   Read the objectives. Determine if you can do them.
2. _____   Restudy the material related to any objectives that you cannot do.
3. _____   Use the SQ3R study procedure to review the material:
    a.   Scan the sections.
    b.   Question yourself again (review the questions you wrote initially).
    c.   Read to answer your questions.
    d.   Recite the answers to yourself.
    e.   Review areas you did not understand.
4. _____   Review all activities, and Self Tests, writing a correct answer for each wrong answer.

SELF TEST 4

Solve each problem using the four-step procedure (each problem, 5 points).

4.01   If 18 is decreased by 6 times the sum of 4 and twice a number, the result is 15 more than three times the sum of the number and 5. Find the number.

4.02   The sides of a triangle can be represented by three consecutive even numbers. If the first side is increased by 1 and the second side is decreased by 1, the triangle becomes isosceles and has a perimeter of 30 in. Find the length of each side of the original triangle.

4.03   Mark is 10 years younger than Larry. Larry's age in 8 years will exceed twice Mark's age 3 years ago by 4 years. How old is each now?

4.04   Mr. West drove his car from home to Chicago at the rate of 40 mph. and returned at a rate of 45 mph. If his time going exceeded his time returning by 30 minutes, find his time going and his time returning.

4.05   Tom, Dick, and Harry weigh 50, 85, and 120 lbs. respectively and use a 12 ft. plank for a teeterboard. Tom sits 5 ft., Dick sits 4 ft., and Harry sits 3 ft. from the fulcrum on the same side. How far must a 200-pound friend sit from the fulcrum to balance them?

4.06   Find 4 consecutive even integers such that the sum of the third and fourth exceeds $\frac{1}{3}$ of the first by the sum of the first and third.

4.07   A sum of $3,500 is invested in two parts. One part brings a return of 5% and the other a return of 8%. The total annual return is $250. Find the amount invested at each rate.

4.08   How many pounds of seed worth 60 cents a pound must be mixed with 300 pounds of seed worth 35¢ a pound to produce a mixture worth 50¢ per pound?

$\frac{32}{40}$

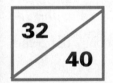

Before taking the LIFEPAC Test, you may want to do one or more of these self checks.

1. _____   Read the objectives. Check to see if you can do them.
2. _____   Restudy the material related to any objectives that you cannot do.
3. _____   Use the SQ3R study procedure to review the material.
4. _____   Review activities, Self Tests, and LIFEPAC Glossary.
5. _____   Restudy areas of weakness indicated by the last Self Test.

GLOSSARY

age problem — A word problem that involves ages of people.

amount formula — $A = p + i$ is a formula used to determine the value of an investment after the interest has been credited.

coin problem — A word problem that involves nickels, dimes, quarters or half-dollars. Sometimes different denominations of bills are also used ($1 bill, $5 bill, and so on).

complementary angles — Two angles whose sum is 90°, a right angle. Each angle is the complement of the other.

consecutive even integers — Even integers that differ by two.

consecutive integers — Integers that differ by one.

consecutive odd integers — Odd integers that differ by two.

even integer — A number that has 2 as one of its factors. If x is an integer, then any even number can be written in the form $2x$.

digits problem — A word problem that involves the digit of an integer.

distance problem — A word problem that involves several distances traveled.

fulcrum — The pivot or support point of a lever.

geometry problem — A word problem that involves geometric figures. Usually a sketch is drawn to help with the solution.

integer problem — A word problem that involves integers. The integers are the counting numbers, their opposites, and zero.

interest — A payment for the use of money borrowed.

interest formula — $i = prt$ is a formula used to compute the interest for a specific principal, rate, and time period.

lever formula — $w_1d_1 = w_2d_2$ is the formula expressing the relationship of the weights and distances in a lever situation.

lever problem — A word problem that deals with the lever principle, which involves a fulcrum and balance. Seesaws are good examples of levers.

mixture problem — A word problem that involves mixing candy, chemicals, or other quantities of different values.

motion problem — A word problem that involves the distance a moving object will travel at a certain average rate for a given period of time.

number problem — An algebraic word problem that provides relationships for finding certain numbers.

odd integer — Any number that does not have 2 as a factor or cannot be divided by 2 with zero remainder. Any odd number can be written as $2n + 1$, where n is an integer.

principal — The amount of money invested at a certain rate of interest. Also, the amount of money borrowed at a certain rate of interest.

rate — The distance an object will travel divided by the time it will travel: $r = \frac{d}{t}$.

supplementary angles — Two angles whose sum is 180°. Each angle is the supplement of the other.

variable — A letter used in a mathematical expression.

verbal problem — A problem stated in words. Its solution requires making a variable assignment, writing and solving an equation, checking the result in the problem, and writing a verbal answer.

word problems — See verbal problem.

MATHEMATICS 904
POLYNOMIALS

CONTENTS

I. ADDITION. 2
   Sums of Terms 2
   Sums of Polynomials 4

II. SUBTRACTION 11
   Differences of Terms 11
   Differences of Polynomials. 14
   Grouping Symbols 18

III. MULTIPLICATION 25
   Products of Monomials. 25
   Products of Polynomials by Monomials. . . . 29
   Products of Polynomials. 32

IV. DIVISION 41
   Quotients of Monomials 41
   Quotients of Polynomials by Monomials . . . 44
   Quotients of Polynomials 46
   GLOSSARY 58

Author: Arthur C. Landrey, M.A.Ed.
Editor-in-Chief: Richard W. Wheeler, M.A.Ed.
Editor: Robin Hintze Kreutzberg, M.B.A.
Consulting Editor: Robert L. Zenor, M.A., M.S.
Revision Editor: Alan Christopherson, M.S.

Alpha Omega Publications®

804 N. 2nd Ave. E., Rock Rapids, IA 51246-1759
© MCMXCVI by Alpha Omega Publications, Inc.   All rights reserved.
LIFEPAC is a registered trademark of Alpha Omega Publications, Inc.

POLYNOMIALS

In this LIFEPAC® you will continue your study in the mathematical system known as *algebra* by learning about a special classification of algebraic expressions—polynomials. In arithmetic, after becoming familiar with the whole numbers, you learned to perform the four basic operations (addition, subtraction, multiplication, and division) with them; later, you did the same with fractions, with decimals, and with integers. Now, in algebra, you will follow the same procedure again with polynomials: become familiar with what they are and then find their sums, differences, products, and quotients.

OBJECTIVES

Read these objectives. The objectives tell you what you will be able to do when you have successfully completed this LIFEPAC. Each section will list according to the numbers below what objectives will be met in that section.

When you have finished this LIFEPAC, you should be able to:

1. Identify and combine like terms.
2. Identify a polynomial by its number of terms.
3. Arrange the terms of a polynomial in ascending or descending powers of a variable.
4. Add polynomials.
5. Subtract polynomials.
6. Multiply polynomials.
7. Divide polynomials.
8. Simplify polynomial expressions having mixed operations.
9. Simplify polynomial expressions requiring the removal of grouping symbols.

Survey the LIFEPAC. Ask yourself some questions about this study. Write your questions here.

_____

_____

_____

_____

_____

_____

I. ADDITION

When you have completed this section, you should be able to:

1. Identify and combine like terms.
2. Identify a polynomial by its number of terms.
3. Arrange the terms of a polynomial in ascending or descending powers of a variable.
4. Add polynomials.

The first operation to be considered is addition, and in this section you will learn to add like terms and to add polynomials. Before that, however, you should become familiar with some basic definitions.

 SUMS OF TERMS

DEFINITION

A *term* (or *monomial*) is a number or a variable, or an indicated product of a number and variable(s).

Models: xy, 0.3, -7a, $\frac{4}{9}$ pq^2, and t are terms.

$\frac{x}{y}$ is not a term under the definition

since it is an indicated quotient of variables.

DEFINITIONS

Like terms have the same variable(s), including the same exponent with each variable.

Constant terms are terms that have no variables.

Models: 5x, -2x, and -$\frac{5}{3}x$ are like terms.

8m, 8n, and 8p are not like terms.

3a^2b^3 and -4.7a^2b^3 are like terms.

6x^2y and 6xy^2 are not like terms.

70, $\frac{2}{3}$, and -1.25 are like terms; they
are called *constant terms* since they
contain no variables.

Write *true* or *false*.

1.1 _____ 6*a* and -60*a* are like terms.

1.2 _____ 2*wxy* and 2*wxz* are like terms.

1.3 _____ a^3b^2c, a^3bc^2, and a^2b^3c are like terms.

1.4 _____ $-5x^4$ and $-5x^4$ are like terms.

1.5 _____ $2x^3$, $2x^2$, and 2*x* are like terms.

1.6 _____ $\frac{1}{3}mn$, 0.58*mn*, and -4*mn* are like terms.

1.7 _____ -46 and 5.2 are like terms.

1.8 _____ -46 and 5.2 are constant terms.

1.9 _____ 7*k*, -2*k*, and $-\frac{1}{5}k$ are like terms.

1.10 _____ 7*k*, -2*k*, and $-\frac{1}{5}k$ are constant terms.

The distributive property is used to add like terms.

PROPERTY

The *distributive property* states that $BA + CA = (B + C)A$.

Models: $4x + 2x = (4 + 2)x = 6x$

$-4y^3 + 5y^3 = (-4 + 5)y^3 = 1y^3 = y^3$

$7abc^2 + (-1.5abc^2) + abc^2 = [7 + (-1.5) + 1]abc^2 = 6.5abc^2$

Notice in the models that the answer is
obtained by adding the numerical parts (or
coefficients) of the like terms, and then by
multiplying that sum by the common variable(s).
This same procedure is used for addition
problems written in a vertical format.

ADDITION

3

Models:

$8a$	$-\dfrac{3}{5}x^2$	$0.2m^3n$
$-5a$		$0.3m^3n$
$\underline{-7a}$	$\dfrac{3}{5}x^2$	$-0.1m^3n$
$-4a$	$\overline{0x^2}=0$	$\underline{m^3n \ (= 1.0m^3n)}$
		$1.4m3n$

►►- Find each sum of like terms.

1.11 $7y + 2y$

1.12 $-3x^4 + 8x^4$

1.13 $5.2ab + (-3.4ab)$

1.14 $-4m + 3m + (-2m)$

1.15 $\dfrac{2}{9}h + (-\dfrac{1}{3}h) + \dfrac{1}{9}h$

1.16 $4c^3d^2 + 3c^3d^2 + c^3d^2$

1.17 $-\dfrac{1}{6}xy + (-\dfrac{2}{3}xy)$

1.18 $-11k + 8k + 4k$

1.19 $-7abc$
          $3abc$
          $\underline{2abc}$

1.20 $4.3pq^2$
          $-2.5pq^2$
          $-3.8pq^2$
          $\underline{pq^2}$

 **SUMS OF POLYNOMIALS**

A *polynomial* is a term or a sum of terms. Polynomials can be one-term, two-term, three-term, and so on.

Models: $-3abc$ is a one-term polynomial (a *monomial*)

$5n + 3$ is a two-term polynomial (a *binomial*).

$4x^2 + x + 1$ is a three-term polynomial (a *trinomial*).

$-5x - 2y + 3z - 8$ is a four term polynomial; the terms
are $-5x$, $-2y$, $3z$ and -8 since it could be written as
$-5x + (-2y) + 3z + (-8)$.

 Label each polynomial as monomial, binomial, or trinomial; or if the polynomial has more than three terms, write the number of terms that the polynomial contains.

1.21 $a^2 + bcd^3$ _____

1.22 $a^2 + b - cd^3$ _____

1.23 a^2bcd^3 _____

1.24 $a^2b - cd^3$ _____

1.25 $a^2 - b + c - d^3$ _____

The terms of a polynomial are usually arranged in an order of either *ascending powers* of one variable or *descending powers* of one variable. You will see as you progress through this LIFEPAC that working with polynomials can be simplified by having them all in the same order.

Model: The polynomial $5xy^3 + 3 + 2x^2y - 4x^3y^2$, when written in ascending powers of y, becomes

$$3 + 2x^2y - 4x^3y^2 + 5xy^3;$$
in descending powers of x, it becomes descending

$$-4x^3y^2 + 2x^2y + 5xy^3 + 3.$$

➡ Write each polynomial in ascending powers of x.

1.26 $-3x + 5x^3 + 1 + x^2$

1.27 $4ax^5 + 5bx^2 - 3$

1.28 $-x^4y^2 + 7x^3y^3 - 3xy^5 + 2x^2y^4$

1.29 $-5x + 2$

1.30 $-5 + 2x$

◖◦• Write each polynomial in descending powers of p.

1.31 $p + p^3 + p^2 + p^4$

1.32 $-5p^4q^2 - 2p^6 + 3q^6$

1.33 $2.4 - 1.6p - 0.8p^3 + p^2$

1.34 $3 - 7p$

1.35 $3p - 7$

To add polynomials, first arrange their terms in the same order. Then, using a vertical format (as shown in the following models), write the polynomials so that like terms are in the same column. Finally, use the distributive property to add any like terms in each column.

Model 1:   Add the polynomials $5x - 2 + y$ and $-3y + 5x + 2$.

Solution: $5x + y - 2$ (or you may write $5x + 1y - 2$)
$\underline{5x - 3y + 2}$
$10x - 2y + 0$ $= 10x - 2y$, the answer.

Model 2:   Find the sum of $-7a^3b + 4a^2b^2 - 2$, $5 + 3a^2b^2$,
$4a^3b + 1 - 8a^2b^2$, and $a^3b + \frac{1}{2}$.

Solution: $-7a^3b + 4a^2b^2 - 2$
$+ 3a^2b^2 + 5$
$4a^3b - 8a^2b^2 + 1$
$\underline{a^3b \qquad + \frac{1}{2}}$
$-2a^3b - a^2b^2 + \frac{9}{2}$, the answer.

Model 3:   Add $m + n - p$, $n + p - q$, and $p + q - r$.

Solution: $m + n - p$

$n + p - q$

$p + q - r$

$\overline{m + 2n + p + 0q - r}$ $= m + 2n + p - r$, the answer

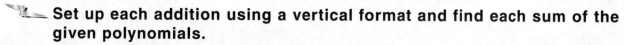 **Set up each addition using a vertical format and find each sum of the given polynomials.**

1.36 $4a^2 + 3a$ and $7a^2 - 2a$

1.37 $7b + 3$, $-4b + 5$, and $-3b + 2$

1.38 $3x^2 + 2x - 5$ and $-4 + 7x^2$

1.39 $p + 3$, $q - 3$, and $p - q$

1.40 $2mn + 4n^2$ and $5m^2 - 7mn$

1.41 $a - b + c, b - c + d$, and $c - d + e$

1.42 $3j + 2.5k$ and $-0.2j - k$

1.43 $\frac{1}{4}m + 2, -4 + \frac{2}{3}m$, and $2 - \frac{1}{3}m$

1.44 $y^2 - 3y + 7, 11 + y$, and $y^2 + 2y$

1.45 $ab + \frac{1}{2}ac - bc$ and $-3ab + bc - 0.5ac$

 Review the material in this section in preparation for the Self Test. The Self Test will check your mastery of this particular section. The items missed on this Self Test will indicate specific area where restudy is needed for mastery.

SELF TEST 1

Write *true* or *false* (each answer, 1 point).

1.01 _____ $2a$, $3a$, and $4a$ are like terms.

1.02 _____ a^2, a^3, and a^4 are like terms.

Find each sum of like terms (each answer, 3 points).

1.03 $4n^5 + 3.5n^5 + (-2.1n^5)$ _____

1.04 $-3xy^3 + 7xy^3 + (-xy^3) + (-3xy^3)$ _____

1.05 $2a^2 + 4a^2 + (-6a^2) + 8a^2$ _____

Label each polynomial as a monomial, binomial, or trinomial (each answer, 3 points).

1.06 x^3y^3 _____

1.07 x^3y^2z _____

1.08 $x^3 - y^2 + z$ _____

Write the following polynomials as directed (each answer, 3 points).

1.09 Write $-7a + 5a^3 - 3 - a^2$ in descending powers of a.

_____

1.010 Write $-4r^3s + 2rs^3 - 3r^2 - 5$ in ascending powers of r.

_____

1.011 Write $4x^2 + x^4 + 3x^3 + 2x$ in descending powers of x.

_____

Find each sum of the given polynomials using a vertical format (each answer, 3 points).

1.012 $5m + 2n$, $n - 3m$, and $7 - 3n$

1.013 $\frac{1}{2}x^2 + \frac{2}{3}y^2$ and $\frac{1}{3}y^2 - xy + 3x^2$

1.014 $ax + by + c$, $2ax - 3by + c$, and $by - c$

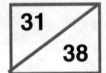

Score _____

Teacher check _____

Initial   Date

II. SUBTRACTION

OBJECTIVES

When you have completed this section, you should be able to:

5. Subtract polynomials.
8. Simplify polynomial expressions having mixed operations.
9. Simplify polynomial expressions requiring the removal of grouping symbols.

The next operation to be considered is subtraction, and in this section you will learn to subtract like terms and to subtract polynomials. You will also learn to simplify expressions involving mixed addition and subtraction as well as how to remove polynomials from grouping symbols. The fundamental idea of this section, however, is that subtraction is not really anything more than a form of addition.

 DIFFERENCES OF TERMS

Subtraction is defined as $A - B = A + (-B)$; that is, to subtract a term, you add its opposite.

DEFINITION

To *subtract* a term, add its opposite.

(The answer in subtraction is called the *difference*.) REMEMBER?

Models:
$$5 - 2 = 5 + (-2) = 3$$
$$5a - 2a = 5a + (-2a) = [5 + (-2)]a = 3a$$
$$-3x^2y - 4x^2y = -3x^2y + (-4x^2y) = [-3 + (-4)]x^2y = -7x^2y$$
$-8 - (-3) = -8 + 3 = -5$, since subtracting -3 means to add the opposite of -3, which is +3.
$$-8x - (-3x) = -8x + 3x = [-8 + 3]x = -5x$$
$$7mn - (-mn) = 7mn + mn = [7 + 1]mn = 8mn$$
$-4a - (-2) = -4a + 2$, which is the answer since the terms are not like terms and cannot be combined.

 Find each difference.

2.1 $9k - 7k$ _____

2.2 $9k - (-7k)$ _____

2.3 $-9k - 7k$ _____

2.4 $-9k - (-7k)$ _____

11

2.5	$15x - 23x$	_____	2.8	$xy^2 - (-2xy^2)$	_____
2.6	$8y^2 - 8y^2$	_____	2.9	$-5mn - (-4mn)$	_____
2.7	$-4ab - ab$	_____	2.10	$7 - (-3b)$	_____

Although addition is a commutative operation, A + B = B + A, subtraction is not, $A - B \neq B - A$. For example, $4t - t = 3t$ and $t - 4t = -3t$; the results, $3t$ and $-3t$, are opposites and are not equal (unless $t = 0$, of course). Thus, subtraction must be set up in the correct order.

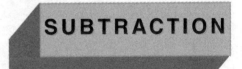

SUBTRACTION

DEFINITION

A *commutative* operation has the same result whatever the order of the operands. Addition is commutative; subtraction is *not* commutative.

Study each of the following translation models.

Models:		
Find the difference of A and B	means $A - B$.
From A take B	means $A - B$.
Take A from B	means $B - A$.
Find A less B	means $A - B$.
Find A less than B	means $B - A$.
Reduce A by B	means $A - B$.
Find A diminished by B	means $A - B$.

Set up each subtraction and find each answer.

2.11 From $4k^2$ take $7k^2$. _____

2.12 Reduce $-5p$ by $4p$. _____

2.13 Find $15abc$ less than abc. _____

2.14 Find $15abc$ less abc. _____

2.15 Take $-3x^2$ from $3x^2$. _____

2.16 Find $40n$ diminished by 0. _____

2.17 Find 0 diminished by $40n$. _____

2.18 Find $-7t$ less $-5u$. _____

2.19 Reduce $-4x$ by $-x$. _____

2.20 Take $-2y^3$ from 3. _____

Some expressions will involve both indicated operations, addition and subtraction. To simplify, you should first convert any subtractions to additions; then collect and combine the like terms.

Model 1:
$$3x^2 + 2x - 5x^2 + 4x - 3x + 7x^2$$
$$= 3x^2 + 2x + (-5x^2) + 4x + (-3x) + 7x^2$$
$$= [3x^2 + (-5x^2) + 7x^2] + [2x + 4x + (-3x)]$$
$$= 5x^2 + 3x$$

Model 2:
$$2a - 3b - (-2b) + a - (-5a) + 7$$
$$= 2a + (-3b) + 2b + a + 5a + 7$$
$$= [2a + a + 5a] + [(-3b) + 2b] + 7$$
$$= 8a + (-b) + 7 = 8a - b + 7 \text{ since}$$
adding $-b$ is the same as subtracting b.

Notice in the preceding model that the final answer is written with only a single sign before b. Your answers should always be simplified in that manner using the definition of subtraction in the form $A + (-B) = A - B$.

Models:
$5x^2 + (-2y)$ becomes $5x^2 - 2y$.
$-2 + (-3b)$ becomes $-2 - 3b$.

Combine like terms and simplify; write each answer in descending powers of a variable when possible.

2.21 $4d + 2d - 3d - (-d)$

2.22 $-7n^3 + 5n - 2n^3 - (-3n) + (-8n)$

2.23 $5x^2 + (-3) - (-2x) + 4 - (-2x^2)$

2.24 $ab - 5ab + 6c - 3ab - 10c$

2.25 $-5k^4 - (-4k^4) - 3k^4 - (-2k^4) - k^4$

DIFFERENCES OF POLYNOMIALS

To subtract a term, you add its opposite; likewise, to subtract a polynomial, you must add its opposite. Since a polynomial is made up of terms, its opposite will be the polynomial made up of the opposites of each of the original terms.

> Models: The opposite of $2x + 3y - z$ is $-2x - 3y + z$.
> The opposite of $-3a^2 + 5$ is $3a^2 - 5$.

To find the difference between two polynomials, $A - B$, find the sum $A + (-B)$.

First, arrange the terms in the same order. Then, using a vertical format, write the opposite of polynomial B below polynomial A so that like terms are in the same column. Finally, combine any like terms in each column as you did in the addition of polynomials.

> Model 1: Find the difference of $5x + 2$ and $-3x + 1$.
>
> Solution: Both polynomials are already in descending powers of x; the subtraction is set up as the addition
>
> $5x + 2$
> $\underline{3x - 1}$ (the opposite of $-3x + 1$)
> $8x + 1$,   the answer.

Model 2:   Take $8a^2 - 3 + 2a$ from $-3 + 5a$.

   Solution: In descending powers of a, the polynomials are $8a^2 + 2a - 3$ and $5a - 3$; the subtraction is set up as the addition

$$\begin{array}{r} 5a - 3 \\ -8a^2 - 2a + 3 \quad \text{(the opposite of } 8a^2 + 2a - 3) \\ \hline -8a^2 + 3a + 0 = -8a^2 + 3a, \text{ the answer.} \end{array}$$

Again, you should remember that subtraction is not commutative; therefore, you must be careful to set up the polynomials in the correct order. (You may want to refer back to the list of subtraction translations given earlier in this section.) Notice how the following two models differ in set-up.

Model 3:   Find $-2m^3 + 4$ less $5 - m$.

   Solution: In descending powers of m, the polynomials are $-2m^3 + 4$ and $-m + 5$, the subtraction is set up as the addition

$$\begin{array}{r} -2m^3 \qquad + 4 \\ m - 5 \quad \text{(the opposite of } -m + 5) \\ \hline -2m^3 + m - 1, \quad \text{the answer.} \end{array}$$

Model 4:   Find $-2m^3 + 4$ less than $5 - m$.

   Solution: This subtraction is set up as the addition

$$\begin{array}{r} -m + 5 \\ 2m^3 \qquad -4 \quad \text{(the opposite of } -2m^3 + 4) \\ \hline 2m^3 - m + 1, \qquad \text{the answer.} \end{array}$$

Notice also that the answers to the two preceding models are opposites.

Model 5:   Reduce 0 by $-8y + 2$.

   Solution: The subtraction is set up as the addition

$$\begin{array}{r} 0 \\ 8y - 2 \quad \text{(the opposite of } -8y + 2) \\ \hline 8y - 2, \qquad \text{the answer.} \end{array}$$

After arranging the terms in descending powers of a variable, give the opposite of each polynomial.

2.26 $-4 + 7x$ _____

2.27 $5y^3 - 3y^5 + 2y^4$ _____

15

2.28 $-2h + 3 - h^2$

2.29 $9 - 12n^2 + 4n^3 - 7n$

2.30 $-8a^3 + 3a - a^2$

Set up each subtraction in a vertical format and find each answer.

2.31 Take $4x + 2$ from $8x + 5$.

2.32 Take $-4 + 3a^2$ from $7a - a^2$

2.33 Reduce $7y + 2y^2 - 7$ by $3 - 4y$

2.34 Reduce $-8 + b^2$ by $5 + b^2$.

2.35 Find $2p^2 + 3p - 4$ less $-2p^2 - 3p + 4$.

2.36 Find $x - y$ less 0.

2.37 Find $x - y$ less than 0.

2.38 Find $k - k^2$ less than $3k^2 + 7$.

2.39 Find $a - 2b + 3c$ diminished by $a - 2b - 3c + d$.

2.40 Find $-2x + 11 + 9x^2$ diminished by itself.

▲▲▶ **In each subtraction, *mentally* find the difference between the upper polynomial and the lower polynomial; check mentally by adding "up."**

    Model: $3n^2 + 7n - 9$

                $-2n^2 - n + 5$ ◀—(Mentally add the opposite of each term.)

                $\overline{5n^2 + 8n - 14}$ Check: Add the answer to the lower polynomial to obtain the upper polynomial.

2.41 $5a + 9$ 2.42 $7x^2 - 3x + 1$ 2.43 $-4mn \qquad + 3n$

      $\underline{2a + 3}$ $\underline{-2x^2 \qquad + 4}$ $\underline{2mn - 4m}$

2.44 $x^4 - 3x^3 + 2x^2 + x - 5$ 2.45 $a - b$

      $\underline{x^4 + 3x^3 \qquad\quad - x - 5}$ $\underline{\quad b - c}$

 # GROUPING SYMBOLS

You have already learned to use a vertical format to find sums and differences of polynomials. These operations may also be done with a horizontal format if the polynomials are enclosed in grouping symbols such as *parentheses* ( ), *brackets* [ ], and *braces* { }. Now you must learn to remove such grouping symbols from the polynomials so that like terms can be combined.

Study the solutions given for the following two models.

Model 1:   Add $2a + 3b$ and $5a - 7b$.

Solution 1: (Vertical format)

$2a + 3b$

$\underline{5a - 7b}$

$7a - 4b$

Solution 2: (Horizontal format)

$(2a + 3b) + (5a - 7b) = 2a + 3b + 5a - 7b$

$= 7a - 4b$

Model 2:   Subtract $5x - 3$ from $-4x + 7$.

Solution: $-4x + 7$ $-4x + 7$

Subtract $\underline{5x - 3}$ ⟶ Add $\underline{-5x + 3}$ (the opposite of $5x - 3$)

$-9x + 10$

Solution 2: $(-4x + 7) - (5x - 3) = (-4x + 7) + (-5x + 3),$

adding the opposite of
$5x - 3$

$= -4x + 7 - 5x + 3$

$= -9x + 10$

The key to removing grouping symbols correctly is the sign (− or +) that is before the grouped polynomial. Notice in Solution 2 of Models 1 and 2 that the following conditions occur:

1.   A plus sign (written or understood) before the grouped polynomial has no effect on that polynomial when the grouping symbols are removed; and

2.   A minus sign before the grouped polynomial results in the opposite of the polynomial when the grouping symbols are removed.

Model 3: Simplify $-(k - 3) + (k - 2)$.

Solution: $-(k - 3) + (k - 2)$

$$= -k + 3 + k - 2$$

$$= 1$$

Model 4: Simplify $(5n^2 + 2) + (-3n^2 - 5) - (-4n^2 + 7)$

Solution: $(5n^2 + 2) + (-3n^2 - 5) - (-4n^2 + 7)$

$$= 5n^2 + 2 - 3n^2 - 5 + 4n^2 - 7$$

$$= 6n^2 - 10$$

When a grouped expression is contained in another grouped expression, remove the innermost set of grouping symbols first. You may have a choice then either of simplifying at that point or of continuing to remove grouping symbols and simplifying at the end of the solution.

Model 5: Simplify $12a - [3a - (2a - 4)]$.

Solutions: $12a - [3a - (2a - 4)]$

$$= 12a - [3a - 2a + 4]$$

$$= 12a - [a + 4]$$

$$= 12a - a - 4$$

$$= 11a - 4$$

or

$$12a - [3a - (2a - 4)]$$

$$= 12a - [3a - 2a + 4]$$

$$= 12a - 3a + 2a - 4$$

$$= 11a - 4$$

Model 6: Simplify $v - \{w - [x - (y - z)]\}$.

Solution: $v - \{w - [x - (y - z)]\}$

$$= v - \{w - [x - y + z]\}$$

$$= v - \{w - x + y - z\}$$

$$= v - w + x - y + z$$

Verbal descriptions of sums and differences of polynomials can now be set up and simplified using these ideas.

Model 7:   From the difference of $5n^2 + 3$ and $4 - 3n$ subtract the sum of $2n^2 - 7$ and $8n + 3n^2$.

Solution:

$$[(5n^2 + 3) - (4 - 3n)] - [(2n^2 - 7) + (8n + 3n^2)]$$
$$= [5n^2 + 3 - 4 + 3n] - [2n^2 - 7 + 8n + 3n^2]$$
$$= 5n^2 + 3 - 4 + 3n - 2n^2 + 7 - 8n - 3n^2$$
$$= -5n + 6$$

Simplify by removing grouping symbols and combining like terms.

2.46 $-(n - 7) + (n - 5)$

2.47 $(3x^2 + 5) + (2x^2 - 9) - (4x^2 + 3)$

2.48 $-(-2a + 13) + (-9a - 2) - (-7a - 3)$

2.49 $2m - [n - (m - 2n)]$

2.50 $3j - \{2k - [5h - (3j + k)]\}$

20

2.51 $(x - y + 1) - (x + y - 1)$

2.52 $n - \{1 - [n - (1 - n) - 1]\}$

2.53 $\{n - 1 - [n - 1 - (n - 1)]\}$

2.54 $a - \{5b - [a - (3b - 2c) + c - (a - 2b - c)]\}$

2.55   Take the difference of $7x^2 + 9$ and $2x^2 - 3x$ from the sum of $5x^2 + 4x + 7$ and $2 - x$.

▶▶▶ **Use the polynomials $Q = 7m + 3n$, $R = 11 - 2m$, $S = n + 5$, and $T = -m - 3n + 8$ to find each of the following sums and/or differences.**

     Model: $[Q + R] - [S - T]$

         Solution: $[(7m + 3n) + (11 - 2m)] - [(n + 5) - (-m - 3n + 8)]$

                     $= [7m + 3n + 11 - 2m] - [n + 5 + m + 3n - 8]$

                     $= 7m + 3n + 11 - 2m - n - 5 - m - 3n + 8$

                     $= 4m - n + 14$, the answer.

2.56 $Q + S - T$

2.57 $R - S + T$

2.58 $R - [S + T]$

2.59 $[Q - R] + [S - T]$

2.60 $Q - [R + S] - T$

Review the material in this section in preparation for the Self Test. This Self Test will check your mastery of this particular section as well as your knowledge of the previous section.

SELF TEST 2

Complete these items (each answer, 3 points).

2.01 Find the sum $-5ab + 7ab + (-9ab) + ab + (-2ab)$.

_____

2.02 Write the polynomial $-4k + 11k^3 - k^2 + 5$ in ascending powers of k.

_____

2.03 Find the difference $11y^3 - (-5y^3)$.

_____

2.04 Take $8x$ from $-4x$.

_____

2.05   Find $-9a^3bc$ less $-7a^3bc$.

Simplify (each answer, 4 points).

2.06   Simplify $5k + (-4k^2) - 13 - 9k - (-7) + 18k^2$, writing the answer in descending powers of k.

2.07   Simplify $(2n + 5) - (3n + 7) + (4n - 9)$.

2.08   Simplify $a - \{b - [c - (d - e) - f] - g\}$.

Solve these problems (each answer, 4 points).

2.09   From $2a - 3b + 4c$ take $4a - 3b + 2c$.

2.010   Find $-x^2 + 10$ less than 0.

2.011   Find the answer mentally and check.

$$3y^3 - 2y^2 + y - 2$$
Subtract $\underline{2y^3 \qquad - y - 1}$

23

2.012 Find the sum of $5m + 3n + p$, $-5p + 3n$, and $2n - m$.

Using the polynomials $Q = 3x^2 + 5x - 2$, $R = 2 - x^2$, **and** $S = 2x + 5$, **perform the indicated operations** (each answer, 4 points).

2.013 $Q - R + S$

2.014 $Q - [R + S]$

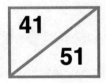

 Score

Teacher check _____

Initial   Date

III. MULTIPLICATION

The third operation to be considered is multiplication, and in this section you will learn to multiply monomials and polynomials. Learning to find such products correctly is important to your success not only in this LIFEPAC, but also in the next one when you will learn the reverse procedure of factoring polynomials.

 PRODUCTS OF MONOMIALS

You will need to learn three basic properties for multiplication; all involve *powers*, which are just shorthand ways of writing products. For example, y^3, read "*y* to the third power," means the product $y \cdot y \cdot y$; the *exponent* 3 indicates the number of times that the *base y* is used as a factor.

DEFINITIONS

A *power* of a number is an abbreviated form of writing a product using a base and an exponent.

The *exponent* is the part of an indicated power that shows the number of times to use the base as a factor.

The *base* is the part of an indicated power that is to be used as a factor.

Study each group of models to see how the exponents are used; then learn each property that follows.

Models;
$$x^5 \bullet x^2 = \overbrace{x \bullet x \bullet x \bullet x \bullet x}^{x^5} \bullet \overbrace{x \bullet x}^{x^2} = x^{5+2} = x^7$$
$$\underbrace{}_{x^7}$$

$$3^3 \bullet 3 = 3^3 \bullet 3^1 = 3^{3+1} = 3^4 \text{ or } 81$$

$$p^3 \bullet q^2 = p \bullet p \bullet p \bullet q \bullet q = p^3 q^2$$

PROPERTY 1

$A^M \bullet A^N = A^{M+N}$; if the bases are the same, then the product is found by keeping that base and adding the exponents.

Since multiplication is both *commutative* (the order of the factors may be changed without changing the product) and *associative* (the grouping of the factors may be changed without changing the product), you may rearrange factors so that products of the same bases are together.

DEFINITION

An *associative* operation has the same result however the operands are grouped. Multiplication and addition are associative.

Models:
$$(xy)^3 = xy \bullet xy \bullet xy = x \bullet x \bullet x \bullet y \bullet y \bullet y = x^3 y^3$$
$$(4pq)^2 = 4pq \bullet 4pq = 4 \bullet 4 \bullet p \bullet p \bullet q \bullet q = 4^2 \bullet p^2 \bullet q^2 = 16p^2 q^2$$
$$(-3k)^5 = (-3)^5 \bullet k^5 = -243k^5$$

PROPERTY 2

$(AB)^M = A^M \bullet B^M$; if a product is raised to a power, then each factor is raised to that power.

Models:
$$(x^5)^4 = x^5 \bullet x^5 \bullet x^5 \bullet x^5 = x^{5+5+5+5} = x^{5 \cdot 4} = x^{20}$$
$$(2^3)^2 = 2^3 \bullet 2^3 = 2^{3+3} = 2^{3 \cdot 2} = 2^6 \text{ or } 64$$
$$(y^7)^3 = y^{7 \cdot 3} = y^{21}$$

PROPERTY 3

$(A^M)^N = A^{MN}$; if a power is itself raised to a power, then the result is found be keeping the same base and multiplying the exponents.

In applying these properties you must remember that if an exponent is not written, it is understood to be 1; also, powers of numerical factors should be found rather than left in exponential form.

✳✳ Find the products.

3.1 $y^5 \cdot y^3$ _____

3.8 $(50y)^2$ _____

3.2 $t^4 \cdot t \cdot t^3$ _____

3.9 $(-7p)^3$ _____

3.3 $d^j \cdot d^k$ _____

3.10 $(jk)^d$ _____

3.4 $2^3 \cdot 2^2$ _____

3.11 $(-4 \cdot 3 \cdot 2)^2$ _____

3.5 $x^5 \cdot x^4 \cdot x^3$ _____

3.12 $(v^6)^5$ _____

3.6 $10 \cdot 10^2 \cdot z^3 \cdot z$ _____

3.13 $(10^2)^3$ _____

3.7 $(fg)^9$ _____

3.14 $(d^j)^k$ _____

Some products will require the use of more than one of the three properties. In the following models the property being used will be identified at each step.

Model 1: $(-5r^4s^5)^3$ $= (-5^1)^3 \cdot (r^4)^3 \cdot (s^5)^3$ by Property 2

$= (-5)^{1 \cdot 3} \, r^{4 \cdot 3} \, s^{5 \cdot 3}$ by Property 3

$= -125r^{12}s^{15}$

Model 2: $(3s^3)^2 \cdot (s^5)^7$ $= (3^1)^2 \cdot (s^3)^2 \cdot (s^5)^7$ by Property 2

$= 3^{\,1 \cdot 2} \, s^{3 \cdot 2} \, s^{5 \cdot 7}$ by Property 3

$= 9 \cdot s^6 \, s^{35}$

$= 9 \cdot s^{6\,+\,35}$ by Property 1

$= 9s^{41}$

▶▶ Find the products. Show your work in the space provided, and circle your answer.

3.15 $(n^3)^2 \cdot (n^5)^4$

3.16 $(4^2)^2 \cdot (x^8)^3 \cdot x$

3.17 $(a^2b^3)^4$

3.18 $(-6mn^2)^3$

3.19 $(3p^4)^3 \cdot (p^2)^7$ 3.20 $(-10x^5yz^{10})^4$

In adding and subtracting monomials, like terms were needed before those operations could actually be performed. This condition is not the case in multiplication. Monomials, whether like terms or unlike terms, are multiplied by finding the product of their numerical factors and the product of their literal factors. The correct use of the three basic properties will again be important.

Models: $9m \cdot 4n = 9 \cdot 4 \cdot m \cdot n = 36mn$

$6x^3 \cdot 5x^2 = 6 \cdot 5 \cdot x^3 \cdot x^2 = 30x^5$

$-3a^4 (-7ab) = -3(-7) \cdot a^4 \cdot ab = 21a^5b$

$-2(-3y^2z)(-4z^3) = -2(-3)(-4) \cdot y^2 \cdot z \cdot z^3 = -24y^2z^4$

$\frac{1}{2}n(6n^4)^2 = \frac{1}{2}n \cdot 36n^8 = \frac{1}{2} \cdot 36 \cdot n \cdot n^8 = 18n^9$

You should be able to do most or all of the work shown in the models mentally rather than writing it out. When multiplying the monomials in the following activities, try to do as much work mentally as possible.

Find the products.

3.21 $5x \cdot 2y$ _____   3.26 $a \cdot ab(abc)^2$ _____

3.22 $-9 \cdot 4n^2$ _____   3.27 $(0.5n^5)^2(10n^7)^3$ _____

3.23 $8y^3(-3y^2)$ _____   3.28 $(xy^2z^3)^4(-xyz)$ _____

3.24 $\frac{1}{5}kq^2 \cdot 10k$ _____   3.29 $-7(-a^2)(-b^3)$ _____

3.25 $(-2x^2)^3 \cdot 3x$ _____   3.30 $(-4kh)^3(-3k^2h^3)^2$ _____

MATHEMATICS

9 0 4

LIFEPAC TEST

64 / 79

Name _____

Date _____

Score _____

MATHEMATICS 904: LIFEPAC TEST

Complete these items (each answer, 2 points).

1. Is $8mn + 8mp + 8np$ a sum of like or unlike terms? _____

2. How many terms are in the polynomial $abcd + e - fg + h^2$? _____

3. Write the polynomial $4k^3 - 7 + 2k^2 + k^4 - 3k$ in ascending powers of k.

Find each sum (each answer, 4 points).

4. $11x^2y + 3x^2y + (-4x^2y) + x^2y + (-16x^2y) + 7x^2y.$ _____

5. $3a - 4b, 7b + c, c - 3a,$ and $a + b - 2c.$

6. $2n^3 + 4n^2 - 7$ and $-n^3 + 8n - 9.$

Find each difference (each answer, 4 points).

7. $-3z^7 - (-5z^7)$ _____

8 $5d^2 + 4d - 3$ less $2d^2 - 3d + 4.$

9. $18 - x$ less than 0.

Remove the grouping symbols and simplify each expression (each answer, 4 points).

10. $-[(2y + 4) - (3y - 7)] - (5 - y)$

11. $m - \{n + [p - (m + n - p)]\}$

Find each product (each answer, 4 points).

12. $(a^3b)^2 \cdot 4ab^3$ _____

13. $-7p^3(4p^2 + 3p - 1)$ _____

14. $(5x^2 + 2x - 3)(x - 1)$

Find each quotient (each answer, 4 points).

15. $42j^4k^2 \div (-3jk)$ _____

16. $(5ab - 10b^2 + 15bc) \div 5b$ _____

17. $(6x^2 - x - 40) \div (5 + 2x)$

Perform the indicated operations and simplify each expression (each answer, 4 points).

18. $2(3y - 7) - 5y(2 - y)$

19. $(2r + 9)(2r - 9) + (2r - 9)^2$

20. $12 - 5 [(a^3 + a^2 - a) \div a] + 5a$

Show your work in finding the remainder when $x^4 + 7$ is divided by $x - 3$ (this problem, 5 points).

21. $\overline{}$

PRODUCTS OF POLYNOMIALS BY MONOMIALS

The distributive property is used in multiplying polynomials. When you have learned this use of the distributive property, then combinations of operations with polynomials will be easier.

Earlier in this LIFEPAC you used the distributive property to combine like terms. Now the same property in the form $A(B +C) = AB + AC$ will be used for multiplying a polynomial of more than one term by a monomial. Also, it is to be noted that $A(B - C) = AB - AC$ is true since subtraction has been defined as a form of addition; that is,

$A (B - C) = A (B + [-C])$ by the definition of subtraction

$= AB + [-AC]$ by the distributive property;

$= AB - AC$ by the definition of subtraction.

Thus, when finding the product of a monomial and a polynomial, you multiply the monomial by each term of the polynomial. Be especially careful with the sign (+ or −) of each term of your answer.

Models: $4(x + y) = 4x + 4y$

$-2m(n + 3) = -2mn - 6m$, since $-2m(+3) = -6m$.

$5y(y^2 - 3) = 5y^3 - 15y$

$-a(a - b) = -a^2 + ab$, since $-a(-b) = +ab$.

$-2x^3(x^2 - 3x + 4) = -2x^5 + 6x^4 - 8x^3$

Find the products.

3.31 $3(m + n)$ _____

3.32 $3(m - n)$ _____

3.33 $5(a + 3)$ _____

3.34 $5(a - 3)$ _____

3.35 $-4(x + 2)$ _____

3.36 $-4(x - 2)$ _____

3.37 $-7(8 + k)$ _____

3.38 $-7(8 - k)$ _____

3.39 $x^3(x^2 + 5x + 1)$ _____

3.40 $-2d(6d + 11)$ _____

3.41 $-\frac{1}{2}y(2y^3 - 8)$ _____

3.42 $-p(p + q - r)$ _____

3.43 $2y^2(3x + 5z)$ _____

3.44 $mnp(mn - mp + np)$ _____

3.45 $-a^2b^2c^2(a + b - c)$ _____

3.46 $-5x^3y^5(-4x^2 + xy - 9y + 3y^2)$ _____

3.47 $a^4(3a^2 - 2a + 1)$ _____

3.48 $a^x(3a^y - 2a + 1)$ _____

3.49 $-2x^a(-4x^b - 2x^3 + 5x)$ _____

3.50 $-7j^3(-3j^7 + 3j^{18})$ _____

Some polynomial expressions will now be presented that use most of the concepts that you have learned so far in this LIFEPAC: combining like terms by addition and subtraction, removing grouping symbols, and multiplying by monomials. Simplifying such expressions will often require you to write out a number of steps; and keeping your work neat and well-organized will be very helpful in obtaining the correct results.

Model 1: $5(a + b) - 3b$

    $= 5a + 5b - 3b$

    $= 5a + 2b$, the answer.

Model 2: $4x(x - 3) - 2x(x - 6)$

    $= 4x^2 - 12x - 2x^2 + 12x$

    $= 2x^2$, the answer.

Model 3: $-5[2y - 3(y + 5)]$

    $= -5[2y - 3y - 15]$

    $= -10y + 15y + 75$

    $= 5y + 75$, the answer.

Model 4: $10 - 2\{m + 4[m - 3(m + n)] + 5n\} - 2(7n)$

    $= 10 - 2\{m + 4[m - 3m - 3n] + 5n\} - 14n$

    $= 10 - 2\{m + 4m - 12m - 12n + 5n\} - 14n$

    $= 10 - 2m - 8m + 24m + 24n - 10n - 14n$

    $= 14m + 10$, the answer.

Notice in Model 4 that it would be incorrect to find $10 - 2$ in the solution even though you may be very tempted to do so. The -2 immediately before the grouping symbol { indicates multiplication; and you will recall that under the *order of operations*, any multiplications or divisions must be performed prior to any subtractions or additions.

Thus, -2 multiplied by m becomes $-2m$, which is not a like term to 10 and cannot be combined with it.

To observe the correct order of operations, perform powers first, then multiplications or divisions, then additions or subtractions.

> REMEMBER?

Show your steps neatly in simplifying each expression.

3.51 $7(n - p) + 5p$

3.52 $4 + 3(x - 2)$

3.53 $8y(y - 4) + 3y(y + 2)$

3.54 $-6[a - 3(a + 4)]$

3.55 $p(p - q) - q(q - p)$

3.56 $3x[2(x + 5) - 7x]$

3.57 $\frac{1}{4}(8m - 4n) + \frac{1}{3}(6m + 3n)$

3.58 $6\{5[4(3z + 2) - 1]\}$

3.59 $8 + 3\{x - 2[x + 5(x + 3)]\}$

3.60 $a - b\{a + b[a - b(a + b)] - ab\} + ab$

 PRODUCTS OF POLYNOMIALS

The distributive property is used more than once when you multiply a polynomial by a polynomial. This section also presents some special products of binomials.

The multiplication of polynomials having more than one term requires the repeated use of the distributive property. For example, when a binomial is multiplied by another binomial, three distributions are necessary as shown in Model 1.

Model 1: $(x + 2)(y + 3)$ $= y(x + 2) + 3(x + 2)$, distributing $(x + 2)$;

$= xy + 2y + 3(x + 2)$, distributing y;

$= xy + 2y + 3x + 6$, distributing 3.

Model 1 illustrates a horizontal format for polynomial multiplication. A vertical format may also be used, but in either case each term of one polynomial must be multiplied by each term of the other polynomial.

Model 2:   Multiply $(2a + 5)(a + 1)$.

Solution 1: (Horizontal format)

$(2a + 5)(a + 1)$ $= a(2a + 5) + 1(2a + 5)$

$= 2a^2 + 5a + 1(2a + 5)$

$= 2a^2 + 5a + 2a + 5$

$= 2a^2 + 7a + 5$

Solution 2: (Vertical format)

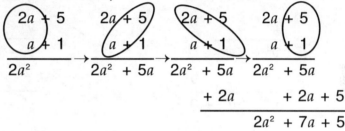

Notice in the vertical format how like terms of the product are placed in the same column to be combined for the final answer. Also, you should see that when a binomial is multiplied by a binomial, the product contains four terms (2 x 2 = 4) before any like terms are combined. Likewise, the product of a trinomial and a binomial will consist of six terms (3 x 2 = 6) before like terms are combined.

Model 3:   Multiply $(5m^2 - 2m + 3)(3m - 4)$

Solution:

$$\begin{array}{r} 5m^2 - 2m + 3 \\ 3m - 4 \\ \hline 15m^3 - 6m^2 + 9m \end{array}$$

$$\begin{array}{r} 5m^2 - 2m + 3 \\ 3m - 4 \\ \hline 15m^3 - 6m^2 + 9m \\ - 20m^2 + 8m - 12 \\ \hline 15m^3 - 26m^2 + 17m - 12 \end{array}$$

Check: Since multiplication is commutative, the product may be checked by reversing the order of the polynomials and multiplying again.

$$\begin{array}{r} 3m - 4 \\ 5m^2 - 2m + 3 \\ \hline 15m^3 - 20m^2 \\ - 6m^2 + 8m \\ + 9m - 12 \\ \hline 15m^3 - 26m^2 + 17m - 12 \text{, the same answer.} \end{array}$$

If the original polynomials are not in the same order, rearrange their terms in descending powers of one of the variables before multiplying.

Model 4:   Multiply $(6 - 2x)(x^2 - 5 + 3x)$.

Solution: $x^2 - 5 + 3x \longrightarrow x^2 + 3x - 5$

$$6 - 2x \longrightarrow -2x + 6$$

$$-2x^3 - 6x^2 + 10x$$

$$6x^2 + 18x - 30$$

$$-2x^3 + 0x^2 + 28x - 30$$

∴ The product is $-2x^3 + 28x - 30$.

Model 5:   Find the cube of $-3 + y^2$.

Solution:

$-3 + y^2$ is $y^2 - 3$, and $(y^2 - 3)^3 = (y^2 - 3)(y^2 - 3)(y^2 - 3)$

$$y^2 - 3$$
$$y^2 - 3$$
$$y^4 - 3y^2$$
$$-3y^2 + 9$$
$$y^4 - 6y^2 + 9$$

$$y^4 - 6y^2 + 9$$
$$y^2 - 3$$
$$y^6 - 6y^4 + 9y^2$$
$$-3y^4 + 18y^2 - 27$$
$$y^6 - 9y^4 + 27y^2 - 27, \text{ the cube.}$$

Find the products.

3.61 $(2x + 9)(x + 1)$

3.62 $(4y - 3)(5y + 3)$

3.63 $(a + 8)(b + 3)$

3.64 $(j + 7)(k - 5)$

3.65 $(mn - 5)(4mn - 1)$

3.66 $(x^2 + 4x + 8)(2x - 1)$

3.67 $(a + b)(a^2 - ab + b^2)$

3.68 $(6 - d)(d^2 - 5 + 3d)$

3.69 $(y + z)^3$

3.70 $(2m - 3n)^2 (2m + 3n)$

SPECIAL PRODUCTS

Two special types of products of binomials should be considered now. The first type is a trinomial that comes from squaring a binomial.

Model 1: $(d + 5)^2$ $= (d + 5)(d + 5)$

$= d(d + 5) + 5(d + 5)$

$= d^2 + 5d + 5d + 25$

$= d^2 + 10d + 25$

This multiplication can be done mentally if you analyze the three terms of the products. The first term, d^2 comes from squaring the first binomial term, $(d)^2$. The middle term, $+ 10d$, comes from multiplying the two binomial terms and then doubling the result, $(d)(+5)(2)$. The last term, $+ 25$, comes from squaring the last binomial term, $(+5)^2$. In general,

$$(A + B)^2 = A^2 + 2AB + B^2.$$

Model 2: $(n - 3)^2$

Solution; Mentally,

square the first term $(n)^2 = n^2$;

multiply the terms,

then double: $(n)(-3)(2) = -6n$;

square the last term: $(-3)^2 = + 9$.

Write the product $n^2 - 6n + 9$.

Of course, you may always check your products by writing out a solution in horizontal or vertical format.

Model 3: $(4t - 11)^2$

Solution: Mentally, do

$$(4t)^2 = 16t^2;$$
$$(4t)(-11)(2) = -88t;$$
$$\text{and } (-11)^2 = +121.$$

Write the product $16t^2 - 88t + 121$.

Check: $(4t - 11)(4t - 11) = 4t(4t - 11) - 11(4t - 11)$
$$= 16t^2 - 44t - 44t + 121$$
$$= 16t^2 - 88t + 121$$

The second special type of product is a binomial that comes from multiplying two binomials.

Model 1: $(g + 4)(g - 4)$
$$= g(g + 4) - 4(g + 4)$$
$$= g^2 + 4g - 4g - 16$$
$$= g^2 + 0g - 16$$
$$= g^2 - 16$$

Model 2: $(5k - 7)(5k + 7)$
$$= 5k(5k - 7) + 7(5k - 7)$$
$$= 25k^2 - 35k + 35k - 49$$
$$= 25k^2 + 0k - 49$$
$$= 25k^2 - 49$$

This type of multiplication also can be done mentally, but you need to have two binomials that differ only in the sign between the terms (one + and one −). The product then is the binomial made up of the squares of the terms separated by a minus sign. In general,

$$(A + B)(A - B) = A^2 - B^2.$$

Again, of course, you may check your product by writing out a solution.

Model 3: $(-3y + 2)(-3y - 2)$

Solution: Mentally, do $(-3y)^2 = 9y^2$ and $(2)^2 = 4$
Write the product $9y^2 - 4$.

Check:
$$-3y + 2$$
$$\underline{-3y - 2}$$
$$9y^2 - 6y$$
$$\underline{ + 6y - 4}$$
$$9y^2 + 0y - 4 = 9y^2 - 4$$

▪ Find each product mentally.

3.71 $(n + 7)^2$ _____

3.72 $(8p + 3)^2$ _____

37

3.73 $(r + s)^2$ _____

3.74 $(a - 5)^2$ _____

3.75 $(2m - 9)^2$ _____

3.76 $(r - s)^2$ _____

3.77 $(t + 9)(t - 9)$ _____

3.78 $(z - 12)(z + 12)$ _____

3.79 $(2j + 7)(2j - 7)$ _____

3.80 $(r + s)(r - s)$ _____

3.81 $(ab + 3)^2$ _____

3.82 $(ab - 3)^2$ _____

3.83 $(ab + 3)(ab - 3)$ _____

3.84 $[(x + 1)(x - 1)]^2$ _____

3.85 $[(-y - 2)(-y + 2)]^2$ _____

 Review the material in this section in preparation for the Self Test. This Self Test will check your mastery of this particular section as well as your knowledge of all previous sections.

SELF TEST 3

Complete these items (each answer, 4 points).

3.01   Find the sum $-7x^3y + 15x^3y + (-11x^3y) + (-x^3y) + 2x^3y$. _____

3.02   Write the polynomial $3ab^2 + 5a^3 - 7b^3 + 4a^2b$ in descending powers of a.

_____

3.03   Find the sum of $3m - 4n - 7$, $5m - n$, and $7n + 2$.

3.04   Find $-5k^4$ less $7k^4$. _____

3.05 Simplify $-3p^3 + 5p + (-2p^2) + (-4) - 12p + 5 - (-8p^3)$, writing the answer in ascending powers of p.

3.06 From $y^3 - 6y^2 + 5y$ take $2y^2 - 3y - 5$.

3.07 Find the answer mentally and check.

$$
\begin{array}{l}
\phantom{\text{Subtract}} \quad 8x - 8y + 9 \\
\text{Subtract} \quad \underline{5x - 8y - z} \\
\end{array}
$$

3.08 Simplify $5t + (t - 3) - [(7t + 5) - (8 - 3t)]$.

3.09 Using the polynomials $H = 2a + b$, $J = 2b + c$, and L $= 2c - a - b$, find $H - J - L$.

3.010 From $3m - 8n + 5p$ subtract the sum of $-m + 7n - p$ and $6m - 9n + 4p$.

3.011 Simplify $b(a + b) - a(a - b)$.

Find each product (each answer, 4 points).

3.012 $(y^2)^5 \cdot y^8$

3.013 $(-3ab^2)^3$

3.014 $1.5m^6 (-2m^2)^4$

3.015 $-2x(x^2 - 3)$

3.016 $y^2z(y + z + yz^2 + 1)$

3.017 $(2p + 7)(3p - 9)$

3.018 $(x + 2y - 3z)^2$

Find each product mentally (each answer, 4 points).

3.019 $(6a + b)^2$ _____

3.020 $(-d + 4)(-d - 4)$ _____

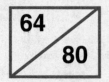

Score _____
Teacher check _____
Initial   Date

IV. DIVISION

7. Divide polynomials.
8. Simplify polynomial expressions having mixed operations.
9. Simplify polynomial expressions requiring the removal of grouping symbols.

The fourth and final operation to be considered is division, and in this section you will learn to divide monomials and polynomials. Also, you will work with some polynomial expressions that require the use of a combination of the operations and procedures learned in this LIFEPAC.

 QUOTIENTS OF MONOMIALS

Division has properties with respect to polynomials, as does multiplication. Division methods for monomials are also presented in this section.

In the section on multiplication you learned three basic properties, one of which was $A^M \bullet A^N = A^{M+N}$; you will now use a similar property in division.

PROPERTY 4

$A^M \div A^N = A^{M-N}$; if the bases are the same, then the quotient is found by keeping the base and subtracting the exponents.

Models:
$$x^5 \div x^3 = x^{5-3} = x^2$$
$$y^{47} \div y^{32} = y^{47-32} = y^{15}$$
$$8^4 \div 8 = 8^4 \div 8^1 = 8^{4-1} = 8^3 = 512$$

$m^9 \div n^7$ cannot be simplified by this property since the bases are different.

$3^2 \div 2^3$ cannot be simplified by this property since the bases are different; but by arithmetic, $3^2 \div 2^3 = 9 \div 8 = 1.125$.

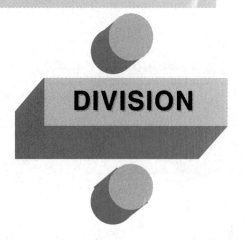

DIVISION

You should recall that division by zero is undefined. Thus, in applying the property it is to be understood that the base, A, cannot be zero.

Now look at the exponents, M and N. If $M > N$, then $M - N$ is a positive number as in the preceding models. If $M < N$, $M - N$ is a negative number; for example,

$y^2 \div y^5 = y^{2-5} = y^{-3}$. Although this example is a correct application of the property, you will not be working with negative exponents at this time. (You may be interested to know, however, that y^{-3} means $\frac{1}{y^3}$, which is not a polynomial term.) If $M = N$, then $M - N$ is zero; you should understand the meaning of zero as an exponent.

Model 1: $2^5 \div 2^5 = 2^{5-5} = 2^0$; but also

$2^5 \div 2^5 = 32 \div 32 = 1$

$\therefore 2^0 = 1$.

In general,

PROPERTY 5 $A^M \div A^M = A^0 = 1$

Again, since division by zero is undefined, the base A $\neq$ 0 in the preceding statement. Thus, the expression 0^0 is undefined and has no meaning. Any other value (numerical or literal) with an exponent of 0 is equal to 1.

Model 2: $z^{17} \div z^{17} = z^0 = 1$ (for $z \neq 0$).

In the next set of activities and in all future activities in this LIFEPAC you are to assume that any indicated divisions are defined.

Find the quotients.

4.1 $n^7 \div n^3$ _____

4.2 $p^{40} \div p^{18}$ _____

4.3 $h^6 \div h$ _____

4.4 $y^r \div y^s$ _____

4.5 $7^5 \div 7^2$ _____

4.6 $6^3 \div 3^2$ _____

4.7 $4^r \div 4^s$ _____

4.8 $x^9 \div x^9$ _____

4.9 $11^3 \div 11^3$ _____

4.10 $y^r \div y^r$ _____

Simplify. Remember that under the order of operations, multiplication or divisions are done as they appear from left to right, unless grouping symbols indicate some other order.

Models; $x^3 \cdot x^2 \div x \quad = x^5 \div x^1 = x^4$

$x^3 \div x^2 \cdot x \quad = x^1 \cdot x^1 = x^2$

$x^3 \div (x^2 \cdot x) = x^3 \div x^3 = x^0 = 1$

4.11 $y^5 \cdot y^3 \div y^2 \ =$ _____

4.12 $y^5 \cdot (y^3 \div y^2) =$ _____

4.13 $y^5 \div y^3 \cdot y^2 \ =$ _____

4.14 $y^5 \div (y^3 \bullet y^2) =$ _____

4.15 $n^6 \div n^5 \bullet n^4 \div n^3 \bullet n^2 \div n =$ _____

4.16 $(n^6 \div n^5) \bullet (n^4 \div n^3) \bullet (n^2 \div n) =$ _____

4.17 $n^6 \bullet n^5 \div n^4 \bullet n^3 \div n^2 \bullet n =$ _____

4.18 $(n^6 \bullet n^5) \div (n^4 \bullet n^3) \div (n^2 \bullet n) =$ _____

4.19 $3^a \bullet 3^b \div 3^c \div 3^d =$ _____

4.20 $(3^a \bullet 3^b) \div (3^c \div 3^d) =$ _____

Monomials are divided by finding the quotient of their numerical factors and the quotient of their literal factors.

Models: $36y^9 \div 4y^7 = [36 \div 4] \, [y^9 \div y^7] = 9y^2$

$28m^4n^3 \div (-7m^2n^2) = [28 \div (-7)] \, [m^4 \div m^2] \, [n^3 \div n^2] = -4m^2n$

$-50a^7b^3c^2 \div (-30ac^2) = [-50 \div (-30)] \, [a^7 \div a] \, [b^3] \, c^2 \div c^2]$

$= \dfrac{5}{3}a^6b^3c^0 = 1.\overline{6}a^6b^3$

Again, as in multiplying monomials, the work shown in the preceding models should be done mentally rather than written out.

Find the quotients.

4.21 $12xy^2 \div 2xy$ _____

4.22 $14a^3b^3c^3 \div 7ab^2c^3$ _____

4.23 $-27m^4n^2 \div (-3m^3)$ _____

4.24 $72a^3bc^2 \div 6abc$ _____

4.25 $-3d^4e^4f^4 \div 9d^2e^2f^2$ _____

4.26 $56m^2n^3p^4 \div (-8n^3p^2)$ _____

4.27 $-40x^3y^3z \div (-2x^2y^3)$ _____

4.28 $-51a^3b^3 \div 3b^2$ _____

4.29 $48a^2b^2 \div 96a^2b^2$ _____

4.30 $-97xyz \div 97xyz$ _____

4.31 $-a^{10}b^{12} \div (-a^9b^{10})$ _____

4.32 $2m^5 \div m^a$

4.33 $12x^a y^b \div (-6x^a y)$

4.34 $-5x^a \div 25x^{a-1}$

4.35 $4z^{a+2} \div (-8z^{a-2})$

 QUOTIENTS OF POLYNOMIALS BY MONOMIALS

To divide a polynomial of more than one term by a monomial, each term of the polynomial is divided by the monomial. Be especially careful with the sign (+ or −) of each term in your answer.

Model 1: $(m^2 + 8m) \div m = [m^2 \div m] + [8m \div m]$

$$= m + 8$$

Model 2:

$(2a + 6b - 10c) \div (-2) = [2a \div (-2)] + [6b \div (-2)] + [-10c \div (-2)]$

$$= 1a + [-3b] + 5c$$

$$= -a - 3b + 5c$$

Model 3:

$(12a^3 b^2 c - 3a^2 c) \div 3a^2 c = [12a^3 b^2 c \div 3a^2 c] + [-3a^2 c \div 3a^2 c]$

$$= 4ab^2 + [-1]$$

$$= 4ab^2 - 1$$

Model 4:

$(-4a^n + 2a^3) \div (-2a) = [-4a^n \div (-2a)] + [2a^3 \div (-2a)]$

$$= 2a^{n-1} + [-a^2]$$

$$= 2a^{n-1} - a^2$$

Find the quotients.

4.36 $(m^2 + 3mn) \div m$ _____

4.37 $(x^2 - 4xy) \div x$ _____

4.38 $(8a^6 - 4a^3) \div 2a^3$ _____

4.39 $(5d + 10p) \div (-5)$ _____

4.40 $(-6n^3 - 2n) \div (-2n)$ _____

4.41 $(5x - 35y + 50) \div 5$ _____

4.42 $(4y^4 - y^3 + 2y^2) \div (-y^2)$ _____

4.43 $(36w^3 - 27w^2) \div 9w$ _____

4.44 $(a^5b^2 - a^3b^3 + a^2b^2) \div a^2b^2$ _____

4.45 $(36x^a - 30x^b) \div (-6x^2)$ _____

Now look at some expressions that will use many of the concepts that you have learned so far in this LIFEPAC: combining like terms by addition and subtraction, multiplication and division by monomials, and removing grouping symbols for simplification. Be sure to follow the order of operations.

Model 1:　　$3(n + 8) - (8n + 6) \div 2$

　　　　　　$= (3n + 24) - (4n + 3)$

　　　　　　$= 3n + 24 - 4n - 3$

　　　　　　$= -n + 21$, the answer.

Model 2:　　$5 - \{5[(18a^3 - 6a^2) \div (-2a)] \div 3a\}$

　　　　　　$= 5 - \{5[-9a^2 + 3a] \div 3a\}$

　　　　　　$= 5 - \{[-45a^2 + 15a] \div 3a\}$

　　　　　　$= 5 - \{-15a + 5\}$

　　　　　　$= 5 + 15a - 5$

　　　　　　$= 15a$, the answer.

✳✳✳**Show your steps neatly in simplifying each expression.**

4.46 $3(y - 7) + (8y + 36) \div 4$

4.47 $(8z - 10) \div (-2) + 5(z - 1)$

4.48 $(a^3 - 5a^2 + 12a) \div a - 3(a + 4)$

4.49 $7 - 3[(n^3 + 8n) \div (-n) + 9n^2]$

4.50 $x - x \{x - x[x - x (x + 1)] \div x^3\}$

 **QUOTIENTS OF POLYNOMIALS**

Division of one polynomial by another requires a process somewhat like long division. Remainders for the problems in this section will be zero at first, and numbers other than zero later in the section.

The final procedure for you to learn in this LIFEPAC is often referred to as long division since it is quite similar to that procedure in arithmetic. Now, however, you will use polynomials instead of just numerical values. You should understand how and why this procedure works.

First, recall the relationship between the operations of multiplication and division. Since 30 • 19 = 570, if 570 is divided by 30, the quotient must be 19; and if 570 is divided by 19, the quotient must be 30.

Likewise, since $(x + 3)(x + 7) = x^2 + 10x + 21$, if $x^2 + 10x + 21$ is divided by $x + 3$, the quotient must be $x + 7$; and if $x^2 + 10x + 21$ is divided by $x + 7$, the quotient must be $x + 3$.

Model 1:   DIVIDEND ÷ DIVISOR = QUOTIENT or $\overset{\text{QUOTIENT}}{\text{DIVISOR}\overline{)\text{DIVIDENED}}}$

Model 2: $570 \div 30 = 19$ or $30\overline{)570}^{\,19}$

Model 3: $570 \div 19 = 30$ or $19\overline{)570}^{\,30}$

Model 4: $(x^2 + 10x + 21) \div (x + 3) = x + 7$ or $x + 3\overline{)x^2 + 10x + 21}^{\,x + 7}$

Model 5: $(x^2 + 10x + 21) \div (x + 7) = x + 3$ or $x + 7\overline{)x^2 + 10x + 21}^{\,x + 3}$

Now let's take the last of the preceding models to see how the quotient $x + 3$ can be obtained through a step-by-step procedure. Keep in mind how long division is performed in arithmetic as you follow this explanation.

Model 5: $(x^2 + 10x + 21) \div (x + 7)$

Solution: ①   Divide the first term of the dividend by the first term of the divisor $[x^2 \div x = x]$, and write the result as the first term of the quotient.

② Multiply (distribute) that term and the divisor $[x(x + 7) = x^2 + 7x]$, and write the result under the dividend with like terms in the same column.

③ Subtract [by mentally adding the opposite of $x^2 + 7x$], and write the result to be used as the new dividend.

④ Divide the first term of this new dividend by the first term of the divisor $[3x \div x = 3]$, and write the result (including the understood plus sign) as the second term of the quotient.

①
$$x + 7\overline{)x^2 + 10x + 21}^{\,x}$$

$$x + 7\overline{)x^2 + 10x + 21}^{\,x}$$
②⟶ $x^2 + 7x$

$$x + 7\overline{)x^2 + 10x + 21}^{\,x}$$
$x^2 + 7x$
③⟶ $3x + 21$

④
$$x + 7\overline{)x^2 + 10x + 21}^{\,x +\ 3}$$
$x^2 + 7x$
$3x + 21$

47

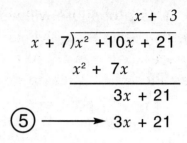

⑤   Multiply (distribute) that term and the divisor [3(x + 7) = 3x + 21], and write the result under the new dividend with like terms in the same column.

$$\begin{array}{r} x + 3 \\ x + 7\overline{)x^2 + 10x + 21} \\ x^2 + 7x \\ \hline 3x + 21 \end{array}$$

⑤ ⟶ 3x + 21

⑥   Subtract [by mentally adding the opposite of 3x + 21]; the remainder is zero in this case.

$$\begin{array}{r} x + 3 \\ x + 7\overline{)x^2 + 10x + 21} \\ x^2 + 7x \\ \hline 3x + 21 \\ 3x + 21 \\ \hline \end{array}$$

⑥ ⟶ 0

Before looking at other models, see if you can complete the following long division to obtain the quotient x + 7 by performing Steps ① through ⑥ when x + 3 is used as the divisor of $x^2 + 10x + 21$.

①   ④

$$x + 3\overline{)x^2 + 10x + 21}$$

② ⟶ ＿＿＿＿＿

③ ⟶

⑤ ⟶

⑥ ⟶

Model 6: $(6y^2 - 5y - 4) \div (3y - 4)$

① $6y^2 \div 3y = 2y)$

② $2y(3y - 4) = 6y^2 - 8y$

③ $(6y^2 - 5y - 4) - (6y^2 - 8y) = 3y - 4$

④ $3y \div 3y = 1$

⑤ $1(3y - 4) = 3y - 4$

⑥ $(3y - 4) - (3y - 4) = 0$

∴ The quotient is 2y + 1.

①   ④

$$\begin{array}{r} 2y + 1 \\ 3y - 4\overline{)6y^2 - 5y - 4} \\ 6y^2 - 8y \\ \hline 3y - 4 \\ 3y - 4 \\ \hline 0 \end{array}$$

② ③ ⑤ ⑥

Check: 3y − 4

        $\underline{2y + 1}$

        $6y^2 - 8y$

            $\underline{+ 3y - 4}$

        $6y^2 - 5y - 4$, the original dividend.

This procedure will work for polynomials of any number of terms; however, when setting up a long division, both the divisor and the dividend should be written in descending powers of a variable. Also, you may find that you want to insert a zero term for each missing power of the variable, or just to leave a space in its position.

Model 7; $(25n^2 - 1) \div (1 - 5n)$

Solution: In descending powers of n, the dividend is $25n^2 + 0n - 1$ and the divisor is $-5n + 1$.

① ④

$$\begin{array}{r} -5n - 1 \\ -5n + 1 \overline{)\, 25n^2 + 0n - 1} \end{array}$$

① $25n^2 \div (-5n) = -5n$

② $-5n(-5n + 1) = 25n^2 - 5n$

③ $(25n^2 + 0n - 1) - (25n^2 - 5n) = 5n - 1$

④ $5n \div (-5n) = -1$

⑤ $-1(-5n + 1) = 5n - 1$

⑥ $(5n - 1) - (5n - 1) = 0$

② $25n^2 - 5n$

③ $5n - 1$

⑤ $5n - 1$

⑥ 0

Of course, not all polynomial divisions work out exactly; some will involve a remainder other than zero. Study the solution of each of the following models and note how the remainder is used in checking the results. The explanatory steps have not been written out, but you should be able to follow the solution as given; the work that is shown is what you should write when doing long division of polynomials.

Model 8: $(23z^2 + 9 + 20z^3 - 13z) \div (2 + 5z^2 - 3z)$

Solution:
$$\begin{array}{r} 4z + 7, \quad R\ -5 \\ 5z^2 - 3z + 2 \overline{)\, 20z^3 + 23z^2 - 13z + 9} \\ \underline{20z^3 - 12z^2 + 8z} \\ 35z^2 - 21z + 9 \\ \underline{35z^2 - 21z + 14} \\ -5 \end{array}$$

Check:
$$5z^2 - 3z + 2$$
$$\underline{4z + 7}$$
$$20z^3 - 12z + 8z$$
$$\underline{+ 35z^2 - 21z + 14}$$
$$20z^3 + 23z^2 - 13z + 14$$
Add Remainder -5
$$\overline{20z^3 + 23z^2 - 13z + 9,}$$ the original dividend in descending powers of z.

49

Model 9: $(p^3 + 11) \div (p + 2)$

$$\begin{array}{r} p^2 - 2p + 4, \ R \ 3 \\ p + 2\overline{)p^3 \qquad\qquad\qquad + 11} \\ \underline{p^3 + 2p^2 \qquad\qquad} \\ -2p^2 \qquad\qquad \\ \underline{-2p^2 - 4p \qquad} \\ 4p + 11 \\ \underline{4p + 8} \\ 3 \end{array}$$

Solution:

Check: $p^2 - 2p + 4$

$$\begin{array}{r} \underline{p + 2} \\ p^3 - 2p^2 + 4p \\ \underline{+ 2p^2 - 4p + 8} \\ p^3 \qquad\qquad + 8 \\ \underline{\text{(Add remainder)} \quad 3} \\ p^3 \qquad\qquad + 11, \text{ the original dividend.} \end{array}$$

Show your work and check for each long division. Circle your answer.

4.51 $(a^2 + 10a + 9) \div (a + 1)$

4.52 $(b^2 + 4b - 21) \div (b + 7)$

4.53 $(c^2 + 2c - 35) \div (c - 5)$

4.54 $(2d^2 + 25d + 33) \div (3 + 2d)$

4.55 $(6f^2 - 13 - 11f) \div (3f - 4)$

4.56 $(4g^2 - 9) \div (2g - 3)$

4.57 $(h^3 - 8j^3) \div (h - 2j)$

4.58 $(6k^2 - 1 - 16k) \div (3k + 1)$

4.59 $(25m^2 - 20m + 4) \div (5m - 2)$

4.60 $(n^4 - 2n^3 - 3n^2 + 7n - 2) \div (n - 2)$

4.61 $(-7 + 20p^2 - 31p) \div (4p - 7)$

4.62 $(q^2 - 39) \div (q - 7)$

4.63 $(r^4 - r^2 + 4) \div (r^2 - r + 2)$

4.64 $(s^3 + t^3) \div (t + s)$

4.65 $(2u^2 - 7) \div (u + 3)$

4.66 $(6v^3 + 13v^2 + 4v - 3) \div (2v + 3v^2 - 1)$

4.67 $(w^3 + 64) \div (4 + w)$

4.68 $(x^3 + 43 - 49x - 7x^2) \div (x^2 - 49)$

4.69 $(y^4 - 1) \div (y + 1)$

4.70 $(z^4 - 1) \div (z - 1)$

 Before you take this last Self Test, you may want to do one or more of these self checks.

SELF TEST 4

Complete these items (each answer, 4 points).

4.01 Find the sum $9mn + (-15mn) + (-3mn) + 7mn + (-mn)$.

4.02 Find the sum of $2x^2 + 3x - 4$, $8 - 3x$ and $-5x^2 + 2$.

4.03 Simplify $5a^2 - (-3a) + (-2a^2) - 7a + 11 - (-2a) - 14$, writing the answer in descending powers of a.

4.04 Find the answer mentally and check:

$$5k^3 \qquad -3k + 7$$
Subtract $\underline{-2k^3 + k^2 \qquad\qquad -9}$

4.05 Using the polynomials $T = xy - 3x + 2y$, $U = 5x - 2xy$, and $V = 8x + y$, find $T - [U - V]$.

4.06 Simplify $5 + 2\{x - 4[3x + 7(2 - x)]\}$.

4.07 Multiply $(6z^2 - 4z + 1)(8 - 3z)$.

4.08 Find the product $(7q - 5)(7q + 5)$ mentally. _____

4.09 Simplify $(14x - 28y) \div [-7(x - 2y)]$.

Find each product (each answer, 4 points).

4.010 $(-5a^2)^3 \cdot a^5$ _____

4.011 $-mnp(3m - 5n + 7p)$ _____

Find each quotient (each answer, 4 points).

4.012 $y^9 \div y^3$ _____

4.013 $2^3 \div 5^2$ _____

4.014 $48a^3bc^2 \div 3abc$ _____

4.015 $-300x^5y^4 \div xy^2$ _____

4.016 $(35n^3 - 30n^2 + 25n) \div (-5n)$ _____

Perform each long division and check. Circle your answer (each answer, 4 points).

4.017 $(10b^2 + b - 1) \div (2b + 3)$

4.018 $(y^3 - 125) \div (y - 5)$

Using the polynomials $X = r + 2$, $Y = 2r - 9$, and $Z = r^2 + 17r + 30$, **perform the indicated operations** (each answer, 4 points).

4.019 $[X \cdot Y - Z] \div X$

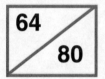

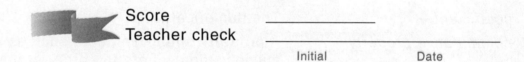

Score _____

Teacher check _____

Initial   Date

 Before taking the LIFEPAC Test, you may want to do one or more of these self checks.

1. Read the objectives. Check to see if you can do them.

2. Restudy the material related to any objective that you cannot do.

3. Use the SQ3R study procedure to review the material.

4. Review activities, Self Tests, and LIFEPAC Glossary.

5. Restudy areas of weakness indicated by the last Self Test.

GLOSSARY

ascending powers—	An arrangement of the terms of a polynomial so that the exponents of a particular variable increase in size.
associative property—	A property of an operation such as addition or multiplication where the grouping of the operands may be changed without changing the result.
base—	The part of an indicated power that is to be used as a factor.
binomial—	A two-term polynomial.
braces—	A pair of grouping symbols, {}, used for enclosing a polynomial.
brackets—	A pair of grouping symbols, [], used for enclosing a polynomial.
coefficient—	The numerical factor of a term.
commutative property—	A property of an operation, such as addition or multiplication, where the order of the operands may be changed without changing the result.
constant term—	A term containing no variables.
descending powers—	An arrangement of the terms of a polynomial so that the exponents of a particular variable decrease in size.
distributive property—	A property used in the form $BA + CA = (B + C)A$ to combine like terms, and in the form $A(B + C) = AB + AC$ to multiply polynomials.
exponent—	The part of an indicated power that shows the number of times the base is to be used as a factor.
like terms—	Terms that have the same variable(s), including the same exponent with each variable.
monomial—	A one-term polynomial.
order of operations—	Unless grouping symbols indicate otherwise, perform powers first, then multiplications or divisions, and finally additions or subtractions, as they appear from left to right. The same order applies within a pair of grouping symbols.
parentheses—	A pair of grouping symbols, ( ), used for enclosing a polynomial.
polynomial—	A term or a sum of terms.
power—	An abbreviated form of writing a product using a base and an exponent. The result of repeated multiplication of a number by itself.
subtraction—	An operation defined in terms of addition as $A - B = A + (-B)$.
term—	A number or a variable, or an indicated product of a number and variable(s).
trinomial—	A three-term polynomial.

MATHEMATICS 905
FACTORS

CONTENTS

I. FINDING THE GREATEST COMMON FACTOR   2

Numerical Terms   2

Literal Terms   6

Polynomials   9

II. FINDING BINOMIAL FACTORS   13

Trinomials   13

Binomials   21

III. FINDING COMPLETE FACTORIZATIONS . . .   26

Second-Degree Polynomials   26

Higher-Degree Polynomials   30

Four-Term Polynomials   33

Word Problems   38

Author:	**Arthur C. Landrey, M.A.Ed.**
Editor-in-Chief:	Richard W. Wheeler, M.A.Ed.
Editor:	Robin Hintze Kreutzberg, M.B.A
Consulting Editor:	Robert L. Zenor, M.A., M.S.
Revision Editor:	Alan Christopherson, M.S.

Alpha Omega Publications®

804 N. 2nd Ave. E., Rock Rapids, IA 51246-1759

FACTORS

In this LIFEPAC® you will continue your study in the mathematical system known as algebra by learning an important procedure—*factoring*. You have already learned that the answer obtained from multiplying numbers or polynomials is called *product*; these numbers or polynomials then are called *factors* of that product. You will need a solid foundation in factoring methods for success in your subsequent study in algebra. In this LIFEPAC you will learn to find greatest common factors, binomial factors, and complete factorizations of polynomials.

OBJECTIVES

Read these objectives. The objectives tell you what you will be able to do when you have successfully completed this LIFEPAC.

When you have finished this LIFEPAC, you should be able to:

1. Factor numerical terms and literal terms.
2. Find the greatest common factor of monomials.
3. Factor polynomials by finding the greatest common factor.
4. Multiply binomials mentally.
5. Factor trinomials of the form $ax^2 + bx + c$.
6. Factor differences of two squares.
7. Factor binomials and trinomials completely.
8. Factor four-term polynomials.
9. Solve verbal problems involving factoring.

Survey the LIFEPAC. Ask yourself some questions about this study. Write your questions here.

_____

_____

_____

_____

_____

_____

_____

_____

I. FINDING THE GREATEST COMMON FACTOR

OBJECTIVES

When you have completed this section, you should be able to:

1. Factor numerical terms and literal terms.
2. Find the greatest common factor of monomials.
3. Factor polynomials by finding the greatest common factor.

Any expression has 1 and itself as factors, of course; if these numbers are its only factors, then the expression is called *prime*. However, if a number or a polynomial is not prime, you need to be able to find its other factors. In this section you will work first with numerical terms, then with literal terms, and finally with polynomials. The key definition for this section is the definition of the greatest common factor.

DEFINITION

The *greatest common factor (GCF)* of two or more expressions is the largest value that will divide each expression exactly.

Models:
The GCF of 8 and 12 is 4 (since 4 is the largest value that will divide both 8 and 12 exactly).

The GCF of 12 and 30 is 6.

The GCF of 8, 12, and 30 is 2.

The GCF of ab and bc is b.

The GCF of $9a$, $12b$, and $16c$ is 1.

-------- NUMERICAL TERMS---------------------------------------

The GCF for numerical terms may be found in two ways. All the factors may be listed; or prime factorizations may be used.

LISTS OF FACTORS

One method for finding the greatest common factor of numerical terms is to list all the factors (positive integral divisors) of each number and then to choose the largest factor that is common to every list.

Model: Find the GCF of 28 and 42 by listing
all the factors.

Solution: The factors of 28 are 1, 2, 4, 7, 14,
and 28.

The factors of 42 are 1, 2, 3, 6, 7, 14,
21, and 42.

The common factors are 1, 2, 7, and
14.

∴ The GCF of 28 and 42 is 14.

List all the factors of each number.

1.1   20   _____

1.2   100   _____

1.3   36   _____

1.4   23   _____

1.5   30   _____

Using the lists you made in Problems 1.1 through 1.5, find the GCF of the following sets of numbers.

1.6   20 and 100   _____

1.7   100 and 36   _____

1.8   36 and 23   _____

1.9   36 and 30   _____

1.10   20, 100, 36, and 30   _____

PRIME FACTORIZATIONS

Another method for finding the greatest common factor of numerical terms
is to obtain the prime factorization of each number and then to use the product of any
common prime factors. If no common prime factors exist, then the GCF is 1.

Model 1:   Find the GCF of 28 and 42 by prime factorizations.

Solution: 28 = 2 • 14   42 = 2 • 21
                    = 2 • 2 • 7   = 2 • 3 • 7

The common prime factors are 2 and 7.

∴ The GCF of 28 and 42 is 2 • 7 = 14.

Model 2:   Find the GCF of 72 and 90.

Solution: 72 = 2 • 36   90 = 2 • 45
                    = 2 • 2 • 18   = 2 • 3 • 15
                    = 2 • 2 • 2 • 9   = 2 • 3 • 3 • 5
                    = 2 • 2 • 2 • 3 • 3

The product of the common prime
factors is 2 • 3 • 3.

∴ The GCF of 72 and 90 is 18.

**Factor each number into the product of primes.**

1.11   210   1.14   170

_____   _____

1.12   27   1.15   325

_____   _____

1.13   198

_____

**Using the prime factorizations from Problems 1.11 - 1.15, find the GCF of the following sets of numbers.**

1.16   210 and 27   _____

1.17   27 and 198   _____

1.18   210 and 170   _____

1.19   198 and 325   _____

1.20   210, 170, and 325   _____

If prime factorizations are written in *exponential form*, then the product of the highest common powers of prime factors will be the GCF of the numerical terms. In the preceding Model 2, $72 = 2^3 \cdot 3^2$ and $90 = 2^1 \cdot 3^2 \cdot 5^1$. The highest common power of 2 is 2^1, and the highest common power of 3 is 3^2. (Five is not a common prime factor.) Thus, the GCF of 72 and 90 is $2^1 \cdot 3^2 = 2 \cdot 9 = 18$.

Model: Find the GCF of 1,560 and 2,548.

Solution:
1,560		2,548	
	$= 2 \cdot 780$		$= 2 \cdot 1,274$
	$= 2 \cdot 2 \cdot 390$		$= 2 \cdot 2 \cdot 637$
	$= 2 \cdot 2 \cdot 2 \cdot 195$		$= 2 \cdot 2 \cdot 7 \cdot 91$
	$= 2 \cdot 2 \cdot 2 \cdot 3 \cdot 65$		$= 2 \cdot 2 \cdot 7 \cdot 7 \cdot 13$
	$= 2 \cdot 2 \cdot 2 \cdot 3 \cdot 5 \cdot 13$		$= 2^2 \cdot 7^2 \cdot 13^1$
	$= 2^3 \cdot 3^1 \cdot 5^1 \cdot 13^1$		

The highest common power of 2 is 2^2.

The highest common power of 13 is 13^1.

$\therefore$ The GCF of 1,560 and 2,548 is $2^2 \cdot 13^1 = 52$.

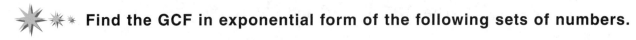 **Find the GCF in exponential form of the following sets of numbers.**

1.21 $2^5 \cdot 5 \cdot 11$ and $2^3 \cdot 5^2 \cdot 7$ _____

1.22 $13 \cdot 17^2 \cdot 19^3 \cdot 23^4$ and $13^4 \cdot 19^3 \cdot 23^2$ _____

1.23   48 and 60   1.25   726 and 1210

_____   _____

1.24   81 and 45

_____

5

To find the greatest common factor of literal terms, apply either of the two methods used for numerical terms.

Model 1:   Find the GCF of x^2y^3 and x^4y.

      Solution 1:   List all the factors. The factors of x^2y^3 are 1, x, x^2, y, y^2, y^3, xy, xy^2, xy^3, x^2y, x^2y^2, and x^2y^3. The factors of x^4y are 1, x, x^2, x^3, x^4, y, xy, x^2y, x^3y, and x^4y.

                The common factors are 1, x, x^2, y, xy, and x^2y.

                ∴ The GCF of x^2y^3 and x^4y is x^2y.

      Solution 2:   Use the exponential forms.

                The literal terms x^2y^3 and x^4y are in exponential form.

                The highest common power of x is x^2.

                The highest common power of y is y^1.

                ∴ The GCF of x^2y^3 and x^4y is $x^2 \cdot y^1 = x^2y$.

The second solution is preferred for literal terms since they are usually written (or can easily be written) in exponential form.

Model 2:   Find the GCF of $aabccc$ and ab^4c^5.

      Solution: First rewrite $aabccc$ as a^2bc^3.

              The highest common power of a is a^1.

              The highest common power of b is b^1.

              The highest common power of c is c^3.

              ∴ The GCF of c^2bc^3 and ab^4c^5 is $a^1 \cdot b^1 \cdot c^3 = abc^3$.

List all the factors of each literal term.

1.26 ab _____

1.27 x^3 _____

1.28 mnp _____

1.29 q^2r _____

Write each literal term in exponential form.

1.30 $kkkkknn$ _____

1.31 $abcbabc$ _____

1.32 $xyyzzz$ _____

Find the GCF of the following sets of literal terms.

1.33 x^5y and x^4y^2 _____

1.34 $abcde$ and $cdefg$ _____

1.35 $m^7n^4p^3$ and $mn^{12}p^5$ _____

1.36 $xxyyyzz$ and $xxxxzzz$ _____

In general, the greatest common factor of two or more monomials is the product of the GCF of the numerical factors and the GCF of the literal factors.

Model 1: Find the GCF of $8m^3n^2$ and $6m^2n^3$.

Solution: The GCF of 8 and 6 is 2.

The GCF of m^3n^2 and m^2n^3 is m^2n^2.

∴ The GCF of $8m^3n^2$ and $6m^2n^3$ is $2 \cdot m^2n^2 = 2m^2n^2$.

Model 2: Find the GCF of $2abc$, $3bcd$, and $4cde$; then write each monomial as the product of the GCF and the remaining factors of that monomial.

Solution: The GCF of 2, 3, and 4 is 1.
The GCF of abc, bcd, and cde is c.
$\therefore$ The GCF of $2abc$, $3bcd$, and $4cde$ is $1 \cdot c = c$.
The monomials are written $2abc = c(2ab)$,
$3bcd = c(3bd)$, and $4cde = c(4de)$.

Model 3: Find the GCF of $-9x^2y^7$, $12x^5y^5$, and $-30x^3y^{10}$; then write each monomial as the product of the GCF and the remaining factors of that monomial.

Solution: The GCF of -9, 12, and -30 is 3.
The GCF of x^2y^7, x^5y^5, and x^3y^{10} is x^2y^5.
$\therefore$ The GCF of $-9x^2y^7$, $12x^5y^5$, and $-30x^3y^{10}$ is $3x^2y^5$.
The monomials are written $-9x^2y^7 = 3x^2y^5 \, (-3y^2)$,
$12x^5y^5 = 3x^2y^5 \, (4x^3)$, and $-30x^3y^{10} = 3x^2y^5 \, (-10xy^5)$.

 Find the GCF of the following sets of monomials.

1.37 $5a$, $5b$, and $5c$ _____

1.38 $4pq$, $3pq$, and $2pq$ _____

1.39 $9x^2y^2$ and $6xy^3$ _____

1.40 $-50m^4n^7$ and $40m^2n^{10}$ _____

 Find the GCF of each pair of monomials; then write each monomial as the product of the GCF and the remaining factors of that monomial.

		GCF	PRODUCTS	
Model:	$8abc$ and $-12ac^2$	$4ac$	$4ac(2b)$	$4ac(-3c)$

1.41 $4wxy$ and $6xyz$ _____ _____ ; _____

1.42 $-10c^2d$ and $15cd^2$ _____ _____ ; _____

1.43 $38m$ and $57n$ _____ _____ ; _____

1.44 $12x^5y^9$ and $-35x^7y^3$ _____ _____ ; _____

1.45 $-80a^3bc^5$ and $-200a^2bc^7$ _____ _____ ; _____

The greatest common factor of a polynomial is the GCF of all the terms that make up that polynomial.

Model 1:   Find the GCF of $8x^3y^4 - 4x^3y^2 - 6x^2y^2 + 2xy^3$.

Solution: The four terms are $8x^3y^4$, $-4x^3y^2$, $-6x^2y^2$, and $2xy^3$.
The GCF of 8, -4, -6, and 2 is 2.
The GCF of x^3y^4, x^3y^2, x^2y^2, and xy^3 is xy^2.
∴ The GCF of the polynomial is $2xy^2$.

The distributive property, $AB + AC = A(B + C)$, is used to factor out or separate the greatest common factor from a polynomial.

Model 2:   Factor $10x + 5y$ by separating the GCF.

Solution: The GCF of $10x + 5y$ is 5, and $10x + 5y = 5 \cdot 2x + 5 \cdot y$
∴ The factorization is $5(2x + y)$.

Model 3:   Factor out the GCF of $9x^3 + 10x^2 - 11x$.

Solution: The GCF is x, and $9x^3 + 10x^2 - 11x = x(9x^2) + x(10x) - x11$
∴ The factorization is $x(9x^2 + 10x - 11)$.

To check the factorization of a polynomial that results from separating the GCF, two steps should be followed. First, be certain that the GCF of the polynomial in the parentheses is 1. Second, be certain that the original polynomial is obtained when the separated GCF is multiplied by the polynomial in the parentheses.

Model 4: $2(3m - 6mn)$ is *not* the correct factorization of $6m - 12mn$ since the GCF of $3m - 6mn$ is $3m$, not 1. The correct factorization is $6m - 12mn = 6m \cdot 1 - 6m \cdot 2n = 6m(1 - 2n)$.

Model 5: $4(-x + 8)$ is *not* the correct factorization of $-4x + 8$ since $4(-x + 8) = -4x + 32$. The correct factorization is $-4x + 8 = 4(-x) + 4(2) = 4(-x + 2)$

You should note that the binomial $-4x + 8$ will often be factored as $-4(x - 2)$ since $-4x \cdot x$ is $-4x$ and $-4(-2)$ is 8.

Model 6: The polynomial $-10a^3 + 15a^2b - 30ab + 5a$ may be factored as $5a(-2a^2 + 3ab - 6b + 1)$ or preferably as $-5a(2a^2 - 3ab + 6b - 1)$

Model 7: Factor $8x^3y^4 - 4x^3y^2 - 6x^2y^2 + 2xy^3$, and check.

Solution: The GCF of this polynomial is $2xy^2$, and $8x^3y^4 - 4x^3y^2 - 6x^2y^2 + 2xy^3 = 2xy^2 \cdot 4x^2y^2 - 2xy^2 \cdot 2x^2 - 2xy^2 \cdot 3x + 2xy^2 \cdot y = 2xy^2(4x^2y^2 - 2x^2 - 3x + y)$.

Check: The GCF of the polynomial in the parentheses is 1, and the product of $2xy^2$ with each term gives the original polynomial.
∴ The factorization is $2xy^2(4x^2y^2 - 2x^2 - 3x + y)$.

✸❋∗ **Factor each polynomial by separating the GCF; check your factors.**

1.46 $14a + 7b$ _____

1.47 $3y^2 - 4y$ _____

1.48 $10x^3 + 8x^2 - 6x$ _____

1.49 $4n^4 + n^3$ _____

1.50 $-3x - 3y - 3z$ _____

1.51 $a^2bc + ab^2c + abc^2$ _____

1.52 $5k^2 - 35k^3$ _____

1.53 $x^4y^2 + x^3y^3$ _____

1.54 $16p^5 - 24p^4$ _____

1.55 $-4d^3 + 28d^2 - 4d$ _____

1.56 $30y^2z + 12yz^2 - 18yz$ _____

1.57 $x^8 + 3x^5$ _____

1.58 $2a^5b + 2a^4b^2 + 2a^3b^3$ _____

1.59 $48m - 80n$ _____

1.60 $-24a^3b^3c^3 - 84a^4b^2c$ _____

Review the material in this section in preparation for the Self Test. The Self Test will check your mastery of this particular section. The items missed on this Self Test will indicate specific areas where restudy is needed for mastery.

SELF TEST 1

Complete these activities (each numbered item, 10 points).

1.01   List all the factors (positive integral divisors) of 48.

_____

1.02   Write the prime factorization of 7700 in exponential form.

_____

1.03   Find the greatest common factor of 270 and 360. (Give your answer in exponential form and in simplified form).

_____   =   _____

1.04   List all the factors of mn^2.

_____

1.05   Write $pqqqqrr$ in exponential form.

_____

1.06   Find the greatest common factor of $8a^3b^2$ and $12ab^4$.

_____

1.07   Write each monomial in Problem 1.06 as the product of the GCF and the remaining factors of the monomial.

_____   ;   _____

11

1.08   Factor $9x - 27y$ by separating the GCF.

_____

1.09   Factor $3a^3 + 7a^5$.

_____

1.010   Factor $-20m^3n^2 + 28m^2n^2 - 44m^2n^3$.

_____

OBJECTIVES

When you have completed this section, you should be able to:

4. Multiply binomials mentally.
5. Factor trinomials of the form multiple. $ax^2 + bx + c$.
6. Factor differences of two squares.

Now that you have learned to factor out a monomial (the GCF) from a polynomial, the next step is to find the binomial factors for a polynomial. In this section you will work first with trinomials and then with a special type of binomials.

--- ---- ---- ---- ---- ---- **TRINOMIALS** ---- ---- ---- ---- ---- ---- ---- ---- ---- ---- ---- ---- ---- ---- ---- ---- ----

Trinomials may result from multiplying binomials. Trinomials can have leading coefficients equal to one or greater than one; trinomials can also be the product of two equal binomial factors. Factorization for each of these cases will be treated in this section.

BINOMIALS WITH TRINOMIAL PRODUCTS

In Mathematics LIFEPAC 904 you learned to multiply binomials such as $(x + 3)(x + 5) = x^2 + 5x + 3x + 15 = x^2 + 8x + 15$. Notice how each term of the trinomial product is formed. The x^2 comes from the product of x and x, which are the *first* terms of the binomials. The 15 comes from the product of 3 and 5, which are the *last* terms of the binomials.

FIRST TERMS = x^2

$(x + 3) (x + 5)$

LAST TERMS = 15

The $8x$ comes from the sum of $5x$ and $3x$, which are the products of the *outer* terms and the *inner* terms, respectively, of the binomials.

OUTER TERMS = $5x$

$(x + 3) (x + 5)$

INNER TERMS = $3x$

13

The first letters of the words *first*, *outer*, *inner*, and *last* form an acronym, *FOIL*, which aids in the mental multiplication of binomials. Only the final product should be written.

Model 1:   Find the product of $(x - 4)(x + 7)$.

Solution: Mentally, think of

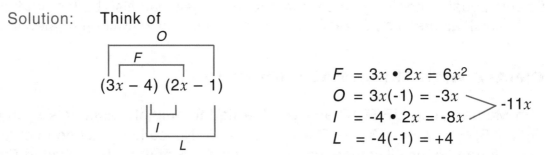

$$\therefore x^2 + 3x - 28 \text{ is the product.}$$

Model 2:   Find the product of $(3x - 4)(2x - 1)$.

Solution: Think of

$$
\begin{aligned}
F &= 3x \cdot 2x = 6x^2 \\
O &= 3x(-1) = -3x \\
I &= -4 \cdot 2x = -8x \\
L &= -4(-1) = +4
\end{aligned}
$$
$\Big\} -11x$

$$\therefore 6x^2 - 11x + 4 \text{ is the product.}$$

Each of these trinomial products consists of a second-degree term, a first-degree term, and a constant term. In the preceding Model 2, $6x^2$ is the second-degree term, $-11x$ is the first-degree term, and 4 is the constant term.

The sign of the second-degree term depends on the *F*-product being positive or negative. The sign of the first-degree term depends on the sum of the *O*-product and *I*-product being positive or negative. The sign of the constant term depends on the *L*-product being positive or negative.

Models: $(x + 2)(x + 3) = x^2 + 5x + 6$

$(-x + 2)(-x + 3) = x^2 - 5x + 6$

$(-x + 2)(x + 3) = -x^2 - x + 6$

$(x - 2)(x - 3) = x^2 - 5x + 6$

$$(x - 2)(x + 3) = x^2 + x - 6$$
$$(-x + 2)(x - 3) = -x^2 + 5x - 6$$
$$(x + 2)(-x - 3) = -x^2 - 5x - 6$$
$$(x + 2)(x - 3) = x^2 - x - 6$$

Notice especially that the sign of the constant term is positive in the first four models when the signs between the terms of the binomials are *alike*, either both + or both − . In the last four models the sign of the constant term is negative when the signs between the terms of the binomials are *unlike*, one + and one − .

Model: Determine whether the sign of the constant term of each product will be positive (+) or negative (-).

a. $(x - 9)(x + 3)$

b. $(2x + 5)(x + 7)$

c. $(-x - 1)(3x - 4)$

d. $(4x + 1)(-3x - 5)$

Solutions:

a. -, since -9 and +3 have unlike signs

b. +, since +5 and +7 have like signs

c. +, since -1 and -4 have like signs

d. -, since +1 and -5 have unlike signs

 Find each trinomial product mentally.

2.1 $(x + 5)(x + 2)$ _____

2.2 $(x - 4)(x - 3)$ _____

2.3 $(y + 7)(y - 1)$ _____

2.4 $(n - 8)(n + 2)$ _____

2.5 $(-a + 3)(a + 4)$ _____

2.6 $(-y - 2)(-y + 6)$ _____

LEADING COEFFICIENT OF ONE

Reversing the procedure for multiplying binomials gives a method for factoring trinomials. Since $(x + 7)(x + 2) = x^2 + 9x + 14$, then the factorization of $x^2 + 9x + 14$ is $(x + 7)(x + 2)$. The method for finding these binomial factors when the coefficient of the second-degree term is 1 is shown in the following models.

(The coefficient is the numerical factor of a term.) REMEMBER?

Model 1:   Find the binomial factors of $x^2 + 9x + 14$.

Solution: $x^2 + 9x + 14 \overset{?}{=} (\quad)(\quad)$

The second degree term comes from the *F*-product $x \cdot x$.

$x^2 + 9x + 14 \overset{?}{=} (x \quad)(x \quad)$

The constant term comes from the *L*-product $7 \cdot 2$.

$x^2 + 9x + 14 \overset{?}{=} (x \quad 7)(x \quad 2)$

The constant term is positive; therefore, the signs between terms of the binomials are alike. Since the positive first-degree term comes from the sum of the *O*-product and the *I*-product, the signs must both be +.

$\therefore x^2 + 9x + 14 = (x + 7)(x + 2)$; check by *FOIL*.

You might have begun factoring by using $(-x)(-x)$ to give the second-degree term x^2; however, this makes the factoring procedure more difficult in the next steps. Also, the constant term 14 might have come from the *L*-product $14 \cdot 1$; however, this pair of factors gives a first-degree term of $15x$ rather than the correct $9x$.

Model 2:   The factors of $x^2 + 15x + 14$ are $(x + 14)(x + 1)$.

Model 3:   Find the binomial factors of $y^2 - 7y + 12$.

Solution: $y^2 - 7y + 12 \overset{?}{=} (\quad)(\quad),$

$\overset{?}{=} (y \quad)(y \quad),$

$\overset{?}{=} (y - \quad)(y - \quad),$ since the constant term is positive (like signs) and the first-degree term is negative. Now 12 can factor as $1 \cdot 12$ or $2 \cdot 6$ or $3 \cdot 4$. Try each possibility:

$$(y - 1)(y - 12) = y^2 - 13y + 12 \neq y^2 - 7y + 12$$

$$(y - 2)(y - 6) = y^2 - 8y + 12 \neq y^2 - 7y + 12$$

$$(y - 3)(y - 4) = y^2 - 7y + 12$$

$$\therefore \text{ The desired factors are } (y - 3)(y - 4).$$

Actually, most or all of the work shown in the solutions should be done mentally rather than written out. Be sure to use *FOIL* to verify your factorizations.

Model 4: Find the binomial factors of $n^2 + 2n - 15$.

Solution: $n^2 + 2n - 15 \overset{?}{=} (n \quad)(n \quad)$

$\overset{?}{=} (n + \quad)(n - \quad)$, since the constant term is negative. Now 15 can factor as $1 \cdot 15$ or $3 \cdot 5$.
$\therefore$ The factors $(n + 5)(n - 3)$ give $+ 2n$ for the first-degree term.

▶▶▶**Find the binomial factors for each trinomial and check by *FOIL*.**

2.7 $y^2 + 5y + 6$ $(\underline{\hspace{3cm}})(\underline{\hspace{3cm}})$

2.8 $x^2 + 13x + 36$ $\underline{\hspace{6cm}}$

2.9 $n^2 - 8n + 15$ $\underline{\hspace{6cm}}$

2.10 $a^2 - a - 20$ $\underline{\hspace{6cm}}$

2.11 $x^2 - 5x - 14$ $\underline{\hspace{6cm}}$

2.12 $y^2 - 8y - 20$ $\underline{\hspace{6cm}}$

2.13 $y^2 + 8y - 20$ $\underline{\hspace{6cm}}$

2.14 $p^2 + 18p + 32$ $\underline{\hspace{6cm}}$

2.15 $p^2 + 12p + 32$ $\underline{\hspace{6cm}}$

2.16 $x^2 - 13x + 12$ $\underline{\hspace{6cm}}$

2.17 $x^2 + 29x - 30$ $\underline{\hspace{6cm}}$

2.18 $m^2 - 10m + 21$ $\underline{\hspace{6cm}}$

2.19 $d^2 - 11d - 80$ $\underline{\hspace{6cm}}$

Find each trinomial product mentally.

2.20 $(2a + 3)(a + 2)$ _____

2.21 $(5a - 7)(2a - 1)$ _____

2.22 $(d - 9)(3d + 7)$ _____

2.23 $(4x + 3)(-2x - 5)$ _____

2.24 $(3y - 2)(2y - 3)$ _____

2.25 $(-2k + 1)(-4k - 1)$ _____

LEADING COEFFICIENT GREATER THAN ONE

When the coefficient of the second-degree term of a trinomial is greater than 1, the factoring procedure may require trying quite a few possibilities.

Model 1:   In the trinomial $6x^2 + 19x + 10$ the coefficient of the second-degree term is 6, which can factor as $6 \cdot 1$ or $3 \cdot 2$.

Model 2:   Factor $6x^2 + 19x + 10$.

Solution: $6x^2 + 19x + 10 \overset{?}{=} (\quad + \quad)(\quad + \quad)$

All of the following possibilities give a first product of $6x^2$ and a last product of 10. To find the correct factors, check the sum of the outer product and the inner product.

	OUTER PRODUCT	INNER PRODUCT	SUM
$(6x + 10)(x + 1)$	$6x$	$10x$	$16x$
$(6x + 1)(x + 10)$	$60x$	$1x$	$61x$
$(6x + 2)(x + 5)$	$30x$	$2x$	$32x$
$(6x + 5)(x + 2)$	$12x$	$5x$	$17x$
$(3x + 10)(2x + 1)$	$3x$	$20x$	$23x$
$(3x + 1)(2x + 10)$	$30x$	$2x$	$32x$
$(3x + 2)(2x + 5)$	$15x$	$4x$	$19x$
$(3x + 5)(2x + 2)$	$6x$	$10x$	$16x$

∴ The factors of $6x^2 + 19x + 10$ are $(3x + 2)(2x + 5)$.

Model 3:   Factor $7y^2 - 18y + 11$.

Solution: $7y^2 - 18y + 11 \stackrel{?}{=} (7y -)(y -)$, since the constant term is positive (like signs) and the first-degree term is negative. The two possibilities are $(7y - 1)(y - 11)$ and $(7y - 11)(y - 1)$. Check by *FOIL* to find the correct factorization.

∴ The factors of $7y^2 - 18y + 11$ are $(7y - 11)(y - 1)$.

Again, much or all of the work shown in the solutions should be done mentally rather than written out. The more you practice, the quicker you will become at finding the correct factorization for a trinomial.

Model 4:   Factor $8x^2 + 23x - 3$.

Solution: $8x^2 + 23x - 3 \stackrel{?}{=} (8x)(x)$ or $(4x)(2x)$

Notice that the constant term is negative, indicating that the signs between the terms of the binomials must be unlike. Consider these possibilities:

	OUTER PRODUCT	INNER PRODUCT	SUM
$(8x + 3)(x - 1)$	$-8x$	$+ 3x$	$-5x$
$(8x + 1)(x - 3)$	$-24x$	$+ 1x$	$-23x$
$(4x + 3)(2x - 1)$	$-4x$	$+ 6x$	$+ 2x$
$(4x + 1)(2x - 3)$	$-12x$	$+ 2x$	$-10x$

Since the second possibility gives a first-degree term of $-23x$ rather than $+23x$, just reverse the + and − signs in the binomials.

∴ The factors of $8x^2 + 23x - 3$ are $(8x - 1)(x + 3)$.

🌑◗◡ **Find the binomial factors for each trinomial and check by *FOIL*.**

2.26 $2x^2 + 7x + 3$ (_____)(_____)

2.27 $8y^2 + 17y + 2$ _____

2.28 $4n^2 - 5n - 6$ _____

2.29 $24a^2 + 5a - 1$ _____

2.30 $6a^2 - 23a - 4$ _____

TRINOMIAL SQUARES

One special type of trinomial you will frequently come across is a *trinomial square*.

> **DEFINITION**
>
> A *trinomial square* is a trinomial that has two equal binomial factors; its second-degree term and its constant term are themselves squares.

Model 1:   The factors of $x^2 + 6x + 9$ are $(x + 3)(x + 3)$.

Thus, $x^2 + 6x + 9$ is a trinomial square.

The binomial factors of a trinomial square should be written in exponential form. In Model 1 the factorization is written $(x + 3)^2$.

Model 2:   Factor $49y^2 - 14y + 1$.

$$\text{Solution:} \quad 49y^2 - 14y + 1 \overset{?}{=} (\quad - \quad)(\quad - \quad)$$
$$= (7y - 1)(7y - 1)$$
$$= (7y - 1)^2$$

Find the binomial factors for each trinomial and check by *FOIL*; write the factors in exponential form for any trinomial squares.

2.31 $5x^2 - 7x + 2$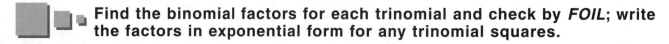

2.32 $8y^2 + 6y + 1$

2.33 $a^2 + 10a + 25$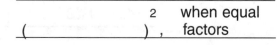

2.34 $15n^2 - 7n - 2$

2.35 $4m^2 - 8m - 5$

2.36 $25y^2 - 30y + 9$

2.37 $3y^2 + 10y - 8$

2.38 $4x^2 + 25x + 6$

2.39 $4n^2 + 28n + 49$

2.40 $5y^2 - 2y - 3$

2.41 $64n^2 - 16n + 1$

2.42 $36x^2 + 60x + 25$ _____

2.43 $7k^2 - 9k - 10$ _____

2.44 $9y^2 - 12y + 4$ _____

2.45 $10m^2 + 11m - 6$ _____

• • • • • • • • • • **BINOMIALS** •

You may recall that the product of two binomials is not always a trinomial.
For example, $(n + 2)(n - 2) = n^2 - 2n + 2n - 4 = n^2 - 4$. Thus, the factorization of $n^2 - 4$
is $(n + 2)(n - 2)$. One method for finding factors of this type is shown in the following
models.

Model 1:   Find the factors of $n^2 - 4$.

Solution: Consider $n^2 - 4$ as a trinomial with a first-degree term of $0n$.
Then use the procedure learned for factoring trinomials.

$n^2 - 4 = n^2 + 0n - 4$.

$\overset{?}{=} (n \quad)(n \quad)$

$\overset{?}{=} (n + \quad)(n - \quad)$, since the constant term is negative
(unlike signs). The outer product and the inner product must
have a sum of $0n$.

∴ The factors of $n^2 - 4$ are $(n + 2)(n - 2)$.

Model 2:   Find the factors of $16a^2 - 9$.

Solution: $16a^2 - 9 = 16a^2 + 0a - 9$

$\overset{?}{=} (\quad + \quad)(\quad - \quad)$; $4a \cdot 4a$ is $16a^2$
and $3 \cdot 3$ is 9.

∴ The factors of $16a^2 - 9$ are $(4a + 3)(4a - 3)$;
check by *FOIL*.

 Factor each binomial as a trinomial with a first-degree term of 0.

2.46 $x^2 - 9 = (x^2 + 0x - 9) =$ ___(_____)(_____)

2.47 $36y^2 - 1$ _____

2.48 $4a^2 - 25$ _____

2.49 $81n^2 - 100$ _____

2.50 $d^2 - 361$ _____

DEFINITION

A binomial such as $n^2 - 4$ or $16n^2 - 9$ is known as a *difference of two squares* since each term is a square and subtraction is indicated between them.

Model 1: $4x^2 - 49$ is a difference of two squares, $(2x)^2 - 7^2$.

$4x^2 + 49$ is *not* a difference of two squares.

$3x^2 - 49$ is *not* a difference of two squares.

Another method for factoring this kind of binomial is suggested by considering $4x^2 - 49$ as the difference of the squares of $2x$ and 7, respectively.

Model 2: Factor $4x^2 - 49$.

Solution 1: Factor as a trinomial with a first-degree term of $0x$.

$$4x^2 - 49 = 4x^2 + 0x - 49$$

$$= (\quad + \quad)(\quad - \quad)$$

$$= (2x + 7)(2x - 7), \text{ the factors.}$$

Solution 2: Factor as a difference of two squares.

$$4x^2 - 49 = (2x)^2 - 7^2$$

$$= (2x + 7)(2x - 7), \text{ the factors}$$

The second solution is more commonly used. Notice that in the factorization of a difference of two squares, the signs between the terms are unlike.

In general, $A^2 - B^2 = (A + B)(A - B)$.

RULE

$A^2 - B^2 = (A + B)(A - B)$ is the factorization of a difference of two squares.

Model 3: Factor $256q^2 - 121r^2$.

Solution: $256q^2 - 121r^2 = (16q)^2 - (11r)^2$

$$= (16q + 11r)(16q - 11r)$$

22

MATHEMATICS

9 0 5

LIFEPAC TEST

84 / 105

Name_____

Date_____

Score_____

MATHEMATICS 905: LIFEPAC TEST

Complete these activities (each answer, 5 points).

1. List all the factors of 70. _____

2. Give the prime factorization of 240 in exponential form.

3. Find the greatest common factor of $15x^2y^3$ and $-18x^3yz$.

4. Factor $3y - 15$ by separating the GCF.

    _____

5. Factor $x^2y + xy^3$. _____

6. Factor $-3m^3 - 5m^2 + m$. _____

7. Find the product $(n + 8)(n - 2)$ mentally.

    _____

8. Find the binomial factors of $k^2 + 13k + 12$.

    _____

9. Factor $p^2 - 8p - 20$. _____

10. Find the product $(-4d + 3)(2d + 1)$ mentally.

    _____

11. Factor $6x^2 - 17x + 5$. _____

12. Factor $25x^2 + 10x + 1$. _____

13. Find the product $(6a + 5)(6a - 5)$ mentally.

    _____

14. Factor $9b^2 - 4$ as a difference of two squares.

    _____

1

15.   Find the product $(a + 5)(a - b)$ mentally.

16.   Factor the four-term polynomial $pq - 3r + pr - 3q$.

Factor each of the following polynomials completely; show your steps (each answer, 5 points).

17. $3x^2 - 15x - 42$

18. $-2bk^2 + 6bk - 2b$

19. $360t + 10t^3 - 120t^2$

20. $y^4 - 16$

21. $-x^2y^2 + x^4 + 9y^2 - 9x^2$

NOTES

Models 4:   Factor $-1 + 0.25t^6$.

Solution: $-1 + 0.25t^6 = 0.25t^6 + (-1)$

$$= 0.25t^6 - 1$$

$$= (0.5t^3)^2 - 1^2$$

$$= (0.5t^3 + 1)(0.5t^3 - 1)$$

▶ ▷ ▸ **Factor each binomial as a difference of two squares.**

2.51 $16y^2 - 25 = (4y)^2 - 5^2 =$ ___(_____)(_____)___

2.52 $a^4 - 9b^2$ _____

2.53 $9a^4 - b^2$ _____

2.54 $64 - x^2$ _____

2.55 $0.04m^2 - n^2$ _____

2.56 $-49 + y^6$ _____

2.57 $x^{10} - y^2$ _____

2.58 $\frac{1}{4}a^2 - \frac{1}{9}y^2$ _____

2.59 $-169p^2 + \frac{4}{169}$ _____

2.60 $1 - 2.25x^8$ _____

Sometimes the factoring procedure will need to be repeated with any resulting binomial factor that is itself a difference of two squares.

Model: Factor $\frac{81}{16}m^4 - n^8$

Solution: $\frac{81}{16}m^4 - n^8 = (\frac{9}{4}m^2)^2 - (n^4)^2$

$$= (\frac{9}{4}m^2 + n^4)(\frac{9}{4}m^2 - n^4)$$

$$= (\frac{9}{4}m^2 + n^4)([\frac{3}{2}m]^2 - [n^2]^2)$$

$$= (\frac{9}{4}m^2 + n^4)(\frac{3}{2}m + n^2)(\frac{3}{2}m - n^2)$$

Notice that the first binomial factor, $\frac{9}{4}m^2 + n^4$, is a sum (not a difference) of two squares and does not factor by this method.

Factor each difference of two squares, repeat the procedure as often as necessary (be sure to give all the final factors in your answer). Check by *FOIL*.

2.61 $n^4 - 1$ _____

2.62 $16 - a^{16}$ _____

2.63 $-\dfrac{1}{81} + x^8$ _____

2.64 $m^4 - n^4$ _____

2.65 $1 - 256y^8$ _____

     Review the material in this section in preparation for the Self Test. This Self Test will check your mastery of this particular section as well as your knowledge of the previous section.

SELF TEST 2

Complete these activities (each answer, 5 points).

2.01   Find the greatest common factor of 572 and 616. (Give your answer in exponential form and in simplified form.)

_____ = _____

2.02   Find the greatest common factor of $-30x^4yz^3$ and $75x^4z^2$.

_____

2.03   Factor $vwx + wxy - xyz$.   _____

2.04   Factor $-50x^3 - 24x^2 + 2x$.   _____

24

2.05   Find the product $(-y + 3)(y - 7)$ mentally.

_____

2.06   Factor $n^2 + 7n - 44$.   _____

2.07   Factor $a^2 + 28a + 27$.   _____

2.08   Find the product $(4p - 3)(5p + 1)$ mentally.

_____

2.09   Factor $2x^2 - 9x - 11$.   _____

2.010   Factor $8n^2 - 26n + 15$.   _____

2.011   Factor $81k^2 + 36k + 4$.   _____

2.012   Find the product $(2y + 3)(2y - 3)$ mentally.

_____

2.013   Factor $k^2 - 81$ as a trinomial with a first degree term of 0.

_____

2.014   Factor $49t^6 - k^8$ as a difference of two squares.

_____

2.015   Factor $625x^4 - 1$ as a difference of two squares, repeating the procedure
        as often as necessary.

_____

Score   _____

Teacher Check _____

Initial   Date

III. FINDING COMPLETE FACTORIZATIONS

OBJECTIVES

When you have completed this section, you should be able to:

7. Factor binomials and trinomials completely.
8. Factor four-term polynomials.
9. Solve verbal problems involving factoring.

You should now know how to perform the two basic factoring procedures, separating the GCF and finding binomial factors. Some polynomials require a combination or repetition of these procedures. In this section you will work first with second-degree polynomials, then with higher-degree polynomials, and then with polynomials having four terms. Word problems involving factoring are the final activity in this section.

══════ SECOND-DEGREE POLYNOMIALS ══════

It is important for you to factor a polynomial completely.

DEFINITION

A *complete factorization* is one in which all polynomial factors (excluding monomial factors) are prime. For example, the factorization of $4x^2 + 8x - 60$ to $4(x^2 + 2x - 15)$ is not complete since the trinomial $x^2 + 2x - 15$ can itself be factored.

Model 1: Write the complete factorization of $4x^2 + 8x - 60$.

Solution: $4x^2 + 8x - 60 = 4(x^2 + 2x - 15)$

$$= 4(x + 5)(x - 3)$$

The factorization is now complete since neither of the binomials can be factored any further.

For a polynomial to be factored correctly, it must be factored completely. However, several ways to reach the complete factorization of a given polynomial may exist.

26

Model 2:   Factor $6x^2 - 15x + 9$.

   Solution 1: $6x^2 - 15x + 9 = (2x - 3)(3x - 3)$

$$= (2x - 3) \bullet 3(x - 1)$$

$$= 3(2x - 3)(x - 1)$$

   Solution 2: $6x^2 - 15x + 9 = (6x - 9)(x - 1)$

$$= 3(2x - 3)(x - 1)$$

   Solution 3: $6x^2 - 15x + 9 = 3(2x^2 - 5x + 3)$

$$= 3(2x - 3)(x - 1)$$

Although all of these solutions give the same factorization, the third solution is preferred. Thus, you should begin by separating the GCF from the polynomial before using any other factoring procedures.

Model 3:   Factor $6y^2 - 726$.

   Solution: $6y^2 - 726 = 6(y^2 - 121)$

$$= 6(y + 11)(y - 11)$$

Model 4:   Factor $250n^2 + 200n + 40$.

   Solution: $250n^2 + 200n + 40 = 10(25n^2 + 20n + 4)$

$$= 10(5n + 2)(5n + 2)$$

$$= 10(5n + 2)^2$$

When factoring second-degree trinomials, you should arrange the terms in descending powers of the variable if they are not already in that order.

Model 5:   Factor $-6 + 20x^2 - 2x$.

   Solution: $-6 + 20x^2 - 2x = 20x^2 - 2x - 6$

$$= 2(10x^2 - x - 3)$$

$$= 2(5x - 3)(2x + 1)$$

Also, if the second-degree term is negative, the factoring will usually be simplified by separating a negative common factor at the beginning of the factorization.

Model 6:   Factor $-y^2 - 5y + 14$.

     Solution: $-y^2 - 5y + 14 = -1(y^2 + 5y - 14)$

$$= -1(y + 7)(y - 2)$$

$$= -(y + 7)(y - 2)$$

Model 7:   Factor $-63a + 14 - 7a^2$.

     Solution: $-63a + 14 - 7a^2 = -7a^2 - 63a + 14$

$= -7(a^2 + 9a - 2)$, which is the complete factorization since $a^2 + 9a - 2$ is prime.

 Give the complete factorization for each polynomial.

3.1 $3x^2 - 6x - 240$

_____

3.2 $25a^2 - 100$

_____

3.3 $4m^2 + 20m - 96$

_____

3.4 $16y^2 + 68y + 42$

_____

3.5 $-p^2 + 6p - 9$

3.6 $-144 + 9n^2$

_____

3.7 $90 + 160k^2 + 240k$

_____

3.8 $10x - 3 - 3x^2$

_____

3.9 $-7y^2 + 7y + 84$

_____

3.10 $35d + 5d^2 - 30$

_____

3.11 $-98n^2 + 2$

_____

3.12 $75t^2 + 12$

3.13 $6y^2 - 48 + 42y$ _____

3.14 $-30x^2 - 7x + 15$ _____

_____

3.15 $-4 + 8a - 4a^2$

_____

-------- **HIGHER-DEGREE POLYNOMIALS** --------------------------

Much of our work has been with second-degree trinomials and binomials. However, the same factoring procedures apply to many higher-degree trinomials and binomials as well. In general, the complete factorization results from following these four steps.

> FOUR STEPS TO COMPLETE FACTORIZATION
>
> 1.   Arrange the terms in descending powers of a variable.
>
> 2.   Separate the GCF (or its negative to make the first term positive).
>
> 3.   If the resulting polynomial has three terms, use the factoring procedures for trinomials.
>
> 4.   If any resulting binomial is a difference of two squares, use $A^2 - B^2 = (A + B)(A - B)$ to factor it. (This step may have to be performed more than once.)

The factorization should be written as the indicated product of all the final factors obtained, including the exponential form of any equal factors. A check should be made at each step of the procedure and/or with the final answer. The four steps are indicated by number as they are used in the following models.

Model 1:   Factor $60 - 3x^4 - 3x^2$.

Solution: $60 - 3x^4 - 3x^2 = -3x^4 - 3x^2 + 60$ by 1

$= -3(x^4 + x^2 - 20)$ by 2

$= -3(x^2 + 5)(x^2 - 4)$ by 3

$= -3(x^2 + 5)(x + 2)(x - 2)$ by 4

Check: $-3(x^2 + 5)(x + 2)(x - 2)$

$= (-3x^2 - 15)(x + 2)(x - 2)$

$= (-3x^3 - 6x^2 - 15x - 30)(x - 2)$

$= -3x^4 + 6x^3 - 6x^3 + 12x^2 - 15x^2 + 30x - 30x + 60$

$= -3x^4 \qquad\qquad\qquad -3x^2 \qquad\quad + 60$

$= 60 - 3x^4 - 3x^2$, the original trinomial.

Model 2:   Factor $16y^7 + 8y^6 + y^5$.

Solution: $16y^7 + 8y^6 + y^5 = y^5(16y^2 + 8y + 1)$ by 2

$= y^5(4y + 1)(4y + 1)$ by 3

$= y^5(4y + 1)^2$

Check: $y^5(4y + 1)^2$

$= y^5(16y^2 + 8y + 1)$

$= 16y^7 + 8y^6 + y^5$, the original trinomial.

Model 3:   Factor $-1 + a^8b^8$.

Solution: $-1 + a^8b^8 = a^8b^8 - 1$ by 1

$= (a^4b^4 + 1)(a^4b^4 - 1)$ by 4

$= (a^4b^4 + 1)(a^2b^2 + 1)(a^2b^2 - 1)$ by 4

$= (a^4b^4 + 1)(a^2b^2 + 1)(ab + 1)(ab - 1)$ by 4

Check: Left for you to do.

31

Write the complete factorization for each polynomial.

3.16 $5x^4 - 30x^2 - 135$

_____

3.17 $12n^3 + 9n^2 + 4n^4$

_____

3.18 $a - ay^4$

_____

3.19 $5x^4 + 8x^2 + 3$

_____

3.20 $7y^6 - 28$

_____

3.21 $-8 + 10x^2 - 2x^4$

_____

3.22 $k^8 - 256$

_____

3.23 $y^4 - 25y^2 + 144$

_____

3.24 $16y^5 + y - 8y^3$

_____

3.25 $-3x^7 - 27x^3$

_____

••••••••••••••••• **FOUR-TERM POLYNOMIALS** •••••••••••••••••••••••••••••••••

Consider the product $(a + b)(c + d)$; the result is $ac + ad + bc + bd$, a polynomial having four terms. Thus, the factorization of $ac + ad + bc + bd$ is $(a + b)(c + d)$. A method for finding these factors is shown in the following model.

Model 1:   Find the factors of $ac + ad + bc + bd$.

Solution 1: Group the four terms into two pairs, then separate the GCF from each pair:

$$ac + ad + bc + bd = (ac + ad) + (bc + bd)$$

$$= a(c + d) + b(c + d)$$

Now you have two terms; $a(c + d)$ is one, and $b(c + d)$ is the other. The GCF of these two terms is the binomial $(c + d)$. If this GCF is separated by the distributive property, then the remaining factor is $(a + b)$.

∴ The factors are $(c + d)(a + b)$; of course, they may also be written as $(a + b)(c + d)$.

Solution 2: The terms may be rearranged, then grouped and factored as shown:

$$ac + ad + bc + bd = ac + bc + ad + bd$$

$$= (ac + bc) + (ad + bd)$$

$$= c(a + b) + d(a + b)$$

$$= (a + b)(c + d), \text{ the factors.}$$

Either of the preceding solutions is acceptable and yields the correct factorization. *The key idea is to group the four terms into pairs that have a common factor.* If the polynomial $ac + ad + bc + bd$ had been rearranged and grouped as $(ac + bd) + (ad + bc)$, then this method would not have worked since each pair has only 1 for a GCF.

Model 2: Factor $xy + 6 + 2x + 3y$.

Solution 1: $xy + 6 + 2x + 3y = xy + 2x + 3y + 6$

$$= (xy + 2x) + (3y + 6)$$

$$= x(y + 2) + 3(y + 2)$$

$$= (y + 2)(x + 3)$$

Solution 2: $xy + 6 + 2x + 3x = xy + 3y + 2x + 6$

$$= (xy + 3y) + (2x + 6)$$

$$= y(x + 3) + 2(x + 3)$$

$$= (x + 3)(y + 2)$$

∴ The factors are $(x + 3)(y + 2)$ by either solution; check by *FOIL*.

If the four-term polynomial has negative terms, special care must be used when grouping the terms and separating each GCF.

Model 3: Factor $ac + ad - bc - bd$.

Solution 1: $ac + ad - bc - bd = (ac + ad) + (-bc - bd)$

$$= a(c + d) - b(c + d)$$

$$= (c + d)(a - b)$$

Solution 2: $ac + ad - bc - bd = ac - bc + ad - bd$

$$= (ac - bc) + (ad - bd)$$

$$= c(a - b) + d\ (a - b)$$

$$= (a - b)(c + d)$$

∴ The factors are $(a - b)(c + d)$ by either solution; check by *FOIL*.

Model 4:   Factor $xy - 3x - 5y + 15$.

Solution 1: $xy - 3x - 5y + 15 = (xy - 3x) + (-5y + 15)$

$$= x(y - 3) - 5\ (y - 3)$$

$$= (y - 3)(x - 5)$$

Solution 2: $xy - 3x - 5y + 15 = xy - 5y - 3x + 15$

$$= (xy - 5y) + (- 3x + 15)$$

$$= y\ (x - 5) - 3\ (x - 5)$$

$$= (x - 5)(y - 3)$$

∴ The factors are $(x - 5)(y - 3)$ by either solution; check by *FOIL*.

✴ ✴ ✴ **Study the solution shown for Model 5. Then see if you can complete a second solution.**

Model 5:   Factor $r^2 - st - rt + rs$.

Solution 1: $r^2 - st - rt + rs = r^2 + rs - rt - st$

$$= (r^2 + rs) + (- rt - st)$$

$$= r(r + s) - t\ (r + s)$$

$$= (r + s)(r - t)$$

3.26   Solution 2: $r^2 - st - rt + rs =$ _____

$=$ _____

$=$ _____

$=$ _____

35

Find the factors for each four-term polynomial, and check by _FOIL_.

3.27 $jm + jn + km + kn$

_____

3.28 $ab + 2a + 3b + 6$

_____

3.29 $x^2 + xy - 2x - 2y$

_____

3.30 $mn - 4m - 5n + 20$

_____

3.31 $ab + 4 + a + 4b$

_____

3.32 $y^2 + 10z - 10y - yz$

_____

3.33 $ab + bc + b^2 + ac$

3.34 $n^3 - n^2 + 3n - 3$

3.35 $pr + qs - qr - ps$

3.36 $z^3 - 2z^2 + 9z - 18$

> **Factor each polynomial completely.**

Model: $x^3 + 5x^2 - 16x - 80$
$= (x^3 + 5x^2) + (-16x - 80)$
$= x^2(x + 5) - 16(x + 5)$
$= (x + 5)(x^2 - 16)$
$= (x + 5)(x + 4)(x - 4)$

3.37 $z^3 + 2z^2 - 9z - 18$

3.38 $a^3 - 3 + 3a^2 - a$

3.39 $5k^2 + 5jk - 15j - 15k$

3.40 $x^6 - 4x^4 - 25x^2 + 100$

_____

3.41 $1 - y^2 - y^4 + y^6$

_____

_____

— · — · — · — · — **WORD PROBLEMS** — · — · — · — · — · — · — · — · — · — · —

Word problems are always a challenge. They serve as a check of how well you have learned any new technique, and they encourage you to put your skills into practice. Notice how the factoring methods you have learned are used to work these exercises.

 Solve these problems. Show your work in the space provided, and circle your answer. Drawings for geometry will help you.

3.42   The area of a rectangle is found by multiplying the length by the width: $A = lw$. A certain rectangle has an area of $x^2 + 7x + 12$. Factor the trinomial to find the length and width of the rectangle.

3.43   Find the length and width of a rectangle with an area of $2x^2 + x - 3$.

3.44   In Problem 3.43, find the numerical values for that length and width if $x = 4$.

3.45   Find the integral values for the length and width of a rectangle with an area of $6x^2 + x - 1$ if $x = 30$.

3.46   The area of a triangle is found by multiplying a base by its altitude (or height), then dividing by 2: $A = \frac{bh}{2}$. A certain triangle has an area of $\frac{2y^2 + 15y + 7}{2}$. Factor the trinomial numerator to find a base and height for the triangle.

3.47   Find a base and height for a triangle with an area of $\frac{(8y^2 - 10y - 3)}{2}$.

3.48   In Problem 3.47, find the numerical value for that base and height if $y = 2$.

3.49   Again in Problem 3.47, what numerical value must y be greater than for such a triangle to exist? (HINT: The dimensions of geometric figures must be greater than zero.)

3.50   The area of a square is found by squaring one of its sides, $(A = s^2)$. A certain square has an area of $z^2 + 18z + 81$. Factor the trinomial to find a side of the square.

3.51   Find a side of a square with an area of $16z^2 - 24z + 9$.

(OPTIONAL)

3.52   In Problem 3.51, what numerical value must z be greater than for such a square to exist?

3.53   The area of a circle is found by multiplying the constant π by the square of the circle's radius: $A = \pi r^2$. A certain circle has an area of $\pi a^2 - 2\pi a + \pi$. Factor the trinomial to find the radius of the circle.

3.54   Find the radius of a circle with an area of $9\pi a^2 + 6\pi a + \pi$.

3.55   The volume of a rectangular box is found by multiplying its length, width, and height: $V = lwh$. A certain box has a volume of $b^3 + 3b^2 - 4b - 12$. Factor the four-term polynomial to find the length, width, and height of the box.

3.56   Find the length, width, and height of a rectangular box with a volume of $50b^3 - 3 - 2b + 75b^2$.

(OPTIONAL)

3.57   In Problem 3.56, what numerical value must b be greater than for such a box to exist?

3.58   A person purchased $5k + 2$ items for a total cost of $35k^2 + 29k + 6$. Find the average cost per item of this purchase.

3.59   Another person bought a certain number of an item at a cost of $4k + 3$ each. Find the number bought if the total cost was $8k^2 + 2k - 3$.

3.60   The number of items purchased by a third person was exactly the same as the cost per item. Find the number purchased and the cost per item if the total cost was $25k^2 - 20k + 4$.

3.61   In Problem 3.60, find the value of k if the number of items purchased was 8.

===

Before you take this last Self Test, you may want to do one or more of these self checks.

1. _____   Read the objectives. Determine if you can do them.
2. _____   Restudy the material related to any objectives that you cannot do.
3. _____   Use the SQ3R study procedure to review the material:
            a. **S**can the sections.
            b. **Q**uestion yourself again (review the questions you wrote initially).
            c. **R**ead to answer your questions.
            d. **R**ecite the answers to yourself.
            e. **R**eview areas you didn't understand.
4. _____   Review all activities and Self Tests, writing a correct answer for each wrong answer.

SELF TEST 3

Complete these activities (each answer, 5 points).

3.01   Find the greatest common factor of $28a^3b^2c$ and $-63a^2b^5$.

3.02   Factor $-5x^2y + 10xy - 15xy^2$.   _____

3.03   Find the product $(n - 3)(-n + 7)$ mentally.

        _____

3.04   Factor $k^2 - 17k + 16$.   _____

42

3.05   Find the product $(-2x + 1)(-3x - 5)$ mentally.

_____

3.06   Factor $20y^2 + 3y - 2$.   _____

3.07   Factor $64a^2 - 48a + 9$.   _____

3.08   Find the product $(11k + 1)(11k - 1)$ mentally.

_____

3.09   Factor $-49 + 16n^2$ as a difference of two squares.

3.010   Factor $a^8 - b^8$ as a difference of two squares, repeating the procedure as many times as necessary.

3.011   Find the product $(p - q)(r + 1)$ mentally.

3.012   Factor the four-term polynomial $mn - 15 + 3m - 5n$.

3.013   Factor $x^3 + 6x^2 - 4x - 24$ completely.

Give the complete factorization for each polynomial (each answer, 5 points).

3.014 $5x^2 + 10x - 40$

3.015 $-3n^2 + 48$

3.016 $2ay^2 + 5ay - 3a$

3.017 $-2k - k^3 - 3k^2$

3.018 $n^8 + 3n^7 + 4n^6$

3.019 $- 2y^4 + 8y^2 + 90$

3.020 $75n + 3n^3$

80 / 100

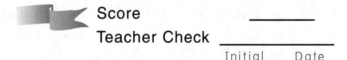

Score _____

Teacher Check _____

Initial   Date

Before taking the LIFEPAC Test, you may want to do one or more of these self checks.

1. _____ Read the objectives. Check to see if you can do them.
2. _____ Restudy the material related to any objective that you cannot do.
3. _____ Use the SQ3R study procedure to review the material.
4. _____ Review activities, Self Tests, and LIFEPAC Glossary.
5. _____ Restudy areas of weakness indicated by the last Self Test.

GLOSSARY

coefficient—	The numerical factor of a term.
complete factorization—	An indicated product in which all polynomial factors (excluding monomial factors) are prime.
degree of a term—	The number of variable factors in the term; for example $7ab$ and $-3x^2$ are second-degree terms and $9y$ is a first-degree term.
degree of a polynomial—	The degree of its highest-degree term.
descending powers—	An arrangement of the terms of a polynomial so that the exponents of a particular variable decrease in size.
difference of two squares—	A polynomial of the form $A^2 - B^2$.
distributive property—	A property used in the form $AB + AC = A(B + C)$ to separate the greatest common factor from a polynomial.
exponential form—	An indicated product in which repeated factors are written as powers.
factors of a polynomial—	Any of the polynomials whose product is the given polynomial.
factor of a term—	An integer or a variable that divides the term exactly.
FOIL—	An acronym for the *First, Outer, Inner,* and *Last* products in the mental multiplication of binomials.
greatest common factor (GCF)—	The largest value that will divide each of a group of expressions exactly.
prime—	A number or a polynomial having only 1 and itself as factors.
prime factorization—	An indicated product in which all factors are prime.
trinomial square—	A polynomial of the form $A^2 + 2AB + B^2$.

NOTES

46

MATHEMATICS 906
ALGEBRAIC FRACTIONS

CONTENTS

I. OPERATIONS **2**

Reducing Fractions **2**

Adding and Subtracting Fractions **10**

Multiplying and Dividing Fractions **17**

Simplifying Complex Fractions **25**

II. OPEN SENTENCES **31**

Solving Equations **31**

Solving Inequalities **40**

Rewriting Formulas **45**

III. WORD PROBLEMS **53**

Work and Single-Number **53**

Motion and Consecutive-Number **58**

Age and Quotient-Remainder **63**

Ratio and Mixture **69**

Author: **Arthur C. Landrey, M.A.Ed.**

Editor-in-Chief: Richard W. Wheeler, M.A.Ed.

Editor: Robin Hintze Kreutzberg, M.B.A.

Consulting Editor: Robert L. Zenor, M.A., M.S.

Revision Editor: Alan Christopherson, M.S.

Alpha Omega Publications®

804 N. 2nd Ave. E., Rock Rapids, IA 51246-1759

MATHEMATICS 900
ALGEBRAIC FRACTIONS

CONTENTS

I. OPERATIONS 2
   Reducing Fractions 2
   Adding and Subtracting Fractions 10
   Multiplying and Dividing Fractions 17
   Simplifying Complex Fractions 25
II. OPEN SENTENCES 31
   Solving Equations 31
   Solving Inequalities ....
   Rewriting Formulas ....
III. WORD PROBLEMS ....
   Work and Single Number 55
   Motion and Consecutive Number ....
   Age and Quotient-Remainder ....
   Ratio and Mixture 69

Author: Arthur C. Landrey, M.A.Ed.
Editor-in-Chief: Richard W. Wheeler, M.A.Ed.
Editor: Robin Hintze Kreutzberg, M.B.A.
Consulting Editor: Robert L. Zenor, M.A., M.S.
Revision Editor: Alan Christopherson, M.S.

Alpha Omega Publications

804 N. 2nd Ave. E., Rock Rapids, IA 51246-1600
© MCMXCVII by Alpha Omega Publications, Inc. All rights reserved.
LIFEPAC is a registered trademark of Alpha Omega Publications, Inc.

ALGEBRAIC FRACTIONS

In this LIFEPAC® you will continue your study in algebra. You will apply what you have learned so far to fractions having polynomial numerators or denominators or both. The factoring techniques that you learned in Mathematics LIFEPAC 905 will be used when performing the basic operations with these fractions. Then you will solve open sentences containing fractions by methods that are quite similar to those you have already used. Finally you will have another opportunity to solve verbal problems, this time in applications that involve fractions.

OBJECTIVES

Read these objectives. The objectives tell you what you will be able to do when you have successfully completed this LIFEPAC.

When you have finished this LIFEPAC, you should be able to:

1. Determine the excluded value(s) for a fraction.
2. Reduce a fraction to lowest terms.
3. Find sums and differences of fractions.
4. Find products and quotients of fractions.
5. Simplify complex fractions.
6. Solve equations containing fractions.
7. Solve inequalities containing fractions.
8. Change the subject of a formula containing fractions.
9. Solve problems requiring the use of fractions.

Survey the LIFEPAC. Ask yourself some questions about this study. Write your questions here.

_____

_____

_____

_____

_____

_____

_____

I. OPERATIONS

OBJECTIVES

When you have completed this section, you should be able to:

1. Determine the excluded value(s) for a fraction.
2. Reduce a fraction to lowest terms.
3. Find sums and differences of fractions.
4. Find products and quotients of fractions.
5. Simplify complex fractions.

As you work through this first section, keep in mind that the basic concepts of reducing, adding, subtracting, multiplying, dividing, and simplifying the fractions of algebra are the same as those used for the fractions of arithmetic.

We will begin by defining algebraic fractions, since we must know what they are in order to be able to work with them.

DEFINITIONS

Algebraic fraction: an indicated quotient of two polynomials written in the form $\frac{A}{B}$. A is the numerator of the algebraic fraction and B is the denominator.

Terms: the numerator and denominator of a fraction.

Models: $\dfrac{2}{x+3}$ $\qquad$ $\dfrac{-y^2-3y+1}{5-2y}$ $\qquad$ $\dfrac{a+b+c}{m-n}$ $\qquad$ $\dfrac{k-3}{7}$

Algebraic fractions can be reduced, using similar methods as for reducing arithmetic fractions. Addition, subtraction, multiplication, division, and simplification are also possible with algebraic fractions.

=============== **REDUCING FRACTIONS** =============================

Algebraic fractions can be reduced by finding the lowest terms. First, however, we need to discuss the circumstances under which algebraic fractions may not even exist!

EXCLUDED VALUES

Since a fraction indicates division ($\frac{A}{B} = A \div B$) and since division by zero is undefined, the denominator of a fraction must be nonzero ($B \neq 0$). If a denominator contains any variables, then a value that would result in zero for that denominator must be *excluded* for the fraction to exist.

In the preceding models, the denominators are $x + 3$, $5 - 2y$, $m - n$, and 7, respectively. The excluded values are $x = $ -3 for the first model (-3 + 3 = 0), $y = 2.5$ for the second ($5 - 2 \cdot 2.5 = 0$), and $m = n$ for the third ($m - m$ or $n - n = 0$); since the denominator of the fourth fraction is the constant 7 and $7 \neq 0$, that fraction has no excluded values.

In determining the excluded values for the fraction $\frac{x-3}{x^2-4}$, you may be able to see immediately that $2^2 - 4 = 0$; thus, $x = 2$ is an excluded value. However, $(-2)^2 - 4 = 0$ is also true; thus, $x = $ -2 is an excluded value as well.

In Mathematics LIFEPAC 905 you learned to factor, and now factoring can be used to find both these excluded values. Since the denominator $x^2 - 4$ is a difference of two squares, it has factors $(x + 2)(x - 2)$. The first factor, $x + 2$, would become zero if $x = $ -2; likewise, the second factor, $x - 2$, would become zero if $x = 2$. The excluded values are then $x = 2$ and $x = $ -2. In this method we have made use of an important property in mathematics.

PROPERTY

If $A \cdot B = 0$, then $A = 0$ or $B = 0$ (or both); if a product of factors is zero, then at least one of the factors must be zero.

3

Model 1: Find the excluded value(s) for the fraction $\dfrac{a + 5}{a(b + 3)(c - 2)}$.

Solution: The denominator is already factored, so each of the three factors is set equal to zero.

$$a = 0 \qquad b + 3 = 0 \qquad\qquad c - 2 = 0$$
$$b = -3 \qquad\qquad c = 2$$

∴ The excluded values are $a = 0$, $b = -3$, and $c = 2$.

Model 2: Find the excluded value(s) for the fraction $\dfrac{7}{d^2 - 5d - 24}$.

Solution: The factors of $d^2 - 5d - 24$ are $(d - 8)(d + 3)$.

$$d - 8 = 0 \qquad d + 3 = 0$$
$$d = 8 \qquad\quad d = -3$$

∴ The excluded values are $d = 8$ and $d = -3$.

Check: If $d = 8$, $d^2 \quad - 5d \quad - 24$
$$= (8)^2 \quad - 5\,(8) \quad - 24$$
$$= 64 \quad - 40 \quad - 24 = 0.$$

If $d = -3$, $d^2 \quad - 5d \quad - 24$
$$= (-3)^2 \quad - 5(-3) \quad - 24$$
$$= 9 \quad + 15 \quad - 24 = 0.$$

Write the excluded value(s) for each fraction, or _none_ if that is the case.

1.1 $\dfrac{a}{b - 2}$ _____

1.2 $\dfrac{4x + 3}{x}$ _____

1.3 $\dfrac{y^2 - y + 5}{y + 4}$ _____

1.4 $\dfrac{3}{5n}$ _____

1.5 $\dfrac{-2x}{17}$ _____

1.6 $\dfrac{a}{3 - 2a}$ _____

1.7 $\dfrac{x + 3}{y(z + 5)}$ _____

1.8 $\dfrac{k^2 + 5k + 1}{k^2 - 9}$ _____

1.9 $\dfrac{7b^3}{b^2 - 7b + 10}$ _____

1.10 $\dfrac{x + 11}{3x^2 + 5x - 2}$ _____

As you work through this LIFEPAC, you are to assume that all fractions do exist; that is, any value(s) that would make a denominator zero are understood to be excluded. However, from time to time (as in the preceding activities), you will be asked to identify these excluded values.

LOWEST TERMS

Now you are ready to begin working with these algebraic fractions. A basic property of fractions will be used in much of this work.

PROPERTY

$\frac{A}{B} = \frac{AC}{BC}$ (or $\frac{AC}{BC} = \frac{A}{B}$) for $C \neq 0$; if the numerator and the denominator of a fraction are both multiplied (or divided) by the same nonzero value, then an *equivalent* fraction is obtained.

In arithmetic you learned that the fraction $\frac{1}{2}$ has the same value as the fraction $\frac{5}{10}$, since both the numerator and the denominator of $\frac{1}{2}$ are multiplied by 5. Similarly, the fraction $\frac{12}{18}$ is equivalent to the fraction $\frac{2}{3}$ since both the numerator and the denominator of $\frac{12}{18}$ are divided by 6; this latter procedure is known as *reducing*. An algebraic fraction is reduced to lowest terms when the greatest common factor of its numerator and denominator is 1.

Model 1:   Reduce $\frac{24m^2n}{21mp^2}$ to lowest terms.

Solution: The GCF of $24m^2n$ and $21mp^2$ is $3m$.
Divide both the numerator and
the denominator by $3m$.

$$\frac{24m^2n \div 3m}{21mp^2 \div 3m} = \frac{8mn}{7p^2},$$
the equivalent reduced fraction since
the GCF of $8mn$ and $7p^2$ is 1.

Model 2:   Reduce $\frac{4y - 20}{12y}$ to lowest terms.

Solution: $4y - 20$ factors into $4(y - 5)$,
and $12y$ is $4 \cdot 3y$. Divide both
the numerator and the denominator
by the common factor 4.

$$\frac{4y - 20}{12y} = \frac{4(y - 5)}{12y}$$

$$= \frac{4(y - 5) \div 4}{12y \div 4}$$

$$= \frac{y - 5}{3y},$$

the equivalent reduced fraction since the GCF of $y - 5$ and $3y$ is 1.

Note: The y's cannot be reduced since y is a term (not a factor) of the numerator $y - 5$. Only common factors can be reduced!

Model 3: Reduce $\frac{r^2 - 3r + 2}{r^2 - 1}$ to lowest terms.

Solution: Since r^2 is a term (not a factor) of both the numerator and denominator, to try to reduce this fraction by dividing by r^2 would be wrong, even though very tempting. You must avoid this type of mistake that so many beginning students make.

Factor the trinomial numerator and the binomial denominator; then divide by the common factor. (This reducing is often shown by drawing lines through these factors.)

$$\frac{r^2 - 3r + 2}{r^2 - 1} = \frac{(r - 2)(r - 1)}{(r + 1)(r - 1)}$$

$$= \frac{(r - 2)\cancel{(r - 1)}}{(r + 1)\cancel{(r - 1)}}$$

$$= \frac{r - 2}{r + 1}$$

Model 4: Reduce $\frac{6m + 6n}{9n + 9m}$ to lowest terms.

Solution: $$\frac{6m + 6n}{9n + 9m} = \frac{6(m + n)}{9(n + m)}$$

$$= \frac{2 \cdot \cancel{3(m + n)}}{3 \cdot \cancel{3(n + m)}}$$

$$= \frac{2}{3}$$

6

In Model 4, the binomials $m + n$ and $n + m$ are equal and reduce as part of the GCF $3(m + n)$. If, however, the binomials had been $m - n$ and $n - m$, they would not have reduced in quite the same way since they are opposites. $\frac{A}{-A} = -1$; if two expressions are opposites, they divide (or reduce) to negative one.

Model 5: Reduce $\dfrac{6m - 6n}{9n - 9m}$ to lowest terms.

Solution: $\dfrac{6m - 6n}{9n - 9m} = \dfrac{6(m - n)}{9(n - m)}$

$$= \dfrac{\overset{2}{\cancel{6}}(\cancel{m - n})^{(-1)}}{\underset{3}{\cancel{9}}(\cancel{n - m})}$$

$$= -\dfrac{2}{3}$$

Note: The (-1) is included in the answer as a minus sign before the fraction.

Model 6: Reduce $\dfrac{16 - a^2}{a^2 + 20 - 9a}$ to lowest terms.

Solution: $\dfrac{16 - a^2}{a^2 + 20 - 9a} = \dfrac{16 - a^2}{a^2 - 9a + 20}$

$$= \dfrac{(4 + a)\overset{(-1)}{\cancel{(4 - a)}}}{(a - 5)\cancel{(a - 4)}}$$

$$= -\dfrac{4 + a}{a - 5}$$

Model 7: Reduce $\dfrac{a + 3b + c}{a^2 - 9b^2}$ to lowest terms.

Solution: $\dfrac{a + 3b + c}{a^2 - 9b^2} = \dfrac{a + 3b + c}{(a + 3b)(a - 3b)}$,

but nothing can be reduced since $a + 3b$ is not a factor of the numerator.

$\therefore$ $\dfrac{a + 3b + c}{a^2 - 9b^2}$ is in lowest terms.

Reduce each fraction to lowest terms.

1.11 $\dfrac{75a^2b}{25ab^2}$

_____

1.15 $\dfrac{38x^2yz^2}{-19xy^2z^3}$

_____

1.12 $\dfrac{12m^4}{28m^3}$

_____

1.16 $\dfrac{6x + 2}{8}$

_____

1.13 $\dfrac{-5jk}{35j^2k^2}$

_____

1.17 $\dfrac{x^3 - x^2}{x^4}$

_____

1.14 $\dfrac{84y^3}{36y^4}$

_____

1.18 $\dfrac{27a}{ab + ac}$

_____

1.19 $\dfrac{y + 5}{2y + 10}$

         _____

1.20 $\dfrac{n + 2}{n^2 - 4}$

         _____

1.21 $\dfrac{5r - 5s}{5r + 5s}$

         _____

1.22 $\dfrac{8a + 8b}{12c + 12d}$

         _____

1.23 $\dfrac{x^2 - y^2}{8x - 8y}$

         _____

1.24 $\dfrac{a + 5}{a^2 - 25}$

         _____

1.25 $\dfrac{7 - y}{y - 7}$

         _____

1.26 $\dfrac{x^2 - 4x - 12}{36 - x^2}$

         _____

1.27 $\dfrac{m^2}{m^2 - n^2}$

         _____

1.28 $\dfrac{-5k + 15}{k^2 - 9}$

         _____

1.29 $\dfrac{(x - 1)^2}{1 - x^2}$

1.30 $\dfrac{12 - 3z^2}{2z^2 - 3z - 2}$

_____   _____

━ ● ━ **ADDING AND SUBTRACTING FRACTIONS** ━ ● ━ ● ━ ●

The procedure used for finding sums and differences of algebraic fractions is like that used in arithmetic. First, each fraction is expressed with the same denominator; next, the numerators are combined into a single numerator and written over that denominator; and finally, the resulting fraction is reduced if possible.

COMMON DENOMINATORS

To start with, consider fractions that already have a common denominator. Study the following models carefully before doing the activities.

Model 1: $\dfrac{x}{7} - \dfrac{3x}{7} + \dfrac{8x}{7}$

$= \dfrac{x - 3x + 8x}{7}$

$= \dfrac{6x}{7}$

Model 2: $\dfrac{7}{a + 2} + \dfrac{1}{a + 2}$

$= \dfrac{7 + 1}{a + 2}$

$= \dfrac{8}{a + 2}$

Model 3: $\dfrac{4m}{9n^2} - \dfrac{7m}{9n^2}$

$= \dfrac{4m - 7m}{9n^2}$

$= \dfrac{\overset{1}{\cancel{-3}m}}{\underset{3}{\cancel{9}n^2}}$

$= \dfrac{-m}{3n^2}$ or $-\dfrac{m}{3n^2}$

10

Model 4:
$$\frac{y + 3}{2y} + \frac{3y - 1}{2y} - \frac{4y + 7}{2y}$$

$$= \frac{(y + 3) + (3y - 1) - (4y + 7)}{2y}$$

$$= \frac{y + 3 + 3y - 1 - 4y - 7}{2y}$$

$$= \frac{-5}{2y} \text{ or } -\frac{5}{2y}$$

Model 5:
$$\frac{4k}{3 - 2k} - \frac{6}{3 - 2k}$$

$$= \frac{4k - 6}{3 - 2k}$$

$$= \frac{2\,(2k \overset{(-1)}{\cancel{3}})}{\underset{1}{\cancel{3 - 2k}}}$$

$$= -2$$

 Find the indicated sums and differences.

1.31　$\dfrac{y}{3} + \dfrac{5y}{3} - \dfrac{4y}{3}$

1.34　$\dfrac{m}{m + n} + \dfrac{n}{m + n}$

_____

_____

1.32　$\dfrac{8}{a} - \dfrac{6}{a} + \dfrac{7}{a}$

1.35　$\dfrac{7x^2}{12w} - \dfrac{3x^2}{12w}$

_____

_____

1.33　$\dfrac{6}{y - z} - \dfrac{2}{y - z}$

1.36　$\dfrac{r^2}{r - s} - \dfrac{s^2}{r - s}$

_____

_____

11

1.37　　$\dfrac{x+2}{10y} + \dfrac{3x-1}{10y} - \dfrac{2x+5}{10y}$

1.39　　$\dfrac{x-y}{x+y} - \dfrac{y-x}{x+y}$

_____

_____

1.38　　$\dfrac{2k}{4k^2-9} + \dfrac{3}{4k^2-9}$

1.40　　$\dfrac{11}{b-7} - \dfrac{2b-3}{b-7}$

_____

_____

LEAST COMMON DENOMINATORS

To combine fractions having different denominators, you must first express them with a common denominator, preferably with the smallest such denominator.

DEFINITION

Least common denominator (LCD): for a group of fractions, the smallest value that has all the denominators as factors.

Model 1:　　Find the LCD for $\dfrac{3}{14x^3} + \dfrac{7}{12x^2}$.

Solution:　　$14x^3 = 2^1 \bullet 7^1 \bullet x^3$ and
$12x^2 = 2^2 \bullet 3^1 \bullet x^2$.

The LCD will be the product of every factor that appears, including the largest exponent of each factor.

∴ The LCD is $2^2 \bullet 3^1 \bullet 7^1 \bullet x^3$
or $84x^3$.

Model 2:   Find the LCD for $\dfrac{n}{n+4} - \dfrac{5}{n-2}$.

Solution: $n + 4$ and $n - 2$ are both
prime, and the LCD will be their product.

∴ The LCD is $(n + 4)(n - 2)$ or $n^2 + 2n - 8$.

Model 3:   Find the LCD for $\dfrac{y+5}{6y^2-6} + \dfrac{7}{8y+8}$.

Solution: $6y^2 - 6 = 6(y^2 - 1)$
$= 2 \cdot 3(y + 1)(y - 1)$

$8y + 8 = 8(y + 1)$
$= 2^3(y + 1)$

∴ The LCD is $2^3 \cdot 3^1(y + 1)(y - 1)$
or $24(y + 1)(y - 1)$.

To express each fraction as an equivalent one having the desired LCD, we will
again use the basic property of fractions: $\dfrac{A}{B} = \dfrac{AC}{BC}$ for $C \neq 0$. The value of the
multiplier C is determined from the factor or factors needed by a denominator to become
the LCD. Once this value has been found, both the numerator and the denominator are
multiplied by it.

Model 4:   Combine $\dfrac{3}{14x^3} + \dfrac{7}{12x^2}$. (See Model 1)

Solution: The LCD is $84x^3$. The multiplier
must be chosen to make each
denominator equal $84x^3$.

$= \dfrac{3}{14x^3}\left[\dfrac{6}{6}\right] + \dfrac{7}{12x^2}\left[\dfrac{7x}{7x}\right]$

$= \dfrac{18}{84x^3} + \dfrac{49x}{84x^3}$

$= \dfrac{18 + 49x}{84x^3}$,   which does not
reduce since
$18 + 49x$ is prime.

Model 5:   Combine $\dfrac{n}{n+4} - \dfrac{5}{n-2}$.

Solution: The LCD is $(n+4)(n-2)$
            or $n^2 + 2n - 8$.

$$= \frac{n}{n+4}\left[\frac{n-2}{n-2}\right] - \frac{5}{n-2}\left[\frac{n+4}{n+4}\right]$$

$$= \frac{n^2 - 2n}{(n+4)(n-2)} - \frac{5n + 20}{(n-2)(n+4)}$$

$$= \frac{(n^2 - 2n) - (5n + 20)}{(n+4)(n-2)}$$

$$= \frac{n^2 - 2n - 5n - 20}{(n+4)(n-2)}$$

$$= \frac{n^2 - 7n - 20}{(n+4)(n-2)}, \text{ which does not reduce.}$$

Note: The answer is usually left as shown, but it may also be

written as $\dfrac{n^2 - 7n - 20}{n^2 + 2n - 8}$.

Model 6:   Combine $\dfrac{y+5}{6y^2-6} + \dfrac{7}{8y+8}$.   (See Model 3)

Solution: The LCD is $24(y+1)(y-1)$.

$$\frac{y+5}{6(y+1)(y-1)}\left[\frac{4}{4}\right] + \frac{7}{8(y+1)}\left[\frac{3(y-1)}{3(y-1)}\right]$$

$$= \frac{4y + 20}{24(y+1)(y-1)} + \frac{21y - 21}{24(y+1)(y-1)}$$

$$= \frac{4y + 20 + 21y - 21}{24(y+1)(y-1)}$$

$$= \frac{25y - 1}{24(y+1)(y-1)}, \text{ the answer.}$$

We may summarize the procedure for adding or subtracting algebraic fractions in these five steps:

1.   Determine the LCD from the prime factorization of the denominator of each fraction;

2.   Change each fraction to an equivalent one having the LCD for its denominator;

3.   Find all numerator products;

4.   Write a single fraction made up of the combined numerators over the LCD; and

5.   Reduce, if possible.

Model 7:   Combine $\dfrac{x-4z}{12} + \dfrac{3x-4z}{4} - \dfrac{2x-y+z}{3}$.

Solution: $12 = 2^2 \cdot 3^1$, $4 = 2^2$, and $3 = 3^1$;
thus, the LCD is $2^2 \cdot 3^1$ or 12.

$$\dfrac{x-4z}{12}\left[\dfrac{1}{1}\right] + \dfrac{3x-4z}{4}\left[\dfrac{3}{3}\right] - \dfrac{2x-y+z}{3}\left[\dfrac{4}{4}\right]$$

$$= \dfrac{x-4z}{12} + \dfrac{9x-12z}{12} - \dfrac{8x-4y+4z}{12}$$

$$= \dfrac{(x-4z)+(9x-12z)-(8x-4y+4z)}{12}$$

$$= \dfrac{x-4z+9x-12z-8x+4y-4z}{12}$$

$$= \dfrac{2x+4y-20z}{12}, \text{ which reduces to}$$

$$= \dfrac{\overset{1}{\cancel{2}}(x+2y-10z)}{\underset{6}{\cancel{12}}}$$

$$= \dfrac{x+2y-10z}{6}, \text{ the answer.}$$

Some special types of denominators may simplify your work.

Model 8:   Combine $5 + \dfrac{2}{a-3} - \dfrac{3}{3-a}$.

Solution: The denominator of 5 is
understood to be 1 and
has no effect on the LCD.
The two denominators
$a-3$ and $3-a$ are just
opposites; if either is multiplied
by -1, the other results.
For example,
$-1(3-a) = -3+a = a-3$.

$\therefore$ The LCD is $a-3$.

$$\dfrac{5}{1}\left[\dfrac{a-3}{a-3}\right] + \dfrac{2}{a-3}\left[\dfrac{1}{1}\right] - \dfrac{3}{3-a}\left[\dfrac{-1}{-1}\right]$$

$$= \dfrac{5a-15}{a-3} + \dfrac{2}{a-3} - \dfrac{-3}{a-3}$$

$$= \dfrac{5a-15+2+3}{a-3}$$

$$= \dfrac{5a-10}{a-3}, \text{ the answer.}$$

Find the indicated sums and differences.

1.41 $\dfrac{x}{2} + \dfrac{y}{3} - \dfrac{z}{4}$

1.45 $\dfrac{y}{y-5} + \dfrac{5}{5-y}$

_____

1.42 $\dfrac{5}{a} - \dfrac{3}{b} + \dfrac{1}{ab}$

1.46 $\dfrac{3}{x+5} - \dfrac{2}{x-3}$

_____

1.43 $\dfrac{4}{7x^2} - \dfrac{3}{2x^3}$

1.47 $\dfrac{x+5}{3} - \dfrac{x-3}{2}$

_____

1.44 $\dfrac{5n+1}{6} + \dfrac{3n-2}{8}$

1.48 $\dfrac{3}{a-5} + \dfrac{a+2}{a}$

_____

1.49 $\dfrac{3k}{k-2} + \dfrac{6}{2-k}$

1.52 $\dfrac{1}{2} + \dfrac{3}{x+4}$

_____

_____

1.50 $\dfrac{b+1}{b+2} - \dfrac{b+3}{b+4}$

1.53 $\dfrac{a+2}{4b} - \dfrac{a-1}{10b} + \dfrac{a-3}{5b}$

_____

_____

1.51 $\dfrac{y}{y^2-49} - \dfrac{7}{y+7}$

1.54 $\dfrac{x}{x+1} - \dfrac{1}{x-1} + \dfrac{2x}{x^2-1}$

_____

_____

1.55 $\dfrac{1}{m^2+3m+2} + \dfrac{2}{m^2+4m+3} - \dfrac{3}{m^2+5m+6}$

_____

✳✳✳✳✳✳✳✳✳✳✳✳✳ **MULTIPLYING AND DIVIDING FRACTIONS** ✳✳✳✳✳✳✳✳✳✳✳✳✳

Products of algebraic fractions are found in the same way as products of arithmetic fractions, according to the following rule.

$\frac{A}{B} \cdot \frac{C}{D} = \frac{AC}{BD}$ ($B \neq 0, D \neq 0$); the product of two fractions is the product

of the numerators over the product of the denominators; the result is to be in

lowest terms.

Model 1: $\frac{x}{y} \cdot \frac{2}{3}$

$= \frac{x \cdot 2}{y \cdot 3}$

$= \frac{2x}{3y}$

Model 2: $-\frac{8}{7m^3} \cdot 28m$

$= -\frac{8}{7m^3} \cdot \frac{28m}{1}$

$= -\frac{8 \cdot \cancel{28m}^{4}}{\cancel{7}\cancel{m^3}_{m^2} \cdot 1}$

$= -\frac{32}{m^2}$

Model 3: $\frac{a^3b^2c}{d^3} \cdot \frac{ab}{c}$

$= \frac{a^3b^2\cancel{c} \cdot ab}{d^3 \cdot \cancel{c}}$

$= \frac{a^4b^3}{d^3}$

Quotients of algebraic fractions are also found in the same way as quotients of arithmetic fractions, according to the following rule.

$\frac{A}{B} \div \frac{E}{F} = \frac{A}{B} \cdot \frac{F}{E}$ ($B \neq 0, F \neq 0, E \neq 0$); the quotient of two fractions is

the product of the first fraction and the *reciprocal* of the second fraction; the

result is to be in lowest terms.

Model 1: $\frac{x}{y} \div \frac{2}{3}$

$= \frac{x}{y} \cdot \frac{3}{2}$

$= \frac{x \cdot 3}{y \cdot 2}$

$= \frac{3x}{2y}$

Model 2: $-\dfrac{8}{7m^3} \div 28m$

$= -\dfrac{8}{7m^3} \bullet \dfrac{1}{28m}$

$= -\dfrac{\overset{2}{\cancel{8}} \bullet 1}{7m^3 \bullet \underset{7}{\cancel{28m}}}$

$= -\dfrac{2}{49m^4}$

Model 3: $\dfrac{a^3b^2c}{d^3} \div \dfrac{ab}{c}$

$= \dfrac{a^3b^2c}{d^3} \bullet \dfrac{c}{ab}$

$= \dfrac{\overset{a^2b}{\cancel{a^3b^2}}c \bullet c}{d^3 \bullet \cancel{ab}}$

$= \dfrac{a^2bc^2}{d^3}$

Note: No reducing is done in a quotient until the second fraction has been *inverted* to its reciprocal and the product rule has been applied. Then any common factors(s) to the numerator and denominator may be reduced.

The two rules may also be applied to products or quotients of more than two fractions. However, in a mixed product and quotient, only invert the fraction immediately after a division sign when changing to multiplication.

Model 1: $\dfrac{A}{B} \bullet \dfrac{C}{D} \bullet \dfrac{E}{F}$

$= \dfrac{ACE}{BDF}$

Model 2: $\dfrac{A}{B} \div \dfrac{C}{D} \bullet \dfrac{E}{F}$

$= \dfrac{A}{B} \bullet \dfrac{D}{C} \bullet \dfrac{E}{F}$

$= \dfrac{ADE}{BCF}$

Model 3: $\dfrac{A}{B} \div \dfrac{C}{D} \div \dfrac{E}{F}$

$\quad = \dfrac{A}{B} \bullet \dfrac{D}{C} \bullet \dfrac{F}{E}$

$\quad = \dfrac{ADF}{BCE}$

Model 4: $\dfrac{5x^3z}{yz^2} \div 2xyz \bullet \dfrac{1}{20x^2} \div \dfrac{3}{8yz}$

$\quad = \dfrac{5x^3z}{yz^2} \bullet \dfrac{1}{2xyz} \bullet \dfrac{1}{20x^2} \bullet \dfrac{8yz}{3}$

$\quad = \dfrac{5x^3z \bullet 1 \bullet 1 \bullet 8yz}{yz^2 \bullet 2xyz \bullet 20x^2 \bullet 3}$

$\quad = \dfrac{\cancel{40x^3yz^2}}{\cancel{120x^3y^2z^3}}{\scriptstyle 3 \quad y \quad z}$

$\quad = \dfrac{1}{3yz}$

Find the indicated products and quotients.

1.56 $\quad \dfrac{a}{7} \bullet \dfrac{b}{2}$

1.59 $\quad -\dfrac{2x^5}{yz^2} \bullet \dfrac{y^2z}{x^4}$

_____

_____

1.57 $\quad \dfrac{11}{d^3} \bullet \left(-\dfrac{7}{d^4}\right)$

1.60 $\quad \dfrac{4m^3}{n^2} \div \dfrac{2m}{n}$

_____

_____

1.58 $\quad \dfrac{15ab}{4} \bullet \dfrac{8}{9a^2b^2}$

1.61 $\quad \dfrac{6a}{8b} \bullet \dfrac{10c}{12d}$

_____

_____

1.62 $\quad \dfrac{6a}{8b} \div \dfrac{10c}{12d}$

1.66 $\quad \dfrac{9z^3}{16xy} \cdot \dfrac{4x}{27z^3}$

_____

_____

1.63 $\quad \dfrac{50p^3q^2}{3} \div 75p^2q^3$

1.67 $\quad \left(-\dfrac{1}{3ab}\right) \div (-3ab)$

_____

_____

1.64 $\quad xyz \div \dfrac{1}{xyz}$

1.68 $\quad \dfrac{3c^2}{ab} \div \dfrac{5b^2}{ac} \div \dfrac{bc}{2a^2}$

_____

_____

1.65 $\quad -\dfrac{a^2b}{b^2c} \div \dfrac{a^2c}{b^2c^2}$

1.69 $\quad \dfrac{5m^3n^2}{2} \div \dfrac{mn^2}{4} \cdot \left(-\dfrac{m^2}{10}\right)$

_____

_____

1.70 $\dfrac{12xy}{z} \div \dfrac{14yz}{x} \cdot 7xyz \div \dfrac{6x}{5y}$

_____

All of the products and quotients considered so far have had monomials for the numerators and denominators. Now we will look at fractions that also involve polynomials of more than one term. The two rules are still used in the same way, but polynomials of more than one term must be factored before any reducing takes place.

Model 1: $\dfrac{9m + 3p}{7} \cdot \dfrac{5}{6m + 2p}$

$= \dfrac{3(3m + p)}{7} \cdot \dfrac{5}{2(3m + p)}$

$= \dfrac{3(\cancel{3m + p}) \cdot 5}{7 \cdot 2 (\cancel{3m + p})}$

$= \dfrac{15}{14}$

Model 2: $\dfrac{a^2 + 2a}{8} \div \dfrac{4 - a^2}{6b}$

$= \dfrac{a^2 + 2a}{8} \cdot \dfrac{6b}{4 - a^2}$

$= \dfrac{a(\cancel{a + 2})}{\cancel{8}^4} \cdot \dfrac{\cancel{6}^3 b}{(\cancel{2 + a})(2 - a)}$

$= \dfrac{3ab}{4(2 - a)}$ or $\dfrac{3ab}{8 - 4a}$

The first of the preceding models shows reducing to a single fraction after the product; the second model shows reducing to a single fraction before the product, which saves writing out one more step in the solution. Just remember that you must have a product (not a quotient) before reducing and that a factor common to any number and any denominator in that product is to be reduced.

Model 3: $\dfrac{2x^2 - 5x - 3}{9 - x^2} \div \dfrac{8x^2 + 2x - 1}{4x^2 + 11x - 3}$

$= \dfrac{2x^2 - 5x - 3}{9 - x^2} \cdot \dfrac{4x^2 + 11x - 3}{8x^2 + 2x - 1}$

$= \dfrac{(\cancel{2x + 1})(\cancel{x - 3})^{(-1)}}{(\cancel{3 + x})(\cancel{3 - x})} \cdot \dfrac{(\cancel{4x - 1})(\cancel{x + 3})}{(\cancel{4x - 1})(\cancel{2x + 1})}$

$= -1$

Model 4: $\dfrac{n^2 - 25}{n^2 - 15n + 50} \div \dfrac{(n-5)^2}{n^2 - 5n} \bullet \dfrac{5n - 50}{n^2 + 5n}$

$= \dfrac{n^2 - 25}{n^2 - 15n + 50} \bullet \dfrac{n^2 - 5n}{(n-5)^2} \bullet \dfrac{5n - 50}{n^2 + 5n}$

$= \dfrac{(n+5)(n-5)}{(n-10)(n-5)} \bullet \dfrac{n(n-5)}{(n-5)(n-5)} \bullet \dfrac{5(n-10)}{n(n+5)}$

$= \dfrac{5}{n-5}$

▶▶▶ Find the indicated products and quotients.

1.71 $\quad \dfrac{3a - 6}{4a^2} \bullet \dfrac{2a}{5a - 10}$

1.75 $\quad \dfrac{7a - a^2}{2a} \div \dfrac{49 - a^2}{2a - 14}$

_____   _____

1.72 $\quad \dfrac{x^2 - y^2}{3x} \bullet \dfrac{3y}{x + y}$

1.76 $\quad \dfrac{y^2 + 3y - 10}{3y + 15} \div (10 - 5y)$

_____   _____

1.73 $\quad \dfrac{k^2 - 36}{k} \bullet \dfrac{k^2}{k - 6}$

1.77 $\quad \dfrac{4a - 4b}{12} \div \dfrac{a^2 - b^2}{3}$

_____   _____

1.74 $\quad \dfrac{3m - 9}{4m + 8} \bullet \dfrac{m^2 + 5m + 6}{m^2 - 9}$

1.78 $\quad \dfrac{2x^2 + x - 3}{9} \bullet \dfrac{(x + 1)^2}{2x^2 + 5x + 3}$

_____   _____

1.79 $\dfrac{6y^2 + y - 2}{6y + 4} \bullet \dfrac{16y + 8}{4y^2 - 1}$

1.81 $\dfrac{n^2 + 5n + 6}{n^2 + 7n + 12} \bullet \dfrac{n^2 + 9n + 20}{n^2 + 11n + 30}$

_____

_____

1.80 $\dfrac{1}{25 - y^2} \div \dfrac{6 - 3y}{y^2 - 7y + 10}$

1.82 $\dfrac{c^2 + 11cd}{c^2 d^2} \div \dfrac{2c + 22d}{11cd^2}$

_____

_____

1.83 $\dfrac{x^2 + 3x - 4}{x^2 - 7x + 6} \div \dfrac{x^3 - 8x^2}{x^2 + 6x} \div \dfrac{x^2 + 10x + 24}{x^2 - 14x + 48}$

_____

1.84 $\dfrac{abc}{a^2 - 3a - 10} \div \dfrac{a^2}{a^2 - 25} \bullet \dfrac{4 - a^2}{9b^2 - 4} \div \dfrac{abc + 5bc}{3ab - 2a}$

_____

1.85 $\dfrac{m^2}{m + n} \bullet \dfrac{n^2}{m - n} \bullet \dfrac{mn}{m^2 + n^2} \div \dfrac{m^2 n^2}{m^2 - n^2}$

_____

You may remember studying complex arithmetic fractions. Algebraic fractions, too, can be complex.

DEFINITION

Complex fraction: a fraction that has at least one fraction in its own numerator or denominator.

Models: $\quad \dfrac{7}{\frac{2}{3}} \qquad \dfrac{\frac{2}{3} + \frac{3}{4}}{\frac{1}{2}} \qquad \dfrac{x - \frac{1}{2}}{3}$

Since any fraction is an indicated quotient ($\frac{A}{B} = A \div B$), the complex fraction $\dfrac{7}{\frac{2}{3}}$ means $7 \div \frac{2}{3} = \frac{7}{1} \cdot \frac{3}{2} = \frac{21}{2}$; the fraction $\frac{21}{2}$ (or the decimal 10.5) is then the simplified form of the complex fraction $\dfrac{7}{\frac{2}{3}}$.

Of the two methods for simplifying a complex fraction, the first has just been described: dividing the numerator by the denominator. However, you need to perform any indicated operations in the numerator and in the denominator before finding their quotient.

Model 1: Simplify $\dfrac{\frac{2}{3} + \frac{3}{4}}{\frac{1}{2}}$.

Solution: $\dfrac{\frac{2}{3} + \frac{3}{4}}{\frac{1}{2}} = \dfrac{\frac{8}{12} + \frac{9}{12}}{\frac{1}{2}}$

$= \dfrac{\frac{17}{12}}{\frac{1}{2}}$

$= \frac{17}{12} \div \frac{1}{2}$

$= \frac{17}{\cancel{12}_{6}} \cdot \frac{\cancel{2}}{1}$

$= \frac{17}{6}$ or $2.8\overline{3}$

Model 2:   Simplify $\dfrac{x-\frac{1}{2}}{3}$.

Solution: $\dfrac{x-\frac{1}{2}}{3} = \dfrac{\frac{2x}{2}-\frac{1}{2}}{3}$

$= \dfrac{\frac{2x-1}{2}}{3}$

$= \dfrac{2x-1}{2} \div 3$

$= \dfrac{2x-1}{2} \bullet \dfrac{1}{3}$

$= \dfrac{2x-1}{6}$

The second method is a shorter procedure for simplifying most complex fractions: Multiply the numerator and the denominator of the complex fraction by the LCD of all the fractions it contains.

Model 3:   Simplify $\dfrac{\frac{2}{3}+\frac{3}{4}}{\frac{1}{2}}$.

Solution: The LCD of $\frac{2}{3}$, $\frac{3}{4}$, and $\frac{1}{2}$ is 12.

$\dfrac{\frac{2}{3}+\frac{3}{4}}{\frac{1}{2}} [\dfrac{12}{12}] = \dfrac{\frac{2}{3} [\cancel{12}]^{4} + \frac{3}{4} [\cancel{12}]^{3}}{\frac{1}{2} [\cancel{12}]^{6}}$

$= \dfrac{8+9}{6}$

$= \dfrac{17}{6}$ or $2.8\overline{3}$

Model 4:   Simplify $\dfrac{x-\frac{1}{2}}{3}$.

Solution: The only fraction is $\frac{1}{2}$, so the LCD is 2.

$\dfrac{x-\frac{1}{2}}{3} [\dfrac{2}{2}] = \dfrac{x [2] - \frac{1}{2} [2]}{3 [2]}$

$= \dfrac{2x-1}{6}$

You can see that the results are the same by either method, and you may use the method of your choice. In some cases you will need to reduce the resulting fraction to lowest terms. Compare the two solutions to the following model:

Model 5: Simplify $\dfrac{\frac{1}{y}+1}{y-\frac{1}{y}}$.

Solutions: Method 1

$$\dfrac{\frac{1}{y}+1}{y-\frac{1}{y}} = \dfrac{\frac{1}{y}+\frac{y}{y}}{\frac{y^2}{y}-\frac{1}{y}}$$

$$= \dfrac{\frac{1+y}{y}}{\frac{y^2-1}{y}}$$

$$= \dfrac{1+y}{y} \div \dfrac{y^2-1}{y}$$

$$= \dfrac{1+y}{y} \cdot \dfrac{y}{y^2-1}$$

$$= \dfrac{1+\cancel{y}}{\cancel{y}} \cdot \dfrac{\cancel{y}}{(y+1)(y-1)}$$

$$= \dfrac{1}{y-1}$$

Method 2

$$\dfrac{\frac{1}{y}+1}{y-\frac{1}{y}}\left[\dfrac{y}{y}\right] = \dfrac{\frac{1}{\cancel{y}}[\cancel{y}]+1[y]}{y[y]-\frac{1}{\cancel{y}}[\cancel{y}]}$$

$$= \dfrac{1+y}{y^2-1}$$

$$= \dfrac{1+\cancel{y}}{(y+1)(y-1)}$$

$$= \dfrac{1}{y-1}$$

✹✹✹ **Simplify each complex fraction.**

1.86 $\dfrac{\frac{1}{4}+x}{\frac{1}{2}}$

1.87 $\dfrac{y-\frac{2}{3}}{y+\frac{1}{5}}$

1.88 $\dfrac{\dfrac{a}{b}+c}{\dfrac{a}{b}-c}$

1.92 $\dfrac{\dfrac{y}{5}+1}{\dfrac{y^2}{25}-1}$

_____ _____

1.89 $\dfrac{2+\dfrac{1}{a}}{\dfrac{2}{a}-a}$

1.93 $\dfrac{a-\dfrac{9}{a}}{1-\dfrac{3}{a}}$

_____ _____

1.90 $\dfrac{\dfrac{x}{2}+\dfrac{x}{3}}{\dfrac{x}{4}}$

1.94 $\dfrac{\dfrac{1}{3}+\dfrac{1}{5}-\dfrac{1}{7}}{\dfrac{1}{x}}$

_____ _____

1.91 $\dfrac{\dfrac{2}{x}+\dfrac{3}{x}}{\dfrac{4}{x}}$

1.95 $\dfrac{\dfrac{n}{12}-\dfrac{2}{9}}{\dfrac{n}{6}}$

_____ _____

1.96 $$\dfrac{m - \dfrac{1}{m}}{m + \dfrac{1}{m}}$$

1.98 $$\dfrac{\dfrac{a}{b} + 2 + \dfrac{b}{a}}{\dfrac{a}{b} - \dfrac{b}{a}}$$

_____   _____

1.97 $$\dfrac{x + \dfrac{1}{2}}{2 + \dfrac{1}{x}}$$

1.99 $$\dfrac{\dfrac{k-3}{4} - \dfrac{7}{k}}{\dfrac{k-7}{4}}$$

_____   _____

Review the material in this section in preparation for the Self Test. The Self Test will check your mastery of this particular section as well as your knowledge of the previous section.

SELF TEST 1

Give the excluded value(s) for each fraction (each answer, 3 points).

1.01 $\dfrac{2}{x\,(x-3)}$ _____

1.02 $\dfrac{y+5}{y^2 + 4y - 32}$ _____

1.03 $\dfrac{-7z}{4z+1}$ _____

Reduce each fraction to lowest terms (each answer, 3 points).

1.04 $\dfrac{6a^2 b^3}{8ab^4}$ _____

1.05 $\dfrac{3 - k}{k - 3}$ _____

1.06 $\dfrac{n^2 - 7n - 44}{n^2 - 121}$ _____

Perform the indicated operations (each answer, 4 points).

1.07 $\dfrac{4x}{2x + y} + \dfrac{2y}{2x + y}$ 1.010 $\dfrac{m}{n} \bullet \dfrac{n}{p} \div \dfrac{p}{q}$

1.08 $\dfrac{d + 3}{8d} - \dfrac{2d + 1}{10d^2}$ 1.011 $\dfrac{4x^2yz^3}{9} \bullet \dfrac{45y}{8x^5z^3}$

1.09 $\dfrac{3}{n^2 - 9} + \dfrac{7}{3 - n}$ 1.012 $\dfrac{k + 5}{k^2 + 3k - 10} \div \dfrac{7k + 14}{4 - k^2}$

Simplify each complex fraction (each answer, 3 points).

1.013 $\dfrac{\frac{1}{x}}{\frac{1}{y}}$ 1.015 $\dfrac{\frac{5}{a} + 1}{\frac{a}{5} - \frac{5}{a}}$

1.014 $\dfrac{\frac{m}{5} - \frac{1}{6}}{\frac{1}{3}}$

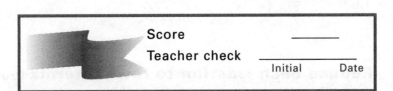

II. OPEN SENTENCES

OBJECTIVES

When you have completed this section, you should be able to:

6. Solve equations containing fractions.
7. Solve inequalities containing fractions.
8. Change the subject of a formula containing fractions.

In the second section of this LIFEPAC, you will learn to solve equations and inequalities for their roots and to rewrite formulas with different subjects. In all these instances you will now be working with open sentences that have algebraic fractions for some or all of their terms.

SOLVING EQUATIONS

In an earlier LIFEPAC, you learned a step-by-step procedure for solving an equation like $5x + 3 = 10 - 2x$ to obtain a *root*, in this case $x = 1$. Now you will have an opportunity to increase your equation-solving ability to ones that contain such algebraic fractions as

$\frac{x}{5} + 3 = 10 - \frac{x}{2}$ or

$\frac{5}{x} + 3 = 10 - \frac{2}{x}$ or

$\frac{5}{x+3} = \frac{10}{2-x}$.

USING THE LCD

Actually, the key to solving an equation having fractions is to eliminate those fractions as the first step of the solution. This step is accomplished by multiplying both sides of the equation by the LCD of all the fractions. After this step is completed, the rest of the procedure is a repeat of what you have already learned.

Model 1:   Solve $\frac{x}{5} + 3 = 10 - \frac{x}{2}$.

Solution: The LCD of $\frac{x}{5}$ and $\frac{x}{2}$ is 10.

$$10 \left[\frac{x}{5} + 3 \right] = 10 \left[10 - \frac{x}{2} \right]$$

$$\overset{2}{\cancel{10}} \left[\frac{x}{\cancel{5}} \right] + 10 [3] = 10 [10] - \overset{5}{\cancel{10}} \left[\frac{x}{\cancel{2}} \right]$$

$$2x + 30 = 100 - 5x$$

$$7x = 70$$

$$x = 10$$

31

Check: Replace x by 10 in the original equation:

$$\frac{10}{5} + 3 \overset{?}{=} 10 - \frac{10}{2}$$

$$2 + 3 \; ? \; 10 - 5$$

$$5 = 5$$

Model 2:   Solve $\frac{5}{x} + 3 = 10 - \frac{2}{x}$.

Solution: The LCD of $\frac{5}{x}$ and $\frac{2}{x}$ is x.

$$x\,[\frac{5}{x} + 3] = x\,[10 - \frac{2}{x}]$$

$$\cancel{x}\,[\frac{5}{\cancel{x}}] + x\,[3] = x\,[10] - \cancel{x}\,[\frac{2}{\cancel{x}}]$$

$$5 + 3x = 10x - 2$$

$$-7x = -7$$

$$x = 1$$

Check: Replace x by 1 in the original equation:

$$\frac{5}{1} + 3 \overset{?}{=} 10 - \frac{2}{1}$$

$$5 + 3 \; ? \; 10 - 2$$

$$8 = 8$$

Model 3:   Solve $\frac{5}{x+3} = \frac{10}{2-x}$.

Solution: The LCD is $(x + 3)(2 - x)$.

$$(x+3)(2-x)[\frac{5}{x+3}] = (x+3)(2-x)\,[\frac{10}{2-x}]$$

$$10 - 5x = 10x + 30$$

$$-15x = 20$$

$$x = -\frac{20}{15}, \text{ which reduces to}$$

$$-\frac{4}{3} \text{ or } -1.\overline{3}$$

Check: Replace x by $-\frac{4}{3}$ in the original equation:

$$\frac{5}{-\frac{4}{3} + 3} \overset{?}{=} \frac{10}{2 - (-\frac{4}{3})}$$

             (These fractions are

$$\frac{5}{-\frac{4}{3} + 3}\,[\frac{3}{3}] \; ? \; \frac{10}{2 + \frac{4}{3}}\,[\frac{3}{3}]$$

             complex fractions.)

$$\frac{15}{-4 + 9} \; ? \; \frac{30}{6 + 4}$$

$$\frac{15}{5} \; ? \; \frac{30}{10}$$

$$3 = 3$$

CROSS-MULTIPLICATION

Model 3, and any equation in the form $\frac{A}{B} = \frac{C}{D}$, can also be solved in a slightly different manner; the LCD is BD, and $B\!\!\!/D\ [\frac{A}{B\!\!\!/}] = B\!\!\!/D\ [\frac{C}{D\!\!\!/}]$ yields the equation $AD = BC$. Thus, the products obtained from multiplying diagonally across the equal sign are themselves equal; for this reason, this procedure is called *cross-multiplication*.

Model 1:   Solve $\frac{5}{x+3} = \frac{10}{2-x}$ by cross-multiplication.

Solution: $\frac{5}{x+3} \;\diagup\!\!\!\!\diagdown\; \frac{10}{2-x}$ $\longrightarrow (x+3)10$ $\longrightarrow 5(2-x)$ } These products are equal.

$$10x + 30 = 10 - 5x$$

$$15x = -20$$

$$x = -\frac{20}{15},$$ which reduces to $-\frac{4}{3}$ or $-1.\overline{3}$, as before.

Model 2:   Solve $\frac{4k-3}{10k+1} = \frac{1}{3}$.

Solution: $\frac{4k-3}{10k+1} \;\diagup\!\!\!\!\diagdown\; \frac{1}{3}$ $\longrightarrow (10k+1)1$ $\longrightarrow (4k-3)3$

$$10k + 1 = 12k - 9$$

$$-2k = -10$$

$$k = 5$$

Check: Replace k by 5 in the original equation:

$$\frac{4(5)-3}{10(5)+1} \stackrel{?}{=} \frac{1}{3}$$

$$\frac{20-3}{50+1} \stackrel{?}{=} \frac{1}{3}$$

$$\frac{17}{51} \stackrel{?}{=} \frac{1}{3}$$

$$\frac{1}{3} = \frac{1}{3}$$

33

Model 3: Solve $11 - \frac{x+6}{2} = \frac{x-20}{3} + x$.

Solution: This equation cannot be solved by cross-multiplication since it is not in the form $\frac{A}{B} = \frac{C}{D}$.
The LCD is 6.

$$6\left[11 - \frac{x+6}{2}\right] = 6\left[\frac{x-20}{3} + x\right]$$

$$6[11] - \overset{3}{\cancel{6}}\left[\frac{x+6}{\cancel{2}}\right] = \overset{2}{\cancel{6}}\left[\frac{x-20}{\cancel{3}}\right] + 6[x]$$

$$66 - 3x - 18 = 2x - 40 + 6x$$

$$-3x + 48 = 8x - 40$$

$$-11x = -88$$

$$x = 8$$

Check: Replace x by 8 in the original equation:

$$11 - \frac{8+6}{2} \overset{?}{=} \frac{8-20}{3} + 8$$

$$11 - \frac{14}{2} \; ? \; \frac{-12}{3} + 8$$

$$11 - 7 \; ? \; -4 + 8$$

$$4 = 4$$

▪ ▪ ▪ Solve each equation and check each root.

2.1 $\frac{x}{9} + 3 = 7 - \frac{x}{3}$

2.3 $\frac{7}{2x} - \frac{5}{3x} = 11$

2.2 $\frac{5}{x} - 1 = \frac{3}{x}$

2.4 $\frac{x+1}{2} - \frac{x+2}{3} = \frac{x+3}{4}$

2.5 $\dfrac{x-1}{3} = \dfrac{x-3}{4}$

2.10 $\dfrac{15}{y+11} - \dfrac{10}{y-3} = 0$

_____

_____

2.6 $\dfrac{y}{5} + \dfrac{3}{10} = \dfrac{y+2}{7}$

2.11 $\dfrac{1}{8k} + \dfrac{1}{5k} - \dfrac{1}{4k} = \dfrac{3}{20}$

_____

_____

2.7 $\dfrac{2}{y+5} = \dfrac{3}{y-1}$

2.12 $\dfrac{4k+3}{6} + \dfrac{4k-8}{9} = \dfrac{5k-4}{3} - \dfrac{k-3}{2}$

_____

_____

2.8 $\dfrac{y}{5} + \dfrac{1}{2} = \dfrac{2y}{5} - \dfrac{1}{10}$

2.13 $\dfrac{3}{k+3} = \dfrac{8}{k-2}$

_____

_____

2.9 $2 - \dfrac{4}{y} = 1 + \dfrac{3}{y}$

2.14 $\dfrac{2k}{k-15} - 3 = 2$

_____

_____

2.15 $\dfrac{1}{k} + \dfrac{1}{2k} + \dfrac{1}{3k} + \dfrac{1}{6k} = 1$

2.20 $\dfrac{a+1}{4} - \dfrac{a+2}{6} + \dfrac{a+3}{9} = 2$

2.16 $\dfrac{a-5}{a+4} = \dfrac{5}{4}$

2.21 $\dfrac{1}{n-4} - \dfrac{2}{n} = \dfrac{3}{4-n}$

2.17 $\dfrac{6}{2a+3} - \dfrac{1}{2a} = \dfrac{1}{a}$

2.22 $\dfrac{20}{n+10} = \dfrac{10}{n+20}$

2.18 $\dfrac{1}{a} + \dfrac{1}{2a} = \dfrac{1}{a-3}$

2.23 $3 + \dfrac{n-5}{7} = \dfrac{n-7}{3} + 5$

2.19 $\dfrac{5}{a} - \dfrac{2}{1-a} = \dfrac{2}{a-1}$

2.24 $\dfrac{1}{n} - \dfrac{6}{2n-3} = \dfrac{4}{3-2n} - \dfrac{2}{2n-3}$

2.25 $\dfrac{17}{n-7} = \dfrac{-17}{7-n}$

LITERAL EQUATIONS

Equations that contain more than one letter, such as $\dfrac{5}{x} + \dfrac{1}{a} = \dfrac{2}{b}$ or $\dfrac{m-n}{y} = \dfrac{m}{m+n}$, can also be solved. These equations are known as *literal equations*.

DEFINITION
Literal equation: an equation containing more than one letter.

In these literal equations, one of the letters (usually x or y) represents the variable, but any other letter is treated as a constant. After eliminating the fractions, collect all terms containing the variable on one side of the equation and all remaining terms on the other side of the equation; finally, solve for the variable.

Model 1:   Solve $\dfrac{5}{x} + \dfrac{1}{a} = \dfrac{2}{b}$ for x.

Solution: The LCD is abx.

$$abx\left[\dfrac{5}{x} + \dfrac{1}{a}\right] = abx\left[\dfrac{2}{b}\right]$$

$$abx\left[\dfrac{5}{x}\right] + abx\left[\dfrac{1}{a}\right] = abx\left[\dfrac{2}{b}\right]$$

$$5ab + bx = 2ax$$

$$5ab = 2ax - bx$$

$$5ab = x(2a - b)$$

$$\dfrac{5ab}{2a - b} = x \text{ or } x = \dfrac{5ab}{2a - b}$$

Model 2:   Solve $\frac{m-n}{y} = \frac{m}{m+n}$ for y.

Solution: Since this equation is in the form

$\frac{A}{B} = \frac{C}{D}$, use cross-multiplication.

$$\frac{m-n}{y} = \frac{m}{m+n} \begin{array}{c} ym \\ (m-n)(m+n) \end{array}$$

$$ym = m^2 - n^2$$

$$y = \frac{m^2 - n^2}{m}$$

▶▶▶ Solve each literal equation for x or y.

2.26 $\frac{3}{x} + \frac{2}{m} = \frac{1}{n}$

2.30 $\frac{y-1}{y+1} = \frac{a-b}{a+b}$

2.27 $\frac{5}{a} - \frac{4}{y} = \frac{1}{b}$

2.31 $\frac{y}{m} + \frac{y}{n} = p$

2.28 $\frac{x}{3-j} = \frac{j}{2}$

2.32 $\frac{x}{j-k} - j = k$

2.29 $\frac{5a}{x} = \frac{5b}{x-1}$

2.33 $\frac{2y+a}{2y+b} = \frac{a}{b}$

2.34 $\dfrac{x}{2a} + \dfrac{x}{3b} = 1$

2.38 $\dfrac{y-a}{a} - \dfrac{y-b}{b} = ab$

_____

_____

2.35 $\dfrac{r}{3} - \dfrac{2}{y} = \dfrac{s}{5}$

2.39 $\dfrac{x}{r-8} + \dfrac{1}{8} = \dfrac{x+1}{8-r}$

_____

_____

2.36 $\dfrac{y}{m} + \dfrac{y-1}{n} = \dfrac{y-2}{mn}$

2.40 $\dfrac{y}{p-q} = \dfrac{y}{p+q}$

_____

_____

2.37 $\dfrac{x}{j-k} - \dfrac{x}{j+k} = 1$

_____

Inequalities with algebraic fractions can be of two different types. The inequality may contain fractions with variables in the numerator or fractions with variables in the denominator. Both types of inequality may be solved, but the procedures differ.

VARIABLE NUMERATORS

You have already learned to solve inequalities in much the same way as equations. Likewise, inequalities having algebraic fractions are solved in much the same way as equations containing fractions. The first step is still to multiply both sides of the inequality by the LCD to eliminate the fractions.

Model 1: Solve $\frac{3x}{4} - \frac{1}{3} > \frac{7}{6}$.

Solution: The LCD is 12.

$$12[\frac{3x}{4} - \frac{1}{3}] > 12[\frac{7}{6}]$$

$$\overset{3}{\cancel{12}}[\frac{3x}{\cancel{4}}] - \overset{4}{\cancel{12}}[\frac{1}{\cancel{3}}] > \overset{2}{\cancel{12}}[\frac{7}{\cancel{6}}]$$

$$9x - 4 > 14$$

$$9x > 18$$

$$x > 2$$

You should recall that the main difference between solving equations and solving inequalities is in the handling of negative numbers in multiplication or division. In solving an equation, negative numbers are used just like positive numbers; but in solving an inequality, the inequality sign must be reversed any time you multiply or divide both sides by a negative number.

Model 2: Solve $\frac{7}{10}n - \frac{5n}{6} \geq \frac{2}{5}$.

Solution: The LCD is 30.

$$30[\frac{7}{10}n - \frac{5n}{6}] \geq 30[\frac{2}{5}]$$

$$\overset{3}{\cancel{30}}[\frac{7}{\cancel{10}}n] - \overset{5}{\cancel{30}}[\frac{5n}{\cancel{6}}] \geq \overset{6}{\cancel{30}}[\frac{2}{\cancel{5}}]$$

$$21n - 25n \geq 12$$

$$-4n \geq 12$$

$$n \leq -3, \text{ since both sides of}$$
$$-4n \geq 12 \text{ are divided by -4.}$$

Solve each inequality.

2.41 $\dfrac{x}{2} - \dfrac{7}{6} < \dfrac{4}{3}$

2.45 $\dfrac{4}{9}z - \dfrac{2z}{3} < \dfrac{1}{2}$

_____ _____

2.42 $\dfrac{y}{3} - \dfrac{3}{4} > \dfrac{1}{2}$

2.46 $\dfrac{a}{2} - 3 \geq 2a$

_____ _____

2.43 $\dfrac{n-2}{5} - \dfrac{n}{3} \leq 2$

2.47 $\dfrac{2m+3}{2} - \dfrac{17}{4} < \dfrac{m+2}{8}$

_____ _____

2.44 $\dfrac{b}{8} + \dfrac{b+3}{6} \geq -3$

2.48 $\dfrac{3}{10}(t + 2) - \dfrac{t}{20} \geq \dfrac{3}{5}$

_____ _____

2.49 $\dfrac{12}{25} - \dfrac{3b}{10} < \dfrac{1}{2} - \dfrac{b}{5}$

2.53 $\dfrac{a+2}{16} - \dfrac{a+3}{12} > \dfrac{a+6}{24}$

_____

_____

2.50 $\dfrac{x}{2} + \dfrac{1}{3} \le 0$

2.54 $\dfrac{d-3}{10} \ge \dfrac{2d+3}{5} + \dfrac{d+3}{3}$

_____

_____

2.51 $\dfrac{4k-1}{3} - \dfrac{2k+1}{7} > k$

2.55 $\dfrac{2z}{3} - \dfrac{3z}{4} + \dfrac{4z}{5} - \dfrac{5z}{6} < 7$

_____

_____

2.52 $\dfrac{y}{4} + 2 - \dfrac{y+1}{6} \ge \dfrac{y+5}{9}$

_____

VARIABLE DENOMINATORS (OPTIONAL)

The solution of an inequality with a variable in the denominator is complicated by the fact that the LCD may be positive or negative. If the LCD is positive, then the solution is as before; but if the LCD is negative, then multiplying both sides of the inequality by that LCD reverses the inequality sign. Thus, you must consider two cases when solving such an inequality.

MATHEMATICS 906: LIFEPAC TEST

Complete these items (each answer, 5 points).

1. Give the excluded value(s) for the fraction $\frac{-7}{x^2 - 2x - 15}$.

   _____

2. Reduce the fraction $\frac{3m^2 - 3n^2}{6m + 6n}$ to lowest terms.

   _____

3. Simplify the complex fraction $\dfrac{\frac{1}{4n} - \frac{1}{2}}{\frac{n}{5} - \frac{1}{20n}}$.

   _____

4. Solve the equation $\frac{4y + 5}{3} = \frac{y - 10}{2}$.

   _____

5. Solve the inequality $\frac{d - 2}{25} > \frac{d}{10} - \frac{1}{2}$.

   _____

6. The formula for the area of a trapezoid with altitude k and bases m and n is $A = \frac{k}{2}(m + n)$. Rewrite this formula with m as the subject.

_____

Perform the indicated operations (each answer, 5 points).

7. $\frac{3}{a^2 b} + \frac{2}{ab^2}$

9. $\frac{k^2 + 9k - 10}{34} \cdot \frac{2}{k^2 - 1}$

_____   _____

8. $\frac{4x - y}{3} - \frac{x + y}{2}$

10. $\frac{8}{r^3 s^2} \div \frac{6}{rs^4}$

_____   _____

Solve any five of the following six problems. The remaining problem may be done as a "bonus" problem. Show your work and circle your answer (each answer, 10 points).

11. One person can do a certain job in twenty-one minutes, and another person can do the same job in twenty-eight minutes. How many minutes will it take them to do the job together?

12. Find two consecutive odd numbers such that the sum of three-sevenths of the first number and one-third of the second number is equal to thirty-eight.

13. The ages of two brothers are in the ratio two to three, but in eight years the ratio of their ages will be three to four. Find their present ages.

14. The sum of two numbers is forty-four; and if the larger number is divided by the smaller number, then the quotient is five and the remainder is two. Find the numbers.

15. Twenty pounds of a salt-water solution contains fifteen per cent salt. How much water must be added to weaken the solution to twelve per cent salt?

16. The distance between two cities is ninety miles, and a woman drives from one city to the other at a rate of forty-five mph. At what rate must she return if the total travel time is three hours and forty minutes?

Model 1:   Solve $2 < \frac{8}{y}$.

Solution: The LCD is y. It may
be positive $(y > 0)$, or
it may be negative $(y < 0)$.

Case i: $y > 0$ and $y\,[2] < y\,[\frac{8}{y}]$
$2y < 8$
$y < 4$

This result, $y > 0$
and $y < 4$, can be
written as $0 < y < 4$.

Case ii: $y < 0$ and $y\,[2] > y\,[\frac{8}{y}]$
$2y > 8$
$y > 4$

This result, $y < 0$ and
$y > 4$, is meaningless
since no values smaller
than zero and (at the
same time) larger than
four exist.

∴ The solution is $0 < y < 4$ (from Case i).

Model 2:   Solve $\frac{3}{z-5} + 2 \geq \frac{5}{z-5}$.

Solution: The LCD is $z - 5$. It
may be positive $(z - 5 > 0)$,
or it may be negative $(z - 5 < 0)$.

Case i: $z - 5 > 0$
$z > 5$

and

$$(z - 5)[\frac{3}{z-5} + 2] \geq (z - 5)[\frac{5}{z-5}]$$

$$(z-5)[\frac{3}{z-5}] + (z - 5)\,2 \geq (z-5)[\frac{5}{z-5}]$$

$$3 + 2z - 10 \geq 5$$
$$2z - 7 \geq 5$$
$$2z \geq 12$$
$$z \geq 6$$

This result, $z > 5$
and (at the same time)
$z \geq 6$, is just $z \geq 6$.

Case ii: $z - 5 < 0$
$z < 5$

and

$$(z - 5) \left[\frac{3}{z-5} + 2 \right] \leq (z - 5) \left[\frac{5}{z-5} \right]$$
$$3 + 2z - 10 \leq 5$$
$$2z - 7 \leq 5$$
$$2z \leq 12$$
$$z \leq 6$$

This result, $z < 5$ and
(at the same time)
$z \leq 6$, is just $z < 5$.
∴ The solution is $z \geq 6$ (from Case i) or
$z < 5$ (from Case ii).

(OPTIONAL) Solve each inequality using two cases.

2.56 $\frac{10}{y} > 5$

2.58 $\frac{2}{x} + 7 < \frac{3}{x} - 1$

2.57 $6 \leq \frac{3}{y}$

2.59 $4 + \frac{5}{x} \geq 5 + \frac{4}{x}$

2.60 $\dfrac{2}{a-3} + 1 \geq \dfrac{3}{a-3}$ **2.63** $-\dfrac{2}{y} + \dfrac{3}{4} > \dfrac{3}{2} + \dfrac{7}{4y}$

2.61 $\dfrac{5}{a+2} - 3 < \dfrac{2}{a+2}$ **2.64** $\dfrac{4n-7}{2n-3} > \dfrac{5}{2n-3}$

2.62 $\dfrac{1}{2} + \dfrac{5}{x} \leq \dfrac{3x-4}{2x}$ **2.65** $\dfrac{37}{3z+6} \leq \dfrac{1}{3} - \dfrac{2z}{z+2}$

REWRITING FORMULAS

You have already learned that a *formula* is an equation that expresses some relationship among certain quantities in mathematics or business or science; you may also recall that a letter isolated on the left side of a formula is known as its *subject*. Formulas that contain fractions are much like the literal equations you worked with earlier in this section; and each result of those equations, the answers to Problems 2.26 through 2.40, can be thought of as a formula whose subject is x or y.

The subject of a formula may be changed by following the same step-by-step procedure used for literal equations to solve for the desired letter.

Model: The formula for the average rate

of speed r in traveling a given

distance d in a given time t is

$r = \frac{d}{t}$.

When this equation is multiplied

by the least common denominator

(t), the result is $tr = d$ or

$d = rt$; the subject of the formula

is now the distance, d.

When the equation $tr = d$ is then

divided by r, the result is $t = \frac{d}{r}$;

the subject of the formula is

now the time, t.

Read through the following list of ten formulas that contain fractions when written with their usual subjects.

1. The average a of two numbers x and y: $a = \frac{x+y}{2}$

2. The average a of three numbers x, y, and z: $a = \frac{x+y+z}{3}$

3. The area A of a triangle with base b and altitude h to that base: $A = \frac{1}{2}bh$

4. The area A of a trapezoid with bases a and b and altitude h:

$$A = \frac{1}{2}(a + b)h$$

5. The Fahrenheit temperature F corresponding to a Celsius temperature C:

$$F = \frac{9}{5}C + 32$$

6. The volume V of a pyramid with base area B and altitude h:

$$V = \frac{Bh}{3}$$

7. The volume V of a cone with base radius r and altitude h:

$$V = \frac{\pi r^2 h}{3}$$

8. The sum S of n terms of an arithmetic progression with first term a and last term l:

$$S = \frac{n}{2}(a + l)$$

9. The sum S of the terms of a finite geometric progression with first term a, last term l, and common ratio r:

$$S = \frac{a - lr}{1 - r}$$

10. The sum S of the terms of an infinite geometric progression with first term a and common ratio r ($|r| < 1$):

$$S = \frac{a}{1 - r}$$

You are no doubt familiar with some of the preceding formulas, and you will probably learn the others in your future studies. (You may even want to inquire about those that interest you at the present time!) However, you should realize that you will be able to rewrite formulas with different subjects without actually understanding the relationships expressed.

Model 1: Rewrite Formula 1 with x as the subject.

Solution: $a = \frac{x + y}{2}$

$$\frac{a}{1} \diagup \frac{x+y}{2} \diagdown \begin{array}{c} x + y \\ 2a \end{array}$$

$$x + y = 2a$$

$$\therefore x = 2a - y$$

Model 2: Rewrite Formula 4 with a as the subject.

Solution: $A = \frac{1}{2}(a + b)h$

The LCD is 2.

$$2[A] = 2[\tfrac{1}{2}(a + b)h]$$

$$2A = ah + bh$$

$$2A - bh = ah$$

$$\frac{2A - bh}{h} = \frac{ah}{h}$$

$$\therefore a = \frac{2A - bh}{h}$$

Model 3:   Rewrite Formula 8 with n as the subject.

Solution: $S = \frac{n}{2}(a + l)$

The LCD is 2.

$$2[S] = 2[\tfrac{n}{2}(a + l)]$$

$$2S = n(a + l)$$

$$\frac{2S}{a + l} = \frac{n(a + l)}{a + l}$$

$$\therefore n = \frac{2S}{a + l}$$

Rewrite each indicated formula with the given subject.

2.66   Formula 1; y 2.68   Formula 3; b

_____   _____

2.67   Formula 2; x 2.69   Formula 3; h

_____   _____

2.70 Formula 4; b	**2.75** Formula 8; a
_____	_____
2.71 Formula 4; h	**2.76** Formula 9; a
_____	_____
2.72 Formula 5; C	**2.77** Formula 9; l
_____	_____
2.73 Formula 6; B	**2.78** Formula 9; r
_____	_____
2.74 Formula 7; h	**2.79** Formula 10; a
_____	_____

 Review the material in this section in preparation for the Self Test. This Self Test will check your mastery of this particular section as well as your knowledge of the previous section.

SELF TEST 2

Complete these items (each answer, 3 points).

2.01   Give the excluded value(s) for the fraction $\frac{m + 5}{mn + 3m}$.

2.02   Reduce the fraction $\frac{x^2 - y^2}{x^2 + 2xy + y^2}$ to lowest terms.

2.03   Simplify the complex fraction $\dfrac{3 + \frac{1}{6y}}{\frac{y}{2}}$.

Perform the indicated operations (each answer, 4 points).

2.04 $\frac{a + b}{a^2 b} + \frac{a - b}{ab^2}$ 2.05 $\frac{x + 1}{x - 8} - \frac{x}{8 - x}$

2.06 $\quad \dfrac{4k^2}{2k+3} \cdot \dfrac{2k^2-5k-12}{8k-32}$

2.07 $\quad \dfrac{9-s^2}{3rs} \div \dfrac{s^2+2s-15}{5rs}$

_____

_____

Solve each equation for x (each answer, 3 points).

2.08 $\quad \dfrac{x}{5} - \dfrac{x}{6} = \dfrac{1}{3}$

2.09 $\quad \dfrac{5}{2x+3} = \dfrac{4}{x}$

_____

_____

2.010 $\quad \dfrac{c-1}{x} + d = cd$

_____

Solve each inequality (each answer, 3 points).

2.011 $\quad \dfrac{n}{9} < \dfrac{n}{2} - \dfrac{1}{3}$

2.012 $\quad \dfrac{y}{4} - \dfrac{y-1}{2} \geq 3$

_____

_____

2.013   (OPTIONAL) $\dfrac{5}{z+1} > 3 + \dfrac{2}{z+1}$

_____

Rewrite each formula with the indicated subject (each answer, 3 points).

2.014 $a = \dfrac{x+y+z}{3}; y$ 2.015 $V = \dfrac{Bh}{3}; h$

_____   _____

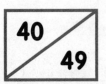

with optional question

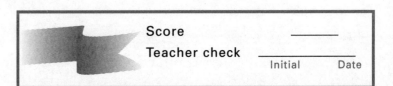

Score _____
Teacher check _____
                    Initial   Date

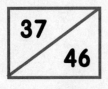

without optional question

III. WORD PROBLEMS

This section consists of various types of verbal problems for which you are to set up and solve equations having algebraic fractions. You will be given a model just before each type of problem is presented for the first time, and any necessary information about the problems will be explained in the solution(s) of that model. You must study the solution(s) carefully and understand the concepts presented before trying to solve the problems that follow.

As you go through this section, you should work all of the problems; and you should do so in the order in which they are given. By working in this orderly fashion, not only will you learn to solve each new type of problem, but also you will be able to review the earlier types. Some of the problems will have equations that are almost identical to those in the models; other problems, although involving the same concepts as the models, will require you to use more creative thought in setting up the equations.

The key to solving any verbal problem is to organize the given information into an equation that fits the problem, and algebra students often have trouble because they immediately try to write an equation without first organizing the given information. Although you will not need to write out as much as is shown in the model solutions, you should always write the *variable assignment* (Let x be...) before setting up the equation for a problem.

▲▽▲▽▲▽▲▽ **WORK AND SINGLE-NUMBER** ▲▽▲▽▲▽▲▽▲▽▲▽▲

The first types of word problems you will study are work problems and single-number problems. Work problems usually deal with how long some person or group of people would take to do a certain job. Single-number problems involve finding a number from clues about certain fractional parts or multiples of the number.

Model 1: One person can do a certain job in forty minutes, and another person can do the same job in one hour. How many minutes will they take to do the job together?

Solution 1: Let m be the number of minutes required to do the job together.

In one minute, the first person would do $\frac{1}{40}$ of the job; in two minutes, $\frac{2}{40}$ of the job; in three minutes,

$\frac{3}{40}$ of the job; and so on. In the m minutes working together, this person would do $\frac{m}{40}$ of the job.

Similarly, since the other person can do the job alone in 1 hour (or 60 minutes), $\frac{1}{60}$ of the job would be done in one minute; $\frac{2}{60}$, in two minutes; $\frac{3}{60}$, in three minutes; and so on. In the m minutes working together, this person would do $\frac{m}{60}$ of the job.

For the job to be completed, the sum of these fractional parts would have to equal 1. Thus, the equation is

$$\frac{m}{40} + \frac{m}{60} = 1.$$

The LCD is 120.

$$120 \left[\frac{m}{40} + \frac{m}{60} \right] = 120 \, [1]$$

$$\overset{3}{\cancel{120}}[\frac{m}{\cancel{40}}] + \overset{2}{\cancel{120}}[\frac{m}{\cancel{60}}] = 120 \, [1]$$

$$3m + 2m = 120$$

$$5m = 120$$

$$m = 24$$

$\therefore$ Together they can do the job in 24 minutes.

Check: In 24 minutes the first person would do $\frac{24}{40}$ (or $\frac{3}{5}$) of the job, the second person would do $\frac{24}{60}$ (or $\frac{2}{5}$) of the job, and together this figure is $\frac{3}{5} + \frac{2}{5}$ or 1 job completed.

Solution 2: Let m be the number of minutes required to do the job together.

In one minute the first person would do $\frac{1}{40}$ of the job and the second person would do $\frac{1}{60}$ of the job. Working together they would do $\frac{1}{m}$ of the job in one minute. Thus, the equation is
$$\frac{1}{40} + \frac{1}{60} = \frac{1}{m}.$$

The LCD is $120m$.

$$120m\left[\frac{1}{40} + \frac{1}{60}\right] = 120m\left[\frac{1}{m}\right]$$

$$\overset{3}{\cancel{120m}}\left[\frac{1}{\cancel{40}}\right] + \overset{2}{\cancel{120m}}\left[\frac{1}{\cancel{60}}\right] = 120\cancel{m}\left[\frac{1}{\cancel{m}}\right]$$

$$3m + 2m = 120$$

$$5m = 120$$

$$m = 24, \text{ as before}$$

(Note: You may use either method of solution for this type of problem.)

Model 2: The sum of four-fifths of a number and one-half of the number exceeds that number by nine. Find the number.

Solution: Let n be the number.

Four-fifths of the number is $\frac{4}{5}n$, and one-half of the number is $\frac{1}{2}n$. The words *exceeds that number by nine* mean the same as *is nine more than that number;* therefore, the equation is set up as shown.

THE SUM	EXCEEDS	THAT NUMBER	BY NINE.

$$\tfrac{4}{5}n + \tfrac{1}{2}n \qquad = \qquad n \qquad + \quad 9$$

The LCD is 10.

$$10[\tfrac{4}{5}\,n + \tfrac{1}{2}\,n] = 10[n + 9]$$

$$\overset{2}{\cancel{10}}\,[\tfrac{4}{\cancel{5}}\,n] + \overset{5}{\cancel{10}}\,[\tfrac{1}{\cancel{2}}\,n] = 10[n] + 10\,[9]$$

$$8n + 5n = 10n + 90$$

$$13n = 10n + 90$$

$$3n = 90$$

$$n = 30$$

∴ The number is thirty.

Check: $\tfrac{4}{5}$ of 30 is 24, $\tfrac{1}{2}$ of 30 is

15; and the sum, 24 + 15 or

39, exceeds 30 by 9.

 **Solve each problem. Show your work and circle your answer.**

3.1   One person can do a certain job in ten minutes, and another person can do the same job in fifteen minutes. How many minutes will they take to do the job together?

3.2   The sum of one-third of a number and three-fourths of the number exceeds that number by one. Find the number.

3.3   One person can do a certain job in six days, a second person can do the same job in two days, and a third person can do this job in three days. How many days will they take to do the job together?

3.4   The difference between one-half of a number and one-sixth of the number is equal to ten more than one-eighth of that number. Find the number.

3.5   Two people together can do a certain job in ten minutes. If one of them can do the job alone in thirty-five minutes, how long will the other person take to do the job alone?

Motion problems and consecutive-number problems are next in your studies. Motion problems usually involve people or vehicles moving in the same or different directions at certain rates of speed. Consecutive-number problems deal with finding sequences of numbers from clues about relationships among the numbers or multiples or fractions of the numbers.

Model 1:   A person drives to a destination at a rate of forty-five miles per hour (mph) and returns over the same route, but with more traffic, at thirty mph. If the round trip takes two hours, how far is the destination?

Solution: Let x be the distance to the destination.

Use the formula $t = \frac{d}{r}$ (time = distance ÷ rate) since we know each rate and since we have assigned the variable x to the distance. The time going to the destination would then be $\frac{x}{45}$; the return trip time would be $\frac{x}{30}$. The total time for the round trip is 2 hours. Thus, the equation is $\frac{x}{45} + \frac{x}{30} = 2$.

The LCD is 90.

$$90 \left[\frac{x}{45} + \frac{x}{30} \right] = 90 \,[2]$$

$$\overset{2}{\cancel{90}} \left[\frac{x}{45} \right] + \overset{3}{\cancel{90}} \left[\frac{x}{30} \right] = 90 \,[2]$$

$$2x + 3x = 180$$

$$5x = 180$$

$$x = 36$$

∴ The destination is thirty-six miles away.

Check: The time going is $\frac{36}{45}$ (or $\frac{4}{5}$) of an hour, the time returning is

$\frac{36}{30}$ (or $\frac{6}{5}$) of an hour, and $\frac{4}{5} + \frac{6}{5}$ is $\frac{10}{5}$ or 2 hours for the

round trip.

Note: You may wish to organize the information in a table such as the one shown.

	DISTANCE (miles)	÷	RATE (mph)	=	TIME
GOING	x		45		$\frac{x}{45}$
RETURNING	x		30		$\frac{x}{30}$
ROUND TRIP					2

The equation is then set up from the TIME column.

Model 2:   Find two consecutive odd numbers such that the sum of two-sevenths of the smaller and one-third of the larger is equal to thirty-one.

Solution: When working with *consecutive* numbers (not specified as all even or all odd), you can use n for the first number, $n + 1$ for the next, $n + 2$ for the third, and so on.

If the first number n is even, then it is followed by an odd number $n + 1$; an even, $n + 2$; an odd, $n + 3$; and so on. Thus, the *consecutive even* numbers would be represented by n, $n + 2$, $n + 4$, and so on.

If the first number n is odd, then it is followed by an even number $n + 1$; an odd, $n + 2$; an even, $n + 3$; and so on. Thus, the *consecutive odd* numbers would be represented by n, $n + 2$, $n + 4$, and so on.

Let n and $n + 2$ be the two consecutive odd numbers. Two-sevenths of the smaller odd number is $\frac{2}{7}n$, and one third of the larger odd number is $\frac{1}{3}(n + 2)$. Thus, the equation is $\frac{2}{7}n + \frac{1}{3}(n + 2) = 31$.

The LCD is 21.

$$21\left[\frac{2}{7}n + \frac{1}{3}(n + 2)\right] = 21[31]$$

$$\overset{3}{\cancel{21}}\left[\frac{2}{7}n\right] + \overset{7}{\cancel{21}}\left[\frac{1}{3}(n + 2)\right] = 21[31]$$

$$6n + 7n + 14 = 651$$

$$13n = 637$$

$$n = 49$$

$$\text{and } n + 2 = 49 + 2 \text{ or } 51$$

∴   The consecutive odd numbers are forty-nine and fifty-one.

Check: $\frac{2}{7}$ of 49 is 14, $\frac{1}{3}$ of 51 is 17, and the sum of 14 + 17 is 31.

 Solve each problem. Show your work and circle your answer.

3.6   A person drives to a destination at a rate of thirty-five mph and returns over the same route at forty mph. How far is the destination if the round trip takes three hours?

3.7   Find two consecutive odd numbers such that the sum of one-fifth of the smaller and four-sevenths of the larger is equal to fifty-nine.

3.8   A person jogs a certain distance at a rate of five mph and gets a ride back over the same route at forty-five mph. How far did the person jog if the round trip takes two hours?

3.9   Find three consecutive even numbers such that the sum of one-half the smallest number, two-thirds the middle number, and three-fourths the largest number is thirty-five.

3.10   Three people together can do a certain job in three hours. If one of them can do the job in six hours and another can do it in ten hours, how long will the third person take to do the job alone?

3.11   Find three consecutive numbers such that the difference between the largest number and three-elevenths of the smallest number is thirty-four.

3.12   A person leaves home at 7:00 a.m. and drives to a destination at a rate of forty mph. After spending one hour at the destination, the person returns at a rate of twenty-five mph and arrives home at 2:30 p.m. How far is the trip to the destination?

The third set of word problems includes age problems and quotient-remainder problems. Age problems deal with finding the respective ages of people from information about them at various time periods. Quotient-remainder problems involve finding two numbers from clues about the way the numbers are related through division.

Model 1:   A boy is now one-fifth as old as his father, and in six years he will be one-third as old as his father is then. Find their present ages.

Solution:

Let f be the father's present age and let $\frac{1}{5} f$ be the boy's present age.

Two time periods must be considered in this problem: now, and six years from now when each person will be 6 years older than he is now. Using the preceding variable assignment for their present ages, the ages of the father and the boy in six years will be $f + 6$ and $\frac{1}{5} f + 6$, respectively.

The relationship of these future ages is that the boy will be one-third as old as his father is then. Thus, the equation is set up:

BOY'S AGE WILL BE $\frac{1}{3}$ OF FATHER'S AGE

$$\frac{1}{5}f + 6 \quad = \quad \frac{1}{3}(f + 6)$$

The LCD is 15.

$$15\left[\frac{1}{5}f + 6\right] = 15\left[\frac{1}{3}(f + 6)\right]$$

$$\overset{3}{\cancel{15}}\left[\frac{1}{\cancel{5}}f\right] + 15[6] = \overset{5}{\cancel{15}}\left[\frac{1}{\cancel{3}}(f + 6)\right]$$

$$3f + 90 = 5f + 30$$

$$-2f = -60$$

$$f = 30$$

$$\text{and } \frac{1}{5}f = \frac{1}{5} \cdot 30 \text{ or } 6$$

∴ The father is now thirty years old, and the boy is now six years old.

Check: For the present ages, 6 is $\frac{1}{5}$ of

30. In six years the father will

be 36, the boy will be 12, and

12 is $\frac{1}{3}$ of 36.

Note: You may wish to organize the information in a table:

	AGE NOW	AGE IN 6 YEARS
FATHER	f	$f + 6$
SON	$\frac{1}{5}f$	$\frac{1}{5}f + 6$

The equation is then set up from the AGE IN 6 YEARS column.

Model 2: The sum of two numbers is fifty-seven; and if the larger number is divided by the smaller number, the quotient is two and the remainder is six. Find the numbers.

Solution: If you know the sum of two numbers and what one of the numbers is, then you can find the other number by subtraction.

For example, if the sum of two numbers is 57 and one of them is 21, then the other number is 57 − 21 or 36. Similarly, if the sum of two numbers is 57 and one of them is n, then the other number is 57 − n. This result gives a way to assign the variable expressions for this type of problem.

Let n be the smaller number, and let 57 − n be the larger number.

For example, suppose you divide 29 by 8

to obtain a quotient of 3 and a

remainder of 5. The result is

the mixed number $3\frac{5}{8}$, and this

relationship can be written as

$\frac{29}{8} = 3 + \frac{5}{8}$. (Notice that the remainder is written over the divisor.)

Thus, the equation for the problem is

$\frac{57 - n}{n} = 2 + \frac{6}{n}$.

The LCD is n.

$n\left[\frac{57-n}{n}\right] = n\left[2 + \frac{6}{n}\right]$

$\not{n}\left[\frac{57-n}{\not{n}}\right] = n[2] + \not{n}\left[\frac{6}{\not{n}}\right]$

$57 - n = 2n + 6$

$-3n = -51$

$n = 17$

and $57 - n = 57 - 17$ or 40

∴ The numbers are seventeen and forty.

Check: The sum 40 + 17 is 57, and

$$17\overline{)40} \quad \begin{array}{l} 2 \leftarrow \text{QUOTIENT} \\ \underline{34} \\ 6 \leftarrow \text{REMAINDER.} \end{array}$$

Solve each problem. Show your work and circle your answer.

3.13   A girl is now one-third as old as her mother, and in three years she will be two-fifths as old as her mother is then. Find their present ages.

3.14   The sum of two numbers is sixty-five. If the larger number is divided by the smaller number, then the quotient is three and the remainder is five. Find the numbers.

3.15   A boy is now two-thirds as old as his sister, and two years ago he was five-eighths as old as she was then. Find their present ages.

3.16   The sum of two numbers is ninety-one. If the larger number is divided by the smaller number, then the quotient is fourteen and the remainder is one. Find the numbers.

3.17   Five years ago a girl was one-half as old as her brother was then, and now she is three years younger than he is. Find their present ages.

3.18   A tank can be filled by one pipe in four hours and by a second pipe in six hours; and when it is full, the tank can be drained by a third pipe in three hours. If the tank is empty and all three pipes are open, in how many hours will the tank be filled?

3.19   When four-sevenths of a number is subtracted from the number, the result is two less than one-half of that number. Find the number.

3.20   A person travels to a destination at a rate of fifty mph and returns the next day at a rate of forty mph. If the time returning is one hour more than the time going, how many miles are traveled in all?

3.21   A man is thirty years old, and his son is thirteen years old. In how many years will the son be three-fourths as old as his father?

3.22   A number is doubled, and then seven is added. When the result is divided by forty, the quotient is two and the remainder is thirty-three. Find the original number.

The last types of word problems in this LIFEPAC are ratio problems and mixture problems. Ratio problems require finding numbers from facts about the ratios they form with one another. Mixture problems deal with amounts of various substances to combine and produce mixtures with specific characteristics.

Model 1:　The ratio of the numerator to the denominator of a certain fraction is one to six. If four is added to the numerator and subtracted from the denominator, the new fraction reduces to one-fourth. Find the original fraction.

Solution:　A *ratio* is another form for a fraction, and the ratio of A to B is written $A{:}B$ or $\frac{A}{B}$. The ratio of the numerator to the denominator in this problem is 1:6 or $\frac{1}{6}$; however, this fact does not mean that the numerator must be 1 and the denominator 6. The fraction might be $\frac{2}{12}$ or $\frac{3}{18}$ or $\frac{1,000}{6,000}$ or any other fraction in the form $\frac{x}{6x}$ that reduces to $\frac{1}{6}$.

Let x be the numerator, and let $6x$ be the denominator; or let $\frac{x}{6x}$ be the original fraction.

Now we are to add 4 to the numerator and subtract 4 from the denominator to obtain the new fraction that is equal to

$\frac{1}{4}$. Thus, the equation is

$\frac{x+4}{6x-4} = \frac{1}{4}$.

Use cross-multiplication.

$$\frac{x+4}{6x-4} \diagdown \frac{1}{4} \quad \begin{array}{l} 6x-4 \\ 4x+16 \end{array}$$

$6x - 4 = 4x + 16$

$2x = 20$

$x = 10$

and $\frac{x}{6x} = \frac{10}{6 \cdot 10}$ or $\frac{10}{60}$

∴   The original fraction

is $\frac{10}{60}$. (DO NOT REDUCE THIS ANSWER!)

Check: The ratio of 10:60 is 1:6, and

$\frac{10+4}{60-4}$ is $\frac{14}{56}$ or $\frac{1}{4}$.

Model 2:   A mixture contains sixty ounces of glycol and water and is thirty per cent glycol.

1.   If the mixture is to be strengthened to forty per cent, how much glycol must be added?

2.   If the mixture is to be weakened to twenty per cent, how much water must be added?

Solutions: To solve either problem, we first need to find the number of ounces of glycol in 60 ounces of the 30% mixture:

30% of 60 = $\frac{30}{100} \cdot 60 = \frac{1,800}{100} = 18$

Thus, the ratio of glycol to total mixture

is $\frac{18}{60}$. This fraction is not reduced

since the mixture actually contains

18 oz. and 60 oz. of these liquids.

Part 1: Let a be the amount of glycol added.

The 18 ounces of glycol in the mixture will then be increased to $18 + a$, and the 60 ounces in the total mixture will be increased to $60 + a$. The new ratio of glycol to the total mixture is then $\frac{18 + a}{60 + a}$, and the problem states that this ratio is to be 40% $= \frac{40}{100} = \frac{2}{5}$. Thus, the equation is

$$\frac{18 + a}{60 + a} = \frac{2}{5}.$$

Use cross-multiplication.

$$\frac{18 + a}{60 + a} \underset{5}{\overset{2}{\times}} \begin{array}{l} 120 + 2a \\ 90 + 5a \end{array}$$

$$120 + 2a = 90 + 5a$$

$$-3a = -30$$

$$a = 10$$

∴ Adding ten ounces of glycol will strengthen the original mixture to forty per cent.

Check: $\frac{18 + 10}{60 + 10} = \frac{28}{70} = \frac{2}{5} = 40\%$

Part 2: Let w be the amount of water added.

The 18 ounces of glycol in the mixture will not be changed by adding water, but the 60 ounces in the total mixture will be increased to $60 + w$.

71

The new ratio of glycol to

the total mixture is then

$\frac{18}{60 + w}$, and this ratio is

to be 20% = $\frac{20}{100}$ = $\frac{1}{5}$. Thus,

the equation is $\frac{18}{60 + w}$ = $\frac{1}{5}$

Use cross-multiplication.

$$\frac{18}{60 + w} = \frac{1}{5} \quad \begin{array}{l} 60 + w \\ 90 \end{array}$$

$$60 + w = 90$$

$$w = 30$$

∴   Adding thirty ounces of water will weaken the original mixture to twenty per cent.

Check: $\frac{18}{60 + 30}$ = $\frac{18}{90}$ = 20%

Note: You should see that the ratios are set up in the form

$\frac{\text{AMOUNT OF GLYCOL}}{\text{AMOUNT OF TOTAL MIXTURE}}$ in

both the preceding equations.

▶▶▶   **Solve each problem. Show your work and circle your answers.**

3.23   The ratio of the numerator to the denominator of a certain fraction is one to four. If three is added to the numerator and subtracted from the denominator, the new fraction reduces to one-third. Find the original fraction.

3.24   A mixture contains forty ounces of glycol and water and is ten per cent glycol. If the mixture is to be strengthened to twenty-five per cent, how much glycol is to be added?

3.25   The ratio of the numerator to the denominator of a certain fraction is three to five. If two is added to the numerator and five is subtracted from the denominator, the new fraction reduces to four-fifths. Find the original fraction.

3.26   A mixture contains one-hundred ounces of glycol and water and is twenty-eight per cent glycol. If the mixture is to be weakened to twenty per cent, how much water must be added?

3.27   The numerator and the denominator of a certain fraction are consecutive odd numbers. If nine is subtracted from the numerator, then the ratio of the numerator to the denominator of the new fraction is two to three. Find the original fraction.

3.28   A mixture contains ninety-two ounces of glycol and water and is forty-five per cent glycol. If the mixture is to be weakened to thirty per cent, how much water must be added?

3.29   In a certain mixture, the ratio of glycol to water is five to three. If ten ounces of glycol are added to the mixture, it becomes seventy per cent glycol. How many ounces of glycol are in the original mixture?

3.30   One person can do a certain job in one-half hour, and another person can do the same job in one hour and ten minutes. How many minutes will they take to do the job together?

3.31   Find three consecutive numbers such that the sum of one-fourth the first and one-fifth the second is five less than one-seventh the third.

3.32   A person drives to a destination at a rate of thirty mph and returns over the same route at fifty mph. How far is the destination if the time returning is one hour less than the time going?

3.33   The present ages of a husband and wife are in the ratio of seven to six, and five years ago the ratio was six to five. Find their ages now.

3.34   The difference of two numbers is seventy-two. If the larger number is divided by the smaller number, then the quotient is seven and the remainder is six. Find the numbers.

3.35   The numerator and the denominator of a fraction are thirteen and fifty, respectively. When a certain number is added to this numerator and subtracted from this denominator, the resulting fraction has a numerator to denominator ratio of two to one. Find the number.

3.36 An automobile's radiator has a capacity of fifteen quarts, and it currently contains twelve quarts of a thirty per cent antifreeze solution.

a. How many quarts of pure antifreeze must be added to strengthen the solution to forty per cent?

b. If the radiator is filled to capacity with pure anti-freeze, what will be the strength (per cent) of this solution?

Before you take this last Self Test, you may want to do one or more of these self checks.

1. _____ Read the objectives. See if you can do them.
2. _____ Restudy the material related to any objectives that you cannot do.
3. _____ Use the SQ3R study procedure to review the material:
   a. **S**can the sections.
   b. **Q**uestion yourself again (review the questions you wrote initially).
   c. **R**ead to answer your questions.
   d. **R**ecite the answers to yourself.
   e. **R**eview areas you did not understand.
4. _____ Review all vocabulary, activities, and Self Tests, writing a correct answer for every wrong answer.

SELF TEST 3

Complete these items (each answer, 3 points).

3.01   Give the excluded value(s) for the fraction $\frac{7 - y}{y^2 + 7y}$.

3.02   Simplify the complex fraction $\dfrac{\frac{n}{3} - \frac{3}{n}}{1 + \frac{n}{3}}$.

3.03   Rewrite the formula $S = \frac{n}{2}(a + l)$ with l as the subject.

Perform the indicated operations (each answer, 4 points).

3.04 $\dfrac{2a + 1}{3a} + \dfrac{5}{4} - \dfrac{2a - 3}{6a^2}$

3.05 $\quad \dfrac{2x^3}{2y^2 - 7y - 4} \div \dfrac{6x^5}{x^2 - y^2} \cdot \dfrac{12 - 3y}{x - y}$

_____

Solve each equation for k (each answer, 3 points).

3.06 $\quad \dfrac{9}{2k - 3} = \dfrac{4}{k + 1}$

_____

3.07 $\quad \dfrac{a}{b} = \dfrac{b}{a} + \dfrac{1}{k}$

_____

Solve each inequality (each answer, 3 points).

3.08 $\quad \dfrac{x}{3} - \dfrac{x - 1}{2} \geq 1$

_____

3.09 (Optional)

$$\frac{8}{y-2} - 3 < \frac{5}{y-2}$$

———————

Solve each problem. Show your work and circle your answer (each answer, 5 points).

3.010 Two people together can do a certain job in twenty minutes. If one of them can do the job alone in forty-five minutes, how long will the other person take to do the job alone?

3.011 The sum of two-thirds of a number and one-fourth of the number exceeds five-sixths of that number by two. Find the number.

3.012   A boy has planned a three-hour bicycle ride. After biking at a rate of fourteen mph for awhile, the bike breaks down and he rides back with his father at a rate of thirty-five mph. How far did the boy ride his bicycle if he returns home one hour after he left?

3.013   Find two consecutive even numbers such that the difference of one-half the larger and two-fifths the smaller is equal to five.

3.014   A girl is now one-fourth as old as her father, and in seven years she will be one-half as old as her father was twelve years ago. Find their present ages.

3.015   The sum of two numbers is eighty-three. If the larger number is divided by the smaller number, then both the quotient and the remainder are six. Find the numbers.

3.016   The ratio of the numerator to the denominator of a certain fraction is five to eight. If five is subtracted from the numerator and four is added to the denominator, the new fraction reduces to one-half. Find the original fraction.

3.017   A mixture contains five quarts of acid and water and is forty per cent acid. If the mixture is to be weakened to thirty per cent, how much water must be added?

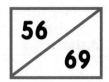

Before taking the LIFEPAC Test, you may want to do one or more of these self checks.

1. _____ Read the objectives. See if you can do them.

2. _____ Restudy the material related to any objectives that you cannot do.

3. _____ Use the SQ3R study procedure to review the material.

4. _____ Review activities, Self Tests, and LIFEPAC vocabulary words.

5. _____ Restudy areas of weakness indicated by the last Self Test.

GLOSSARY

algebraic fraction —
An indicated quotient of two polynomials written in the form $\frac{A}{B}$.

complex fraction —
A fraction that has at least one fraction in its own numerator or denominator.

consecutive numbers —
Integers that can be represented by n, $n + 1$, $n + 2$, $n + 3$, and so on; if all even (or all odd), they can be represented by n, $n + 2$, $n + 4$, $n + 6$, and so on.

cross-multiplication —
A procedure used to multiply diagonally across the equal sign of an equation of the form $\frac{A}{B} = \frac{C}{D}$; the result is $AD = BC$.

equivalent fraction —
The result of multiplying or dividing both the numerator and the denominator of a fraction by the same nonzero value.

excluded value —
Any value that would result in zero in the denominator of a fraction.

formula —
An equation that expresses some relationship among certain quantities in mathematics or business or science.

glycol —
A chemical used in making solvent, automobile antifreeze, and printing ink.

invert —
To replace a fraction with its reciprocal.

least common denominator (LCD) —
The smallest value into which each denominator of a group of fractions can be divided exactly.

literal equation —
An equation containing letters in which one letter is treated as a variable and any other letter is treated as a constant.

ratio —
An indicated quotient written in the form $A{:}B$ or $\frac{A}{B}$.

reciprocals —
Two fractions whose product is the number 1; the reciprocal of $\frac{A}{B}$ is $\frac{B}{A}$.

reduce to lowest terms —
To convert a fraction to an equivalent one with numerator and denominator that have a greatest common factor of 1.

root —
A value that makes an open sentence true.

subject —
The letter for which a formula is solved.

term —
When a fraction is in the form $\frac{A}{B}$, A and B are the terms of the fraction.

variable assignment —
A written indication of what a letter or a literal expression represents in the set-up of a verbal problem.

MATHEMATICS 907
RADICAL EXPRESSIONS

CONTENTS

I. REAL NUMBERS 2

Rational Numbers 2

Irrational Numbers 20

Completeness 25

II. OPERATIONS 32

Simplifying Radicals 32

Combining Radicals 45

Multiplying Radicals 53

Dividing Radicals 60

III. EQUATIONS 68

Solving for Irrational Roots 68

Solving Radical Equations 77

Author: **Arthur C. Landrey, M.A.Ed.**
Editor-in-Chief: Richard W. Wheeler, M.A.Ed.
Editor: Robin Hintze Kreutzberg, M.B.A.
Consulting Editor: Robert L. Zenor, M.A., M.S.
Revision Editor: Alan Christopherson, M.S.

Alpha Omega Publications®

804 N. 2nd Ave. E., Rock Rapids, IA 51246-1759

MATHEMATICS 907
RADICAL EXPRESSIONS

In this LIFEPAC® you will continue your study in the mathematical system of algebra by learning first about *real numbers* and then about *radical expressions*. After becoming familiar with radical expressions, you will learn to simplify them and to perform the four basic operations (addition, subtraction, multiplication, and division) with them. Finally, you will learn to solve equations containing these expressions.

OBJECTIVES

Read these objectives. The objectives tell you what you will be able to do when you have successfully completed this LIFEPAC.

When you have finished this LIFEPAC, you should be able to:

1. Identify and work with rational numbers.

2. Identify and work with irrational numbers.

3. Draw number-line graphs of open sentences involving real numbers.

4. Simplify radical expressions.

5. Combine (add and subtract) radical expressions.

6. Multiply radical expressions.

7. Divide radical expressions.

8. Solve equations having irrational roots.

9. Solve equations containing radical expressions.

Survey the LIFEPAC. Ask yourself some questions about this study. Write your questions here.

_____

_____

_____

_____

_____

_____

OBJECTIVES

When you have completed this section, you should be able to:

1. Identify and work with rational numbers.

2. Identify and work with irrational numbers.

3. Draw number-line graphs of open sentences involving real numbers.

In this section, you will study the fundamental set of numbers for beginning algebra and geometry—the *real numbers*. You will learn about two other sets, the *rational numbers* and the *irrational numbers*, that make up the real numbers. You will also learn a new property that applies to no other numbers you have studied so far—*completeness*; this property will be used in graphing the real numbers.

RATIONAL NUMBERS

You will begin by classifying some numbers that you are quite familiar with already. You will need to discover what numbers are actually included in this classification according to the definition. Conversion between the different forms that a rational number may take should help to understand the classification better. Then you will be ready to graph rational numbers and study their properties.

DEFINITIONS AND CONVERSIONS

The following definition outlines the classification of numbers known as rational numbers.

DEFINITION

A *rational number* is a number that can be written as a ratio of two integers in the form $\frac{A}{B}$ with $B \neq 0$.

Model 1: $\frac{2}{9}$ is a rational number since it is the ratio

of the integers 2 and 9.

Model 2: $4\frac{1}{5}$ is a rational number since it can be written as $\frac{21}{5}$, the ratio of the integers 21 and 5.

Model 3: $-\frac{3}{8}$ is a rational number since it can be written as $\frac{-3}{8}$, the ratio of the integers -3 and 8.

Model 4: 0.283 is a rational number since it can be written as $\frac{283}{1,000}$, the ratio of the integers 283 and 1,000.

Model 5: -81.7 is a rational number since it can be written as $-81\frac{7}{10} = -\frac{817}{10} = \frac{817}{-10}$, the ratio of the integers 817 and -10.

Model 6: 17 is a rational number since it can be written as $\frac{17}{1}$, the ratio of the integers 17 and 1.

Model 7: 0 is a rational number since it can be written as $\frac{0}{1}$, the ratio of the integers 0 and 1.

Model 8: -6 is a rational number since it can be written as $-\frac{6}{1} = \frac{-6}{1}$, the ratio of the integers -6 and 1.

From the models, you can see that the common fractions, mixed numbers, and decimals of arithmetic (as well as their negatives) are included in the rational numbers. Also, you can see that the integers themselves are included in the rational numbers.

You may be wondering which numbers are *not* included in this classification. Such numbers will be considered in detail later in this section, but at the present time you should know that not all decimals are rational and not all fractions are rational. For example, a number that you have probably worked with, π, cannot be written as the ratio of two integers and is not rational; therefore, neither is a fraction such as $\frac{\pi}{6}$ rational. You may have used an *approximation* for π , such as 3.14 or $\frac{22}{7}$, in evaluating formulas. These approximations are themselves rational, but π is not!

A fraction that is rational can be converted to an equivalent decimal form, and a decimal that is rational can be converted to an equivalent fraction form. The two equivalent forms, of course, must have the same sign.

Model 1:   Convert $\frac{5}{8}$ and $-\frac{5}{8}$ to decimals.

   Solution: $\frac{5}{8} = 5 \div 8 = 0.625$,

   a *terminating* decimal.

   $\therefore \quad \frac{5}{8} = 0.625$ and $-\frac{5}{8} = -0.625$

Model 2:   Convert -0.24 to a fraction.

   Solution: $-0.24 = -\frac{24}{100} = -\frac{4 \cdot 6}{4 \cdot 25}$

   $\therefore \quad -0.24 = -\frac{6}{25}$

Model 3:   Convert $\frac{1}{3}$ to a decimal.

   Solution: $\frac{1}{3} = 1 \div 3 = 0.3333...$,

   a *repeating* decimal.

   $\therefore \quad \frac{1}{3} = .0\overline{3}$

The decimal $0.\overline{3}$ is said to have a *period* of 1 since one number place continues without end; the decimal $-0.363636... = -0.\overline{36}$ has a period of 2 since two number places continue without end. The line drawn above a repeating decimal is called the *repetend bar*, and it should be over the exact number of places in the period of the decimal.

Models: $0.12341234... = 0.\overline{1234}$ and has a period of 4.

$0.12343434... = 0.12\overline{34}$ and has a period of 2.

$0.12344444... = 0.123\overline{4}$ and has a period of 1.

We saw that the rational number $\frac{1}{3}$ converts to $0.\overline{3}$, but how does $0.\overline{3}$ convert back to $\frac{1}{3}$? The decimal 0.3 converts to $\frac{3}{10}$, but $\frac{1}{3} \neq \frac{3}{10}$; thus, $0.\overline{3} \neq \frac{3}{10}$ either. The following solutions show a procedure for converting repeating decimals to fractions.

Model 1:   Convert $0.\overline{3}$ to a fraction.

Solution: Let $n = 0.\overline{3} = 0.333...$

Then $10n = 10(0.333...) = 3.33...$, since multiplying a decimal by ten moves the decimal point one place to the right.

Now subtract: $10n = 3.33...$

$\underline{\quad 1n = 0.33... \quad}$

$9n = 3.00...$

or $9n = 3$

and $n = \frac{3}{9}$ or $\dfrac{\cancel{3} \cdot 1}{\cancel{3} \cdot 3}$

$\therefore 0.\overline{3} = \frac{1}{3}$

(Note: The period of $0.\overline{3}$ is 1, and n is multiplied by $10^1 = 10$.)

Model 2:   Convert $-0.\overline{36}$ to a fraction.

Solution: Since the given decimal is negative, its equivalent fraction will

be negative also.

Let $n = 0.\overline{36} = 0.363636...$

Then $100n = 100(0.363636...) = 36.3636...$ since multiplying

a decimal by one hundred moves the decimal point two places to

the right.

Now subtract: $100n = 36.3636...$

$$\begin{array}{r} 1n = 0.3636... \\ \hline 99n = 36.0000... \end{array}$$

or $99n = 36$

and $n = \dfrac{36}{99}$ or $\dfrac{\cancel{9} \cdot 4}{\cancel{9} \cdot 11}$

$\therefore$ Since $0.\overline{36} = \dfrac{4}{11}$, then $-0.\overline{36} = -\dfrac{4}{11}$.

(Note: The period of $0.\overline{36}$ is 2, and n is multiplied by $10^2 = 100$.)

Some other results of this procedure are shown in the following models. Try to find a relationship between the repeating decimal, its period, and its equivalent unreduced fraction.

Models: $0.\overline{1} = \dfrac{1}{9}$ $0.\overline{01} = \dfrac{1}{99}$ $0.\overline{001} = \dfrac{1}{999}$

$0.\overline{5} = \dfrac{5}{9}$ $0.\overline{53} = \dfrac{53}{99}$ $0.\overline{531} = \dfrac{531}{999} = \dfrac{59}{111}$

You have seen that a repeating decimal as well as a terminating decimal can be written as the ratio of two integers in the form $\dfrac{A}{B}$; both types then are rational numbers. Actually, a terminating decimal is just a special type of repeating decimal—one that repeats zero; for example, $0.815 = 0.815000...$ and $-5.3 = -5.3000....$ Keeping this fact in mind, consider the following alternate definition and see how it applies to the models from the beginning of this section.

DEFINITION

A *rational number* is a number that can be written as a repeating decimal.

Models: $\frac{2}{9} = 0.\overline{2}$

$4\frac{1}{5} = 4.20\overline{0}$

$-\frac{3}{8} = -0.3750\overline{0}$

$0.283 = 0.2830\overline{0}$

$-81.7 = -81.70\overline{0}$

$17 = 17.\overline{0}$

$0 = 0.\overline{0}$

$-6 = -6.\overline{0}$

 Write each rational number as the ratio of two integers in the form $\frac{A}{B}$ **and then as a repeating decimal.**

Model: $4.3 = \frac{43}{10} = 4.30\overline{0}$

1.1 $\frac{3}{4}$ = _____ = _____

1.2 $-7\frac{1}{3}$ = _____ = _____

1.3 $8\frac{1}{2}$ = _____ = _____

1.4   -6.59   = _____ = _____

1.5   10   = _____ = _____

 Convert each fraction to its equivalent decimal form.

1.6 $\frac{3}{5}$ = _____   1.7 $\frac{33}{50}$ = _____

7

1.8 $\frac{2}{3}$ = _____   1.12 $-\frac{52}{125}$ = _____

1.9 $\frac{1}{15}$ = _____   1.13 $-\frac{5}{12}$ = _____

1.10 $\frac{20}{33}$ = _____   1.14 $-\frac{12}{5}$ = _____

1.11 $-\frac{83}{200}$ = _____   1.15 $-\frac{21}{37}$ = _____

 Convert each decimal to its equivalent reduced fraction form.

1.16   0.7   = _____   1.22   -0.63   = _____

1.17 $0.\overline{7}$ = _____   1.23 $-0.\overline{63}$ = _____

1.18   -0.8   = _____   1.24   0.135   = _____

1.19 $-0.\overline{8}$ = _____   1.25 $0.\overline{135}$ = _____

1.20   0.25   = _____   1.26   0.9   = _____

1.21 $0.\overline{25}$ = _____   1.27 $0.\overline{9}$ = _____

Model: $.2\overline{5}$

Solution: Let $n = 0.2\overline{5} = 0.25555...$

Then $10n = 2.55...$ and $100n = 25.55...$

Now subtract: $100n = 25.55...$

$$\underline{10n = 2.55...}$$

$$90n = 23.00...$$

or $90n = 23$

and $n = \frac{23}{90}$

$\therefore 0.2\overline{5} = \frac{23}{90}$

Convert each decimal to its equivalent reduced fraction form. Show your work as in the preceding model.

1.28 $0.8\overline{7}$

1.29 $-0.3\overline{8}$

1.30 $0.0\overline{9}$

GRAPHS AND ORDER

Now that rational numbers have been explained, you should be able to graph them on the number line. First, however, a review of some of the basic ideas of graphing may be helpful.

The small vertical line segments drawn on the number line are only reference marks (not graphed points); and the spacing between them, as well as the numbers written below them, may be changed for convenience in graphing.

Models:

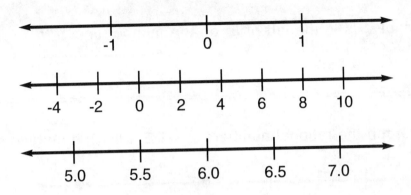

All three lines shown can be thought of as the same number line, but with different reference marks; no points are graphed on these lines.

A point is graphed on the number line by placing a heavy dot on (or between) the appropriate reference mark(s). A darkened arrowhead is used at the end(s) of the line represented on the paper to show a continuation of points.

Model 1:   The graph of the integers is shown.

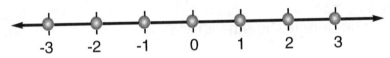

Model 2:   The graph of the odd integers larger than -2 is shown.

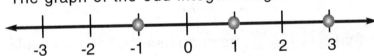

You have already learned that all the integers are rational numbers since each can be written as the ratio of itself to 1 and as a decimal that repeats zero. From the graph, the order of the integers can be seen to be ...-3 < -2 < -1 < 0 < 1 < 2 < 3...; that is, an integer is less than another integer if it is to the left of the other integer on the number line.

Although infinitely many integers are in the rational numbers, infinitely many nonintegers are also rational, such as $1\frac{1}{4}$ and $-0.\overline{56}$. A nonintegral rational number that would be between two reference marks on the number line is graphed by placing a heavy dot on the approximate corresponding point and writing the number above the dot. The *order* of both integral and nonintegral rational numbers can be determined from the relative positions of their points on the line.

10

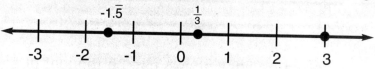

Model 1: Graph the rational numbers $\frac{1}{3}$, $-1.\overline{5}$, and 3; then give their order.

Solution:

$-1.\overline{5} < \frac{1}{3} < 3$ is their order.

Model 2: Graph the rational numbers $1\frac{7}{10}$, 0, $-\frac{1}{2}$, and $1\frac{5}{8}$; then give their order.

Solution: You can easily graph 0 and $-\frac{1}{2}$ and determine their order; you can also see that they are less than the other two numbers, which lie between 1 and 2. But which of the two positive numbers is the smaller?

If the fractions are written with a positive common denominator, then the numerators can be compared. Since $\frac{7}{10}\left(\frac{4}{4}\right) = \frac{28}{40}$ and $\frac{5}{8}\left(\frac{5}{5}\right) = \frac{25}{40}$, you can see that $1\frac{5}{8}$ is smaller than $1\frac{7}{10}$. Thus, the numbers can be graphed in order.

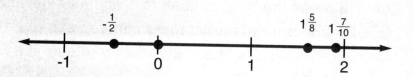

$-\frac{1}{2} < 0 < 1\frac{5}{8} < 1\frac{7}{10}$ is their order.

In many cases, fractions may be more quickly converted to their equivalent decimal forms (rather than written with a common denominator) when finding their order. For example, in the preceding model $1\frac{7}{10} = 1.7$, $1\frac{5}{8} = 1.625$, and $1.625 < 1.7$; therefore, $1\frac{5}{8} < 1\frac{7}{10}$.

Model 3:   Give the order of the rational numbers $5.\overline{6}$, $\frac{28}{5}$, $5\frac{5}{6}$, and 5.7.

Solution: The decimal forms are $5.\overline{6}$, $\frac{28}{5} = 5.6$, $5\frac{5}{6} = 5.8\overline{3}$, and 5.7, respectively; and $5.6 < 5.\overline{6} < 5.7 < 5.8\overline{3}$.

∴ The order is $\frac{28}{5} < 5.\overline{6} < 5.7 < 5\frac{5}{6}$.

Model 4:   Give the order of the rational numbers -2, $-\frac{19}{10}$, $-(1.4)^2$, and $-2\frac{1}{99}$.

Solution: The decimal forms are $-2 = -2.\overline{0}$, $-\frac{19}{10} = -1.9$, $-(1.4)^2 = -1.96$, and $-2\frac{1}{99} = -2.\overline{01}$, respectively; and $-2.\overline{01} < -2.\overline{0} < -1.96 < -1.9$.

∴ The order is $-2\frac{1}{99} < -2 < -(1.4)^2 < -\frac{19}{10}$.

Using a number line may be helpful in ordering negative decimal numbers such as the ones in this model.

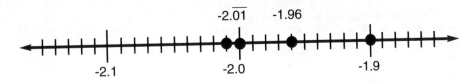

 Graph the rational numbers indicated and give their order (smallest to largest) in each case.

1.31   The positive even integers

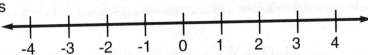

Order: _____

1.32 3.5, -2.3, 0

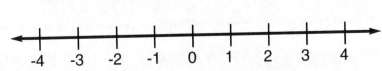

Order: _____

1.33 $-\frac{3}{4}$, -3, $1\frac{1}{2}$, $1\frac{2}{3}$

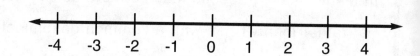

Order: _____

1.34 $2.\overline{8}$, -1.5, 0.7, -0.7

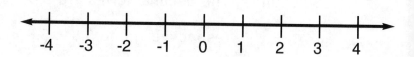

Order: _____

1.35 $\frac{1}{5}$, 3.2, $-1\frac{2}{3}$, -2

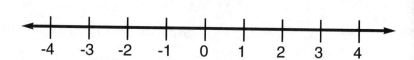

Order: _____

 Give the order of the rational numbers in each case.

1.36 $2.\overline{5}$, $\frac{5}{2}$, 2.6   _____

1.37   -4.1, $-\frac{103}{25}$, $-(1.9)^2$ _____

1.38 $1\frac{2}{3}$, $(1.3)^2$, $\frac{8}{5}$, $1\frac{13}{20}$ _____

1.39   0, -0.1, 0.1, $-0.\overline{1}$ _____

1.40 $8\frac{3}{11}$, $\frac{25}{3}$, 8.3, $8.\overline{30}$ _____

PROPERTIES

The fact that the rational numbers include nonintegers as well as integers results in their having additional properties. For example, the rational numbers are *closed* under defined division, but the integers are not.

Model: The quotient of -4 and 5 is -4 ÷ 5 = $-\frac{4}{5}$ or -0.8, which is rational even though it is not an integer.

Both the integers and the rational numbers are closed under the operations of addition, subtraction, and multiplication.

Also, only in some instances can you find an integer between two integers; but in all instances you can find a rational number between two rational numbers. Thus, the rational numbers are *dense*; but the integers are not.

Model: Between the integers -2 and 3, you can find the integers -1, 0, 1, and 2.

Between the integers 9 and 10, you cannot find another integer.

Between the rational numbers 9 and 10, you can find rational numbers such as 9.001, $9\frac{1}{2}$, $\frac{68}{7}$, and $9.\overline{8}$.

One such rational number X that can easily be found between A and B is their average: $\frac{A + B}{2}$. On the number line, the point that corresponds to $\frac{A + B}{2}$ is midway between the points corresponding to A and B.

Model: Start with the rational numbers 0 and 1; between them is their average, $\frac{0 + 1}{2}$ or $\frac{1}{2}$.

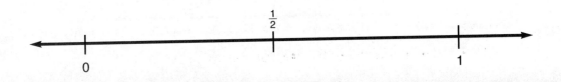

Between $\frac{1}{2}$ and 1 is their average:

$$\frac{\frac{1}{2}+1}{2} \text{ or } \frac{\frac{3}{2}}{2} \text{ or } \frac{3}{4}$$

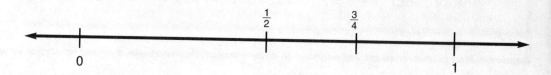

Between $\frac{3}{4}$ and 1 is their average:

$$\frac{\frac{3}{4}+1}{2} \text{ or } \frac{\frac{7}{4}}{2} \text{ or } \frac{7}{8}$$

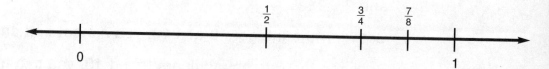

Between $\frac{7}{8}$ and 1 is their average:

$$\frac{\frac{7}{8}+1}{2} \text{ or } \frac{\frac{15}{8}}{2} \text{ or } \frac{15}{16}.$$ This process can be continued without end.

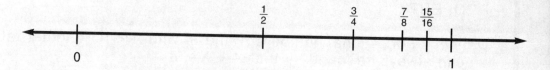

Thus, infinitely many rational numbers occur between 0 and 1. (Do you think this statement is true for any rational numbers A and B?)

Of course, other rational numbers are between A and B beside their average. The following models will show how the number line can be used to help in finding such numbers. You will need to understand one basic idea first: the distance between two points on the number line is the difference between the numbers (larger minus smaller) corresponding to those points.

For example, on the number line shown below, the distance from A to B is $B - A$; the distance from A to X is $X - A$; and the distance from X to B is $B - X$.

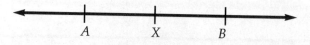

Model: 1:   Find the number two-thirds of the way between 10 and 70.

Solution: We are trying to find X on the number line shown.

The distance from 10 to 70 is 70 − 10 or 60.

The distance from 10 to X is X − 10.

The distance from 10 to X is $\frac{2}{3}$ of the distance from 10 to 70; thus, the equation is

$$X - 10 = \frac{2}{3} \bullet 60$$

Solve for X: $X - 10 = \frac{2}{3} \bullet \overset{20}{6\!\!\!/0}$

$$X - 10 = 40$$

$$X = 50$$

∴ 50 is two-thirds of the way between 10 and 70.

Model 2:   Find the number three-fifths of the way between $1\frac{1}{3}$ and $2\frac{1}{4}$.

Solution: We are trying to find X on the number line shown.

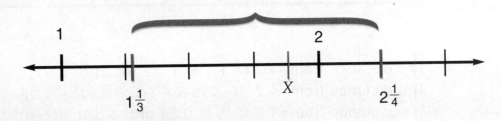

The distance from $1\frac{1}{3}$ to $2\frac{1}{4}$ is $2\frac{1}{4}$ − $1\frac{1}{3}$ or $\frac{11}{12}$.

The distance from $1\frac{1}{3}$ to X is $X - 1\frac{1}{3}$ or $X - \frac{4}{3}$.

The distance from $1\frac{1}{3}$ to X is $\frac{3}{5}$ of the distance from $1\frac{1}{3}$ to $2\frac{1}{4}$; thus, the equation is

$$X - \frac{4}{3} = \frac{3}{5} \cdot \frac{11}{12}$$

Solve for X:
$$X - \frac{4}{3} = \frac{\cancel{3}}{5} \cdot \frac{11}{\cancel{12}_4}$$

$$X - \frac{4}{3} = \frac{11}{20}$$

The LCD is 60.

$$60[X - \frac{4}{3}] = 60 \,[\overset{3}{\cancel{\frac{11}{20}}}]$$

$$60X - 80 = 33$$

$$60X = 113$$

$$X = \frac{113}{60} \text{ or } 1\frac{53}{60}$$

∴ $1\frac{53}{60}$ is three-fifths of the way between $1\frac{1}{3}$ and $2\frac{1}{4}$.

Model 3: Find the number 0.28 of the way between -4.2 and 1.7.

Solution: We are trying to find X on the number line shown.

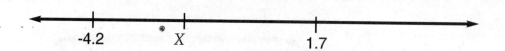

The distance from -4.2 to 1.7 is $1.7 - (-4.2)$ or 5.9.
The distance from -4.2 to X is $X - (-4.2)$ or $X + 4.2$.
The distance from -4.2 to X is 0.28 of the distance from -4.2 to 1.7; thus, the equation is

$$X + 4.2 = 0.28(5.9)$$
Solve for X:
$$X + 4.2 = 1.652$$
$$X = -2.548$$

∴ -2.548 is 0.28 of the way between -4.2 and 1.7.

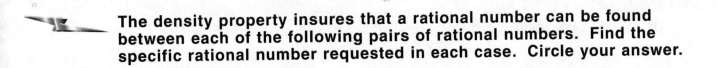

The density property insures that a rational number can be found between each of the following pairs of rational numbers. Find the specific rational number requested in each case. Circle your answer.

1.41   One-fourth of the way between 67 and 83.

1.42   Five-sixths of the way between -12 and 18.

1.43   0.4 of the way between 15 and 50.

1.44   0.61 of the way between -20 and -10.

1.45   One-third of the way between $1\frac{1}{4}$ and $2\frac{3}{4}$.

1.46   Two-sevenths of the way between 3.36 and 3.5.

1.47   0.75 of the way between 0 and 10.

1.48   0.75 of the way between -10 and 0.

1.49   Three-eighths of the way between -3 and 9.

1.50   Midway between 1.79 and 5.33.

You have learned that a rational number has an infinite decimal representation that repeats, and you have worked only with these numbers so far in this LIFEPAC. Now you will observe some numbers that are not included in the rational classification. Square roots often fit this description, as you will see. Graphs of these numbers will also be shown.

DEFINITIONS AND ROUNDING

The following definition outlines the classification of numbers that are *not* rational numbers and are, therefore, called *irrational* numbers.

DEFINITION

An *irrational number* is a number with an infinite decimal representation that does not repeat.

Model 1:   0.10110111011110... is an irrational number since its infinite decimal does not repeat; it would continue with five 1's and a 0, then six 1's and a 0, and so on.

Model 2:   -1.23456789101112... is an irrational number since its infinite decimal does not repeat; it would continue with the digits 13, then 14, and then 15, and so on.

At no time in either of these models could a portion of the decimal representation be written under a repetend bar.

Although the two preceding models may not be very useful irrational numbers, they do illustrate ways in which nonrepeating decimals can be formed. And since such decimals could be formed without limit, you should see that infinitely many irrational numbers exist just as infinitely many rational numbers exist.

One very important irrational number, π, was mentioned earlier in this section. The number π is the ratio of the circumference of a circle to the diameter, and it is found in many area and volume formulas. The nonrepeating decimal representation of π is 3.1415926..., and this number can be rounded to a rational approximation of any desired accuracy for use in evaluating formulas.

The rules for rounding decimals, whether rational or irrational, are given for you to follow.

1. When rounding to a certain number of places, look at the digit immediately after the last decimal place to be kept.

2. If this digit is 0, 1, 2, 3, or 4, leave the last place to be kept as it is and drop all the remaining digits.

3. If this next digit is 5, 6, 7, 8, or 9, add 1 to the last place to be kept and drop all the remaining digits.

Model:

$$\pi = 3.1415926\ldots$$

To the nearest tenth or to one decimal place, $\pi \doteq 3.1$ since the next digit is 4. (The symbol $\doteq$ means "is approximately equal to.")

To the nearest hundredth or to two decimal places, $\pi \doteq 3.14$ since the next digit is 1.

To the nearest thousandth or to three decimal places, $\pi \doteq 3.142$ since the next digit is 5.

To the nearest ten-thousandth or to four decimal places, $\pi \doteq 3.1416$ since the next digit is 9.

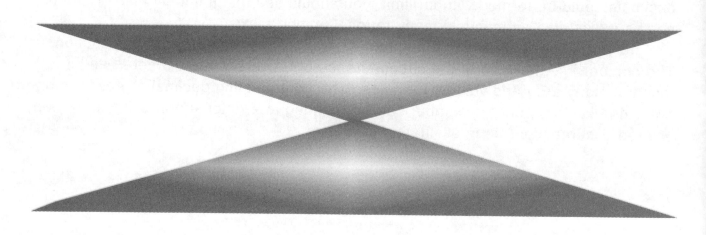

a. Tell whether each of the following infinite decimals indicates a rational or irrational number.

b. If the number is rational, write it using a repetend bar; then round every number to the nearest hundredth.

Models: -0.783783783...   a. <u>rational</u>   b. <u>-0.$\overline{783}$ $\doteq$ -0.78</u>

            51.626626662...   a. <u>irrational</u>   b. <u>$\doteq$ 51.63</u>

1.51   4.617617617...   a. _____   b. _____

1.52   -7.6544444...   a. _____   b. _____

1.53   -0.353353335...   a. _____   b. _____

1.54   573.19999...   a. _____   b. _____

1.55   0.2468101214...   a. _____   b. _____

1.56   -13.060060006...   a. _____   b. _____

1.57   -13.60606060...   a. _____   b. _____

1.58   25.2627282930...   a. _____   b. _____

1.59   -3.838838883...   a. _____   b. _____

1.60   99.999099909990...   a. _____   b. _____

SQUARE ROOTS

Suppose that we wish to find the positive number whose square is 30. Since $5^2 = 25$ and $6^2 = 36$, the number must be between 5 and 6. Use a calculator to verify the square of each of the following numbers.

$$(5.1)^2 = 26.01$$
$$(5.2)^2 = 27.04$$
$$(5.3)^2 = 28.09$$
$$(5.4)^2 = 29.16$$
$$(5.5)^2 = 30.25$$

Now since $29.16 < 30 < 30.25$, we can conclude that the number must be between 5.4 and 5.5. Continuing to try squares in this way, we can obtain the hundredths place, then the thousandths place, and so on of the desired decimal number, as shown on the next page.

$$(5.47)^2 = 29.9209$$
$$(5.477)^2 = 29.997529$$
$$(5.4772)^2 = 29.99971984$$
$$(5.47722)^2 = 29.9999389284$$
$$\vdots$$

This sequence of squares gets closer and closer to 30, but will never reach exactly 30. The number we are looking for is an infinite nonrepeating decimal known as the positive *square root* of 30; this irrational number is written as

$$\sqrt{30} = 5.47722557\ldots.$$

Use the $\sqrt{}$ key on a calculator to verify this result.

The negative square root of 30 is written as

$$-\sqrt{30} = -5.47722557\ldots;$$

this statement is true since $(-5.47722557\ldots)^2 = 30$. However, $\sqrt{-30}$ will have no meaning for us at this time since no rational or irrational number will square to yield a negative number.

The following list contains the positive square roots of the first ten counting numbers.

$$\sqrt{1} = 1 \qquad\qquad \sqrt{6} = 2.44948974\ldots$$

$$\sqrt{2} = 1.41421356\ldots \qquad\qquad \sqrt{7} = 2.64575131\ldots$$

$$\sqrt{3} = 1.73205080\ldots \qquad\qquad \sqrt{8} = 2.82842712\ldots$$

$$\sqrt{4} = 2 \qquad\qquad \sqrt{9} = 3$$

$$\sqrt{5} = 2.23606797\ldots \qquad\qquad \sqrt{10} = 3.1622776\ldots$$

From this list you can see that not all indicated square roots are irrational; square roots of numbers having two equal rational factors are themselves rational.

Model 1: $11^2 = 121$;

$\sqrt{121} = 11$ is rational.

Model 2: $\left(\frac{7}{9}\right)^2 = \frac{49}{81}$;

$\sqrt{\frac{49}{81}} = \frac{7}{9}$ is rational.

Model 3: $(1.04)^2 = 1.0816$;

$\sqrt{1.0816} = 1.04$ is rational.

Model 4: $(6.\overline{3})^2 = 40.\overline{1}$;

$\sqrt{40.\overline{1}} = 6.\overline{3}$ is rational.

23

a. Find each of the following square roots, using a calculator when necessary; b. then indicate whether each is rational or irrational.

1.61 $\sqrt{25}$ a._____   b._____

1.62 $\sqrt{26}$ a._____   b._____

1.63 $\sqrt{\dfrac{4}{9}}$ a._____   b._____

1.64 $\sqrt{32.\overline{1}}$ a._____   b._____

1.65 $\sqrt{32.1}$ a._____   b._____

1.66 $\sqrt{1.522756}$ a._____   b._____

1.67 $\sqrt{400}$ a._____   b._____

1.68 $\sqrt{4,000}$ a._____   b._____

1.69 $\sqrt{0.04}$ a._____   b._____

1.70 $\sqrt{\dfrac{1}{64}}$ a._____   b._____

GRAPHS AND ORDER

An irrational number can be graphed on the number line by placing a heavy dot on the approximate corresponding point and writing the number above the dot.

Model: The graph of π is shown.

The order of irrational numbers can be determined by observing the relative positions of their points on the number line, or by comparing their decimal representations, or both.

Model: Give the order of the irrational numbers -3.010010001…,

-$\sqrt{10}$, and -π.

Solution: The decimal representations are -3.010010001…,

-$\sqrt{10}$ = -3.1622776…, and -π = -3.1415926…, respectively;

and -3.1622776… < -3.1415926… < -3.010010001….

On the number line,

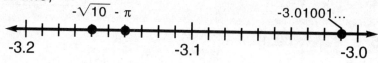

∴ The order is -$\sqrt{10}$ < -π < -3.010010001…

Graph each irrational number on the given number line.

1.71 $\sqrt{17}$

1.72   -$\sqrt{18}$

1.73 $\frac{\pi}{2}$

1.74   -2.818818881…

Give the order of the preceding four irrational numbers (1.71 through 1.74).

1.75   _____ < _____ < _____ < _____

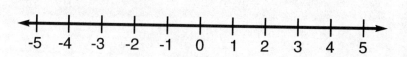 COMPLETENESS

Consider the numbers that are between -2 and 3, inclusive. If we want only counting numbers, then the graph is Figure 1; if we want whole numbers, then the graph is Figure 2; and if we want integers, then the graph is Figure 3.

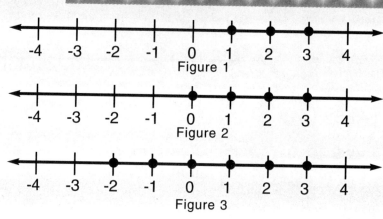

Figure 1

Figure 2

Figure 3

Can we make a graph if we want the rational numbers between -2 and 3, inclusive? We cannot show all of the infinitely many rational numbers between -2 and 3 by individual dots. We cannot use a solid line segment of points, such as Figure 4, because we must allow for "holes" at the points that correspond to irrational numbers such as $-\sqrt{2}$ and 0.313233343... and $\frac{\pi}{3}$. (The same problem arises when we try to graph only the irrational numbers because we will have "holes" at the points that correspond to the rational numbers between -2 and 3.)

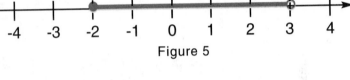
Figure 4

The meaning of the graph in Figure 4, then, is that it shows the points corresponding to both the rational numbers and the irrational numbers between -2 and 3, inclusive. If we do not want to include 3, then the graph becomes Figure 5; and if we only want the numbers *between* -2 and 3 (noninclusive), then the graph is Figure 6. The use of a circle instead of a dot in these instances indicates that each number corresponding to a circled point is not included in the result.

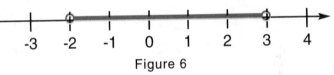
Figure 5

Therefore, we cannot make a graph for only the rational numbers between -2 and 3. However, the rational numbers and the irrational numbers together make up the *real numbers*, which have a special property that allows us to make solid graphs such as the preceding ones.

Figure 6

PROPERTY

Completeness: Each real number has one point on the number line, and each point on the number line has one real number.

Thus, a more correct name for the number line that you have been using is the real-number line; and every infinite decimal, whether repeating (rational) or nonrepeating (irrational) can be represented by a point on that line.

From this time on, you are to assume that variables represent real numbers unless you are specifically told otherwise.

Model 1: The graph of $x \geq 4\frac{1}{2}$ is

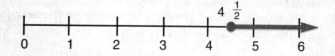

Model 2: The graph of $x < 4\frac{1}{2}$ is

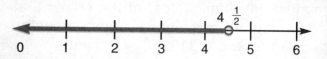

Model 3: The graph of $-\pi < y \leq 0$ is

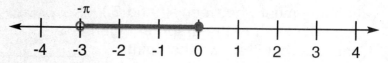

Model 4: The graph of $-\pi < y \leq 0$ for even integers is

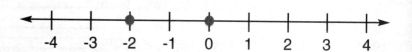

Model 5: The graph of $|z| = 1.\overline{7}$ is

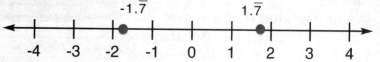

Model 6: The graph of $|z| \geq 1.\overline{7}$ is

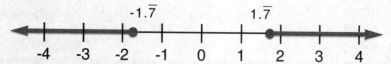

Model 7: The graph of $|z| < 1.\overline{7}$ is

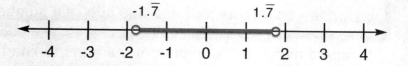

Draw the graph for each of the following conditions.

1.76 $x \le 3\frac{1}{3}$

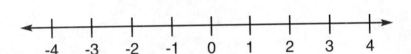

1.77 $x > -2.2$

1.78 $-1 < y \le \pi$

1.79 $|y| = 5\frac{3}{8}$

1.80 $|n| \le 3$

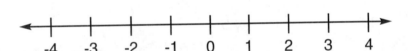

1.81 $|n| \le 3$ for odd integers

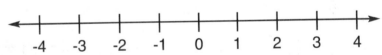

1.82 $|n| > 3$

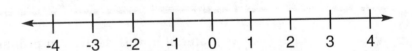

1.83 $a \ge \sqrt{71}$

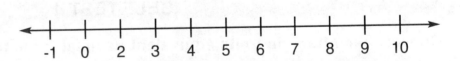

1.84 $-2 \le t < 2$

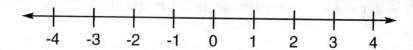

1.85 $-2 \le t < 2$ for integers

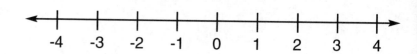

1.86 $1 < |k| < 4$ for integers

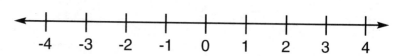

1.87 $1 < |k| < 4$

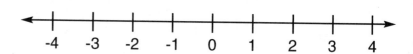

1.88 $|z| = \sqrt{5}$

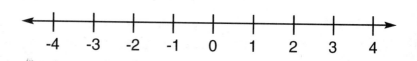

1.89 $|z| = -\sqrt{5}$

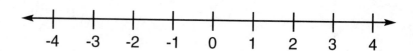

1.90 $-3\frac{1}{2} < b < 0.\overline{6}$

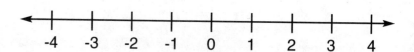

 Review the material in this section in preparation for the Self Test. The Self Test will check your mastery of this particular section. The items missed on this Self Test will indicate specific areas where restudy is needed for mastery.

SELF TEST 1

Convert each fraction to its equivalent decimal form, (each answer, 3 points).

1.01 $\frac{2}{5}$ = _____

1.02 $-\frac{16}{33}$ = _____

1.03 $\frac{19}{16}$ = _____

29

Convert each decimal to its equivalent reduced fraction form (each answer, 3 points).

1.04   -0.72 = _____

1.05 $0.\overline{72}$ = _____

1.06 $0.7\overline{2}$ = _____

Graph the given rational numbers (each location, 1 point).

1.07 $-3\frac{1}{3}$, 0, 1.6

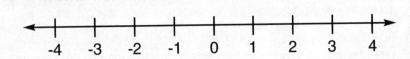

1.08   2.4, $-\frac{5}{4}$, $3.\overline{8}$

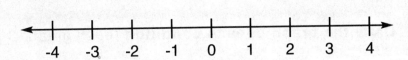

Write the order of the given rational numbers (each numbered item, 3 points).

1.09 -3, $\frac{1}{3}$, 0.3   _____ < _____ < _____

1.010 $5.\overline{40}$, $(\frac{7}{3})^2$, $5\frac{2}{5}$ _____ < _____ < _____

Find the rational number (each answer, 3 points).

1.011   One-sixth of the way between 7 and 16.

1.012   0.8 of the way between -0.5 and $4\frac{1}{2}$.

Tell whether each infinite decimal is rational or irrational (each answer, 2 points).

1.013   -7.234567...   _____

1.014   -7.232323...   _____

Round each number to the nearest hundredth (each answer, 2 points).

1.015 $0.\overline{61}$ _____   1.016   0.292292229... _____

a. Find each square root; b. then tell whether each is rational or irrational (each answer, 3 points).

1.017 $\sqrt{\dfrac{25}{49}}$ =   a._____   b._____

1.018 $\sqrt{32.49}$ =   a._____   b._____

Draw the graph of each condition (each graph, 3 points).

1.019 $y < 1.\overline{8}$

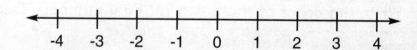

1.020 $|h| \geq \sqrt{13}$

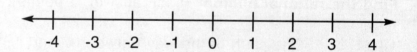

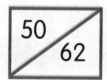

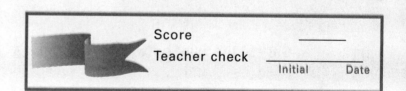

Score   _____
Teacher check   _____
Initial   Date

31

OBJECTIVES

When you have completed this section, you should be able to:

4. Simplify radical expressions.

5. Combine (add and subtract) radical expressions.

6. Multiply radical expressions.

7. Divide radical expressions.

Earlier in this LIFEPAC, we looked for a positive number whose square was 30; and we found that this number, the positive square root of 30, or $\sqrt{30}$, was irrational. However, other square roots such as $\sqrt{121}$ and $\sqrt{40.1}$ were seen to be rational.

Although you will be working almost exclusively with square roots, you should realize that cube roots (such as $\sqrt[3]{8}$), fourth roots (such as $\sqrt[4]{15}$), fifth roots, and so on also exist. Real numbers written in this form are called *radical expressions*, and they may be rational or irrational. In this section, you will first learn how to simplify these expressions and then how to add, subtract, multiply, and divide them.

SIMPLIFYING RADICALS

To simplify radicals, you must know what radicals are. Definitions and examples of roots will prepare you for working with the properties that allow radicals to be simplified.

ROOTS

We shall begin by taking a look at the basic terms and ideas for roots that will be used throughout this section. Remember that we are working with real numbers in all cases, whether rational or irrational.

DEFINITIONS

The *radical expression* $\sqrt[N]{A}$ is read, "the N th root of A" where N is the *index*, A is the *radicand*, and $\sqrt{}$ is the *radical sign*.

Model 1: $\sqrt[2]{9}$ or just $\sqrt{9}$ is read, "the second (or square) root of nine," where the index is 2 and the radicand is 9.

Model 2: $\sqrt[3]{27}$ is read, "the third (or cube) root of twenty-seven," where the index is 3 and the radicand is 27.

Model 3: $\sqrt[5]{-32}$ is read, "the fifth root of negative thirty-two," where the index is 5 and the radicand is -32.

Model 4: $-\sqrt[5]{32}$ is read, "the opposite of the fifth root of thirty-two," where the index is 5 and the radicand is 32.

DEFINITION

If $X^N = A$, then X is an *Nth root* of A.

Model 1: $7^2 = 49$, so 7 is a square root of 49: $\sqrt{49} = 7$.

Model 2: $(-7)^2 = 49$, so -7 is a square root of 49: $-\sqrt{49} = -7$.

The positive (or *principal*) square root is indicated by the radical sign itself; a negative square root must be shown as the opposite of the principal square root.

To indicate both square roots, write $\pm\sqrt{49} = \pm7$; the symbol $\pm$ is read "plus or minus."

Model 3: $4^3 = 64$; therefore, 4 is a cube root of 64: $\sqrt[3]{64} = 4$.

Model 4: $(-4)^3 = -64$; therefore, -4 is a cube root of -64: $\sqrt[3]{-64} = -4$.

You must be particularly careful if the index is even (square roots, fourth roots, sixth roots, etc.), because then the radicand cannot be negative. For example, $\sqrt{-49}$ is *undefined* since no real number squares can be -49 (or any other negative number).

The following list of the squares and cubes of nonzero integers is given for your reference, and you should become very familiar with at least the listed squares so that you will be able to simplify radicals more quickly.

Squares:

$$1^2 = 1 \qquad 6^2 = 36 \qquad 11^2 = 121$$
$$2^2 = 4 \qquad 7^2 = 49 \qquad 12^2 = 144$$
$$3^2 = 9 \qquad 8^2 = 64 \qquad 13^2 = 169$$
$$4^2 = 16 \qquad 9^2 = 81 \qquad 14^2 = 196$$
$$5^2 = 25 \qquad 10^2 = 100 \qquad 15^2 = 225$$

Cubes:

$$1^3 = 1 \qquad\qquad (-1)^3 = -1$$
$$2^3 = 8 \qquad\qquad (-2)^3 = -8$$
$$3^3 = 27 \qquad\qquad (-3)^3 = -27$$
$$4^3 = 64 \qquad\qquad (-4)^3 = -64$$
$$5^3 = 125 \qquad\qquad (-5)^3 = -125$$
$$6^3 = 216 \qquad\qquad (-6)^3 = -216$$
$$7^3 = 343 \qquad\qquad (-7)^3 = -343$$
$$8^3 = 512 \qquad\qquad (-8)^3 = -512$$
$$9^3 = 729 \qquad\qquad (-9)^3 = -729$$
$$10^3 = 1,000 \qquad\qquad (-10)^3 = -1,000$$

 Using the preceding lists, find the indicated roots; if the root is not a real number, write *undefined.*

2.1 $\sqrt{4}$ _____   2.11 $\sqrt[3]{-216}$ _____

2.2 $-\sqrt{81}$ _____   2.12 $-\sqrt[3]{216}$ _____

2.3 $\pm\sqrt{169}$ _____   2.13 $\sqrt{64}$ _____

2.4 $\sqrt{-196}$ _____   2.14 $\sqrt[3]{64}$ _____

2.5 $\sqrt[3]{27}$ _____   2.15 $\sqrt{-64}$ _____

2.6 $\sqrt[3]{-125}$ _____   2.16 $\sqrt[3]{-64}$ _____

2.7 $\sqrt[3]{729}$ _____   2.17 $-\sqrt{225}$ _____

2.8 $-\sqrt[3]{1,000}$ _____   2.18 $\pm\sqrt{100}$ _____

2.9 $\sqrt{-1}$ _____   2.19 $-\sqrt[3]{-8}$ _____

2.10 $\sqrt[3]{-1}$ _____   2.20 $-\sqrt{-144}$ _____

Find the numerical value for each of the following expressions.

Models: $7\sqrt{9} - 5\sqrt{4} =$

$7 \cdot 3 - 5 \cdot 2 =$

$21 - 10 =$

11

$\frac{1}{3}\sqrt[3]{216} + \frac{1}{2}\sqrt[3]{-64} =$

$\frac{1}{3} \cdot 6 + \frac{1}{2}(-4) =$

$2 + (-2) =$

0

2.21 $3\sqrt{25} + 2\sqrt{49}$

2.22 $\sqrt[3]{343} + \frac{3}{4}\sqrt[3]{-8}$

2.23 $\sqrt{121} - \sqrt[3]{512}$

2.24 $-\frac{1}{5}\sqrt[3]{125} + \frac{1}{7}\sqrt{196}$

2.25 $\frac{2}{3}\sqrt{81} - \sqrt[3]{-27} - \frac{4}{3}\sqrt[3]{729}$

Much of our work will be with radical expressions containing variables, so we need to know how the roots of variables are handled. Study the following lists of the squares and cubes of powers of a variable x.

Squares:

$(x^1)^2$	$=$	x^2
$(x^2)^2$	$=$	x^4
$(x^3)^2$	$=$	x^6
$(x^4)^2$	$=$	x^8
$(x^5)^2$	$=$	x^{10}

$(x^6)^2$	$=$	x^{12}
$(x^7)^2$	$=$	x^{14}
$(x^8)^2$	$=$	x^{16}
$(x^9)^2$	$=$	x^{18}
$(x^{10})^2$	$=$	x^{20}

Note: The exponents of the squares are multiples of 2.

Cubes:

$(x^1)^3$	$=$	x^3
$(x^2)^3$	$=$	x^6
$(x^3)^3$	$=$	x^9
$(x^4)^3$	$=$	x^{12}
$(x^5)^3$	$=$	x^{15}

$(x^6)^3$	$=$	x^{18}
$(x^7)^3$	$=$	x^{21}
$(x^8)^3$	$=$	x^{24}
$(x^9)^3$	$=$	x^{27}
$(x^{10})^3$	$=$	x^{30}

Note: The exponents of the cubes are multiples of 3.

IMPORTANT: In this LIFEPAC, we shall assume that all variables in radical expressions represent positive numbers.

For square roots, the exponent of the result is one-half the exponent of the radicand.

Model 1: $(x^1)^2 = x^2$; therefore, x^1 is a square root of x^2:

$\sqrt{x^2} = x^1$ or x.

Model 2: $(x^2)^2 = x^4$; therefore, x^2 is a square root of x^4:

$\sqrt{x^4} = x^2$.

Model 3: $(x^3)^2 = x^6$; therefore, x^3 is a square root of x^6:

$\sqrt{x^6} = x^3$.

Model 4: $(x^4)^2 = x^8$; therefore, x^4 is a square root of x^8:

$\sqrt{x^8} = x^4$.

For cube roots, the exponent of the result is one-third the exponent of the radicand.

Model 1: $(x^1)^3 = x^3$; therefore, x^1 is a cube root of x^3:

$$\sqrt[3]{x^3} = x^1 \text{ or } x .$$

Model 2: $(x^2)^3 = x^6$; therefore, x^2 is a cube root of x^6:

$$\sqrt[3]{x^6} = x^2.$$

Model 3: $(x^3)^3 = x^9$; therefore, x^3 is a cube root of x^9:

$$\sqrt[3]{x^9} = x^3.$$

Model 4: $(x^4)^3 = x^{12}$; therefore, x^4 is a cube root of x^{12}:

$$\sqrt[3]{x^{12}} = x^4.$$

 Find the indicated roots.

2.26 $\sqrt{x^{10}}$ _____   2.31 $\sqrt[3]{n^{75}}$ _____

2.27 $\sqrt{y^{12}}$ _____   2.32 $\sqrt{m^{24}}$ _____

2.28 $\sqrt[3]{x^{15}}$ _____   2.33 $\sqrt[3]{m^{24}}$ _____

2.29 $\sqrt[3]{y^{18}}$ _____   2.34 $\sqrt{(a + b)^2}$ _____

2.30 $\sqrt{n^{100}}$ _____   2.35 $\sqrt[3]{(a + b + c)^3}$ _____

Model 1: $\sqrt{9a^4b^2} = 3a^2b$ since $(3a^2b)^2 = 9a^4b^2$.

Model 2: $\sqrt[3]{-343y^{12}} = -7y^4$ since $(-7y^4)^3 = -343y^{12}$.

Find the indicated roots.

2.36 $\sqrt{25x^2}$ _____

2.37 $\sqrt{144a^2b^4c^6}$ _____

2.38 $\sqrt[3]{8n^3}$ _____

2.39 $\sqrt[3]{512y^9z^6}$ _____

2.40 $\sqrt{121m^8n^4}$ _____

2.41 $\sqrt[3]{-1,000k^{15}}$ _____

2.42 $\sqrt{16p^{16}}$ _____

2.43 $\sqrt[3]{-27n^{27}}$ _____

2.44 $\sqrt{64d^{12}}$ _____

2.45 $\sqrt[3]{64d^{12}}$ _____

PROPERTIES

The numerical roots that you have found so far in this section have all been rational, and you now need to learn to simplify irrational roots as well. From this point on, you will be simplifying only square roots; but the procedures can be used for cube roots, fourth roots, and so on. One of the basic properties of radical expressions deals with multiplication.

> **PROPERTY**
>
> For A and B positive, $\sqrt{AB} = \sqrt{A}\sqrt{B}$.

Model 1: $\sqrt{36} = 6$ and $\sqrt{36} = \sqrt{9}\sqrt{4} = 3 \cdot 2 = 6$; in this case the root is rational.

Model 2: $\sqrt{12} = 3.4641016...$, and $\sqrt{12} = \sqrt{4 \cdot 3} = \sqrt{4}\sqrt{3} = 2\sqrt{3}$; in this case the root is irrational.

Although an irrational root can be written as an infinite nonrepeating decimal, this process is not what is meant by simplification. Thus, in the preceding model, $2\sqrt{3}$, not 3.4641016..., is considered to be the simplified form of $\sqrt{12}$; however, if 12 is written as 6 • 2 instead of 4 • 3, then the result $\sqrt{12} = \sqrt{6}\sqrt{2}$ is not in simplified form either. The key idea in simplification is for one of the factors to be a square; in fact, it should be the largest square factor of the original radicand.

Model 1:   Simplify $\sqrt{48}$.

Solution: 48 can be factored as 2 • 24 or 3 • 16 or 4 • 12 or 6 • 8. Two of the pairs contain squares, 3 • 16 and 4 • 12, but 16 > 4.

$\therefore \sqrt{48} = \sqrt{16 \cdot 3} = \sqrt{16}\sqrt{3} = 4\sqrt{3}$, the simplified form.

Notes: 1 • 48 is omitted as a pair of factors since 1 is a factor of every number and it does not help in simplification. ($\sqrt{1} = 1$)

If the pair 4 • 12 had been used ($\sqrt{48} = \sqrt{4 \cdot 12} = \sqrt{4}\sqrt{12} = 2\sqrt{12}$), you would have to continue to simplify $2\sqrt{12}$ as follows: $2\sqrt{12} = 2\sqrt{4 \cdot 3} = 2\sqrt{4}\sqrt{3} = 2 \cdot 2\sqrt{3} = 4\sqrt{3}$, the simplified form.

For a radical expression to be in simplified form, the radicand cannot be a square or have any square factor (other than 1). The more familiar you become with the squares 1, 4, 9, 16, ... , the quicker you will be at simplifying radicals.

Model 2: $\sqrt{500} = \sqrt{100}\sqrt{5} = 10\sqrt{5}$

Model 3: $5\sqrt{288} = 5\sqrt{144}\sqrt{2} = 5 \cdot 12\sqrt{2} = 60\sqrt{2}$

Model 4: $\sqrt{30}$ is simplified as much as possible since 30 has no square factor other than 1.

In summary, if a positive integer P factors to integers $M^2 \cdot N$, where M^2 is the largest square factor of P, then $M\sqrt{N}$ is the simplified radical form of $\sqrt{P}$.

a. Give the infinite nonrepeating decimal for each irrational square root;
b. Then show your steps in obtaining the simplified radical form of each root.

		DECIMAL FORM	SIMPLIFIED FORM

Model: $\sqrt{32}$ a. $\sqrt{32} = 5.6568542...$ b. $\sqrt{32} = \sqrt{16}\sqrt{2} = 4\sqrt{2}$

2.46 $\sqrt{24}$ a._____   b._____

2.47 $\sqrt{75}$ a._____   b._____

2.48 $\sqrt{55}$ a._____   b._____

2.49 $\sqrt{28}$ a._____   b._____

2.50 $\sqrt{300}$ a._____   b._____

Show your steps in simplifying each radical expression.

2.51 $3\sqrt{45}$ _____

2.52 $\frac{1}{2}\sqrt{40}$ _____

2.53 $-\frac{1}{2}\sqrt{80}$ _____

2.54 $\frac{3}{14}\sqrt{98}$ _____

2.55 $-\frac{5}{2}\sqrt{128}$ _____

The same procedure is used to simplify radical expressions containing monomials with variable factors. Again we use the property $\sqrt{AB} = \sqrt{A}\sqrt{B}$, and again the radicand of the simplified form must not be a square or have any square factor (other than 1).

Model 1:   Simplify $\sqrt{x^7}$.

Solution: x^7 can be factored as $x \bullet x^6$ or $x^2 \bullet x^5$ or $x^3 \bullet x^4$.

All three pairs contain squares, and x^6 is the largest square factor.

$\therefore \sqrt{x^7} = \sqrt{x^6}\sqrt{x} = x^3\sqrt{x}$, the simplified form.

Note: If the pair $x^3 \bullet x^4$ had been used

$(\sqrt{x^7} = \sqrt{x^4}\sqrt{x^3} = x^2\sqrt{x^3})$,

40

you would have to continue to
simplify $x^2\sqrt{x^3}$ in this way:

$= x^2\sqrt{x^2}\sqrt{x} \quad = x^2\sqrt{x^2} \cdot \sqrt{x}$

$= x^2 \cdot x \cdot \sqrt{x}$

$= x^3\sqrt{x}$, the simplified form.

The following models show roots of monomials with both numerical and variable factors; study each simplification carefully before working the activities.

Model 2: $\quad \sqrt{3m^2} = \sqrt{m^2}\sqrt{3} = m\sqrt{3}$

Model 3: $\quad -\sqrt{16n} = -\sqrt{16}\sqrt{n} = -4\sqrt{n}$

Model 4: $\quad \frac{1}{2}\sqrt{24z^3} = \frac{1}{2}\sqrt{4z^2}\sqrt{6z} = \frac{1}{2}\sqrt{4z^2} \cdot \sqrt{6z} = \frac{1}{2} \cdot 2z\sqrt{6z} = z\sqrt{6z}$

Model 5: $\quad 3z\sqrt{50xy^8z^5} = 3z\sqrt{25y^8z^4}\sqrt{2xz} = 3z \cdot 5y^4z^2\sqrt{2xz}$

$\qquad\qquad = 15y^4z^3\sqrt{2xz}$

Show your steps in simplifying each radical expression.

2.56 $\qquad \sqrt{60a^3}$ _____

2.57 $\qquad 2\sqrt{48x^2y^3}$ _____

2.58 $\qquad -\sqrt{m^4n^7}$ _____

2.59 $\qquad r\sqrt{5r^2}$ _____

2.60 $\qquad \frac{1}{5}\sqrt{75xy^2z^3}$ _____

2.61 $\qquad -\sqrt{49ab}$ _____

2.62 $\qquad \frac{1}{2}\sqrt{1{,}000n^4}$ _____

2.63 $\qquad 2x\sqrt{20x^{20}}$ _____

2.64 $\qquad -\frac{5}{6}\sqrt{72p}$ _____

2.65 $\qquad \sqrt{363a^5b^2}$ _____

The two other requirements for a simplified radical both involve fractions. The first requirement is that a radical is not to contain a fraction; thus, $\sqrt{\frac{49}{81}}$ and $\sqrt{\frac{2}{9}}$ and $\sqrt{\frac{5}{7}}$ are not in simplified form. You have already used the property $\sqrt{AB} = \sqrt{A}\sqrt{B}$ in simplifying, and another basic property of radical expressions will now be needed.

PROPERTY

For positive A and B, $\sqrt{\frac{A}{B}} = \frac{\sqrt{A}}{\sqrt{B}}$.

Model 1: $\sqrt{\frac{49}{81}} = \frac{\sqrt{49}}{\sqrt{81}} = \frac{7}{9}$, a rational root.

Model 2: $\sqrt{\frac{2}{9}} = \frac{\sqrt{2}}{\sqrt{9}} = \frac{\sqrt{2}}{3}$, an irrational root.

Model 3: $\sqrt{\frac{5}{7}} = \frac{\sqrt{5}}{\sqrt{7}}$, also an irrational root.

Now $\frac{7}{9}$ is the simplified form of $\sqrt{\frac{49}{81}}$, and $\frac{\sqrt{2}}{3}$ is the simplified form of $\sqrt{\frac{2}{9}}$. However, $\frac{\sqrt{5}}{\sqrt{7}}$ is not considered to be the simplified form of $\sqrt{\frac{5}{7}}$ since the second requirement is that a denominator is not to contain a radical. In order to meet this condition, the original fraction must have a denominator that is a square before using the property $\sqrt{\frac{A}{B}} = \frac{\sqrt{A}}{\sqrt{B}}$.

Model 1: Simplify $\sqrt{\frac{5}{7}}$.

Solution: We need to convert $\frac{5}{7}$ to an equivalent fraction having a denominator of 49 (a square divisible by 7).

$$\sqrt{\frac{5}{7}} = \sqrt{\frac{5}{7} \cdot \frac{7}{7}} = \sqrt{\frac{35}{49}} = \frac{\sqrt{35}}{\sqrt{49}} = \frac{\sqrt{35}}{7},$$

the simplified form.

Note: This answer may also be written as $\frac{1}{7}\sqrt{35}$, and any problems of this type may be written as a fraction times the radical.

Be sure to check the radicand in the numerator to see if it has a square factor (other than 1); if it does, you must simplify the radical using the property $\sqrt{AB} = \sqrt{A}\sqrt{B}$ as before.

Model 2: Simplify $\sqrt{2.4}$.

Solution: Write the decimal in fraction form, $2.4 = 2\frac{4}{10} = 2\frac{2}{5} = \frac{12}{5}$;

then $\sqrt{2.4} = \sqrt{\frac{12}{5}} = \sqrt{\frac{12}{5} \cdot \frac{5}{5}} = \sqrt{\frac{60}{25}} =$

$\frac{\sqrt{60}}{\sqrt{25}} = \frac{\sqrt{4}\sqrt{15}}{\sqrt{25}} = \frac{2\sqrt{15}}{5}$.

Model 3: Simplify $-3\sqrt{0.\overline{7}}$.

Solution: $0.\overline{7} = \frac{7}{9}$; then $-3\sqrt{0.\overline{7}} = -3\sqrt{\frac{7}{9}} = -3 \cdot \frac{\sqrt{7}}{\sqrt{9}} = \overset{(-1)}{-\cancel{3}} \cdot \frac{\sqrt{7}}{\cancel{3}} = -\sqrt{7}$.

Model 4: Simplify $\sqrt{\frac{3}{8}}$.

Solution 1: $\sqrt{\frac{3}{8}} = \sqrt{\frac{3}{8} \cdot \frac{8}{8}} = \sqrt{\frac{24}{64}} = \frac{\sqrt{24}}{\sqrt{64}} = \frac{\sqrt{4}\sqrt{6}}{\sqrt{64}} = \frac{\overset{}{2}\sqrt{6}}{\underset{4}{8}} = \frac{\sqrt{6}}{4}$.

Solution 2: $\sqrt{\frac{3}{8}} = \sqrt{\frac{3}{8} \cdot \frac{2}{2}} = \sqrt{\frac{6}{16}} = \frac{\sqrt{6}}{\sqrt{16}} = \frac{\sqrt{6}}{4}$.

Note: The second solution is shorter since the smallest possible square multiple of 8(16) is obtained for the denominator.

a. Show your steps in simplifying each radical expression;
b. then tell whether each result is rational or irrational.

2.66 $8\sqrt{\frac{9}{4}}$ a._____ b._____

2.67 $\sqrt{\frac{5}{16}}$ a._____ b._____

2.68 $-\sqrt{\frac{4}{7}}$ a._____ b._____

2.69	$-10\sqrt{\dfrac{2}{5}}$	a._____	b._____
2.70	$\sqrt{\dfrac{1}{18}}$	a._____	b._____
2.71	$\sqrt{2.25}$	a._____	b._____
2.72	$\sqrt{5.6}$	a._____	b._____
2.73	$-\dfrac{1}{2}\sqrt{1.\overline{7}}$	a._____	b._____
2.74	$-4\sqrt{\dfrac{7}{8}}$	a._____	b._____
2.75	$\sqrt{1\dfrac{5}{27}}$	a._____	b._____

Show your steps in simplifying each radical expression.

Model 1: $\quad -9\sqrt{\dfrac{17}{a}} = -9\sqrt{\dfrac{17}{a}\bullet\dfrac{a}{a}} = -9\bullet\dfrac{\sqrt{17a}}{\sqrt{a^2}} = -\dfrac{9}{1}\bullet\dfrac{\sqrt{17a}}{\sqrt{a^2}} = -\dfrac{9\sqrt{17a}}{a}$

Model 2: $\quad \sqrt{\dfrac{32m}{n^5}} = \sqrt{\dfrac{32m}{n^5}\bullet\dfrac{n}{n}} = \sqrt{\dfrac{32mn}{n^6}} = \dfrac{\sqrt{16}\sqrt{2mn}}{\sqrt{n^6}} = \dfrac{4\sqrt{2mn}}{n^3}$

2.76	$2\sqrt{\dfrac{3y}{7}}$	_____
2.77	$-18\sqrt{\dfrac{7a^2}{36}}$	_____
2.78	$\dfrac{1}{3}\sqrt{\dfrac{7}{32x^2}}$	_____
2.79	$\sqrt{\dfrac{n}{18}}$	_____
2.80	$\sqrt{\dfrac{5}{m}}$	_____
2.81	$\sqrt{\dfrac{a^2c}{b^3}}$	_____
2.82	$-\dfrac{2x}{3}\sqrt{\dfrac{1}{12x}}$	_____
2.83	$\sqrt{\dfrac{7}{121a^4}}$	_____
2.84	$20\sqrt{\dfrac{9x}{50y}}$	_____
2.85	$\sqrt{\dfrac{25}{32a^3b}}$	_____

Remember the three requirements for simplified radical expressions:

1. No radicand can be a square or have any square factor (other than 1).
2. No fraction can be within a radical sign.
3. No radical can be in a denominator.

For answers involving radicals to be correct, the radical expressions must be simplified.

COMBINING RADICALS

Radical expressions are added and subtracted in much the same way as terms: only like terms can be combined, and only like radicals can be combined. First we need a definition.

DEFINITION

Like radicals are expressions having the same root index and the same radicand.

Model 1: $\sqrt{3}$, $4\sqrt{3}$, and $-\frac{1}{2}\sqrt{3}$ are like radicals.

Model 2: $-7\sqrt[3]{5a}$, $\frac{\sqrt[3]{5a}}{4}$, and $\sqrt[3]{5a}$ are like radicals.

Model 3: $\sqrt{2}$, $\sqrt[3]{2}$, and $\sqrt[4]{2}$ are not like radicals.

Model 4: $\sqrt[5]{x^2}$, $\sqrt[5]{y^2}$, and $\sqrt[5]{z^2}$ are not like radicals.

Model 5: $7\sqrt{14}$ and $14\sqrt{7}$ are not like radicals.

Model 6: $3\sqrt{x}$, $\sqrt{3x}$, and $x\sqrt{3}$ are not like radicals.

You should recall that terms such as $-4x^3$ and $15x^3$ are combined by using the distributive property in the form $BA + CA = (B + C)A$; similarly, radical expressions such as $-4\sqrt[3]{x}$ and $15\sqrt[3]{x}$ are combined by using this same property.

MATHEMATICS

9 0 7

LIFEPAC TEST

$$\frac{56}{70}$$

Name _____

Date _____

Score _____

MATHEMATICS 907: LIFEPAC TEST

Complete these items (each answer, 2 points).

1. Convert the fraction $\frac{17}{20}$ to its equivalent decimal form.

   _____

2. Convert the decimal $0.\overline{14}$ to its equivalent fraction form.

   _____

Complete these items (each numbered item, 3 points).

3. Give the order of the rational numbers $(\frac{8}{5})^2$, $2.5\overline{6}$, $2\frac{1}{2}$.

   _____ < _____ < _____

4. Find the rational number $\frac{3}{4}$ of the way between -3 and 3.

5. Is the real number $\sqrt{1.21}$ rational or irrational? _____

   Why? _____

6. Is the real number $\sqrt{12.1}$ rational or irrational? _____

   Why? _____

7. Draw the graph of $x \geq -1.3$.

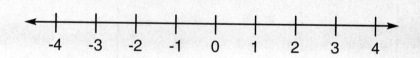

8. Draw the graph of $|y| < \pi$.

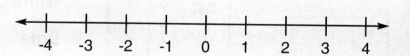

Perform any indicated operation(s), and give the simplified form of each expression (each answer, 4 points).

9. $-3\sqrt{84x^3}$ _____

10. $\sqrt{\dfrac{7}{18}}$ _____

11. $\sqrt{9a^2} + \sqrt{49b} - a + \sqrt{b}$ _____

12. $\sqrt{12} - \dfrac{2}{5}\sqrt{75}$ _____

13. $(-8\sqrt{2})(\dfrac{1}{2}\sqrt{32})$ _____

14. $(x - \sqrt{7})^2$ _____

15. $\dfrac{8\sqrt{6mn} + 6\sqrt{8mn}}{2\sqrt{2mn}}$ _____

16. $\dfrac{y\sqrt{6}}{6\sqrt{y}}$ _____

Complete this item (this answer, 4 points).

17. Solve the equation $\dfrac{x}{2} + 1 = \sqrt{3}$ for both the exact irrational root and its rational approximation to the nearest tenth.

2

Solve and check each radical equation (each answer, 4 points).

18. $\sqrt{y} + 5 = 0$

19. $7 - \sqrt{3z + 2} = 4$

20. Solve $\sqrt{m - 7} = n + 3$ for m.

BONUS: Solve $r = \sqrt{\dfrac{A}{\pi h}}$ for h.

3

Model:	LIKE TERMS	LIKE RADICALS
	$-4x^3 + 15x^3$	$-4\sqrt[3]{x} + 15\sqrt[3]{x}$
	$= (-4 + 15)x^3$	$= (-4 + 15)\sqrt[3]{x}$
	$= 11x^3$	$= 11\sqrt[3]{x}$

You should realize that the radical expression $\sqrt[N]{A}$ actually means $1\sqrt[N]{A}$ (even though the number 1 is not written) and that $0\sqrt[N]{A}$ is 0. Again, this idea is the same as with variables when x means $1x$ and when $0x$ is 0.

Model 1: $7\sqrt{3} - 2\sqrt{3} + \sqrt{3}$

$= 7\sqrt{3} - 2\sqrt{3} + 1\sqrt{3}$

$= (7 - 2 + 1)\sqrt{3}$

$= 6\sqrt{3}$, the answer.

Model 2: $4x\sqrt[3]{2y} + 3x\sqrt[3]{2y} - 7x\sqrt[3]{2y}$

$= (4 + 3 - 7)x\sqrt[3]{2y}$

$= 0x\sqrt[3]{2y}$

$= 0$, the answer.

In an indicated sum or difference of radicals, the like radicals (as well as the like terms) may be grouped together to be combined. Although the steps are shown in the following model, most or all of the work should be done mentally.

Model 3: $5\sqrt{2a} + 3\sqrt{3b} - 7\sqrt{2a} - 5c + 2\sqrt{2a} - \sqrt{3b} + c$

$= 5\sqrt{2a} - 7\sqrt{2a} + 2\sqrt{2a} + 3\sqrt{3b} - \sqrt{3b} - 5c + c$

$= (5 - 7 + 2)\sqrt{2a} + (3 - 1)\sqrt{3b} + (-5 + 1)c$

$= 0\sqrt{2a} + 2\sqrt{3b} + (-4c)$

$= 2\sqrt{3b} - 4c$, the answer.

 Combine like radicals (and like terms) in each of the following expressions.

2.86 $2\sqrt{5} + 5\sqrt{5}$ _____

2.87 $2a\sqrt{b} - 5a\sqrt{b}$ _____

2.88 $2\sqrt{k} + \sqrt{k} - 3\sqrt{k}$ _____

2.89 $\sqrt{x} - 4\sqrt{x} + \sqrt{x}$ _____

2.90 $r\sqrt{t} + s\sqrt{t}$ _____

2.91 $2\sqrt{3} + 5x + 3\sqrt{3} - 2x$ _____

2.92 $a\sqrt{x} + b\sqrt{y} - c\sqrt{x}$ _____

2.93 $7\sqrt{2a} - 3\sqrt{2a} + b\sqrt{2a}$ _____

2.94 $4m + 5\sqrt{n} - m + 6m - 3\sqrt{n}$ _____

2.95 $j\sqrt{k} + l - m\sqrt{k} - n$ _____

At first glance you might not think that $-\sqrt{48}$ and $\sqrt{27}$ can be combined; however, you must write all radical expressions in simplified form before making any conclusions.

Model 1: $-\sqrt{48} + \sqrt{27}$

     $= -\sqrt{16}\,\sqrt{3} + \sqrt{9}\,\sqrt{3}$

     $= -4\sqrt{3} + 3\sqrt{3}$

     $= -1\sqrt{3}$

     $= -\sqrt{3}$, the answer.

Model 2: $\sqrt{12a^2} + \sqrt{8b} - \sqrt{75a^2}$

     $= \sqrt{4a^2}\,\sqrt{3} + \sqrt{4}\,\sqrt{2b} - \sqrt{25a^2}\,\sqrt{3}$

     $= 2a\sqrt{3} + 2\sqrt{2b} - 5a\sqrt{3}$

     $= (2 - 5)a\sqrt{3} + 2\sqrt{2b}$

     $= -3a\sqrt{3} + 2\sqrt{2b}$

Model 3:
$$5x\sqrt{20} - \sqrt{405y^2}$$
$$= 5x\sqrt{4}\sqrt{5} - \sqrt{81y^2}\sqrt{5}$$
$$= 5x \cdot 2\sqrt{5} - 9y\sqrt{5}$$
$$= 10x\sqrt{5} - 9y\sqrt{5}$$
$$= (10x - 9y)\sqrt{5}$$

Model 4:
$$3\sqrt{24k^3} + \tfrac{2}{3}\sqrt{54k^3}$$
$$= 3\sqrt{4k^2}\sqrt{6k} + \tfrac{2}{3}\sqrt{9k^2}\sqrt{6k}$$
$$= 3 \cdot 2k\sqrt{6k} + \tfrac{2}{3}\,3k\sqrt{6k}$$
$$= 6k\sqrt{6k} + 2k\sqrt{6k} = (6k + 2k)\sqrt{6k}$$
$$= 8k\sqrt{6k}$$

For each indicated sum and/or difference, simplify the radicals and combine when possible; show your work.

2.96 $\sqrt{9m^2n^2} + 2\sqrt{m^2n^2} - 3mn$

2.97 $2\sqrt{x} - 3\sqrt{x^3} + 5\sqrt{x}$

2.98 $\sqrt{3y^2} + 4\sqrt{12y^2} - y\sqrt{75}$

2.99　　　　$3\sqrt{27} + \sqrt{8} - 2\sqrt{75}$

2.100　　　　$\sqrt{48n^3} + \sqrt{9n} - \sqrt{3n}$

2.101　　　　$3\sqrt{63} - 2\sqrt{175}$

2.102　　　　$\sqrt{16a} - \sqrt{49a} + \sqrt{81a}$

2.103 $\quad 5x\sqrt{72} + \sqrt{8x^2}$

2.104 $\quad a\sqrt{125y} - b\sqrt{45y}$

2.105 $\quad \sqrt{36a} + \sqrt{a^3} + \sqrt{a^2b}$

2.106 $\quad \frac{1}{3}\sqrt{45} - \frac{1}{2}\sqrt{12} + \sqrt{20} + \frac{2}{3}\sqrt{27}$

2.107 $\sqrt{m^2p} + \sqrt{n^2p} - \sqrt{m^2n^2p}$

2.108 $2\sqrt{18x^3} - 3\sqrt{8x^3}$

2.109 $a\sqrt{500b^3} + 2\sqrt{125a^3b^2}$

2.110 $3\sqrt{\dfrac{3}{5}} + 2\sqrt{\dfrac{5}{3}}$

2.111 $2\sqrt{18} + 3\sqrt{50} - 5\sqrt{8}$

2.112 $\quad 8x + \sqrt{1} - \sqrt{9y} - \sqrt{9x^2}$

2.113 $\quad 2a\sqrt{b} - \sqrt{b^2c} - \sqrt{4a^2b}$

2.114 $\quad -\sqrt{147} + \sqrt{192} - \sqrt{243}$

2.115 $\quad 2\sqrt{\dfrac{a}{2}} - 3\sqrt{\dfrac{b}{3}} + 4\sqrt{\dfrac{c}{4}}$

In a previous section we used the property $\sqrt{AB} = \sqrt{A}\sqrt{B}$ to simplify radical expressions; now we will use this same property in the reverse order to find products of radicals.

PROPERTY

For positive A and B, $\sqrt{A} \cdot \sqrt{B} = \sqrt{AB}$.

Model 1: $\sqrt{4} \cdot \sqrt{25} = 2 \cdot 5 = 10$ and $\sqrt{4} \cdot \sqrt{25} = \sqrt{4 \cdot 25} = \sqrt{100} = 10$; in this case, the product of two rational numbers is rational.

Model 2: $3\sqrt{5} \cdot \sqrt{13} = 3\sqrt{5 \cdot 13} = 3\sqrt{65}$; in this case, the product of two irrational numbers is irrational.

Model 3: $(4\sqrt{12})(-\frac{1}{3}\sqrt{3}) = (4)(-\frac{1}{3})\sqrt{12 \cdot 3} = -\frac{4}{3}\sqrt{36} = -\frac{4}{3} \cdot \overset{2}{\cancel{6}} = -8$; in this case, the product of two irrational numbers is rational.

Model 4: $(\sqrt{15})^2 = \sqrt{15} \cdot \sqrt{15} = \sqrt{15 \cdot 15} = \sqrt{225} = 15$; in this case, the square of an irrational number is rational, and the result is just the radicand of the irrational root.

Model 4 illustrates a property that can shorten our work in finding certain products.

PROPERTY

For positive A, $(\sqrt{A})^2$ or $\sqrt{A} \cdot \sqrt{A} = A$.

Model 1: $\frac{1}{2}\sqrt{41} \cdot 10\sqrt{41} = \frac{1}{\cancel{2}} \cdot \overset{5}{\cancel{10}} \cdot \sqrt{41} \cdot \sqrt{41} = 5 \cdot 41 = 205$

Model 2: $(-\frac{2}{3}\sqrt{30})^2 = (-\frac{2}{3})^2 (\sqrt{30})^2 = \frac{4}{\underset{3}{\cancel{9}}} \cdot \overset{10}{\cancel{30}} = \frac{40}{3}$ or $13.\overline{3}$

Products of radical expressions having variables are found in the same manner.

Model 3: $8\sqrt{2n} \cdot \sqrt{50n^3} = 8\sqrt{2n \cdot 50n^3} = 8\sqrt{100n^4} = 8 \cdot 10n^2 = 80n^2$

Model 4: $2y\sqrt{3z} \cdot 11\sqrt{7} = 2y \cdot 11\sqrt{3z \cdot 7} = 22y\sqrt{21z}$

Model 5: $(\frac{x}{6}\sqrt{6x})^2 = (\frac{x}{6})^2 (\sqrt{6x})^2 = \frac{x^2}{\underset{6}{\cancel{36}}} \cdot \cancel{6}x = \frac{x^3}{6}$

Model 6: $a\sqrt{3} \cdot b\sqrt{5} \cdot c\sqrt{10} = abc\sqrt{3 \cdot 5 \cdot 10} = abc\sqrt{150}$; but this

radicand has a square factor of 25, so we must simplify:

$abc\sqrt{150} = abc\sqrt{25}\sqrt{6} = 5abc\sqrt{6}$.

Model 7: $\sqrt{6x} \cdot \sqrt{15x} = \sqrt{6x \cdot 15x} = \sqrt{90x^2} = \sqrt{9x^2}\sqrt{10} = 3x\sqrt{10}$.

 Find the products. Be sure your answers are in simplified radical form.

2.116 $\sqrt{20} \cdot \sqrt{5}$ _____

2.117 $4\sqrt{3} \cdot \sqrt{27}$ _____

2.118 $(-\frac{1}{2}\sqrt{2})(-6\sqrt{18})$ _____

2.119 $\sqrt{2x} \cdot \sqrt{3y}$ _____

2.120 $-6\sqrt{7} \cdot 4\sqrt{5}$ _____

2.121 $2\sqrt{ab} \cdot 3\sqrt{cd}$ _____

2.122 $(\sqrt{97})^2$ _____

2.123 $5\sqrt{a} \cdot 11\sqrt{a}$ _____

2.124 $(x\sqrt{3})^2$ _____

2.125 $2\sqrt{7} \cdot 5\sqrt{7}$ _____

2.126 $(-\sqrt{7})^2$ _____

2.127 $-(\sqrt{7})^2$ _____

2.128 $(-\frac{2}{3}\sqrt{6})(9\sqrt{3})$ _____

2.129 $\sqrt{xy} \cdot \sqrt{yz}$ _____

2.130 $\frac{1}{3}\sqrt{18n^2} \cdot \sqrt{2n}$ _____

You will need to use the distributive property in the form $A(B + C) = AB + AC$ to find some products of radical expressions; the procedure is similar to that used in multiplying polynomials.

Model 1: $4\sqrt{2}(3\sqrt{5} + \sqrt{2}) = 4\sqrt{2} \cdot 3\sqrt{5} + 4\sqrt{2} \cdot \sqrt{2}$

$$= 12\sqrt{10} + 4 \cdot 2$$

$$= 12\sqrt{10} + 8$$

Model 2: $\sqrt{xyz}(a\sqrt{x} - b\sqrt{y} + c\sqrt{z})$

$$= \sqrt{xyz} \cdot a\sqrt{x} - \sqrt{xyz} \cdot b\sqrt{y} + \sqrt{xyz} \cdot c\sqrt{z}$$

$$= a\sqrt{x^2yz} - b\sqrt{xy^2z} + c\sqrt{xyz^2}$$

$$= a\sqrt{x^2}\sqrt{yz} - b\sqrt{y^2}\sqrt{xz} + c\sqrt{z^2}\sqrt{xy}$$

$$= ax\sqrt{yz} - by\sqrt{xz} + cz\sqrt{xy}$$

Model 3: $(5\sqrt{7} - \sqrt{2})^2$

$$= (5\sqrt{7} - \sqrt{2})(5\sqrt{7} - \sqrt{2})$$

$$= 5\sqrt{7} \cdot 5\sqrt{7} - 5\sqrt{7} \cdot \sqrt{2} - \sqrt{2} \cdot 5\sqrt{7} + \sqrt{2} \cdot \sqrt{2} \text{ (by FOIL)}$$

$$= 25 \cdot 7 - 5\sqrt{14} - 5\sqrt{14} + 2$$

$$= 177 - 10\sqrt{14}$$

Find each product (in simplified form).

2.131 $\quad \sqrt{y}\,(2 - \sqrt{y}\,)$

2.132 $\quad \sqrt{3}\,(\sqrt{3} + x\,)$

2.133 $\quad \sqrt{a}\,(2\sqrt{a} - \sqrt{b}\,)$

2.134 $\quad (\sqrt{5} + 4)\,(\sqrt{5} - 2)$

2.135 $(x + 2\sqrt{3})^2$

2.136 $(5\sqrt{2} - 1)^2$

2.137 $(2a\sqrt{b} - 3c)(3a\sqrt{b} + 5c)$

2.138 $(x\sqrt{y} + z)(x\sqrt{y} - z)$

2.139 $3\sqrt{2}\,(3\sqrt{8} - 4\sqrt{2}\,)$

2.140 $(3\sqrt{x} + 2\sqrt{3}\,)(2\sqrt{x} - 4\sqrt{3}\,)$

2.141 $(2\sqrt{5} - 3\sqrt{2}\,)^2$

2.142 $(\sqrt{0.08} + \sqrt{0.0032}\,) \cdot \sqrt{2}$

2.143 $(\sqrt{a} + \sqrt{b})^3$ HINT: Find $(\sqrt{a} + \sqrt{b})(\sqrt{a} + \sqrt{b})$, then

multiply the result by $(\sqrt{a} + \sqrt{b})$.

2.144 $(\sqrt{3} + \sqrt{2})^3$

2.145 $(5\sqrt{6} - 4\sqrt{2})^3$

Division of radicals is the final operation with radicals in this LIFEPAC. After the properties have been presented, the method will be shown for removing radicals from the denominator of a fraction.

PROPERTIES

Earlier we used the property $\sqrt{\frac{A}{B}} = \frac{\sqrt{A}}{\sqrt{B}}$ to simplify radical expressions involving fractions. Now we will use this same property in the reverse order to find quotients of radicals.

PROPERTY

For positive A and B, $\frac{\sqrt{A}}{\sqrt{B}} = \sqrt{\frac{A}{B}}$.

Model 1: $\frac{\sqrt{36}}{\sqrt{4}} = \frac{6}{2} = 3$ and $\frac{\sqrt{36}}{\sqrt{4}} = \sqrt{\frac{36}{4}} = \sqrt{9} = 3$; in this case, the quotient of two rational numbers is rational.

Model 2: $\frac{6\sqrt{56}}{3\sqrt{8}} = \frac{6}{3}\sqrt{\frac{56}{8}} = 2\sqrt{7}$; in this case, the quotient of two irrational numbers is irrational.

Model 3: $\frac{2\sqrt{2}}{3\sqrt{98}} = \frac{2}{3}\sqrt{\frac{2}{98}} = \frac{2}{3}\sqrt{\frac{1}{49}} = \frac{2}{3} \cdot \frac{1}{7} = \frac{2}{21}$; in this case, the quotient of two irrational numbers is rational.

Model 4: $\frac{\sqrt{25}}{\sqrt{25}} = \sqrt{\frac{25}{25}} = \sqrt{1} = 1$ and $\frac{\sqrt{26}}{\sqrt{26}} = \sqrt{\frac{26}{26}} = \sqrt{1} = 1$; in these cases, the quotients of a rational number by itself and an irrational number by itself are both equal to 1.

PROPERTY

For positive A, $\frac{\sqrt{A}}{\sqrt{A}} = 1$.

Quotients of radical expressions having variables are found in the same manner.

Model 1: $\dfrac{5\sqrt{12x^3}}{\sqrt{3x}} = \dfrac{5}{1}\sqrt{\dfrac{12x^3}{3x}} = 5\sqrt{4x^2} = 5 \cdot 2x = 10x$

Model 2: $\dfrac{-3a\sqrt{32b^2}}{b\sqrt{16}} = \dfrac{-3a}{b}\sqrt{\dfrac{32b^2}{16}} = -\dfrac{3a}{b}\sqrt{2b^2}$; but this radicand

has a square factor of b^2, so we must simplify:

$$-\dfrac{3a}{b}\sqrt{2b^2} = -\dfrac{3a}{b}\sqrt{b^2}\sqrt{2} = -\dfrac{3a}{\cancel{b}} \cdot \cancel{b}\sqrt{2} = -3a\sqrt{2}$$

Model 3: $\dfrac{\sqrt{50y^4z^5}}{-10\sqrt{yz}} = \dfrac{1}{-10}\sqrt{\dfrac{50y^4z^5}{yz}} = -\dfrac{1}{10}\sqrt{50y^3z^4} = -\dfrac{1}{10}\sqrt{25y^2z^4}\sqrt{2y}$

$$= \dfrac{1}{\cancel{2}\cancel{10}} \cdot 5yz^2\sqrt{2y}$$

$$= -\dfrac{yz^2}{2}\sqrt{2y}$$

If the dividend has indicated sums or differences of radicals, find the quotient of each of them with the divisor.

Model 1: $\dfrac{\sqrt{28} + \sqrt{14}}{\sqrt{7}} = \dfrac{\sqrt{28}}{\sqrt{7}} + \dfrac{\sqrt{14}}{\sqrt{7}} = \sqrt{4} + \sqrt{2} = 2 + \sqrt{2}$

Model 2: $\dfrac{15\sqrt{n^3} - 9\sqrt{n^2} + 6\sqrt{n}}{-3\sqrt{n}}$

$$= \dfrac{15\sqrt{n^3}}{-3\sqrt{n}} - \dfrac{9\sqrt{n^2}}{-3\sqrt{n}} + \dfrac{6\sqrt{n}}{-3\sqrt{n}}$$

$$= -5\sqrt{n^2} - (-3\sqrt{n}) + (-2 \cdot 1)$$

$$= -5n + 3\sqrt{n} - 2$$

▶▶▶ **Find the quotients. Be sure your answers are in simplified radical form.**

2.146 $\dfrac{\sqrt{50}}{\sqrt{2}}$ _____

2.147 $\dfrac{7\sqrt{6}}{\sqrt{2}}$ _____

2.148 $\dfrac{-12\sqrt{30}}{3\sqrt{6}}$ _____

2.149 $\dfrac{\sqrt{80}}{2\sqrt{5}}$ _____

2.150 $\dfrac{-4\sqrt{3}}{-\sqrt{48}}$ _____

2.151 $\dfrac{\sqrt{8y}}{\sqrt{y}}$ _____

2.152 $\dfrac{\sqrt{32x^3y^5}}{-5\sqrt{2xy}}$ _____

2.153 $\dfrac{\sqrt{60a^{18}b}}{\sqrt{3a^2}}$ _____

2.154 $\dfrac{\sqrt{15a^6}}{\sqrt{3a^4}}$ _____

2.155 $\dfrac{3\sqrt{m^5} + 5\sqrt{m^3}}{\sqrt{m}}$ _____

2.156 $\dfrac{\sqrt{0.08} + \sqrt{0.0032}}{\sqrt{2}}$ _____

2.157 $\dfrac{3\sqrt{22}}{6\sqrt{2}}$ _____

2.158 $\dfrac{\sqrt{x^3y^2}}{\sqrt{9x^7}}$ _____

2.159 $\dfrac{\sqrt{3y}}{\sqrt{y}}$ _____

2.160 $\dfrac{21\sqrt{5}}{-7\sqrt{125}}$ _____

2.161 $\dfrac{\sqrt{abc} - \sqrt{bcd}}{\sqrt{bc}}$ _____

2.162 $\dfrac{\sqrt{18a} + \sqrt{50a} - \sqrt{72a}}{\sqrt{2a}}$ _____

2.163 $\dfrac{\sqrt{60} - \sqrt{240}}{\sqrt{6}}$ _____

2.164 $\dfrac{8\sqrt{x^7} - 6\sqrt{x^5}}{2\sqrt{x^3}}$ _____

2.165 $\dfrac{20\sqrt{38}}{8\sqrt{19} - 6\sqrt{19}}$ _____

RATIONALIZATION OF DENOMINATORS

If an indicated quotient results in a fraction within a radical sign or in a radical in the denominator of a fraction, then that answer is not in simplified form.

You have already learned one method for simplifying fractions within radicals.

Model 1: Find the quotient of $\sqrt{3}$ and $\sqrt{7}$.

Solution 1: $\dfrac{\sqrt{3}}{\sqrt{7}} = \sqrt{\dfrac{3}{7}} = \sqrt{\dfrac{3}{7} \cdot \dfrac{7}{7}} = \sqrt{\dfrac{21}{49}} = \dfrac{\sqrt{21}}{\sqrt{49}} = \dfrac{\sqrt{21}}{7}$

Solution 2: $\dfrac{\sqrt{3}}{\sqrt{7}} = \dfrac{\sqrt{3}}{\sqrt{7}} \; \dfrac{\sqrt{7}}{\sqrt{7}} = \dfrac{\sqrt{21}}{7}$; this procedure is known

as *rationalizing the denominator* since the irrational denominator

$\sqrt{7}$ becomes the rational denominator 7.

Study the following models to see how the denominator is rationalized in each case.

Model 2: $\dfrac{3}{\sqrt{8}} = \dfrac{3}{\sqrt{8}} \cdot \dfrac{\sqrt{2}}{\sqrt{2}} = \dfrac{3\sqrt{2}}{\sqrt{16}} = \dfrac{3\sqrt{2}}{4}$

Model 3: $\dfrac{5\sqrt{x}}{\sqrt{5y}} = \dfrac{5\sqrt{x}}{\sqrt{5y}} \cdot \dfrac{\sqrt{5y}}{\sqrt{5y}} = \dfrac{5\sqrt{5xy}}{5y} = \dfrac{\sqrt{5xy}}{y}$

Model 4: $\dfrac{-2\sqrt{a}}{3\sqrt{bc^3}} = \dfrac{-2\sqrt{a}}{3\sqrt{bc^3}} \cdot \dfrac{\sqrt{bc}}{\sqrt{bc}} = \dfrac{-2\sqrt{abc}}{3\sqrt{b^2c^4}} = -\dfrac{2\sqrt{abc}}{3bc^2}$

Model 5: $\dfrac{\sqrt{8}-10}{\sqrt{12}} = \dfrac{\sqrt{8}-10}{\sqrt{12}} \cdot \dfrac{\sqrt{3}}{\sqrt{3}} = \dfrac{\sqrt{24}-10\sqrt{3}}{\sqrt{36}} = \dfrac{\sqrt{24}-10\sqrt{3}}{6}$, but

$\sqrt{24} = \sqrt{4}\sqrt{6} = 2\sqrt{6}$; the quotient is simplified as follows:

$\dfrac{\sqrt{24}-10\sqrt{3}}{6} = \dfrac{2\sqrt{6}-10\sqrt{3}}{6} = \dfrac{\cancel{2}(\sqrt{6}-5\sqrt{3})}{\cancel{6}_3} = \dfrac{\sqrt{6}-5\sqrt{3}}{3}$

 Find each quotient (in simplified form).

2.166 $\dfrac{4}{\sqrt{5}}$ _____

2.167 $\dfrac{\sqrt{7}}{2\sqrt{11}}$ _____

2.168 $\dfrac{7}{\sqrt{x}}$ _____

2.169 $\dfrac{-30}{\sqrt{8}}$ _____

2.170 $\dfrac{2\sqrt{3}}{3\sqrt{5}}$ _____

2.171 $\dfrac{\sqrt{m}}{\sqrt{9n^3}}$ _____

2.172 $\dfrac{6 - \sqrt{18}}{\sqrt{27}}$ _____

2.173 $\dfrac{5\sqrt{x} + \sqrt{5y}}{\sqrt{20x}}$ _____

2.174 $\dfrac{-4}{3\sqrt{2}}$ _____

2.175 $\dfrac{3 - \sqrt{3}}{\sqrt{3}}$ _____

2.176 $\dfrac{ab}{\sqrt{b}}$ _____

2.177 $\dfrac{\sqrt{3} + \sqrt{y}}{\sqrt{12y}}$ _____

2.178 $\dfrac{\sqrt{a} - \sqrt{b}}{\sqrt{ab}}$ _____

2.179 $\dfrac{3x^2}{-\sqrt{18}}$ _____

2.180 $\dfrac{-7\sqrt{m}}{\sqrt{7m^3}}$ _____

Review the material in this section in preparation for the Self Test. This Self Test will check your mastery of this particular section as well as your knowledge of the previous section.

SELF TEST 2

Complete these items (each answer, 2 points).

2.01 Convert the fraction $\frac{15}{8}$ to its equivalent decimal form.

_____

2.02 Convert the decimal $0.\overline{81}$ to its equivalent fraction form.

_____

Complete these items (each numbered item, 3 points).

2.03   Give the order of the rational numbers $\frac{42}{19}$, 2.1, and $2\frac{1}{9}$.

$$\underline{\hspace{4em}} < \underline{\hspace{4em}} < \underline{\hspace{4em}}$$

2.04   Find the rational number $\frac{2}{3}$ of the way between 1 and 7.5.

2.05   Draw the graph of $-\pi \leq x < 2\frac{3}{4}$.

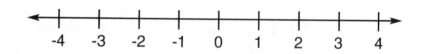

a. Tell whether each of the following real numbers is rational or irrational;
b. then round each to the nearest tenth (each answer, 2 points).

2.06   3.616116111...   a._____   b._____

2.07 $-0.2\overline{8}$ a._____   b._____

Find each indicated root (each answer, 3 points).

2.08 $\sqrt{36a^{10}b^2}$ _____

2.09 $\sqrt[3]{-8x^3y^6}$ _____

Show your steps in obtaining the simplified radical form of each expression (each answer, 4 points).

2.010 $\sqrt{125}$ _____

2.011 $-\frac{2}{3}\sqrt{63x^3}$ _____

2.012 $\sqrt{\frac{5}{8}}$ _____

2.013 $\frac{y}{x}\sqrt{\frac{1}{2y}}$ _____

Combine like radicals in each expression (each answer, 4 points).

2.014 $5a\sqrt{2} + 3a\sqrt{2}$ _____

2.015 $m\sqrt{p} + n\sqrt{p} - \sqrt{p}$ _____

Simplify radicals and combine when possible (each answer, 4 points).

2.016 $\sqrt{45} + \sqrt{20} - \sqrt{5}$

2.017 $\sqrt{12x^2} - \frac{x}{5}\sqrt{75} + \sqrt{3x}$

Find each product and simplify (each answer, 4 points).

2.018 $(3\sqrt{5})(-\frac{1}{6}\sqrt{7})$ _____

2.019 $a\sqrt{b} \bullet b\sqrt{c} \bullet c\sqrt{ab}$ _____

2.020 $\sqrt{2x}\,(7 + \sqrt{2x})$ _____

2.021 $(5 + \sqrt{3})^2$ _____

Find each quotient and simplify (each answer, 4 points).

2.022 $\dfrac{-5\sqrt{12}}{2\sqrt{3}}$ _____

2.023 $\dfrac{\sqrt{96x^3}}{\sqrt{2x}}$ _____

2.024 $\dfrac{\sqrt{a^2b}+\sqrt{ab^2}}{\sqrt{ab}}$ _____

2.025 $\dfrac{8+\sqrt{6}}{\sqrt{2}}$ _____

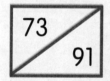

Score _____

Teacher check _____

              Initial   Date

OBJECTIVES

When you have completed this section, you should be able to:

8. Solve equations having irrational roots.

9. Solve equations containing radical expressions.

In this final section, you will apply what you have learned in the two preceding sections of this LIFEPAC to solve equations. You will solve some in which the answers contain radicals and some in which the equations themselves contain radicals.

SOLVING FOR IRRATIONAL ROOTS

In previous LIFEPACS you solved many equations having answers (roots) that were integers or rational numbers. Now you will be able to solve equations that have irrational answers as well. Any answer that contains a radical must be simplified as you have just learned; for your review, the three requirements for simplified radical expressions are listed again:

1. No radicand can be a square or have any square factor (other than 1).
2. No fraction can be within a radical sign.
3. No radical can be in a denominator.

Compare the solutions of the four equations in the following models.

Model 1:
$$3x - 2 = 7$$
$$3x = 9$$
$$x = 3$$

Model 2:
$$3x - \sqrt{2} = 7$$
$$3x = 7 + \sqrt{2}$$
$$x = \frac{7 + \sqrt{2}}{3}$$

Model 3:
$$\sqrt{3}\,x - 2 = 7$$
$$\sqrt{3}\,x = 9$$
$$x = \frac{9}{\sqrt{3}} = \frac{9}{\sqrt{3}} \cdot \frac{\sqrt{3}}{\sqrt{3}} = \frac{9\sqrt{3}}{3} = 3\sqrt{3}$$

Model 4:
$$\sqrt{3}\,x - \sqrt{2} = 7$$
$$\sqrt{3}\,x = 7 + \sqrt{2}$$
$$x = \frac{7 + \sqrt{2}}{\sqrt{3}} = \frac{7 + \sqrt{2}}{\sqrt{3}} \cdot \frac{\sqrt{3}}{\sqrt{3}} = \frac{7\sqrt{3} + \sqrt{6}}{3}$$

Model 1 has a rational root, but the other three models have irrational roots. Although the four equations are somewhat similar, the answers are certainly different. To see this fact more clearly, we shall determine a rational approximation for each irrational answer by finding the infinite nonrepeating decimal, performing any indicated operations, and rounding the resulting decimal. Use a calculator to verify these results.

EQUATION	EXACT ROOT	RATIONAL APPROXIMATION TO THE NEAREST TENTH
$3x - 2 = 7$	3	
$3x - \sqrt{2} = 7$	$\dfrac{7 + \sqrt{2}}{3}$	$\dfrac{7 + 1.414...}{3}$ $= \dfrac{8.414...}{3}$ $= 2.804...$ $\doteq 2.8$
$\sqrt{3}x - 2 = 7$	$3\sqrt{3}$	$3(1.732...)$ $= 5.196$ $\doteq 5.2$
$\sqrt{3}x - \sqrt{2} = 7$	$\dfrac{7\sqrt{3} + \sqrt{6}}{3}$	$\dfrac{7(1.732...) + 2.449...}{3}$ $= \dfrac{12.124... + 2.449...}{3}$ $= \dfrac{14.573...}{3}$ $= 4.857...$ $\doteq 4.9$

Model: Solve the equation $4 - \frac{\sqrt{5}}{2}n = \sqrt{11}$ for both the exact irrational root and its rational approximation to the nearest tenth.

Solution: $4 - \frac{\sqrt{5}}{2}n = \sqrt{11}$

The LCD is 2.

$$2\left[4 - \frac{\sqrt{5}}{2}n\right] = 2[\sqrt{11}]$$

$$8 - \sqrt{5}n = 2\sqrt{11}$$

$$-\sqrt{5}n = 2\sqrt{11} - 8$$

$$n = \frac{2\sqrt{11} - 8}{-\sqrt{5}}$$

$$n = \frac{2\sqrt{11} - 8}{-\sqrt{5}} \cdot \frac{\sqrt{5}}{\sqrt{5}}$$

$$= \frac{2\sqrt{55} - 8\sqrt{5}}{-5} ,$$

and $\dfrac{2\sqrt{55} - 8\sqrt{5}}{-5} = \dfrac{2(7.416...) - 8(2.236...)}{-5}$

$$= 0.611...$$

$$\doteq 0.6.$$

$\therefore$ The exact answer is $-\dfrac{2\sqrt{55} - 8\sqrt{5}}{5}$, and the approximate answer is 0.6.

When you write an expression such as $\sqrt{15}y$, you must be careful that the radical sign does not extend over the variable since the expression $\sqrt{15y}$ has a different meaning. For this reason, $y\sqrt{15}$ is often written instead of $\sqrt{15}y$.

Solve each question for both the exact irrational root and its rational approximation to the nearest tenth. Circle your answers.

3.1 $\qquad a + \sqrt{2} = 7$

3.2 $b - 5 = \sqrt{19}$

3.3 $4d + 1 = \sqrt{3}$

3.4 $\sqrt{7} - 2f = 4$

3.5 $\qquad \sqrt{3}q + 2 = \sqrt{5}$

3.6 $\qquad 3h + \sqrt{2} = \sqrt{5}$

3.7 $\qquad \frac{k}{3} - \sqrt{11} = 4$

3.8 $\qquad \dfrac{m}{\sqrt{3}} - 11 = 4$

3.9 $\qquad 8n = \sqrt{6}$

3.10 $\qquad \sqrt{8}p = 6$

3.11 $q\sqrt{8} = \sqrt{6}$

3.12 $\dfrac{\sqrt{2}}{3}r + 1 = 23$

3.13 $\dfrac{\sqrt{2}}{3}s + 1 = \sqrt{23}$

3.14 $\quad\sqrt{52} - t = 72$

3.15 $\quad 52 - u = \sqrt{72}$

3.16 $\quad 5 - \dfrac{\sqrt{17}}{5}v = 1$

3.17 $\quad\sqrt{4}w + \sqrt{9}w = \sqrt{13}$

3.18 $\sqrt{12}(\sqrt{3} - x) = 15$

3.19 $\dfrac{y - \sqrt{2}}{3} = \dfrac{1}{2}$

3.20 $\pi z - \sqrt{10} = 0$

Now you will look at two types of equations involving radical expressions. The first equations have literal radicands; the second equations have literal constants.

RADICAL EQUATIONS

A radical equation contains a variable within a radical sign. Of course, you should already be in the habit of checking the root(s) for any equation that you solve; however, for this type of equation, the check is essential.

DEFINITION

A *radical equation* is an equation having a variable within a radical sign.

Model 1: $2\sqrt{x} = 17$ is a radical equation.

Model 2: $\sqrt{2x} = 17$ is a radical equation.

Model 3: $\sqrt{2}x = 17$ is not a radical equation.

The following steps are to be used in solving a radical equation:
1. Isolate the radical expression containing the variable on one side of the equation.
2. Square both sides of the equation to eliminate that radical.
3. Solve for the variable.
4. Check the root in the original equation.

Study the solutions to these four equations carefully.

Model 1: $\sqrt{y} - 7 = 0$

$$\sqrt{y} = 7$$

$$(\sqrt{y})^2 = 7^2$$

$$y = 49$$

Check: $\sqrt{49} - 7 \overset{?}{=} 0$

$$7 - 7$$

$$0 \;\checkmark$$

∴ The root is 49.

Model 2: $\sqrt{y + 1} - 7 = 0$

$$\sqrt{y + 1} = 0$$

$$(\sqrt{y + 1})^2 = 7^2$$

$$y + 1 = 49$$

$$y = 48$$

Check: $\sqrt{48 + 1} - 7 \overset{?}{=} 0$

$$\sqrt{49} - 7$$

$$7 - 7$$

$$0 \sqrt{}$$

$\therefore$ The root is 48.

Model 3: $\sqrt{2z - 1} = 8$

$$(\sqrt{2z - 1})^2 = 8^2$$

$$2z - 1 = 64$$

$$2z = 65$$

$$z = \frac{65}{2} \text{ or } 32.5$$

Check: $\sqrt{2(32.5) - 1} \overset{?}{=} 8$

$$\sqrt{65 - 1}$$

$$\sqrt{64}$$

$$8 \sqrt{}$$

$\therefore$ The root is 32.5.

Model 4: $3\sqrt{z} + 2 = 1$

$$3\sqrt{z} = -1$$

$$(3\sqrt{z})^2 = (-1)^2$$

$$9z = 1$$

$$z = \frac{1}{9}$$

78

Check: $3\sqrt{\frac{1}{9}} + 2 \overset{?}{=} 1$

$\cancel{3} \cdot \frac{1}{\cancel{3}} + 2$

$1 + 2$

$3 \neq 1$

$\therefore$ This equation has no root.

The fact that Model 4 has no root should point out the importance of checking radical equations. Before reading on, look again at the solution of $3\sqrt{z} + 2 = 1$ to see if you can find an early step that would tell you that no root for this equation exists. (HINT: Remember that the radical sign, $\sqrt{}$, indicates the principal square root).

If you identified the step $3\sqrt{z} = -1$, then you were correct. 3 is positive and $\sqrt{z}$ is positive (the principal square root of z); and the product of two positive values must be positive. Thus, $3\sqrt{z}$ could never be -1. At this step you can conclude that the equation has no root.

If the variable appears more than once in an equation, the procedure may be modified slightly.

Model 1: $\sqrt{3x - 1} - \sqrt{x + 2} = 0$

$\sqrt{3x - 1} = \sqrt{x + 2}$

$(\sqrt{3x - 1})^2 = (\sqrt{x + 2})^2$

$3x - 1 = x + 2$

$2x = 3$

$= \frac{3}{2}$ or 1.5

Check: $\sqrt{3(1.5) - 1} - \sqrt{1.5 + 2} \overset{?}{=} 0$

$\sqrt{4.5 - 1} - \sqrt{1.5 + 2}$

$\sqrt{3.5} - \sqrt{3.5}$

$0\sqrt{}$

$\therefore$ The root is 1.5.

Model 2: $x - \sqrt{x^2 - 4} = 2$

$$-\sqrt{x^2 - 4} = 2 - x$$

$$(-\sqrt{x^2 - 4})^2 = (2 - x)^2$$

$$x^2 - 4 = 4 - 4x + x^2$$

$$-4 = 4 - 4x$$

$$-8 = -4x$$

$$2 = x$$

Check: $2 - \sqrt{2^2 - 4} \overset{?}{=} 2$

$$2 - \sqrt{4 - 4}$$

$$2 - \sqrt{0}$$

$$2 - 0$$

$$2 \checkmark$$

∴The root is 2.

 Solve and check each radical equation.

3.21 $\sqrt{a} - 5 = 0$

3.22 $\sqrt{a + 1} - 5 = 0$

3.23 $\quad$ $\sqrt{a} + 1 + 5 = 0$

3.24 $\quad$ $\sqrt{a + 5} = 0$

3.25 $\quad$ $\sqrt{3x + 1} = 7$

3.26 $\quad$ $\sqrt{3x - 1} = 7$

3.27 $\sqrt{3x} + 1 = 7$

3.28 $3\sqrt{x} + 1 = 7$

3.29 $\sqrt{2y - 5} + 4 = 8$

3.30 $\sqrt{2y - 5} + 8 = 4$

3.31 $\quad\sqrt{7a - 10} - \sqrt{2a + 5} = 0$

3.32 $\quad\sqrt{5m + 3} - \sqrt{3m + 5} = 0$

3.33 $\quad y - \sqrt{y^2 - 9} = 3$

3.34 $\quad\sqrt{x^2 - 25} + 5 = x$

3.35 $\qquad \sqrt{z^2 + 5} - 2 = z$

LITERAL EQUATIONS

The solution procedure can also be used to solve literal radical equations for a particular variable.

Model 1: Solve $k = \sqrt{\dfrac{n}{3}}$ for n.

Solution: $\qquad (k)^2 = (\sqrt{\tfrac{n}{3}})^2$

$$k^2 = \tfrac{n}{3}$$

$$3 \cdot k^2 = \cancel{3} \cdot \tfrac{n}{\cancel{3}} \text{ or } n = 3k^2$$

Model 2: Solve $\quad a - 1 = \sqrt{2b + 3}$ for b.

Solution: $\quad (a - 1)^2 = (\sqrt{2b + 3})^2$

$$a^2 - 2a + 1 = 2b + 3$$

$$a^2 - 2a - 2 = 2b \quad \text{or} \quad b = \frac{a^2 - 2a - 2}{2}$$

Note: $(a - 1)^2$ means $(a - 1)(a - 1)$, and $(a - 1)^2 \neq a^2 + 1$.

 Solve each equation for the indicated variable.

3.36 $\qquad m = \sqrt{\dfrac{p}{2}}$ for p.

3.37 $2a = \sqrt{\dfrac{b}{7}}$ for b.

3.38 $r = \sqrt{\dfrac{s}{t}}$ for s.

3.39 $r = \sqrt{\dfrac{s}{t}}$ for t.

3.40 $y - 1 = \sqrt{3z + 2}$ for z.

3.41 $\qquad d + 3 = \sqrt{2k - 5}$ for k.

3.42 $\qquad \sqrt{a + 9} = b + 3$ for a.

3.43 $\qquad \sqrt{m - 10n} = n - 5$ for m.

3.44 $\qquad \sqrt{\dfrac{a - 3b}{2}} = c$ for a.

3.45 $\qquad \sqrt{\dfrac{a - 3b}{2}} = c$ for b.

Before you take this last Self Test, you may want to do one or more of these self checks.

1. _____ Read the objectives. See if you can do them.
2. _____ Restudy the material related to any objectives that you cannot do.
3. _____ Use the SQ3R study procedure to review the material:
   a. **S**can the sections.
   b. **Q**uestion yourself (review the questions you wrote initially).
   c. **R**ead to answer your questions.
   d. **R**ecite the answers to yourself.
   e. **R**eview areas you did not understand.
4. _____ Review all vocabulary, activities, and Self Tests, writing a correct answer for every wrong answer.

SELF TEST 3

Give an example of a real number in infinite decimal form for each item (each answer, 2 points).

3.01   A rational number   _____

3.02   An irrational number   _____

Complete these items (each answer, 3 points).

3.03   Find the rational number $0.\overline{3}$ of the way between $-\frac{1}{2}$ and 4.

3.04   Draw the graph of $|x| > \sqrt{5}$.

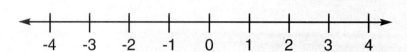

Perform any indicated operation(s) and give the simplified radical form for each expression (each answer, 4 points).

3.05 $\sqrt[3]{-27a^3b^{12}}$ _____

3.06 $\sqrt{108x^5y^6}$ _____

3.07 $4\sqrt{n^2} + \sqrt{m^2n} - \sqrt{4n^2} - \sqrt{mn^2}$ _____

3.08 $\frac{1}{6}\sqrt{6}(3\sqrt{2}-2\sqrt{3})$ _____

3.09 $\frac{\sqrt{5x}}{x\sqrt{20}}$ _____

Solve each equation for both the exact irrational root and its rational approximation to the nearest hundredth (each numbered item, 4 points).

3.010 $x + 5 = \sqrt{37}$

3.011 $\frac{m}{2} - \sqrt{5} = 3$

3.012 $\pi y - 1 = \sqrt{8}$

Solve and check each radical equation (each answer, 4 points).

3.013 $3 - \sqrt{x} = 0$

3.014 $\sqrt{2y - 1} - 1 = 2$

3.015 $\sqrt{z^2 + 8z} + 4 = z$

Solve each equation for the indicated variable (each answer, 4 points).

3.016 $r = \sqrt{\dfrac{A}{\pi}}$ for A.

3.017 $a + 1 = \sqrt{b + 1}$ for b.

3.018 $\sqrt{\dfrac{5m - n}{3}} = p$ for n.

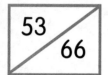

53
66

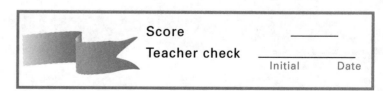

Before taking the LIFEPAC Test, you may want to do one or more of these self checks.

1. _____ Read the objectives. See if you can do them.
2. _____ Restudy the material related to any objectives that you cannot do.
3. _____ Use the SQ3R study procedure to review the material.
4. _____ Review activities, Self Tests, and LIFEPAC vocabulary words.
5. _____ Restudy areas of weakness indicated by the last Self Test.

GLOSSARY

approximation — A nonexact value that is accurate enough for a specific purpose.

closure — A property that holds when an operation is performed on numbers in a set and the result is always a number of that set.

completeness — A property that holds only with the real numbers: a one-to-one correspondence exists between the real numbers and the points on the number line.

cube root — A value whose cube is the given quantity.

density — A property that holds when a third number of a set can always be found between any two numbers of that set.

index — The number written over a radical sign that indicates which root is to be found; if omitted, it is understood to be 2.

irrational number — A real number that cannot be written as a ratio of two integers or as a repeating decimal.

like radicals — Expressions having the same root index and the same radicand.

Nth root — A value whose *N*th power is the given quantity.

order — A comparison of the relative sizes of numbers or of their relative positions on the number line.

period — The number of digits that repeat in a rational decimal expression.

principal square root — The positive square root of a quantity.

radical equation — An equation having a variable within a radical sign.

radical expression — An indicated *N*th root of a quantity.

radical sign — The sign $\sqrt{}$ indicating that a root is to be found.

radicand —	The quantity within a radical sign.
rational number —	A real number that can be written as a ratio of two integers or as a repeating decimal.
real number —	A number that can be written as an infinite decimal expression; it may be rational or irrational.
repeating decimal —	A real (and rational) number whose infinite decimal expression has a digit or a group of digits that continue without end.
repetend bar —	The line drawn above the repeating digit(s) of a rational decimal expression.
square root —	A value whose square is the given quantity.
terminating decimal —	A real (and rational) number whose infinite decimal expression repeats zero.

MATHEMATICS 908
GRAPHING

CONTENTS

I. USING TWO VARIABLES 2

 Equations 2

 The Real–Number Plane 7

 Translations 12

II. APPLYING GRAPHING TECHNIQUES 22

 Lines 22

 Inequalities 51

 Absolute Values 58

III. WRITING EQUATIONS OF LINES 72

 Given Two Points 72

 Given One Point and the Slope 79

 Given the Graph 82

 Given a Related Line 84

Authors: Arthur C. Landrey, M.A.Ed.
                            Robert L. Zenor, M.A., M.S.

Editor-In-Chief: Richard W. Wheeler, M.A.Ed.
Editor: Robin Hintze Kreutzberg, M.B.A.
Consulting Editor: Rudolph Moore, Ph.D.
Revision Editor: Alan Christopherson, M.S.

Alpha Omega Publications®

804 N. 2nd Ave. E., Rock Rapids, IA 51246-1759
© MCMXCVI by Alpha Omega Publications, Inc.   All rights reserved.
LIFEPAC is a registered trademark of Alpha Omega Publications, Inc.

GRAPHING

In this LIFEPAC® you will continue your study in the mathematical system of algebra by learning about graphing. After seeing how two variables are used, you will learn the various techniques for showing the solutions to open sentences on the real-number plane. Finally, you will learn to write the equations of lines drawn in this plane.

OBJECTIVES

Read these objectives. The objectives tell you what you will be able to do when you have successfully completed this LIFEPAC.

When you have finished this LIFEPAC, you should be able to:

1. Find ordered-pair solutions for two-variable equations.

2. Locate points on the real-number plane.

3. Translate verbal statements to equations.

4. Draw the graphs for linear equations, linear inequalities, and open sentences involving absolute values.

5. Find the equations of lines from given information.

Survey the LIFEPAC. Ask yourself some questions about this study. Write your questions here.

_____

_____

_____

_____

_____

_____

_____

_____

I. USING TWO VARIABLES

OBJECTIVES

1. Find ordered-pair solutions for two-variable equations.
2. Locate points on the real-number plane.
3. Translate verbal statements to equations.

In this first section you will learn the introductory concepts and definitions needed for graphing: solving two-variable equations, plotting points on the real-number plane, and translating verbal sentences to equations.

EQUATIONS

You have already learned to find numerical answers for equations having one variable, such as $x + 2 = 5$, $3m + 2 = 7$, and $4 - |t| = 1.2$. For example, you know that the equation, $x + 2 = 5$, has exactly one integral solution, $x = 3$; but what about the equation, $x + y = 5$? Is $x = 3$ still a solution? Is 3 the only value for x that will give a solution? Let us investigate further.

The equation, $x + y = 5$, indicates that the sum of x and y is five. If x is 3, then the sum of 3 and y must be five; therefore y must be 2. Thus, $x = 3$ is a solution only when $y = 2$. Now 3 and 2 are certainly not the only two numbers having a sum of five; 1 and 4, 5 and 0, and -23 and 28 are just three examples of other pairs of integers with sums of five. Certain pairs of rational numbers (such as $3\frac{1}{3}$ and $1.\overline{6}$) and irrational numbers (such as $\sqrt{3} - 8$ and $13 - \sqrt{3}$) also have a sum of five. In fact, infinitely many real number solutions exist to the equation $x + y = 5$.

When an equation contains two variables, you must look for a relationship between those variables rather than just for the value(s) of a single variable. The solutions for such equations will be pairs of numbers that make true sentences. These solutions are called *ordered pairs* since the numbers are written in the alphabetical order of the two variables.

Model 1:   Find several ordered–pair solutions for $x + y = 5$

2

Solution: The ordered pairs are written as (x, y) since x is before y in the alphabet:

$$(3, 2),\ \ (1, 4),\ (5, 0),\ (\text{-}23, 28),\ (3\tfrac{1}{3},\ 1.\overline{6}),\ (\sqrt{3} - 8,\ 13 - \sqrt{3}).$$

You should notice that if the numbers are reversed in the solutions of Model 1, the resulting ordered pairs will also be solutions of $x + y = 5$. This situation is not always true.

Model 2:   Find three solutions for $2a - b = 1$.

Solution: You may use any real values you wish for one of the variables (usually the one nearer the beginning of the alphabet). Substitute each of the chosen values in the equation and solve for the remaining variable.

Suppose we choose 5, $\tfrac{1}{2}$, and 0 for a:

$$a = 5: \qquad 2 \cdot 5 - b = 1$$
$$10 - b = 1$$
$$b = 9$$

$$a = \tfrac{1}{2}: \qquad 2 \cdot \tfrac{1}{2} - b = 1$$
$$1 - b = 1$$
$$b = 0$$

$$a = 0: \qquad 2 \cdot 0 - b = 1$$
$$0 - b = 1$$
$$b = \text{-}1$$

$\therefore$ Three ordered-pair solutions of $2a - b = 1$ are $(5, 9)$, $(\tfrac{1}{2}, 0)$, and $(0, \text{-}1)$. They are in the order (a, b).

These ordered pairs cannot be reversed and still be solutions for $2a - b = 1$.

$(9, 5)$ is not a solution since $2 \cdot 9 - 5 \neq 1$.

$(0, \tfrac{1}{2})$ is not a solution since $2 \cdot 0 - \tfrac{1}{2} \neq 1$.

$(\text{-}1, 0)$ is not a solution since $2(\text{-}1) - 0 \neq 1$.

You must be very careful to put your pairs of numbers in the correct order when writing solutions to two-variable equations. The ordered pairs that make an equation true are said to *satisfy* that equation.

Complete the following activities.

Find the value of y for the given value of x in each of the following equations. Then write the ordered pairs.

1.1 $x + y = 10$

x	y	(x, y)
0		
2		
4		

1.2 $x - y = 8$

x	y	(x, y)
10		
8		
6		

Complete the ordered–pair solutions for each of the following equations.

1.3 $2x + y = 6$

$A = \quad \{(1, \underline{\quad}), \quad (0, \underline{\quad}), \quad (-1, \underline{\quad})...\}$

1.4 $\frac{x}{3} + y = 15$

$B = \quad \{(0, \underline{\quad}), \quad (3, \underline{\quad}), \quad (6, \underline{\quad})...\}$

1.5 $y = 2x - 3$

$C = \quad \{(-2, \underline{\quad}), \quad (0, \underline{\quad}), \quad (2, \underline{\quad})...\}$

Find three ordered–pair solutions for each of the following equations.

1.6 $x - y = 1$ a. _____ b. _____ c. _____

1.7 $x + y = -1$ a. _____ b. _____ c. _____

1.8 $2x - y = 7$ a. _____ b. _____ c. _____

1.9 $x + 2y = 0$ a. _____ b. _____ c. _____

1.10 $y - 3x + 1 = 0$ a. _____ b. _____ c. _____

Sometimes you may wish to find solutions by first changing the form of the original equation so that the variable nearer the end of the alphabet is written alone on one side of the equation.

Model 1:   Solve $y - 2x = 7$ for y.

Solution: $y - 2x = 7$
   $y = 7 + 2x$ or $y = 2x + 7$

4

Model 2:   Solve $a + 2b = 5$ for b.

Solution:
$$a + 2b = 5$$
$$2b = 5 - a$$
$$b = \frac{5 - a}{2} \text{ or } b = \frac{-a + 5}{2}$$

Model 3:   Solve $m - \frac{n}{2} = 1$ for n.

Solution:
$$2\left[m - \frac{n}{2} \right] = 2[\,1\,]$$
$$2m - n = 2$$
$$-n = -2m + 2$$
$$-1[\,-n\,] = -1[\,-2m + 2\,]$$
$$n = 2m - 2$$

 Solve each of the following equations for the variable indicated.

1.11 $3x + y = 1$ for y: _____

1.12 $x + 2y = -6$ for y: _____

1.13 $3a + 2b = 6$ for b: _____

1.14 $\frac{2r}{3} - 3s = 10$ for s: _____

1.15 $5x - 2y = 11$ for y: _____

DEFINITION

For a two–variable equation, the *domain* is the set of numbers to be used for the first (alphabetical) variable.

The elements of a set are listed between braces: { }.

The symbol $\in$ means *is an element of the set*.

Sets are often named with capital letters.

REMEMBER?

5

Model 1: Find the ordered pairs that satisfy the equation $3m + 2n = 7$ when the domain of m is $\{-5, 0, 3\frac{2}{3}\}$.

Solution: First solve for n:

$$3m + 2n = 7$$
$$2n = 7 - 3m$$
$$n = \frac{7 - 3m}{2}$$

Then complete the table:

m	-5	0	$3\frac{3}{2}$ or $\frac{11}{3}$
$\dfrac{7 - 3m}{2}$	$\dfrac{7 - 3(-5)}{2}$ $\dfrac{7 + 15}{2}$ $\dfrac{22}{2}$	$\dfrac{7 - 3 \cdot 0}{2}$ $\dfrac{7 - 0}{2}$ $\dfrac{7}{2}$	$\dfrac{7 - 3 \cdot \frac{11}{3}}{2}$ $\dfrac{7 - 11}{2}$ $\dfrac{-4}{2}$
n	11	$3\frac{1}{2}$	-2

∴ The ordered pairs are $(-5, 11)$, $(0, 3\frac{1}{2})$, and $(3\frac{2}{3}, -2)$.

Model 2: Find the ordered pairs that satisfy the equation $4s - |t| = 1.2$ when $s \in \{-2, 0.3, 1\}$.

Solution: Solve for $|t|$:

$$4s - |t| = 1.2$$
$$-|t| = 1.2 - 4s$$
$$|t| = -1.2 + 4s$$
$$\text{or } |t| = 4s - 1.2$$

Complete the table:

s	-2	0.3	1
$4s - 1.2$	$4(-2) \quad - \quad 1.2$ $-8 \quad - \quad 1.2$	$4(0.3) \quad - \quad 1.2$ $1.2 \quad - \quad 1.2$	$4(1) \quad - \quad 1.2$ $4 \quad - \quad 1.2$
$|t|$	-9.2	0	2.8
t	no values (since $|t|$ cannot be negative)	0	-2.8 or 2.8

∴ $(0.3, 0)$, $(1, -2.8)$, and $(1, 2.8)$ are solutions of $4s - |t| = 1.2$.

6

 **a. Solve each of the following equations for y; b. find the ordered pairs that satisfy the equation for the given domain.**

1.16 $x - y = 1$ $x \in \{-1, 0, 1\}$

       a. $y =$ _____   b. ____(-1, ___), (0, ___), (1, ___)____

1.17 $2x + y = 10$ $x \in \{\frac{1}{2}, \frac{1}{4}, \frac{1}{8}\}$

       a. $y =$ _____   b. _____

1.18 $\frac{3x}{5} + 2y = -1$ $x \in \{0, 5, 10\}$

       a. $y =$ _____   b. _____

1.19 $7x - 2y + 2 = 0$ $x \in \{0.5\ \ 1.5\ \ 2.5\}$

       a. $y =$ _____   b. _____

1.20 $\frac{x}{2} + \frac{y}{3} = \frac{1}{5}$ $x \in \{\frac{1}{3}, \frac{-1}{3}, 0\}$

       a. $y =$ _____   b. _____

 **Find three ordered–pair solutions for each of the following equations by selecting three convenient elements of the domain.**

1.21 $y = \frac{3x}{2} - 4$ _____

1.22 $2x + 3y = 5$ _____

1.23 $\frac{2x}{7} - \frac{y}{2} = 7$ _____

1.24 $|x| + y = 6$ _____

1.25 $|x| + |y| = 1$ _____

THE REAL–NUMBER PLANE

In Mathematics LIFEPAC 907, you learned to graph the solution points of one-variable equations on the *real-number line*. In this LIFEPAC you will be graphing the solution points of two-variable equations on the *real-number plane*. First, however, you need to learn the terminology and procedures of graphing.

Two reference lines or *axes* are drawn in the plane, one horizontally and one vertically, meeting at a common zero point called the *origin*. Each axis is a number line for one of the two variables. Since x and y are the letters used most frequently, the horizontal axis is known as the *x-axis* and the vertical axis is known as the *y-axis*.

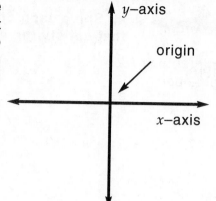

On the x-axis, positive numbers are to the right of the origin, and negative numbers are to the left of the origin. On the y-axis, positive numbers are above the origin, and negative numbers are below the origin. The axes separate the plane into four regions called *quadrants*, which are labeled with Roman numerals as indicated in the diagram.

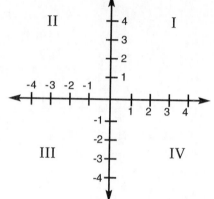

An ordered pair of numbers in the form (x, y) is used to locate any point in the plane. The value of x indicates the horizontal direction and distance of the point from the origin, and the value of y indicates the vertical direction and distance of the point from the origin. Of course, the ordered pair $(0, 0)$ represents the origin itself.

Suppose we wish to locate the point corresponding to the ordered pair (4, -2) on the plane at the right. (Note: A complete grid of intersecting lines is used so that points may be found more easily and accurately.) The first number indicates that the point is four units to the right of the origin; the second number indicates that the point is two units below the origin. Thus, to find the point (4, -2), begin at the origin and move four units right then two units down. You arrive at point *J* in Quadrant IV; a heavy dot is used to show (or *plot*) the point on the plane.

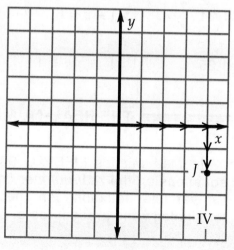

8

The order of the numbers written in the pair, as well as the order of movements from the origin, is very important. To see this fact, notice that point K corresponding to the ordered pair (-2, 4) is in Quadrant II and certainly is not the same point as J.

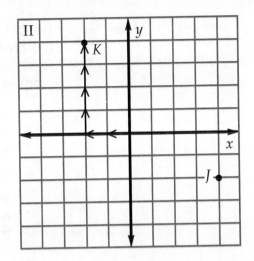

Model 1:   Plot the point corresponding to the ordered pair (-5, -1) and describe its location.

Solution: Begin at the origin and move five units left then one unit down.

This point is located in Quadrant III.

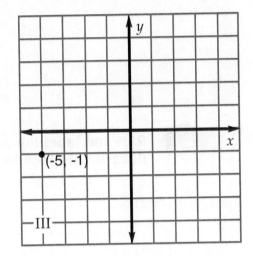

Model 2:   Plot the point for (0, -3) and describe its location.

Solution: The first value of 0 indicates that no horizontal movement is to be made. Thus, the point corresponding to (0, -3) is three units below the origin on the y-axis.

This point is located between Quadrants III and IV.

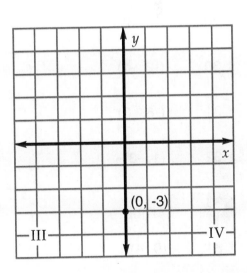

Model 3:   Describe the locations and name the ordered pairs corresponding to points L, M, and N in the diagram.

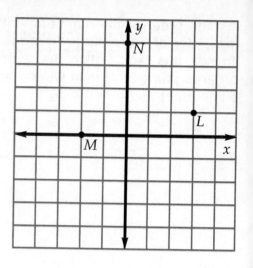

Solution: Point L—beginning at the origin, move 3 units right then 1 unit up; thus, the ordered pair is (3, 1).

Point M—beginning at the origin, move 2 units left then 0 units vertically; thus, the ordered pair is (-2, 0).

Point N—beginning at the origin, move 0 units horizontally then 4 units up; thus, the ordered pair is (0, 4).

 Plot and label the point corresponding to each given ordered pair; then describe its location.

1.26   (4, 3)

_____

1.27   (3, 4)

_____

1.28   (-2, 5)

_____

1.29   (-5, 3)

_____

1.30   (-2, -1)

_____

1.31   (-6, -3)

_____

1.32   (1, -3)

_____

1.33   (3, -3)

_____

1.34   (0, 4)

_____

1.35   (4, 0)

_____

1.36   (0, -2)

_____

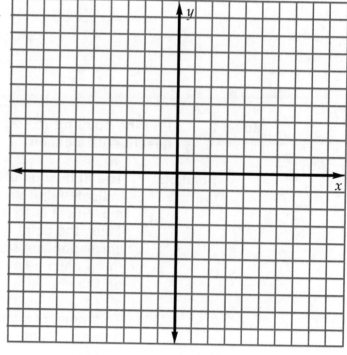

10

**a. Name the ordered pair corresponding to each point given on the graph;
b. describe its location.**

1.37   a. Point _A_   _____

      b. _____

1.38   a. Point _B_   _____

      b. _____

1.39   a. Point _C_   _____

      b. _____

1.40   a. Point _D_   _____

      b. _____

1.41   a. Point _E_   _____

      b. _____

1.42   a. Point _F_   _____

      b. _____

1.43   a. Point _G_   _____

      b. _____

1.44   a. Point _H_   _____

      b. _____

1.45   a. Point _I_   _____

      b. _____

1.46   a. Point _J_   _____

      b. _____

1.47   a. Point _K_   _____

      b. _____

1.48   a. Point _L_   _____

      b. _____

1.49   a. Point _M_   _____

      b. _____

1.50   a. Point _N_   _____

      b. _____

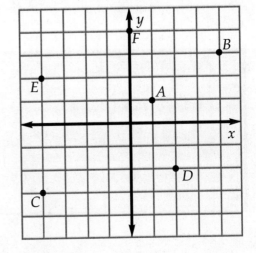

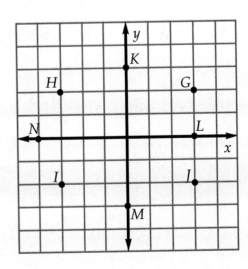

11

Now let us see how verbal statements can be translated to two-variable equations and then how points corresponding to their ordered-pair solutions can be graphed. First you need two definitions.

DEFINITION

The first number (or x-value) of an ordered pair is called *abscissa*.

The second number (or y-value) of an ordered pair is called *ordinate*.

Together, the abscissa and the ordinate are called the *coordinates*.

Model 1:   Points having positive abscissas and negative ordinates are all found in which quadrant?

     Solution: A positive abscissa indicates a positive x-value, and a negative ordinate indicates a negative y-value. Thus, the ordered pairs of these points are of the form (+, -). Beginning at the origin, move to the right, then downward.

           ∴ All (+, -) points are in Quadrant IV.

Model 2:   Describe the location of all points having an abscissa of zero and a positive ordinate.

     Solution: The ordered pairs of these points are of the form (0, +) and are found between Quadrants I and II.

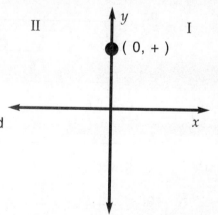

Describe the location of all points having the given coordinates.

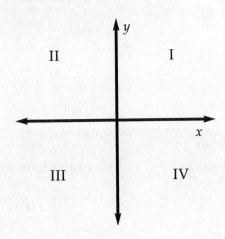

Quadrants:

Model: Positive abscissa, nonzero ordinate

Solution: Points are (+, +), (+, −)   <u>Quadrants I & IV</u>

1.51   Positive abscissa, positive ordinate   _____

1.52   Negative abscissa, negative ordinate   _____

1.53   Zero abscissa, negative ordinate   _____

1.54   Positive abscissa, zero ordinate   _____

1.55   Negative abscissa, positive ordinate   _____

1.56   Zero abscissa, zero ordinate   _____

1.57   Negative abscissa, zero ordinate   _____

1.58   Nonzero abscissa, positive ordinate   _____

1.59   Nonzero abscissa, negative ordinate   _____

1.60   Negative abscissa, nonzero ordinate   _____

1.61   Abscissa and ordinate have the same sign   _____

1.62   Abscissa and ordinate have opposite signs   _____

Any time the word *abscissa* appears in a verbal statement, it may be translated to the letter x. Any time the word *ordinate* appears in a verbal statement, it may be translated to the letter y. Study the following models to see how a relationship expressed verbally can be translated to an equation.

Model 1:   The ordinate is four less than the abscissa.

Solution: THE ORDINATE ⓘⓢ FOUR LESS THAN THE ABSCISSA
                        ↓   ↓
                        y $=$

$x - 4$ is the translation.

Model 2:   The sum of twice the abscissa and the ordinate is 13.

Solution: $2x + y = 13$ is the translation.

 For each of the following sentences, write a translation using x and y.

1.63   The ordinate is two more than the abscissa.   _____

1.64   The ordinate is three less than twice the abscissa.   _____

1.65   The sum of the abscissa and the ordinate is six.   _____

1.66   The difference between the ordinate and the

abscissa is two.   _____

1.67   Twice the abscissa increased by three times the

ordinate is ten.   _____

1.68   The ordinate exceeds half the abscissa by two.   _____

14

Once a verbal statement has been translated to a two-variable equation, ordered-pair solutions can be found, as shown previously in this LIFEPAC. The points corresponding to these ordered pairs can then be graphed on the real-number plane.

Model 1: Graph three points for "the ordinate is four less than the abscissa."

Solution: The translation is $y = x - 4$. First choose three values for x; then substitute each value into the equation and solve for y.

If you select $x = 3$: $y = 3 - 4 = -1$
If you select $x = 0$: $y = 0 - 4 = -4$
If you select $x = 5$: $y = 5 - 4 = 1$

Checks: (3, -1)

$y = x - 4$
$-1 \overset{?}{=} 3 - 4$
$\underline{\quad -1 \ \surd \quad}$

(0, -4)

$y = x - 4$
$-4 \overset{?}{=} 0 - 4$
$\underline{\quad -4 \ \surd \quad}$

(5, 1)

$y = x - 4$
$1 \overset{?}{=} 5 - 4$
$\underline{\quad 1 \ \surd \quad}$

Finally, plot the points for
(3, -1), (0, -4), and (5, 1).

As shown in Model 1, when the domain is not given, then you may use any real values for x that you desire; you may wish to choose values that will result in ordered pairs whose points are easy to plot. If the domain of x is given, then you must use those specified values.

15

Model 2: For $x \in \{-3, 0, 5\}$, graph the points whose ordered pairs correspond to "the difference of the abscissa and twice the ordinate is seven."

Solution: The translation is $x - 2y = 7$. First solve this equation for y:

$$x - 2y = 7$$
$$-2y = 7 - x$$
$$y = \frac{7 - x}{-2}$$

Then, using the given domain, find the three ordered pairs:

x	-3	0	5
$\dfrac{7-x}{-2}$	$\dfrac{7-(-3)}{-2}$	$\dfrac{7-0}{-2}$	$\dfrac{7-5}{-2}$
	$\dfrac{10}{-2}$	$\dfrac{7}{-2}$	$\dfrac{2}{-2}$
y	-5	-3.5	-1
(x, y)	(-3, -5)	(0, -3.5)	(5, -1)

Checks: (-3, -5)

$$x - 2y = 7$$
$$-3 - 2(-5) \overset{?}{=} 7$$
$$-3 + 10$$
$$\underline{7 \ \surd}$$

(0, -3,5)

$$x - 2y = 7$$
$$0 - 2(-3,5) \overset{?}{=} 7$$
$$0 + 7$$
$$\underline{7 \ \surd}$$

(5, -1)

$$x - 2y = 7$$
$$5 - 2(-1) \overset{?}{=} 7$$
$$5 + 2$$
$$7 \ \surd$$

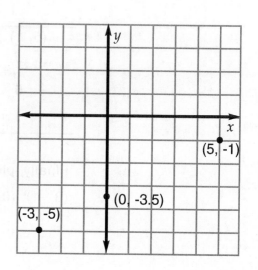

Finally, plot the points.

For each of the following problems, find three ordered pairs and graph them.

1.69 $x + y = 6$ and $x \in \{0, 1, -1\}$

_____   _____   _____

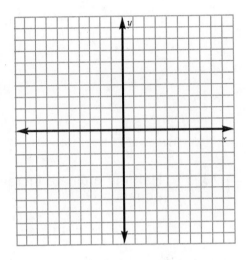

1.70 $y = 2x - 3$ and $x \in \{0, -1, 2\}$

_____   _____   _____

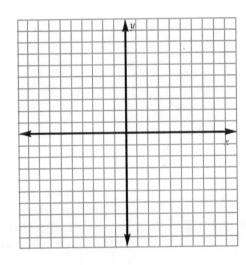

1.71   The ordinate equals the abscissa, and $x \in \{-3, 0, 3\}$.

_____   _____   _____

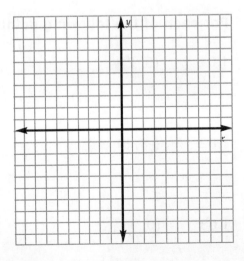

1.72   The ordinate is three more than twice the abscissa.

_____ _____ _____

1.73   Half the ordinate increased by one-third the abscissa
        equals six.

_____ _____ _____

Review the material in this section in preparation for the Self Test. This Self Test will check your mastery of this particular section. The items missed on this Self Test will indicate specific areas where restudy is needed for mastery.

SELF TEST 1

For each of the following points, describe its location on a grid (each answer, 3 points).

1.01   (6, 2)   _____

1.02   (-3, 5)   _____

1.03   (0, 1)   _____

1.04   (0, 0)   _____

1.05   (-6, -6)   _____

Name the ordered pair corresponding to each point on the graph (each answer, 3 points).

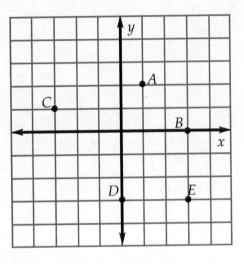

1.06   Point A _____

1.07   Point B _____

1.08   Point C _____

1.09   Point D _____

1.010   Point E _____

For each of the following sentences, write a translation using x and y (each answer, 3 points).

1.011   The ordinate is one-half the abscissa.   _____

1.012   The abscissa less the ordinate is one.   _____

1.013   The product of the abscissa and ordinate is ten.   _____

For each of the following equations, solve for y (each answer, 3 points).

1.014 $x + y = 6$ _____

1.015 $\frac{x}{2} - y + 6 = 0$ _____

1.016 $2x + 3y = 10$ _____

For each of the following equations, a. solve for y; b. find three ordered pairs; and c. graph the points (a. 3 points; b. 3 points; c. 4 points).

1.017   The ordinate is twice the abscissa.

c.

a. _____

b. _____   _____   _____

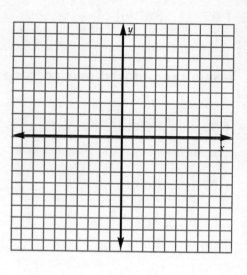

1.018 $x + y = 0$

c.

a. _____

b. _____   _____   _____

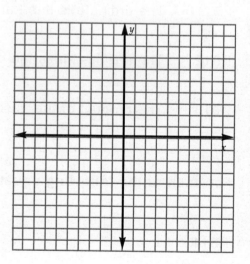

1.019 $x + \frac{y}{2} = 1$ and $x \in \{-2, 0, 2\}$

     a. _____

     b. _____   _____   _____

c

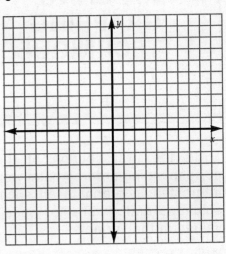

1.020 $3x - 2y = -1$

     a. _____

     b. _____   _____   _____

c.

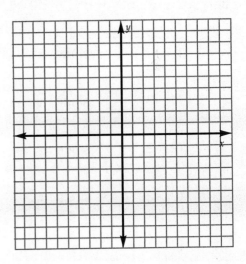

<table>
<tr><td>71</td></tr>
<tr><td>88</td></tr>
</table>

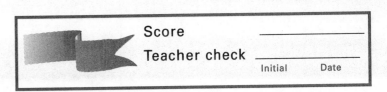

Score _____

Teacher check _____
               Initial   Date

II. APPLYING GRAPHING TECHNIQUES

OBJECTIVES

4. Draw the graphs for linear equations, linear inequalities, and open sentences involving absolute values.

In the first section of this LIFEPAC, you learned to graph several points whose corresponding ordered pairs were solutions to a two-variable equation; in this section we will be interested in graphing all such points for an equation or an inequality. You will also find solutions and graphs for special types of equations and inequalities that contain absolute values of the variables.

LINES

Graphs of lines are defined by linear equation, that is, equations in which the variables are of the first degree. You also need to learn about the x- and y-intercepts and the slope of a line.

LINEAR EQUATIONS

You have already seen that three solutions for equation, $x - 2y = 7$, are (-3, -5), (0, -3.5), and (5, -1); the points for these ordered pairs are graphed again in the diagram. Four other solutions for this equation are given in the following list:

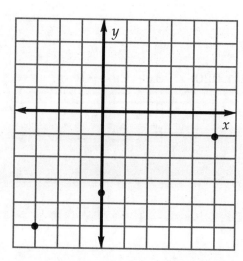

$$(-1, -4) \quad \text{since } x - 2y = -1 - 2(-4)$$
$$= -1 + 8 = 7$$
$$(1, -3) \quad \text{since } x - 2y = 1 - 2(-3)$$
$$= 1 + 6 = 7$$
$$(2, -2\tfrac{1}{2}) \quad \text{since } x - 2y = 2 - 2(-2\tfrac{1}{2})$$
$$= 2 + 5 = 7$$
$$(3, -2) \quad \text{since } x - 2y = 3 - 2(-2)$$
$$= 3 + 4 = 7$$

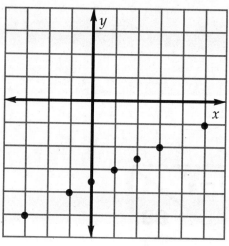

When the four points corresponding to these ordered pairs are included with the previous ones, the result is the seven-point graph shown.

Some other solutions are shown. (You should verify that each ordered pair does indeed satisfy $x - 2y = 7$.)

$(-3\frac{1}{2}, -5\frac{1}{4})$, $(-2, -4\frac{1}{2})$, $(-0.5, -3.75)$, $(\frac{1}{2}, -3\frac{1}{4})$,

$(4, -1\frac{1}{2})$, $(5.5, -0.75)$

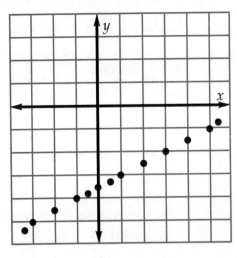

When these points are included with the previous ones, the result is the graph shown at the right. A (straight) line could be drawn through these thirteen points. The points are said to be *collinear*.

If we were to find more solutions (using both rational and irrational numbers), each point obtained would be collinear with those shown on the graph. Thus, if the domain of x is all the real numbers, then the graph for the equation, $x - 2y = 7$, is the "solid" lines of points shown. This line continues without end in both directions and represents all the points having ordered pairs that satisfy the equation.

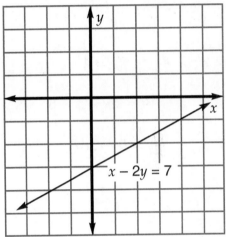

DEFINITIONS

A *linear equation* is an open sentence whose graph is a line, and the *general form* for such an equation is $Ax + By + C = 0$.

A and B are called the *coefficients* of x and y, respectively; C is called the *constant*.

Note: We shall be working only with rational coefficients and constants; therefore A, B, and C are to be integers, with the first nonzero coefficient being positive. Also, A, B, and C are to be *relatively prime*; that is, their greatest common factor must be 1.

Model 1:   Write $x - 2y = 7$ in the general form and identify A, B, and C.

Solution: $x - 2y = 7$

$\therefore x - 2y - 7 = 0$ is the general form;

$A = 1$, $B = -2$, and $C = -7$.

Model 2:   Write $y = \frac{1}{4} - \frac{2}{5}x$ in the general form and identify A, B, and C.

Solution:

$$y = \frac{1}{4} - \frac{2}{5}x$$

$$20[y] = 20[\frac{1}{4} - \frac{2}{5}x]$$

$$20y = 5 - 8x$$

$$\therefore \; 8x + 20y - 5 = 0 \text{ is the general form;}$$

$$A = 8, B = 20, \text{ and } C = -5.$$

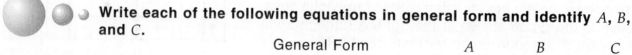 **Write each of the following equations in general form and identify** A, B, **and** C.

		General Form	A	B	C
2.1	$2x + y = 6$	_____	____	____	____
2.2	$y + 2x = 4$	_____	____	____	____
2.3	$3y - 2x - 1 = 0$	_____	____	____	____
2.4	$y = 6 - 2x$	_____	____	____	____
2.5	$x = 3y + 1$	_____	____	____	____
2.6	$7 = x - \frac{y}{3}$	_____	____	____	____
2.7	$x = 6$	_____	____	____	____
2.8	$\frac{x}{2} = 6 - y$	_____	____	____	____
2.9	$y = x$	_____	____	____	____
2.10	$y - 8 = 0$	_____	____	____	____

Actually, you do not need to plot as many points as are shown at the beginning of this section to be able to draw the line for a linear equation. In fact, two points determine a line; at least three points should be found, however, so that you can check to see that they are collinear.

Model 1:   Graph the line for $2x + 3y + 6 = 0$.

Solution: First, solve for y.

$$2x + 3y + 6 = 0$$

$$3y = -2x - 6$$

$$y = \frac{-2x - 6}{3}$$

Then pick at least three values for x. (Again you may choose any real values for x that you wish, but try to pick values that are easy to work with and to graph.) Solve for each corresponding y:

x	-3	0	3
$\dfrac{-2x-6}{3}$	$\dfrac{-2(-3)-6}{3}$	$\dfrac{-2(0)-6}{3}$	$\dfrac{-2(3)-6}{3}$
	$\dfrac{6-6}{3}$	$\dfrac{0-6}{3}$	$\dfrac{-6-6}{3}$
	$\dfrac{0}{3}$	$\dfrac{-6}{3}$	$\dfrac{-12}{3}$
y	0	-2	-4
(x, y)	(-3, 0)	(0, -2)	(3, -4)

Now plot three points and check to see that they are collinear; if so, draw the line that passes through them. (Be sure to use a straightedge.)

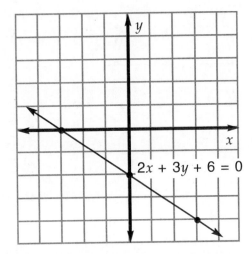

Model 2:   Graph the line for $x + 4 = 0$.

Solution: When this equation is written as $x + 0y + 4 = 0$, you can see that y has no effect since any y-value is multiplied by zero.
Solve for x: $x + 4 = 0$
$\qquad\qquad\quad x = -4$

Plot at least three points having an abscissa of -4, such as (-4, -2), (-4, 0), and (-4, 4); draw the line through them.

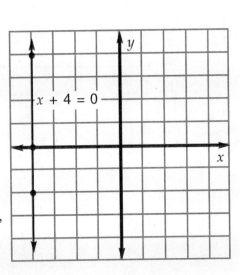

25

a. Solve each of the following equations for y (or for x if there is no y-term); b. find three points; and c. draw the line through the three points.

2.11 $x + y = 2$

        a. _____

        b. _____   _____   _____

c.

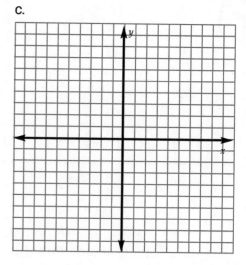

2.12 $y - x = 3$

        a. _____

        b. _____   _____   _____

c.

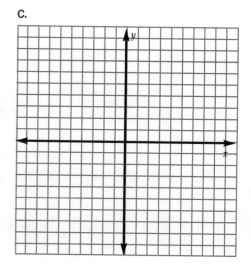

2.13 $x - 5 = 0$

        a. _____

        b. _____   _____   _____

c.

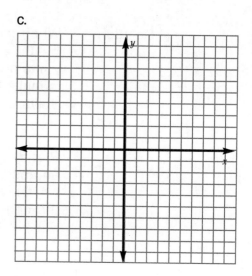

2.14 $y + 2 = 0$

a. _____

b. _____ _____ _____

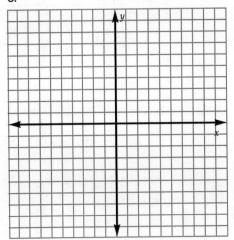

c.

2.15 $2x + y = 4$

a. _____

b. _____ _____ _____

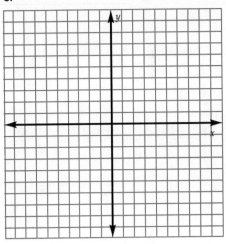

c.

2.16 $2x - y = 2$

a. _____

b. _____ _____ _____

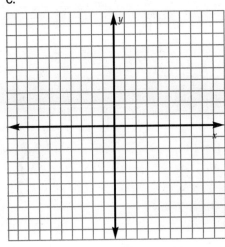

c.

2.17 $x + 2y = 6$

a. _____

b. _____   _____   _____

c.

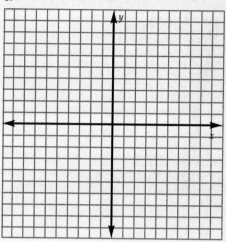

2.18 $2x - 3y = 6$

a. _____

b. _____   _____   _____

c.

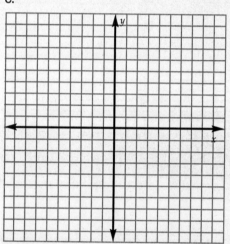

2.19 $5x + 2y = 3$

a. _____

b. _____   _____   _____

c.

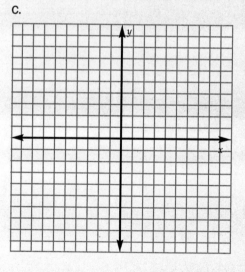

2.20 $3x = 1 - \frac{y}{2}$

a. _____   c.

b. _____ _____ _____

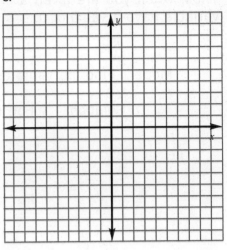

INTERCEPTS

A second method for graphing a line is perhaps the easiest and quickest way of all; however, it cannot be used for all linear equations. First let us see how and when it can be used. The following definitions should be learned.

DEFINITIONS

The *x–intercept* of a line is the *x*-value (*abscissa*) of the point where the line crosses the *x*-axis.

The *y–intercept* of a line is the *y*-value (*ordinate*) of the point where the line crosses the *y*-axis.

Model: The line shown crosses the *x*-axis at (-2, 0),
and it crosses the *y*-axis at (0, 3).

∴   The *x*-intercept is -2 and the
y-intercept is 3.

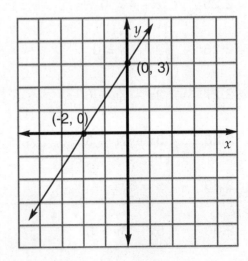

You should notice in the preceding model that the x-intercept occurs at the point (-2, 0) when the y-value is zero. Similarly, the y-intercept occurs at the point (0, 3) when the x-value is zero. Thus, when you are given a linear equation, you can find each intercept by letting the other variable have a value of 0.

Model: Find the x-intercept and the y-intercept of the line for $2x + y = 4$.

Solution: For the x-intercept, let $y = 0$ in the linear equation $2x + y = 4$;
$$2x + 0 = 4$$
$$2x = 4$$
$$x = 2$$

For the y-intercept, let $x = 0$ in the linear equation $2x + y = 4$;
$$2 \cdot 0 + y = 4$$
$$0 + y = 4$$
$$y = 4$$

∴ The x-intercept is 2 and the y-intercept is 4.

 For each of the following equations, find the x–intercept and the y–intercept of the corresponding line.

		x–intercept	y–intercept
2.21	$x + y = 7$	a. _____	b. _____
2.22	$x - y - 5 = 0$	a. _____	b. _____
2.23	$x = 10 - 2y$	a. _____	b. _____
2.24	$y = 3x - 9$	a. _____	b. _____
2.25	$x + 4 = 0$	a. _____	b. _____
2.26	$2y - 3 = 0$	a. _____	b. _____
2.27	$2x + 3y = 6$	a. _____	b. _____
2.28	$3x + 2y - 5 = 0$	a. _____	b. _____
2.29	$x = 3y$	a. _____	b. _____
2.30	$5x - 6y = 0$	a. _____	b. _____

Once each intercept is known, you can plot it on the appropriate axis. The line drawn through the two points where the intercepts occur will be the graph for the given linear equation.

Model: Using the intercept method, graph the line for $2x + y = 4$.

Solution: The x-intercept is 2, so plot the point (2, 0).

STEP 1:

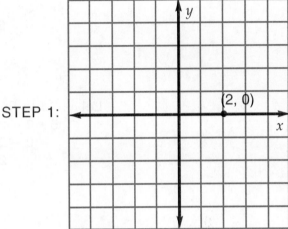

The y-intercept is 4, so plot the point (0, 4).

STEP 2:

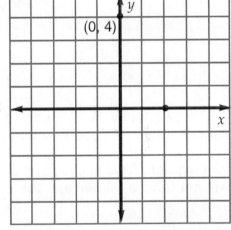

Draw the line through these two points.

STEP 3:

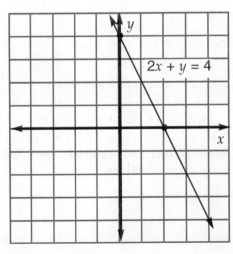

If an intercept is not an integer, then you will need to estimate the corresponding point's position on the axis.

Model: Using the intercept method, graph the line
for $5x - 2y - 8 = 0$.

Solution: Let $y = 0$ to find the x-intercept:
$$5x - 2 \bullet 0 - 8 = 0$$
$$5x - 0 - 8 = 0$$
$$5x - 8 = 0$$
$$5x = 8$$
$$x = \frac{8}{5} \text{ or } 1\frac{3}{5}$$

Let $x = 0$ to find the y-intercept:
$$5 \bullet 0 - 2y - 8 = 0$$
$$0 - 2y - 8 = 0$$
$$-2y - 8 = 0$$
$$-2y = 8$$
$$y = -4$$

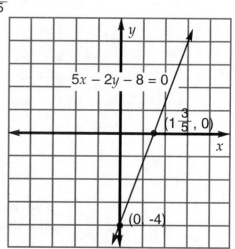

Plot the points $(1\frac{3}{5}, 0)$ and $(0, -4)$
and draw the line
through them.

Three types of linear equations require special consideration. As you saw earlier (Model 2 on page 25), an equation of the form $x = K$ (some constant) has a vertical line for its graph. This line is parallel to the y-axis and, of course, will not have a y-intercept; the x-intercept will be K.

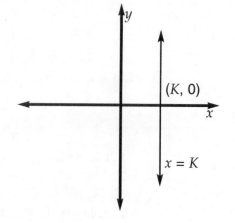

Likewise, an equation of the form $y = K$ (some constant) has a horizontal line for its graph. This line is parallel to the x-axis and, of course, will not have an x-intercept; the y-intercept will be K.

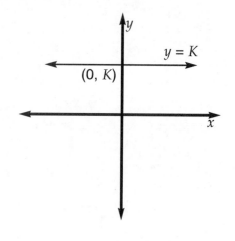

Finally, an equation such as $3x + y = 0$ requires the use of some method of graphing other than intercepts since both the x-intercept and the y-intercept are zero. This line passes through the origin and you need to find at least one other point to determine it.

Model: Graph the line for $3x + y = 0$.

Solution: Both intercepts are zero, so plot the point $(0, 0)$.

STEP 1:

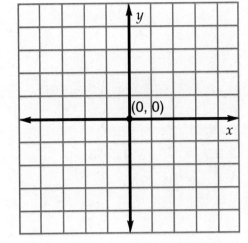

Now solve the equation for y and choose a value for x:
$$3x + y = 0$$
$$y = -3x$$
If $x = 2$, then $y = -3 \cdot 2$ or -6. Plot $(2, -6)$ and draw the line.

STEP 2:

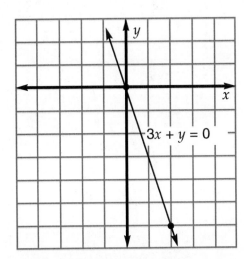

For each of the following equations, construct the graphs using the x- and y-intercepts. If both intercepts are zero, find at least one other point.

2.31 $x - y = 3$

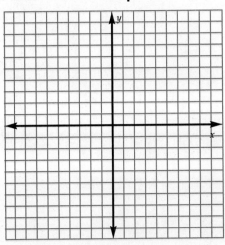

33

2.32 $x + 2y - 4 = 0$

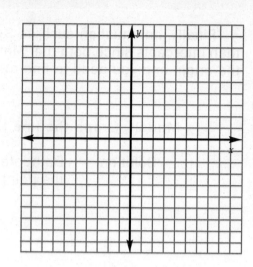

2.33 $2x - 3y = 6$

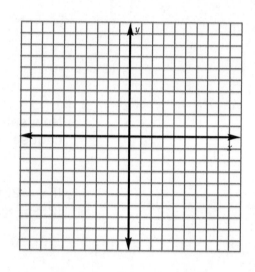

2.34 $2x = 4 - 3y$

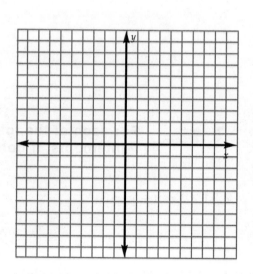

2.35 $3x = 2y$

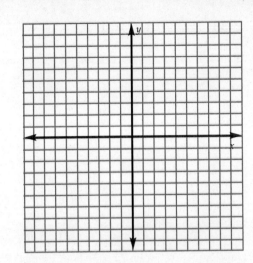

2.36 $x + 1 = y$

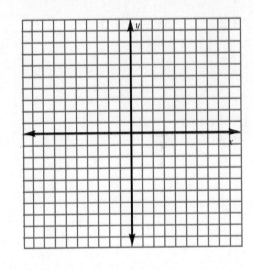

2.37 $1 - 2x = 3y$

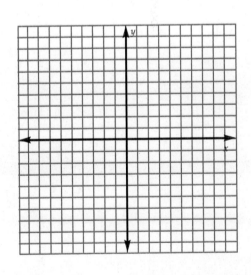

2.38 $2y + 6 = 0$

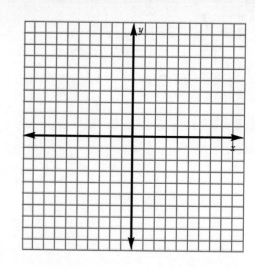

2.39 $3x - 3 = 0$

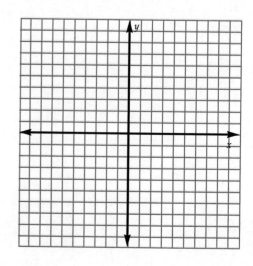

2.40 $5x + 2y = 7$

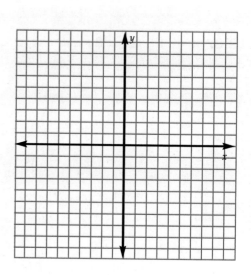

SLOPE

A third method of graphing uses one point and the concept of the steepness or slope of a line. This concept is important in advanced mathematics as well as in algebra, and practical applications of slope are many.

Model 1:   The pitch (or slope) of a road can be expressed as a per cent. For the diagram at the right, the pitch is 1:3 since the roof rises 4' in the 12' run, and $4:12 = \frac{4}{12} = \frac{1}{3} = 1:3$.

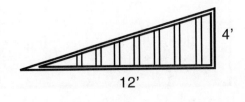

Model 2:   The grade (or slope) of a road can be expressed as a per cent. For the diagram at the right, the downgrade (left to right) is 8% since the road drops 12' in the 150' run, and $\frac{12}{150} = \frac{2}{25} = 0.08 = 8\%$.

In the preceding models, the amount of rise or drop is not so important as is the *rate* of the rise or drop as compared to the run. In each case, the fraction is formed in this way:

$$\text{slope} = \frac{\text{rise (or drop)}}{\text{run}}$$

If a rise is to be considered as positive, then a drop must be considered as negative. In Model 2, this negative value was implied by the word downgrade, so the fraction could also have been set up as $\frac{-12}{150} = \frac{-2}{5} = -8\%$. (We must be sure to look at a situation from left to right when determining whether it has a rise or a drop.) Notice that the rise or drop is the vertical change, and the run is the horizontal change.

▶▶▶ **Find the missing numbers.**

	rise	run	slope (reduced fraction)	% slope
2.41	3	12	a. _____	b. _____
2.42	2	20	a. _____	b. _____
2.43	a. _____	50	$\frac{1}{2}$	b. _____
2.44	14	a. _____	b. _____	30%
2.45	a. _____	120	b. _____	5%

37

Let us now find the slope of a line that is graphed on the real-number plane. We shall use the following definition.

DEFINITION

The *slope* of a line is the ratio of the rise or drop to the run of the line or

$$\text{slope} \ = \ \frac{\text{vertical change}}{\text{horizontal change}}$$

If the slope is rising, it is positive; if it is falling, it is negative. Always measure from left to right.

Model: Find the slope of the line through the points (-2, 3) and (4, -1).

Solution: Plot the points and draw the line through these points. (This line is *falling*.)

STEP 1:

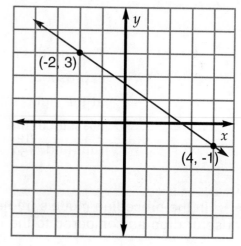

Now moving from left to right, count the vertical change, then the horizontal change required to get from (-2, 3) to (4, -1).

STEP 2:

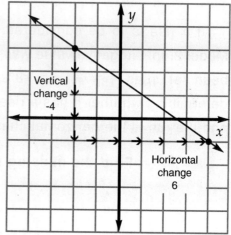

Finally, write the ratio of the vertical change to the horizontal change and simplify the resulting fraction:

$$\frac{\text{vertical change}}{\text{horizontal change}} \ = \ \frac{-4}{6} \ = \ -\frac{2}{3}$$

∴ The slope is $-\frac{2}{3}$.

38

Plot each of the following pairs of points and draw the line through the points. Find the slope of the line as in the preceding model. Reduce all fractions to lowest terms.

2.46   (1, 2) and (2, 5)

$\dfrac{\text{vertical change}}{\text{horizontal change}}$ = _____

slope = _____

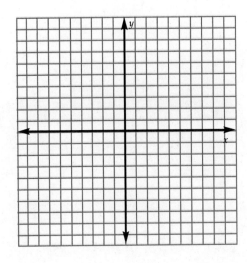

2.47   (1, 2) and (2, 1)

$\dfrac{\text{vertical change}}{\text{horizontal change}}$ = _____

slope = _____

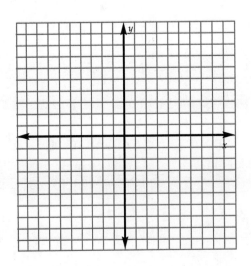

2.48   (0, 0) and (3, 5)

$\dfrac{\text{vertical change}}{\text{horizontal change}}$ = _____

slope = _____

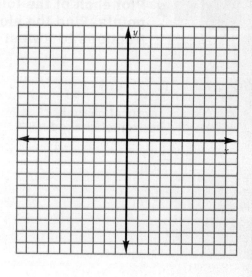

2.49   (-3, 0) and (2, 7)

$\dfrac{\text{vertical change}}{\text{horizontal change}}$ = _____

slope = _____

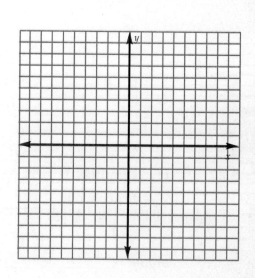

2.50   (-4, -4) and (0, 4)

$\dfrac{\text{vertical change}}{\text{horizontal change}}$ = _____

slope = _____

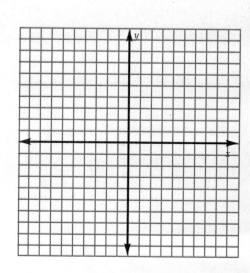

In the preceding exercises, the vertical and horizontal changes were found by counting the number of units moved in each direction on the grid. Another way is to subtract the ordinates (y-values) to find the vertical change and to subtract the abscissas (x-values) to find the horizontal change.

Model 1: Find the slope of the line through the points (-2, 3) and (4, -1).

Solution: The ordinates are 3 and -1;

their difference is -1 – 3 or -4.

The abscissas are -2 and 4; their difference is 4 – (-2) or 6.

Their ratio is $\frac{-4}{6} = -\frac{2}{3}$.

∴ The slope is $-\frac{2}{3}$, as before.

When the slope is found in this manner, the difference of ordinates is referred to as Δy and the difference of abscissas is referred to as Δx. The Greek letter Δ ("delta") is the fourth letter of the Greek alphabet, corresponding to our fourth letter d (for difference).

Model 2: Find the slope of the line through (0, -1) and (3, 5).

Solution: Plot the points and draw the line through these points.
(This line is *rising*.)

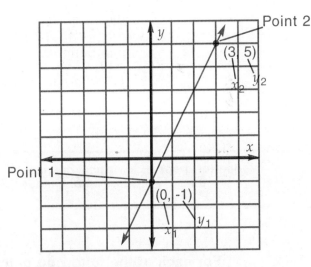

Find Δy and Δx:
$\Delta y = y_2 - y_1 = 5 - (-1) = 6$

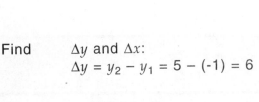

(0, -1) , (3, 5)

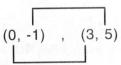

$\Delta x = x_2 - x_1 = 3 - 0 = 3$

Finally, write the ratio of Δy to Δx and simplify the resulting fraction:

$\frac{\Delta y}{\Delta x} = \frac{6}{3} = 2$

∴   The slope is 2.

NOTE: Remember, always measure from left to right. Therefore, you subtract the coordinates of Point 2 from the coordinates of Point 1 to determine the Δ values.

$\Delta x = x_2 - x_1$

$\Delta y = y_2 - y_1$

41

Model 3:   Find the slope of the line through (1, 3) and (4, 3). (This line is *horizontal*).

Solution: $\Delta y = 3 - 3 = 0$

(1, 3) , (4, 3)

$\Delta x = 4 - 1 = 3$

$\dfrac{\Delta y}{\Delta x} = \dfrac{0}{3} = 0$

∴ The slope is 0.

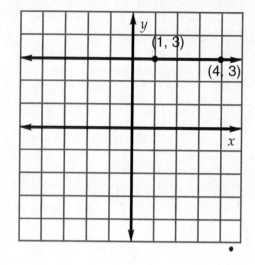

Model 4:   Find the slope of the line through (-2, 4) and (-2, -2). (This line is *vertical*).

Solution: $\Delta y = -2 - 4 = -6$

(-2, 4) , (-2, -2)

$\Delta x = -2 - (-2) = 0$

$\dfrac{\Delta y}{\Delta x} = \dfrac{-6}{0}$, but division by zero is undefined.

∴ The slope is undefined.

To summarize:

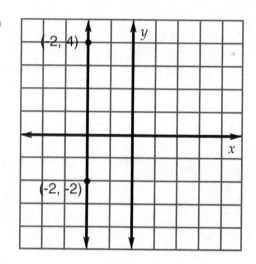

$$\text{slope} = \frac{\text{rise (or drop)}}{\text{run}} = \frac{\text{vertical change}}{\text{horizontal change}} = \frac{\Delta y}{\Delta x} = \frac{y_2 - y_1}{x_2 - x_1}$$

For each of the following pairs of points, find Δy, Δx, and the slope of the line through the points.

	Point	Δy	Δx	Slope (in simplest form)
2.51	(0, 0), (6, 8)	a. _____	b. _____	c. _____
2.52	(1, 3), (4, 7)	a. _____	b. _____	c. _____
2.53	(-2, 1), (0, 0)	a. _____	b. _____	c. _____

42

2.54	(1, 1), (2, 1)	a. _____	b. _____	c. _____
2.55	(-3, -5), (0, 10)	a. _____	b. _____	c. _____
2.56	(6, 6), (7, 7)	a. _____	b. _____	c. _____
2.57	(8, 1), (8, -4)	a. _____	b. _____	c. _____
2.58	(0, 0), (-5, -6)	a. _____	b. _____	c. _____
2.59	(0, 32), (100, 212)	a. _____	b. _____	c. _____
2.60	(-1, -2), (-5, -8)	a. _____	b. _____	c. _____

Now that you understand the meaning of the slope of a line, let us see how it can be used in graphing. When two points are given, you can draw the line through them and find their slope (as in the preceding activities). When one point and the slope are given, you can also find a second point and then draw the desired line.

Model 1: Draw the line having a slope of $\frac{3}{2}$ and passing through (-4, -1).

Solution: First, plot the given point.

STEP 1:

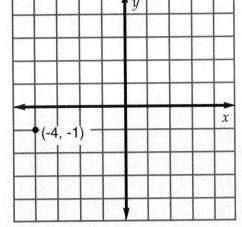

Then, use the given slope $\frac{\Delta y}{\Delta x} = \frac{3}{2}$ to "rise" 3 units and "run" 2 units from (-4, -1) on the grid to obtain another point.
Finally, draw the line through the given point and the second point, (-2, 2).

STEP 2:

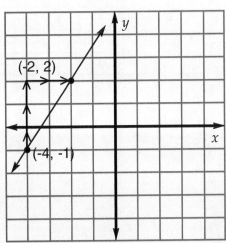

43

Checks: The given slope is positive and
            the resulting line is rising.

$$\Delta y = 2 - (-1) = 3$$

(-4, -1) , (-2, 2)

$$\Delta x = -2 - (-4) = 2$$

Thus, $\frac{\Delta y}{\Delta x} = \frac{3}{2}$, the given slope.

Model 2:   Draw the line having an undefined slope
            and whose x-intercept is 3.

Solution: An x-intercept of 3 indicates the
            point (3, 0). Since the slope is
            undefined, the line is vertical.

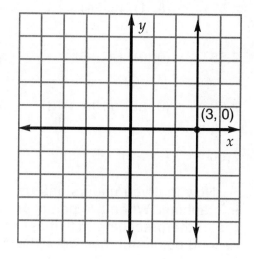

 For each of the following exercises, graph a line using the given point and slope.

2.61   (0, 0), $\frac{2}{3}$

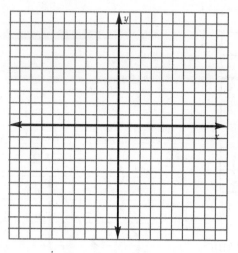

2.62   (-1, 2), 3

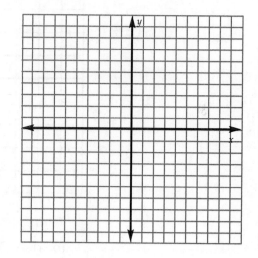

44

2.63 $(0, -2)$, $-\dfrac{2}{3}$

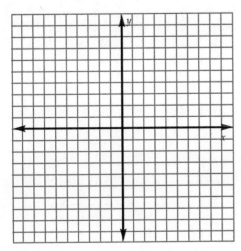

2.64 $(-2, -3)$, $-\dfrac{1}{4}$

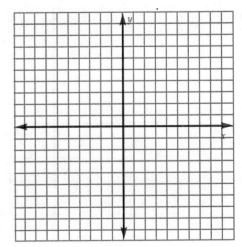

2.65 $(2, -4)$, $-\dfrac{3}{2}$

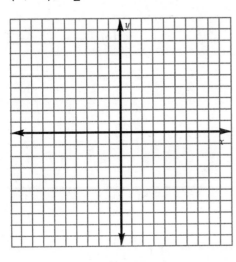

2.66 $(-3, 5)$, 1

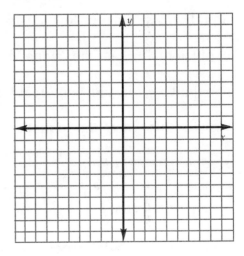

2.67 $(0, 6)$, -1

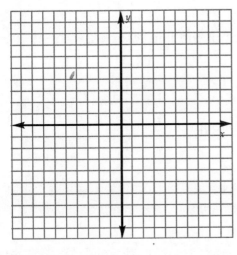

2.68 $(-2, 3)$, 0

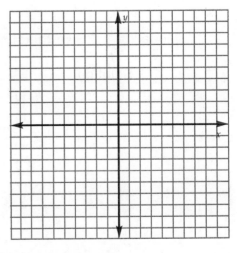

2.69   (1, 0), no slope (or undefined slope)

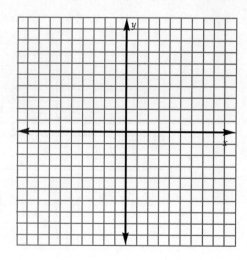

The point/slope method can also be used when a linear equation, $Ax + By + C = 0$, is given. If this equation is solved for y, as shown, then the coefficient $-\frac{A}{B}$ is the slope of the line and the constant $-\frac{C}{B}$ is the y-intercept of the line. When written this way, the equation is said to be in *slope/y-intercept form.*

$$Ax + By + C = 0$$

$$By = -Ax - C$$

$$y = \frac{-Ax - C}{B}$$

$$y = -\frac{A}{B}x - \frac{C}{B}$$

DEFINITION

The *slope/y-intercept form* of a linear equation is $y = mx + b$.

The letter m represents the slope of the line, and the letter b represents the y-intercept of the line.

Model 1:   Give the slope and the y-intercept of the line for $y = 3x - 5$.

Solution: $y = mx + b$
$y = 3x - 5$

∴ The slope is 3; the y-intercept is -5.

46

MATHEMATICS

9 0 8

LIFEPAC TEST

81 / 101

Name _____

Date _____

Score _____

MATHEMATICS 908: LIFEPAC TEST

Complete each statement by referring to the diagram (each answer, 2 points).

1.   Point A is located in quadrant _____ .

2.   Point B is called the _____ .

3.   Point C has a. _____ abscissa

        and a b. _____ ordinate.

4.   The ordinate of point D is _____ .

5.   Line l passes through quadrants

        a. _____ and has a b. _____ slope.

6.   Line m is parallel to the y-axis, and its slope is _____ .

7.   The coordinates of the point where lines l and m meet are both _____ .

8.   Translate using x and y: The difference of the ordinate and twice the abscissa is

        seven. _____

9.   Find the intercepts for $5x = y - 10$.

        x-intercept: _____ y-intercept: _____

10.   Find the slope of the line through (-2, 7) and (4, 9). (Show your work.)

        slope: _____

11.   Write the equation $3x - 5y + 10 = 0$ in slope/y-intercept form and identify m and b.

        Slope/y-intercept form = _____

        $m =$ _____ $b =$ _____

12.   Write the equation $x = \dfrac{1}{3}y$ in general form and identify A, B, and C.

        General form = _____

        $A =$ _____ $B =$ _____ $C =$ _____

1

Draw the graph of each equation or inequality (each graph, 5 points).

13. $y = -\frac{4}{3}x + 2$

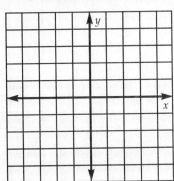

14. $x - 4y = 0$

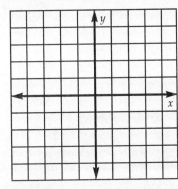

15. $3 + x \le 0$

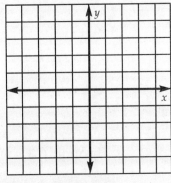

16. $3x - 2y < 6$

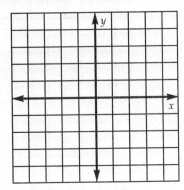

17. $|y| = 4$

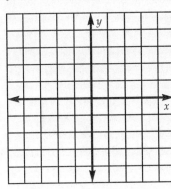

18. $y \ge |x - 2|$

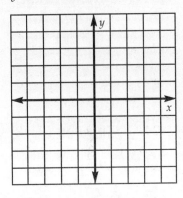

For problems 19 and 20, refer to the line shown in the diagram (each answer, 3 points).

19. Find the slope (in simplified form).

_____

20. Find the equation in general form. (Show your work neatly.)

•

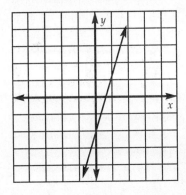

Graph each line from the given information; then find the equation in general form for each line (each numbered answer, 5 points).

21. Through (4, -1) and (-2, 3)

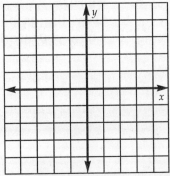

2

22. x-intercept -1 and y-intercept 2

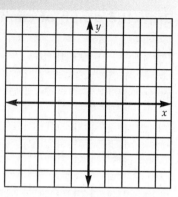

23. Through (-3, -1) with slope $\dfrac{3}{5}$

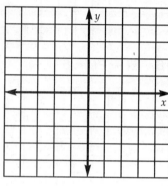

24. Through (0, -2) with slope 0

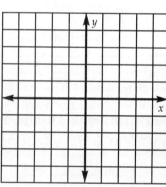

25. Through (1, 2) and parallel to $4x + y - 1 = 0$ (draw both lines, then find the equation.)

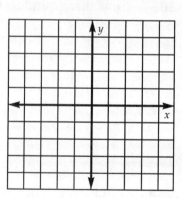

26. BONUS
Draw the graph for $5(x - 2y) - 2(x + y) \geq 6$.
Show your work.

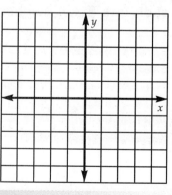

3

Model 2:   Find the slope and the y-intercept of the line for $6 - 3y = 2x$.

Solution: Solve for y to write the equation in the slope/y-intercept form:

$$6 - 3y = 2x$$
$$-3y = 2x - 6$$
$$y = \frac{2x - 6}{-3}$$
$$y = -\frac{2}{3}x + 2$$

$\therefore$ The slope is $-\frac{2}{3}$; the y-intercept is 2.

 Write each equation in slope/y-intercept form; then identify the slope and the y-intercept.

		$y = mx + b$ form	slope	y-intercept
2.70	$y = 2x - 3$	a. _____	b. _____	c. _____
2.71	$y = 7 - 2x$	a. _____	b. _____	c. _____
2.72	$y = \frac{x}{2} - 1$	a. _____	b. _____	c. _____
2.73	$y = \frac{3x}{2} + 4$	a. _____	b. _____	c. _____
2.74	$y = x$	a. _____	b. _____	c. _____
2.75	$y = \frac{1}{2} - \frac{5x}{2}$	a. _____	b. _____	c. _____
2.76	$y = 6$	a. _____	b. _____	c. _____
2.77	$2x - \frac{1}{2} = y$	a. _____	b. _____	c. _____
2.78	$y = 5 - \frac{x}{5}$	a. _____	b. _____	c. _____
2.79	$y = \frac{2x}{6} - \frac{1}{3}$	a. _____	b. _____	c. _____
2.80	$y = \frac{4x}{-5}$	a. _____	b. _____	c. _____
2.81	$x + y = 6$	a. _____	b. _____	c. _____
2.82	$2x - y = 0$	a. _____	b. _____	c. _____
2.83	$3x + 2y = 6$	a. _____	b. _____	c. _____
2.84	$y - x = -1$	a. _____	b. _____	c. _____
2.85	$3x - y = 1$	a. _____	b. _____	c. _____
2.86	$x + 3y = 10$	a. _____	b. _____	c. _____

2.87 $5x - 2y + 3 = 0$ a. _____ b. _____ c. _____

2.88 $7x + 3y = 21$ a. _____ b. _____ c. _____

2.89 $3x + 9 = 0$ a. _____ b. _____ c. _____

2.90 $3y - 6 = 0$ a. _____ b. _____ c. _____

Model 3:   Find the slope and the y-intercept of the line for $4x + y + 2 = 0$; then draw the line.

Solution: Solve for y:

$$4x + y + 2 = 0$$
$$y = -4x - 2$$
$$\therefore m = -4 \text{ and } b = -2$$

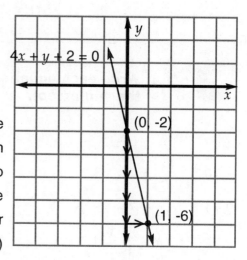

A y-intercept of $b = -2$ indicates the point (0, -2). Plot this point; then use the slope m = -4 or $\frac{\Delta y}{\Delta x} = \frac{-4}{1}$ to obtain another point. (Since the slope is negative, you "drop" four units and "run" one unit from (0, -2) on the grid.) Draw the line determined by these two points.

Check: Verify that both points satisfy the original equation:

$$(0, -2): \ 4x + y + 2 = 0$$
$$4 \cdot 0 + (-2) + 2 \overset{?}{=} 0$$
$$0 + (-2) + 2$$
$$-2 + 2$$
$$0 \checkmark$$

$$(1, -6): \ 4x + y + 2 = 0$$
$$4 \cdot 1 + (-6) + 2 \overset{?}{=} 0$$
$$4 + (-6) + 2$$
$$-2 + 2$$
$$0 \checkmark$$

For each of the following questions, construct the graph using the slope and the y-intercept.

2.91 $x + y = 2$

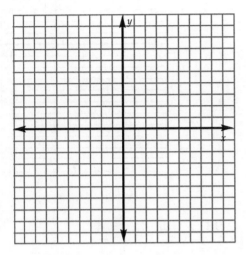

2.92 $2x - y + 4 = 0$

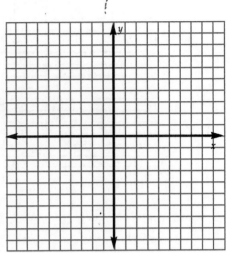

2.93 $x + 2y = 0$

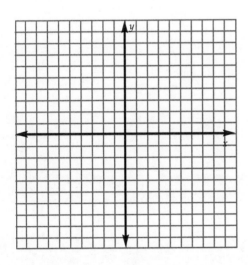

2.94 $3y = 2x - 6$

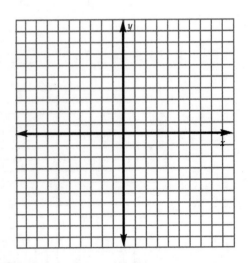

2.95 $3x - 6 = 0$

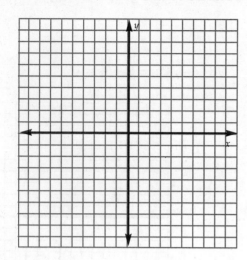

2.96 $x - y - 3 = 0$

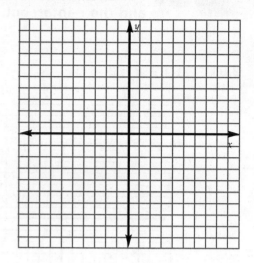

2.97 $2y + 4 = 0$

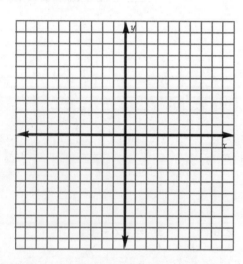

2.98 $y - 2x = 4$

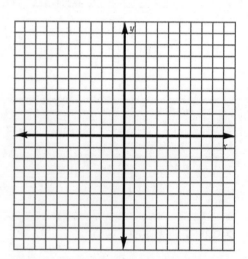

2.99 $5x - 2y = 3$

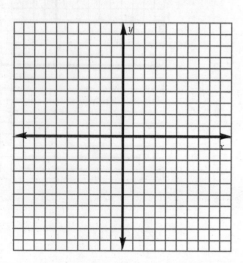

The methods you have learned for graphing linear equations can also be applied to graphing *linear inequalities*. However, several additional concepts should be considered.

DEFINITION

A *linear inequality* is an open sentence of the form $Ax + By + C < 0$ or $Ax + By + C > 0$.

Notice that a line drawn in a plane separates the points of the plane into three groups: all points on the line; all points to one side of the line (a *half-plane*); and all points to the other side of the line (also a half-plane).

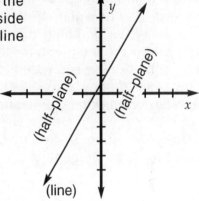

For example, when the line for $x = 2$ is drawn in the real-number plane, the plane is separated into three regions: the line itself, on which all points have abscissas of 2; the left half-plane, in which all points have abscissas less than 2; and the right half-plane, in which all points have abscissas greater than 2. The inequality for each half-plane is indicated in the diagram at the right.

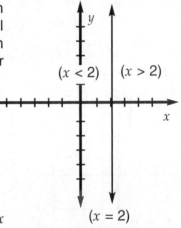

Since every point in the left half-plane satisfies the inequality $x < 2$, then every point must be indicated when the graph of $x < 2$ is drawn. This indication is made by drawing a series of parallel lines or shading in the appropriate half plane. The line for $x = 2$ is the *boundary* for this half-plane, but the points on the line do not satisfy $x < 2$. When the boundary is not to be included, it is drawn as a dashed line. The completed graph for $x < 2$ is shown at the right.

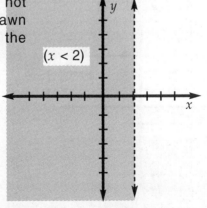

Similarly, shading the right-half plane indicates that every point in that region satisfies the inequality $x > 2$. Again the boundary is dashed since the points on the line ($x = 2$) do not satisfy $x > 2$. The completed graph is shown at the right.

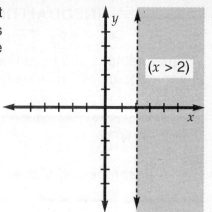

$(x > 2)$

Often a linear equation and a linear inequality are combined by using $\leq$ or $\geq$ in an open sentence; for example, $x \geq 2$ means $x > 2$ or $x = 2$. When graphing this type of open sentence, points that satisfy either the inequality or the equation must be indicated. As before, a half-plane is shaded for $x > 2$; but now the boundary line will be solid to show that these points are included for $x = 2$. The completed graph for $x \geq 2$ is shown at the right.

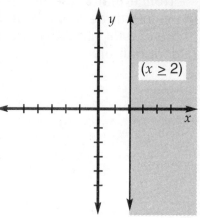

$(x \geq 2)$

(Note: An open sentence containing $\leq$ or $\geq$ is usually also referred to as an inequality.)

Compare the following graphs.

$$4x - y - 1 = 0$$

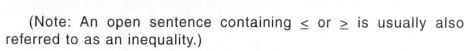

$4x - y - 1 < 0$

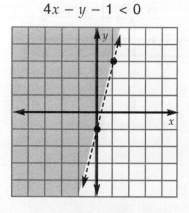

$4x - y - 1 \leq 0$

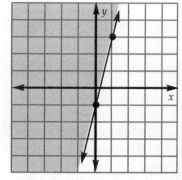

$4x - y - 1 > 0$

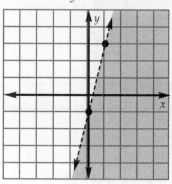

$4x - y - 1 \geq 0$

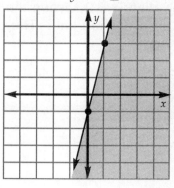

The procedure for graphing a linear inequality has three steps.

1. Replace <, >, ≤, or ≥ by = to find the boundary.

2. Make the line dashed when < or >, and make the line solid when ≤ or ≥.

3. Shade the half-plane whose points satisfy the original inequality.

This procedure is explained in detail in the solutions of the next two models; study them carefully.

Model 1:   Graph $2 - y < 0$.

Solution: 1. Use $2 - y = 0$ to find the boundary.

Solving for y,

$$2 - y = 0$$
$$-y = -2$$
$$y = 2.$$

2. Graph the horizontal line for $y = 2$, making it dashed since the original inequality contains <.

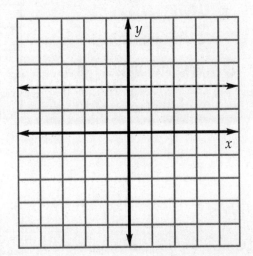

3. One way to determine which half-plane to shade is to test any point on either side of the boundary to see if its abscissa and ordinate satisfy the original inequality. If so, then shade the half-plane in which the point lies; if not, then try a point in the other half-plane.

Try a point below the line such as (4, 1):

$$2 - y < 0$$
$$2 - 1 \overset{?}{<} 0$$
$$1 \overset{?}{<} 0; \text{ this statement}$$

is false.

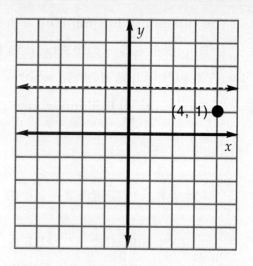

$$2 - y < 0$$

Now try a point above the line such as (-3, 5):

$$2 - y < 0$$
$$2 - 5 \overset{?}{<} 0$$
$$-3 \overset{?}{<} 0; \text{ this statement is}$$

true, so shade the upper half-plane.

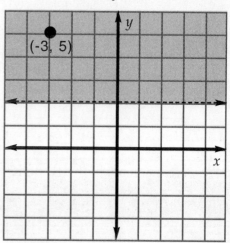

Model 2:   Graph $5x + 2y \leq 6$.

Solution: 1. Use $5x + 2y = 6$ to find the boundary. Solving for y,

$$5x + 2y = 6$$
$$2y = -5x + 6$$
$$y = \frac{-5x + 6}{2}$$
$$y = -\frac{5}{2}x + 3.$$

Plot the y-intercept, 3; then use the slope, $-\frac{5}{2}$, to find the second point.

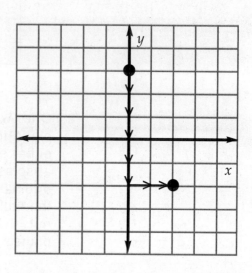

54

2. Graph the boundary line through these two points, making it solid since the original inequality contains ≤.

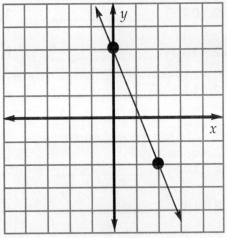

3. Test a point in the lower left half-plane such as (0, 0):

$$5x + 2y \overset{\leq}{?} 6$$

$$5 \cdot 0 + 2 \cdot 0 \overset{\leq}{?} 6$$

$$0 + 0 \overset{\leq}{?} 6$$

$$0 \overset{\leq}{?} 6; \text{ this}$$

statement is true, so shade this half-plane.

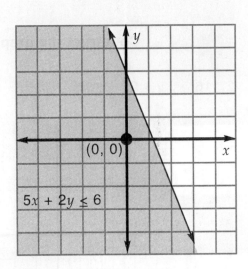

 For each of the following inequalities, indicate whether the boundary line should be dashed or solid.

2.100 $x + y < 2$ _____

2.101 $2x - y > 3$ _____

2.102 $x \leq y$ _____

2.103 $3x \geq y + 1$ _____

2.104 $2 > x - y$ _____

2.105 $x \leq 5$ _____

 For each of the following exercises, test the given point to see if it satisfies the inequality. Write *true* or *false*.

2.106   _____ $x + y < 2$,   (1, 1)

2.107   _____ $x - y > 0$,   (-1, 1)

2.108   _____ $x > y$,   (5, 5)

2.109 _____ $3x - y \leq 1$, (6, 20)

2.110 _____ $x + 2y \geq 3$, (1, 1)

2.111 _____ $y \leq 6$, (2, 5)

2.112 _____ $x \geq -3$, (0, -2)

2.113 _____ $5x - 2y + 1 > 0$, (-2, -1)

2.114 _____ $10x + 11y < 5$, (-2, -3)

2.115 _____ $2x - 3y \geq 5$, $(\frac{1}{2}, \frac{1}{3})$

 Construct the graph of each of the following inequalities.

2.116 $y > 2$

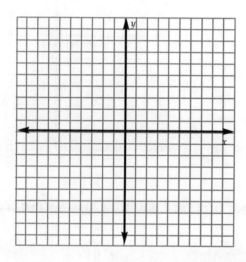

2.117 $y \leq -2$

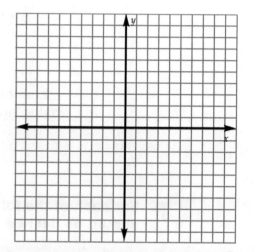

2.118 $x < -1$

2.119 $x + y > 1$

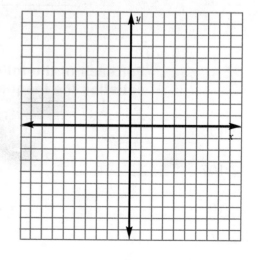

2.120 $x - y < 2$

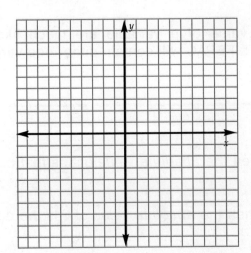

2.121 $y \le x - 2$

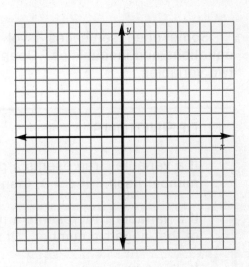

2.122 $y \ge 2x - 3$

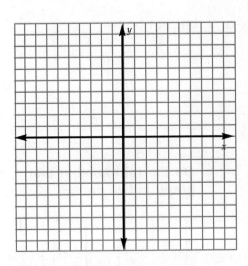

2.123 $3x - y > 0$

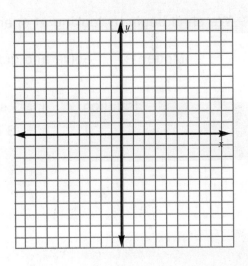

2.124 $3x - 2y \ge 6$

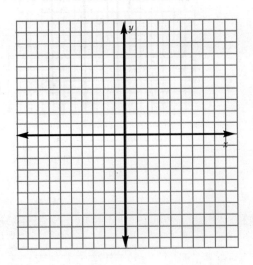

Some open sentences involving the absolute value of a variable are much like linear equations and inequalities. Open sentences in this LIFEPAC will contain either one variable or two variables.

DEFINITIONS

If a variable z represents a positive number, then the *absolute value* of z is that positive number itself. (If $z > 0$, then $|z| = z$.)

If a variable z represents a negative number, then the *absolute value* of z is the opposite of that negative number. (If $z < 0$, then $|z| = -z$.)

If a variable z represents zero, then the *absolute value* of z is zero. (If $z = 0$, then $|z| = 0$.)

ONE-VARIABLE SENTENCES

We shall begin by looking at open sentences using x or y, but not both.

Model 1: Solve and graph $|x| = 3$.

Solution: $x = 3$ since $|3| = 3.$; or
$x = -3$ since $|-3| = -(-3) = 3$.

On the real-number plane, the graph is two lines.

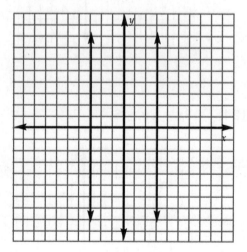

On the real-number line, the graph is two points.

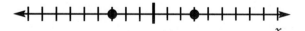

Model 2:   Solve and graph |x| < 3.

Solution: Each real value between -3 and 3 has an absolute value that
is less than 3. Here are several examples:

x = 1.98 since |-1.98| = -(-1.98) = 1.98 < 3

x = 0 since |0|= 0 < 3

x = $\sqrt{5}$ since |$\sqrt{5}$| = $\sqrt{5}$ = 2.236067977 . . . < 3

The solution is written: -3 < x < 3.

On the real-number plane, the graph is a region between but not including the boundary lines x = -3 and x = 3.

On the real-number line, the graph is a line segment between but not including the endpoints -3 and 3.

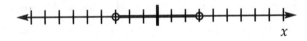

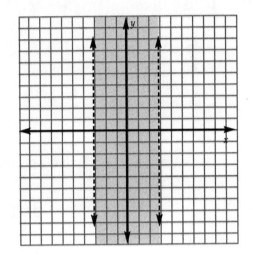

Model 3:   Solve and graph |y| − 3 ≥ 0.

Solution: |y| − 3 ≥ 0 may be written |y| ≥ 3. Any real value greater than
or equal to 3 or any real value less than or equal to -3
satisfies |y| ≥ 3.

This solution is written: y ≥ 3 or y ≤ -3.

On the real-number line, the graph is the two rays shown, including both endpoints.

On the real-number plane, the graph is the two half-planes shown, including both boundary lines.

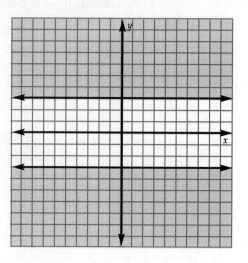

Model 4:   Solve and graph $|2y + 3| < 7$.

Solution: By the definition of absolute value, $|2y + 3| = 2y + 3$ when the binomial is positive and $|2y + 3| = -(2y + 3)$ when the binomial is negative. In both cases the absolute value must be less than 7, so solve the two inequalities.

$2y + 3 < 7$ and $-(2y + 3) < 7$
$2y < 4$ $-2y - 3 < 7$
$y < 2$ $-2y < 10$
                    $y > -5$

Thus, any real value less than 2 and greater than -5 satisfies $|2y + 3| < 7$. (You should try several values.) This solution is written: $-5 < y < 2$.

60

On the real-number line, the graph is a line segment between but not including the endpoints 2 and -5.

On the real-number plane, the graph is a region between but not including the boundary lines $y = 2$ and $y = -5$.

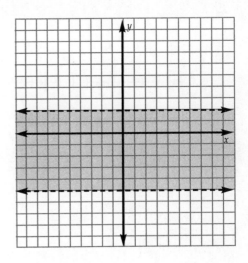

Before advancing to the activities, go back and look again at the graphs for each of the preceding four models. Notice especially the similarities between the one-dimensional (number-line) graph and the two-dimensional (number-plane) graph of each solution.

 Graph each of the following absolute-value equations or inequalities on both a number line and a number plane, as shown in the models.

2.125 $|x| = 2$

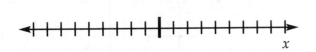

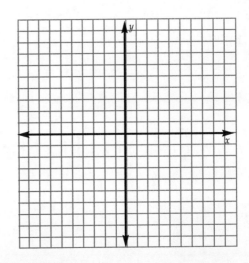

2.126 $|x - 1| = 3$

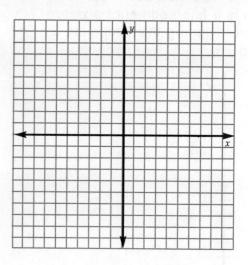

2.127 $|y + 2| = 5$

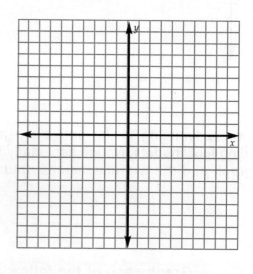

2.128 $|x| - 1 \leq 0$

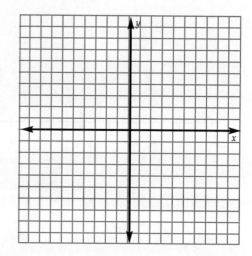

2.129 $|x| \geq 3$

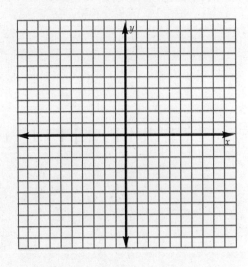

2.130 $|y + 1| \leq 5$

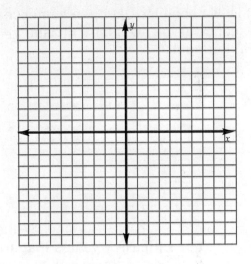

2.131 $|2x + 3| < 5$

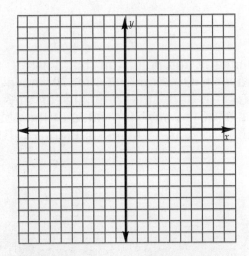

63

$|2x - 4| \geq 6$

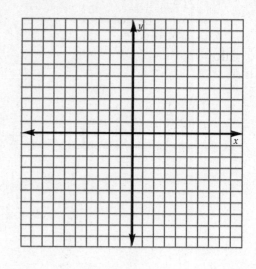

TWO-VARIABLE SENTENCES

Now we shall look at open sentences using both x and y. To start, consider the lines for $y = x$ and $y = -x$ graphed on the same grid at the right.

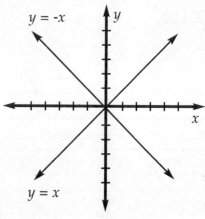

The points on the "V" formed by the origin and the rays in Quadrants I and II have y-values that are never negative; in fact, the ordinate of any of these points is the absolute value of the abscissa of a point. The equation for this "up-V" is then $y = |x|$.

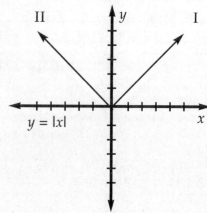

Similarly, the points on the "down-V" formed by the origin and the rays in Quadrants III and IV have y-values that are never positive; in fact, the ordinate of any of these points is the opposite of the absolute value of the abscissa of that point. The equation for this "down-V" is then $y = -|x|$.

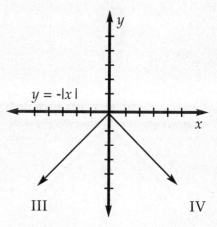

By the same type of reasoning, you should see that the equation of the "right-V" of Quadrants I and IV is $x = |y|$ and that the equation of the "left-V" of Quadrants II and III is $x = -|y|$. (If you think for a while, you may even be able to see that the equation of the whole "X" would be $|x| = |y|$.)

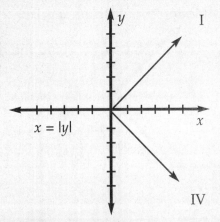

$x = |y|$

Thus, when working with a two-variable open sentence involving the absolute value of one of the variables, look for a V-graph. If the open sentence is an inequality, you need to test points "inside" and "outside" the dashed or solid V-graph to determine which region to shade.

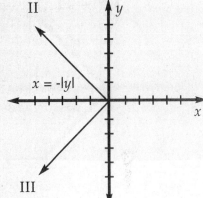

$x = -|y|$

Model 1:   Graph $x + |y| - 3 = 0$.

Solution: First, solve for x:

$x + |y| - 3 = 0$

$x + |y| = 3$

$x = 3 - |y|$

Then, complete a table using convenient values for y:

y	-2	-1	0	1	2
$3 - |y|$	$3 - |-2|$ $3 - 2$ 1	$3 - |-1|$ $3 - 1$ 2	$3 - |0|$ $3 - 0$ 3	$3 - |1|$ $3 - 1$ 2	$3 - |2|$ $3 - 2$ 1
(x, y)	$(1, -2)$	$(2, -1)$	$(3, 0)$	$(2, 1)$	$(1, 2)$

Finally, plot the points and draw the graph.

$x + |y| - 3 = 0$

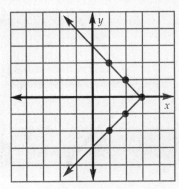

65

Model 2:   Graph $y > |x + 2|$.

Solution: Find the dashed boundary $y = |x + 2|$.

x	-4	-3	-2	-1	0	1	2
$|x + 2|$	$|-4 + 2|$	$|-3 + 2|$	$|-2 + 2|$	$|-1 + 2|$	$|0 + 2|$	$|1 + 2|$	$|2 + 2|$
	$|-2|$	$|-1|$	$|0|$	$|1|$	$|2|$	$|3|$	$|4|$
	2	1	0	1	2	3	4
(x, y)	(-4, 2)	(-3, 1)	(-2, 0)	(-1, 1)	(0, 2)	(1, 3)	(2, 4)

STEP 1:

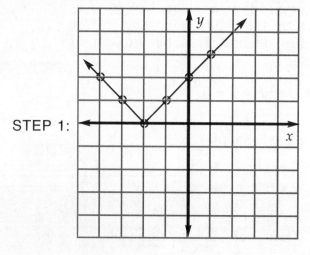

Test a point "inside," such as (0, 3):

$$y \;>\; |x + 2|$$
$$3 \;\overset{?}{>}\; |0 + 3|$$
$$3 \;\overset{?}{>}\; 2; \text{ this statement is true,}$$

so shade inside the V-graph.

STEP 2:

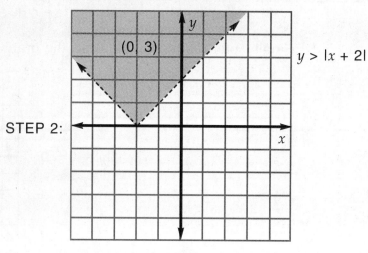

$y > |x + 2|$

Graph each of the following equations and inequalities.

2.133 $y = |x|$

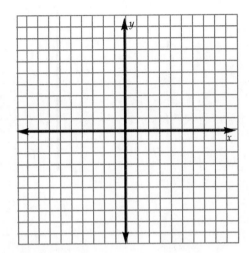

2.134 $y \geq |x + 1|$

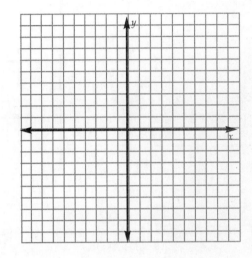

2.135 $y \leq |x|$

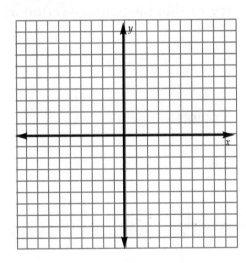

2.136 $y < |x + 3|$

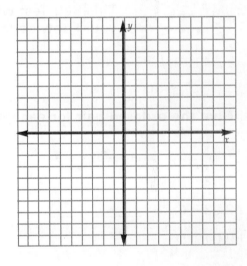

2.137 $x + |y| = 2$

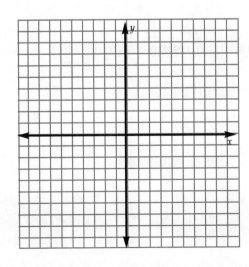

2.138 $x - |y| < 2$

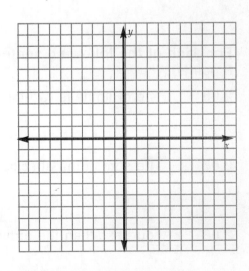

2.139 $|x| + y \leq 0$ 2.140 $|y| \leq |x|$

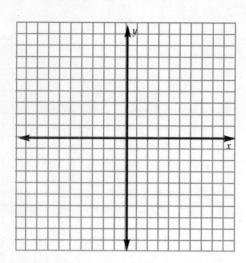   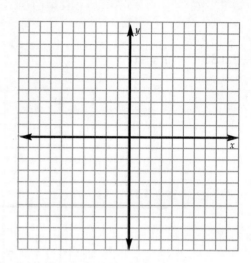

   Review the material in this section in preparation for the Self Test. This Self Test will check your mastery of this particular section as well as your knowledge of the previous section.

SELF TEST 2

Give the ordered pair for each point (each answer, 2 points).

2.01   A   _____

2.02   B   _____

2.03   C   _____

2.04   D   _____

2.05   E   _____

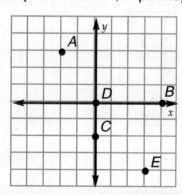

For each of the following sentences, write a translation using x and y (each answer, 3 points).

2.06   The ordinate is two-thirds the abscissa increased by ten.

_____

2.07   The sum of the abscissa and twice the ordinate is equal to five.

_____

2.08   Four less than the ordinate equals half the abscissa. _____

a. Solve each equation for y; b. then find three ordered pairs using $x \in \{-2, 0, 1\}$ (each equation, 2 points; each ordered pair, 2 points).

2.09 $3x - 2y = 5$ a. $y =$ _____

b. _____ , _____ , _____

2.010 $x + 4y + 1 = 0$ a. $y =$ _____

b. _____ , _____ , _____

Complete each statement (each answer, 2 points).

2.011   All points having positive abscissas and positive ordinates are located

_____ .

2.012   All points having negative abscissas and zero ordinates are located

_____ .

2.013   All points in Quadrants III and IV have _____ ordinates.

Write each equation in general form and identify A, B, and C (each numbered answer, 2 points).

	General Form	A	B	C
2.014 $y = 6 - 2x$	_____	_____	_____	_____
2.015 $y = \dfrac{3x}{2} - 1$	_____	_____	_____	_____
2.016 $4 - \dfrac{y}{3} = 0$	_____	_____	_____	_____

Write each equation in slope/y-intercept form and identify m and b (each numbered answer, 2 points).

	Slope/y-intercept form	m	b
2.017 $3x + y = 7$	_____	_____	_____
2.018 $5x + 2y + 1 = 0$	_____	_____	_____
2.019 $2y - x = 6$	_____	_____	_____

Find the x-intercept and the y-intercept for each equation (each numbered answer, 2 points).

2.020 $5x - 2y = 10$ _____   _____

2.021 $y = 3x - 4$ _____   _____

Find the slope of the line through each pair of points (each answer, 3 points).

2.022   (1, 2), (3, 8)   _____

2.023   (-4, 1), (3, 0)   _____

2.024   (-2, 5), (-2, -3)   _____

Draw the graph of each equation or inequality (each graph, 5 points).

2.025 $y = -2x + 3$

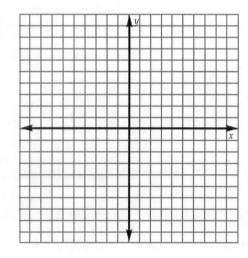

2.026 $y = \dfrac{x}{3} + 1$

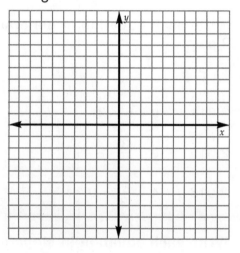

2.027 $x + y = 3$

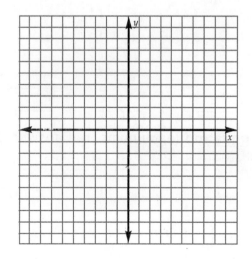

2.028 $x - 2y - 4 = 0$

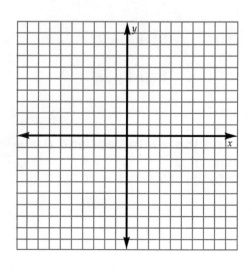

2.029 $x + y < 1$

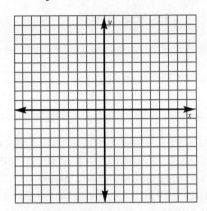

2.030 $y \geq 3x - 3$

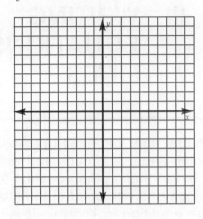

2.031 $y - 3 \leq 0$

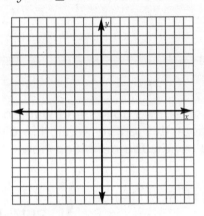

2.032 $x + 2 \geq 1$

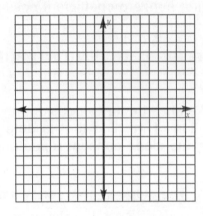

2.033 $|y - 1| = 2$

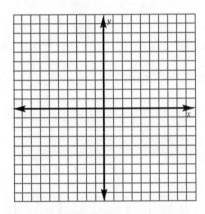

2.034 $y = |x|$

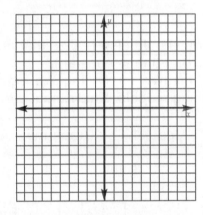

2.035 $y \leq |x + 2|$

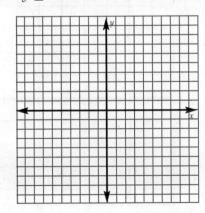

Score _____

Teacher check _____

Initial   Date

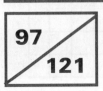

97 / 121

71

III. WRITING EQUATIONS OF LINES

OBJECTIVE

5. Find the equations of lines from given information.

By the time you have reached this point in the LIFEPAC, you should know quite a bit about graphing lines. Although you will continue to draw graphs in this section, the main emphasis will shift to finding the equation for a line from some given information—two points of the line, the slope and one point of the line, a graph of the line, or the relation of the line to another line whose equation is known. In all of these cases, you will learn to write the equation for the desired line in the general form ($Ax + By + C = 0$, with A, B, and C relatively-prime integers and the first nonzero coefficient positive.)

=== **GIVEN TWO POINTS** ===

We shall begin by considering situations where we are given two points and want to find the equation of the line that is determined by them. Throughout this entire section, we shall be using the slope concept repeatedly, so perhaps we should review the definition now.

$\Bigg($ The slope m between two points is the ratio of their vertical change to their horizontal change; that is, $m = \dfrac{\Delta y}{\Delta x}$. $\Bigg)$ **REMEMBER?**

You should also realize that any two points of a line may be used to find the slope since the slope of a line is constant.

A method for finding the equation of a line is described in detail in the solutions to the following models. Study them carefully.

Model 1:　　Graph the line through (-3, -4) and (2, 5), and find its equation.

Solution:　　First, plot the two points and draw the line determined by them.

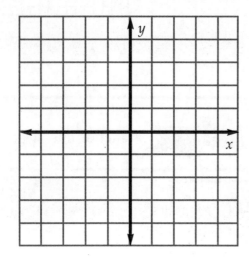
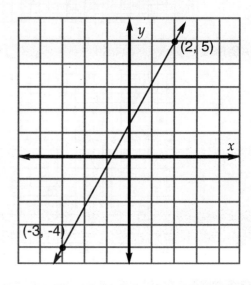

72

Next, find the slope of this line; notice that it will be positive since this line is rising.

$$\Delta y = 5 - (-4) = 9$$

(-3, -4) , (2, 5) and

$$\Delta x = 2 - (-3) = 5$$

$$m = \frac{9}{5}$$

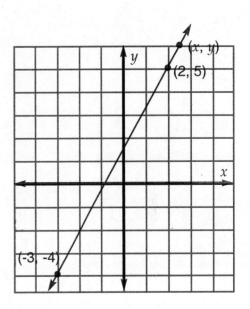

(This slope may also be found by counting units on the graph.)

The equation of a line uses the letters x and y to represent the abscissa and ordinate, respectively, of any point on the line. So choose some other point on the line and mark it as (x, y).

Now, find the slope between this point and either of the two known points:

$$\Delta y = y - 5$$

(2, 5) , (x, y) and

$$\Delta x = x - 2$$

$$m = \frac{y - 5}{x - 2}$$

Since the slope of a line is constant, $\frac{y - 5}{x - 2}$ must have the same value as we obtained earlier, $\frac{9}{5}$. Set up this relationship, use cross-multiplication, and write the resulting equation in the general form:

$$9(x - 2)$$

$$\frac{y - 5}{x - 2} = \frac{9}{5}$$

$$5(y - 5)$$

$$9x - 18 = 5y - 25$$

$$9x - 5y + 7 = 0$$

73

∴   The equation of the line through (-3, -4) and (2, 5) is $9x - 5y + 7 = 0$. The same equation results whether you choose (2, 5) or (-3, -4).

Check: Show that both of the given points satisfy the equation $9x - 5y + 7 = 0$.

$$(-3, -4): \quad 9(-3) - 5(-4) \quad + \quad 7 \overset{?}{=} 0$$
$$-27 + 20 \quad + \quad 7$$
$$-7 \quad + \quad 7$$
$$0 \quad \checkmark$$

$$(2, 5): \quad 9 \bullet 2 - 5 \bullet 5 + 7 \overset{?}{=} 0$$
$$18 - 25 + 7$$
$$-7 + 7$$
$$0 \quad \checkmark$$

Model 2:   A line has a y-intercept of -1 and passes through (-3, 5). Graph the line and find its equation.

Solution: The graph is shown.

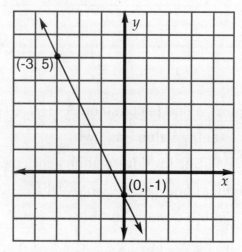

Since this line is a falling line, you should expect the slope to be negative.

$$\Delta y = -1 - 5 = -6$$

(-3, 5) , (0, -1) and

$$\Delta x = 0 - (-3) = 3$$

$$m = \frac{-6}{3} = -2 \text{ (Always reduce this fraction!)}$$

74

You may position the point (x, y) anywhere on the line when finding the slope between it and another point.

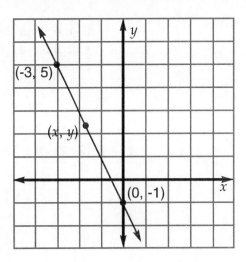

$$\Delta y = y - 5$$

$$(-3, 5) \; , \; (x, y) \text{ and}$$

$$\Delta x = x - (-3) = x + 3$$

$$m = \frac{y - 5}{x + 3}$$

The two expressions for m must be equal.

$$\frac{y - 5}{x + 3} = -2 \quad \left(\text{Use } \frac{-2}{1} \text{ for cross-multiplication.}\right)$$

$$-2x - 6 = y - 5$$

$$0 = 2x + y + 1$$

$\therefore \;\; 2x + y + 1 = 0$ is the equation of the line through $(-3, 5)$ and $(0, -1)$.

(You should check the two points in this equation to verify that the equation is correct.)

Model 3:   Graph the line through $(2, 2)$ and $(2, -3)$ and find its equation.

Solution: The graph is shown.

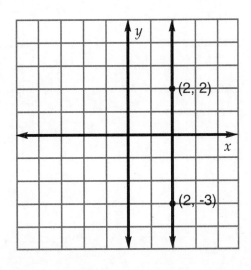

Since this line is a vertical line, you should expect the slope to be undefined.

$$\Delta y = -3 - 2 = -5$$

(2, 2) , (2, -3) and

$$\Delta x = 2 - 2 = 0$$

$$m = \frac{-5}{0}$$

The equation for any vertical line is $x = K$, and in this case the value of K (the abscissa of any point on the line) is 2.

$$x = 2$$

$\therefore \; x - 2 = 0$ is the equation of the line through (2, 2) and (2, -3) in general form.

 **Graph the line that passes through the two points, and write the equation of the line. Show your work as in the preceding models. (NOTE: All equations are to be written in general form.)**

3.1 (1, 1), (5, 5)

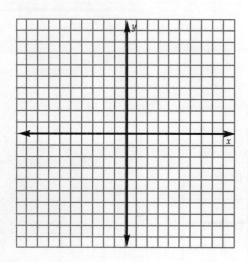

3.2 (1, 2), (4, 5)

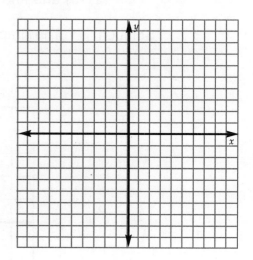

3.3   (1, 6), (6, 2)

3.4   x-intercept of 5,
       y-intercept of 5

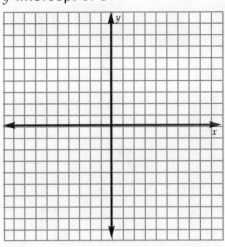

_____   _____

3.5   (-2, 1), (2, 1)

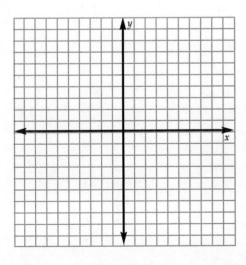

3.6   x-intercept of -2,
       y-intercept of -3

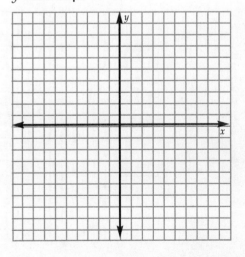

_____(1, 6), (6, 2)_____   _____x-intercept of 5_____

3.7 y-intercept of 2, (5, 2)

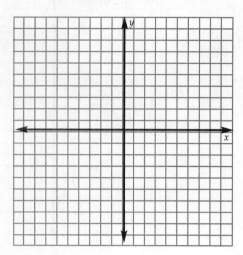

3.8 x-intercept of 2, (2, 6)

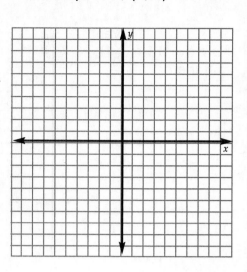

_____

_____

3.9   (1, 5), (-1, -5)

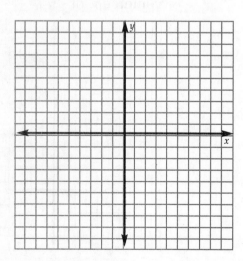

_____

If you are given the numerical value for the slope of a line, then, of course, you need not compute it from points. Knowing one point that the line passes through is all that is needed to find the equation in this situation.

Model 1:　Graph and find the equation of the line having a slope of -3 and passing through (2, 4).

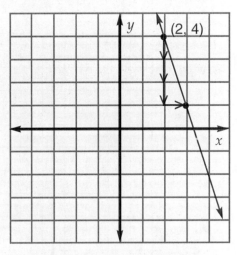

Solution:　Plot the point (2, 4), and use the slope $\frac{\Delta y}{\Delta x} = \frac{-3}{1}$ to find a second point. Draw the line through these points.

Using (x, y) to represent any point on the line, proceed as before.

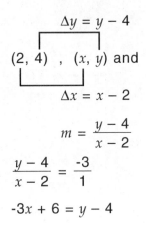

$$\Delta y = y - 4$$

(2, 4) , (x, y) and

$$\Delta x = x - 2$$

$$m = \frac{y - 4}{x - 2}$$

$$\frac{y - 4}{x - 2} = \frac{-3}{1}$$

$$-3x + 6 = y - 4$$

∴ $3x + y - 10 = 0$ is the equation of this line in general form.

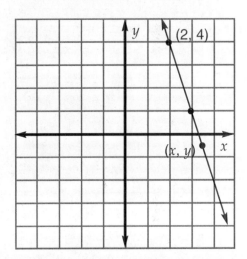

Model 2:　A line has a y-intercept of 3 and a slope of 0. Graph this line and find its equation.

Solution:　The graph is shown; a zero slope indicates a horizontal line. The equation for any horizontal line is $y = K$, and in this case the value of K (the ordinate of any point on the line) is 3.

$$y = 3$$

∴ $y - 3 = 0$ is the equation of this line in general form.

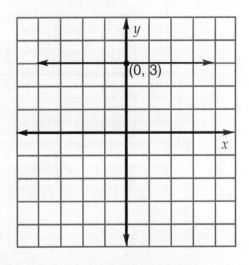

For each of the following points and slopes, graph the line and find its equation. Show your work as in the preceding models (and write each equation in general form).

3.10   (0, 0), 1

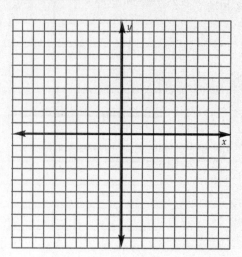

_____

3.11   (1, 1), 2

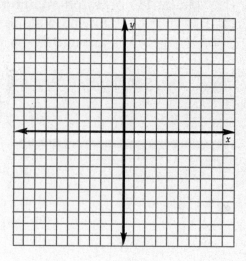

_____

3.12   (-2, 1), 3

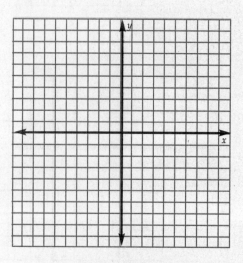

_____

3.13   (2, 2), -2

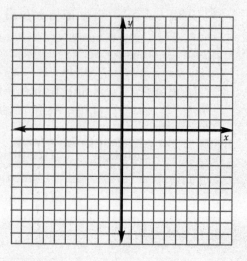

_____

3.14   (-3, -3), -1

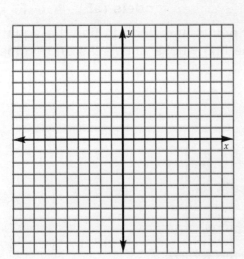

_____

3.15   (5, 2), 0

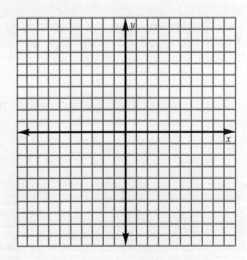

_____

3.16   (-5, -1), $\dfrac{-2}{3}$

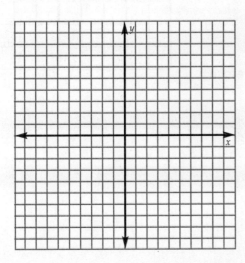

_____

3.17 x-intercept of 2,
        undefined slope

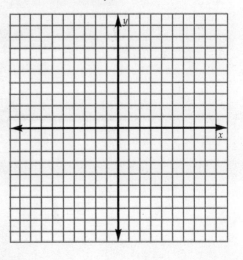

_____

You should now be able to use your knowledge of points and slope to find the equation of a line from its graph. You will want to find points on the line whose abscissas and ordinates are integers in these situations.

Model: Find the equation of this line

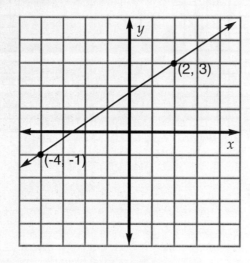

Solution: Locate (-4, -1) and (2, 3) on the line.

Find the slope of the line using these two points.

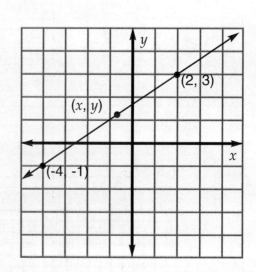

$$\Delta y = 3 - (-1) = 4$$

(-4, -1) , (2, 3) and

$$\Delta x = 2 - (-4) = 6$$

$$m = \frac{4}{6} = \frac{2}{3}$$

Using (x, y), proceed as before.

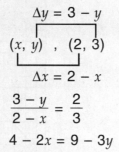

$$\Delta y = 3 - y$$

(x, y) , (2, 3)

$$\Delta x = 2 - x$$

$$\frac{3 - y}{2 - x} = \frac{2}{3}$$

$$4 - 2x = 9 - 3y$$

$\therefore$ $2x - 3y + 5 = 0$ is the

equation of this line in

general form.

Find the equation for each of the following lines. Show your work as in the preceding model.

3.18

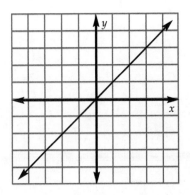

3.19

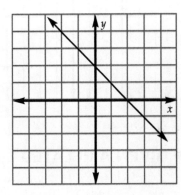

3.20

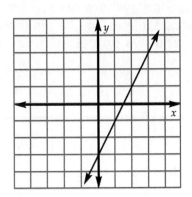

3.21

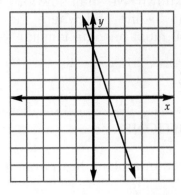

3.22

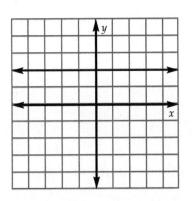

3.23

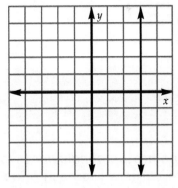

3.24

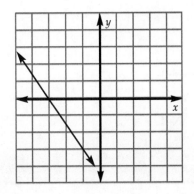

3.25

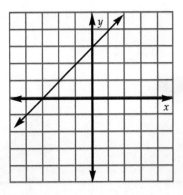

3.26

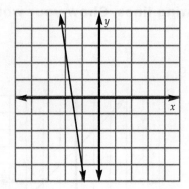

═══════════ **GIVEN A RELATED LINE** ═══════════

We can also find the equation for a line that is related in some way to another line whose equation is known. We shall now look at two of these situations: where the known line is parallel to the unknown line and where the known line is perpendicular to the unknown line. First, however, you must become familiar with two definitions and two properties from geometry.

DEFINITIONS

Two lines in a plane are *parallel* (symbol | |) when they have no point in common.

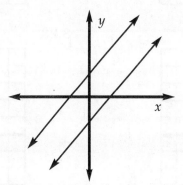

Two lines are *perpendicular* (symbol ⊥)when they cross at right angles ("square corners") to each other.

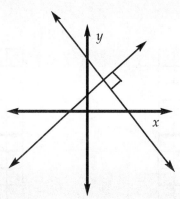

Model 1: A line passes through (-2, 5) and is parallel to the line for

$4x + 3y - 9 = 0$.

Graph the line and write its equation.

Solution: Find the slope of the known line from its equation.

$$4x + 3y - 9 = 0$$
$$3y = -4x + 9$$
$$y = -\frac{4}{3}x + 3$$

$\therefore$ The slope is $m = -\frac{4}{3}$.

Since the line we are looking for is parallel to the known line, its slope will also be $-\frac{4}{3}$. Using this slope and the given point (-2, 5), proceed as before.

The graph is shown.

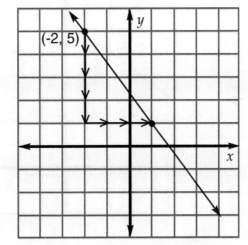

$$\Delta y = y - 5$$

(-2, 5) , (x, y) and

$$\Delta x = x - (-2) \text{ or } x + 2$$

$$m = \frac{y - 5}{x + 2}$$

85

$$\frac{y-5}{x+2} = \frac{4}{-3}$$

$$4x + 8 = -3y + 15$$

$\therefore$ $4x + 3y - 7 = 0$ is the equation in general form.

Model 2: A line passes through (-2, 5) and is perpendicular to the line for $4x + 3y - 9 = 0$. Graph the line and write its equation.

Solution: As in Model 1, the slope of the known line is $-\frac{4}{3}$.

Since the two lines are to be perpendicular, the slope of the line we are looking for will be the opposite of the reciprocal of the slope of the known line.

The reciprocal of $-\frac{4}{3}$ is $-\frac{3}{4}$; its opposite is $\frac{3}{4}$. Using this slope and the given point (-2, 5), proceed as before. The graph is shown.

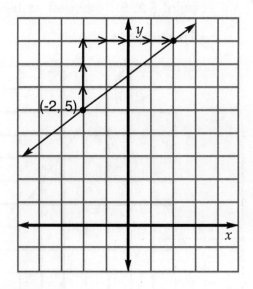

$$\frac{y-5}{x+2} = \frac{3}{4}$$

$$3x + 6 = 4y - 20$$

$\therefore$ $3x - 4y + 26 = 0$ is the equation in general form.

Given a point and the equation of a line, graph the parallel or perpendicular line and find its equation. Show your work as in the preceding models.

3.27   (2, 4), | | to $y = x$

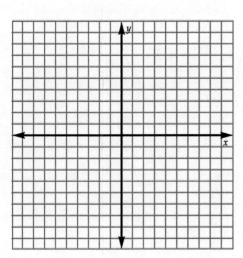

_____

3.28   (2, 2), $\perp$ to $y = x$

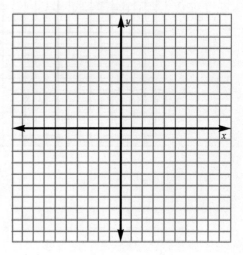

_____

3.29   (-1, 5), | | to $x + y = 10$

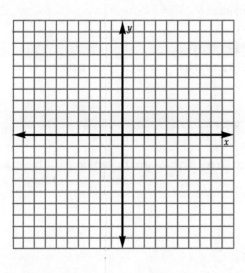

_____

3.30   (4, -1), $\perp$ to $2x - y - 7 = 0$

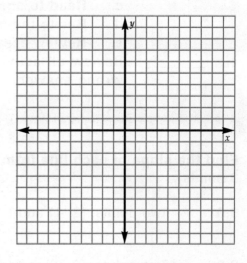

_____

3.31 $(0, 0)$, | | to $3x + 2y - 6 = 0$

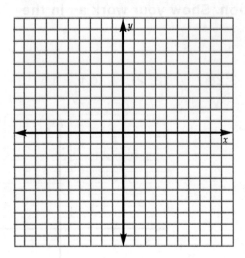

_____

Before you take this last Self Test, you may want to do one or more of these self checks.

1. _____ Read the objectives. Determine if you can do them.
2. _____ Restudy the material related to any objectives that you cannot do.
3. _____ Use the SQ3R study procedure to review the material:
    a. **S**can the sections.
    b. **Q**uestion yourself again (review the questions you wrote initially).
    c. **R**ead to answer your questions.
    d. **R**ecite the answers to yourself.
    e. **R**eview areas you did not understand.
4. _____ Review all activities, and Self Tests, writing a correct answer for every wrong answer.

SELF TEST 3

Find the slope of each line from the given information; show your work (each answer, 3 points).

3.01   Two points, (2, 1) and (-3, 6)

3.02   Two points, (0, 0) and (4, -7)

3.03   Two points, (-5, 3) and (2, 3)

3.04   Two points, (1, 4) and (1, 2)

3.05   Equation $5y + 6x - 2 = 0$

3.06   Equation $2x - 7y - 12 = 0$

3.07   Equation $y = 2x + 5$

3.08   Equation $y - \dfrac{2}{3} = 0$

3.09   3.010

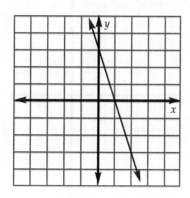   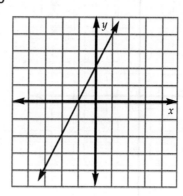

Construct the graph of each of the following equations and inequalities (each graph, 5 points).

3.011 $3x - y - 1 = 0$ 3.012 $2x - y \leq 3$

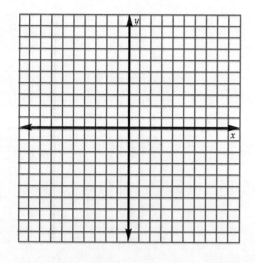   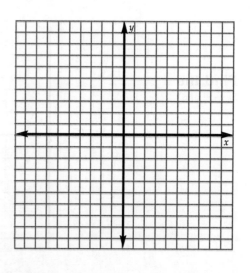

3.013 $y \geq |x - 1|$

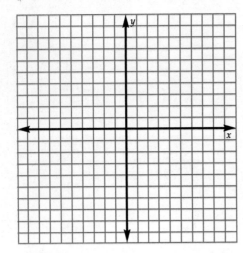

3.014 $y = \dfrac{-3x}{5} + 1$

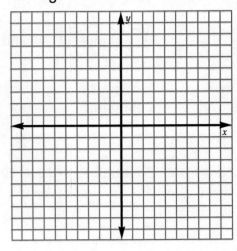

3.015 $x - y = 3$

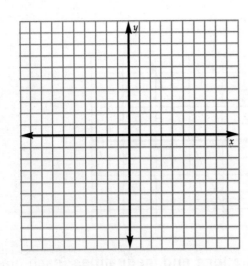

3.016 $x - y - 2 \geq 0$

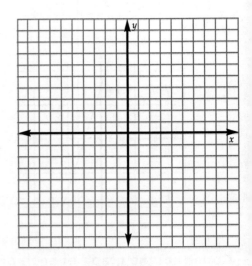

3.017 $-x > y$

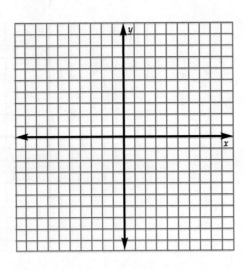

3.018 $x - |y| < 2$

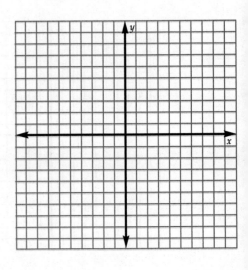

90

Find the equation (in general form) of each line from the given information; show your work (each answer, 3 points).

3.019   Two points, (3, 2) and (-4, 5)

3.020   Two points, (-1, 2) and (5, 2)

3.021   Point (1, -2) and slope $\frac{1}{3}$

3.022   Point (-3, 0) and slope 0

3.023   Slope -2 and y-intercept 8

3.024   Horizontal line through (5, 12)

3.025   Slope 4 and x-intercept -1

3.026   Vertical line through (6, 1)

3.027   3.028

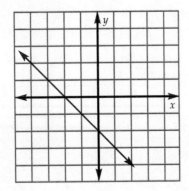   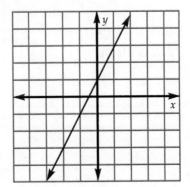

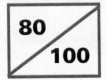   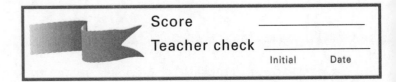

GLOSSARY

abscissa — The first value of an ordered pair, usually x.

absolute value — $|z| = z$ for $z \geq 0$ and $|z| = -z$ for $z < 0$.

axes — Two reference lines drawn in the real-number plane, usually at right angles to each other.

coefficient — The numerical factor of a term.

collinear — Points through which a (straight) line can be drawn.

constant — A term that contains no variable.

coordinates — The abscissa and the ordinate of a point of real-number plane.

domain — The value(s) to be used for the first alphabetical variable of an open sentence.

general form of an equation — $Ax + By + C = 0$, where A, B, and C are relatively prime integers, with the first nonzero coefficient positive.

half-plane — All the points on one side of a line.

linear equation — An open sentence whose graph is a line.

linear inequality — An open sentence whose graph is a shaded half-plane bounded by a line.

ordered pair — Two values written in the alphabetical order of the variables they represent.

ordinate — The second value of an ordered pair, usually y.

origin — The common zero point of the axes.

parallel — Two lines in a plane having no common point.

perpendicular — Two lines meeting at right angles.

plot — To indicate a point's position on the real-number plane.

quadrants — The four regions into which the axes separate the real-number plane.

satisfy — To make an open sentence true.

slope — The ratio of the vertical change to the horizontal change of a line.

slope/y-intercept form of an equation — $y = mx + b$, with m the slope and b the y-intercept.

x-axis — The horizontal reference line on the real-number plane.

x-intercept — The abscissa of the point where a line crosses the x-axis.

y-axis — The vertical reference line on the real-number plane.

y-intercept — The ordinate of the point where a line crosses the y-axis.

MATHEMATICS 909
SYSTEMS

CONTENTS

I. GRAPHICAL SOLUTIONS 2
  Equations 2
  Inequalities 14
II. ALGEBRAIC SOLUTIONS 23
  Opposite-Coefficients Method 23
  Comparison Method 29
  Substitution Method 33
  (OPTIONAL) Determinants Method 37
III. WORD PROBLEMS 46
  Number Problems 47
  Age Problems 49
  Coin Problems 51
  Digit Problems 53
  Fraction Problems 55
  Miscellaneous Problems 58

Authors: Arthur C. Landrey, M.A.Ed.
                             Robert L. Zenor, M.A., M.S.

Editor-in-Chief: Richard W. Wheeler, M.A.Ed.
Editor: Robin Hintze Kreutzberg, M.B.A.
Consulting Editor: Robert L. Zenor, M.A., M.S.
Revision Editor: Alan Christopherson, M.S.

Alpha Omega Publications®

804 N. 2nd Ave. E., Rock Rapids, IA 51246-1759
© MCMXCVI by Alpha Omega Publications, Inc.   All rights reserved.
LIFEPAC is a registered trademark of Alpha Omega Publications, Inc.

MATHEMATICS 906
SYSTEMS

CONTENTS

I. GRAPHICAL SOLUTIONS ... 2

   Equations ... 7

   Inequalities ... 14

II. ALGEBRAIC SOLUTIONS ... 22

   Opposite-Coefficients Method ... 23

   Comparison Method ... 28

   Substitution Method ... 32

   (OPTIONAL) Determinants Method ... 37

III. WORD PROBLEMS ... 46

   Number Problems ... 47

   Age Problems ... 49

   Coin Problems ... 51

   Digit Problems ... 53

   Fraction Problems ... 55

   Miscellaneous Problems ... 56

Author: Arthur C. Landrey, M.A. Ed.

     Robert J. Zenor, M.A., M.S.

Editor-in-Chief: Richard W. Wheeler, M.A. Ed.

Editor: Edith Marie Reifsnyder, B.A.

Consulting Editor: Robert L. Zenor, M.A., M.S.

Illustrator: Thomas R. Cannon, B.S.

Alpha Omega Publications

804 N. 2nd Ave. E., Rock Rapids, IA 51246-1759

© MCMXCVII by Alpha Omega Publications, Inc. All rights reserved.

SYSTEMS

In this LIFEPAC®, you will continue your study in *algebra* by learning to find any common solutions to groups of open sentences called *systems*—first graphically using the techniques of the preceding LIFEPAC, then algebraically using several different methods. Finally, you will see how systems can be set up to solve verbal problems of various types.

OBJECTIVES

Read these objectives. The objectives tell you what you will be able to do when you have successfully completed this LIFEPAC.

When you have finished this LIFEPAC, you should be able to:

1. Identify the equations of systems as consistent, equivalent, or inconsistent.

2. Solve systems of linear equations and inequalities by graphing.

3. Solve systems of linear equations by the methods of opposite-coefficients, comparison, substitution, and (OPTIONAL) determinants.

4. Solve problems using systems of linear equations.

Survey the LIFEPAC. Ask yourself some questions about this study. Write your questions here.

_____

_____

_____

_____

_____

_____

_____

I. GRAPHICAL SOLUTIONS

SECTION OBJECTIVES

Review these objectives. When you have completed this section, you should be able to:

1. Identify the equations of systems as consistent, equivalent, or inconsistent.
2. Solve systems of linear equations and inequalities by graphing.

You are already familiar with the procedures for drawing the graph of a linear equation or a linear inequality on the real-number plane. In this section, we shall graph more than one such open sentence on the same grid and then determine whether ordered pairs exist that satisfy the system. You will need to draw your graphs as accurately as possible.

EQUATIONS

We shall begin by looking at systems made up of two-variable linear equations. You need to learn several terms and then learn the procedures for solving these systems graphically.

TERMINOLOGY

A system of two linear equations is classified by the number of ordered pairs that satisfy both equations. Since the graph of each linear equation is a line, three possible situations can occur. These cases are shown in the following models.

Model 1: Lines m and n *intersect* at one common point P.

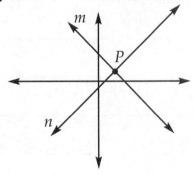

Model 2: Lines q and r *coincide*, having all (infinitely many) common points.

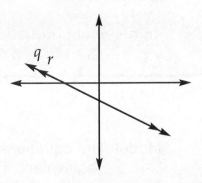

Model 3: Lines s and t are *parallel*, having no common point.

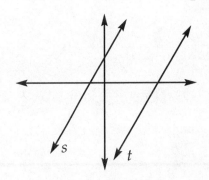

The equations of each of these three systems are identified as *consistent*, *equivalent*, and *inconsistent*, respectively. The set of the ordered pair(s) corresponding to any common point(s) is written as the *solution set* for each system.

DEFINITION

In a system, equations having a common solution are *consistent*.

Model: The equations for lines e and f are consistent. The solution set for this system is $\{(-3, 2)\}$, since the common point is V.

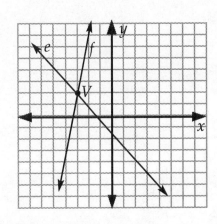

Model: The equations for lines g and h are equivalent. The solution set for this system is the infinite set of ordered pairs for all points on the line.

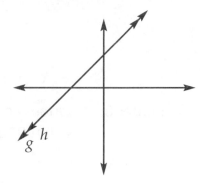

Model: The equations for lines k and l are inconsistent. The solution set for this system is $\varnothing$ (the empty set).

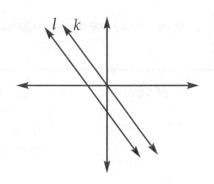

For each of the following pairs of lines, write a. the type of equations (consistent, equivalent, or inconsistent) and b. the solution set of each system.

1.1   a._____

      b._____

1.2   a._____

      b._____

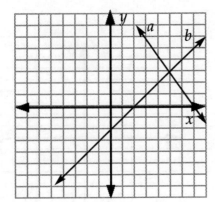

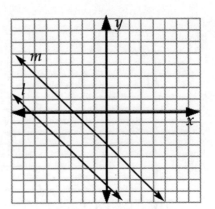

1.3   a._____

      b._____

1.4   a._____

      b._____

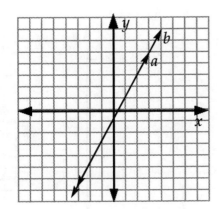

For each of the following pairs of lines, write a. the type of equations
(consistent, equivalent, or inconsistent) and b. the solution set of
each system.

1.5   a._____

        b._____

1.6   a._____

        b._____

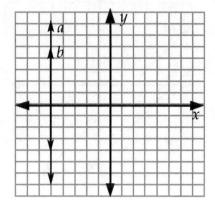

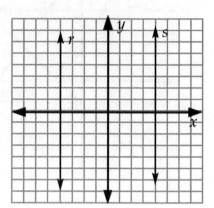

1.7   a._____

        b._____

1.8   a._____

        b._____

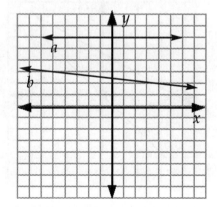

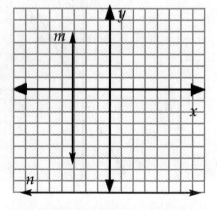

1.9   a._____

        b._____

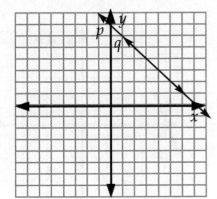

1.10   a._____

        b._____

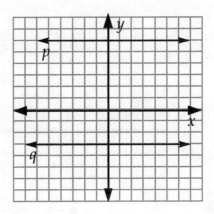

1.11   a._____

        b._____

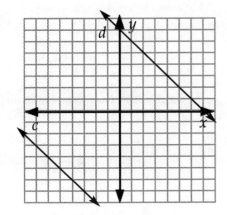

1.12   a._____

        b._____

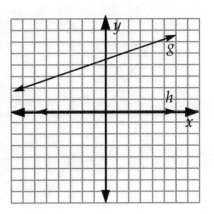

1.13   a._____

         b._____

1.14   a._____

         b._____

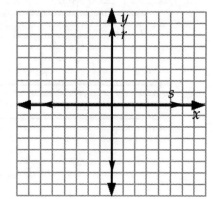

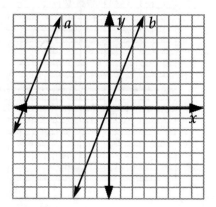

1.15   a._____

         b._____

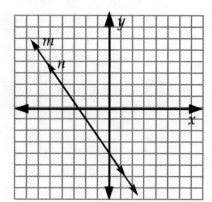

GRAPHS

Now we shall draw the graphs of linear equations to solve a system. This section will be a review of the techniques you learned in Mathematics LIFEPAC 908, except that you will be graphing two lines on the same number-plane grid.

Model 1:   Graph and describe the system

$$\begin{cases} y = -\frac{2}{3}x + 1 \\ 4x + 6y + 8 = 0. \end{cases}$$

Solution: Step 1. The first equation, $y = -\frac{2}{3}x + 1$, is in slope, y-intercept form. Draw the line through (0, 1) and with a slope of $-\frac{2}{3}$.

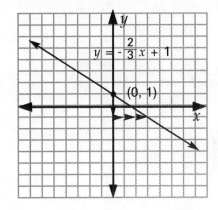

Step 2. Use the intercepts method to graph the second equation, $4x + 6y + 8 = 0$. (When $y = 0$, the x-intercept is -2; and when $x = 0$, the y-intercept is $-\frac{4}{3}$ or $-1.\overline{3}$.)

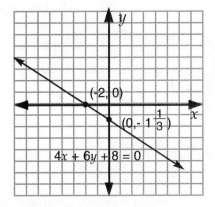

Step 3. Since the lines are parallel, the equations are inconsistent and the solution set of this system is $\varnothing$.

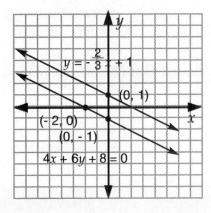

Model 2:   Graph and describe the system

$$\begin{cases} y - 3 = 0 \\ 3x - y = 0. \end{cases}$$

Solution: Step 1. The first equation, $y - 3 = 0$, (or $y = 3$) gives the horizontal line 3 units above the x-axis.

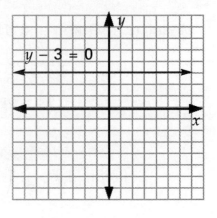

Step 2. You can set up a table of values to find points on the line for the second equation, $3x - y = 0$ (or $3x = y$).

x	2	-1	0
y	6	-3	0

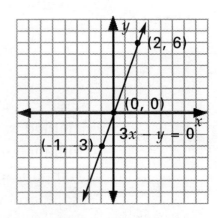

Step 3. Since the lines intersect in one point, the equations are consistent and the solution set of this system is {(1, 3)}.

Checks: $y - 3 = 0$ $3x - y = 0$
           $3 - 3\ ?\ 0$ $3 \cdot 1 - 3\ ?\ 0$
           $0 = 0\ \checkmark$ $3 - 3\ ?\ 0$
                               $0 = 0\ \checkmark$

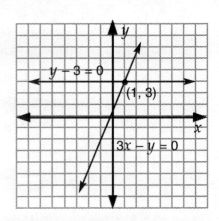

10

Model 3:　Graph and describe the system

$$\begin{cases} 3x - 5y = 15 \\ y = \dfrac{3}{5}x - 3. \end{cases}$$

Solution:　Step 1. Use the intercepts method to graph the first equation, $3x - 5y = 15$. (When $y = 0$, the x-intercept is 5; and when $x = 0$, the y-intercept is -3.)

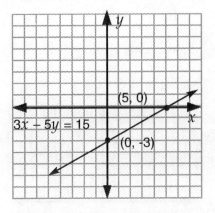

Step 2. The second equation, $y = \dfrac{3}{5}x - 3$, is in slope, y-intercept form. Draw the line through (0, -3) and with a slope of $\dfrac{3}{5}$.

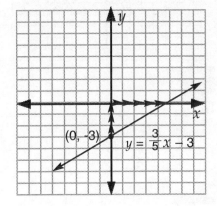

Step 3. Since the lines coincide, the equations are equivalent and the solution set for this system is $\{(x, y): 3x - 5y - 15 = 0\}$.

Note:
The solution set for a system of equivalent equations is written $\{(x, y): Ax + By + C = 0\}$, where $Ax + By + C = 0$ is the general form of the equation for the lines that coincide.

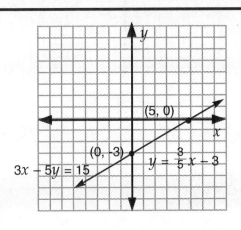

a. Solve the following systems by graphing. b. Identify the equations by type in each case.

1.16 $\begin{cases} x + y = 4 \\ x - y = 6 \end{cases}$

a._____

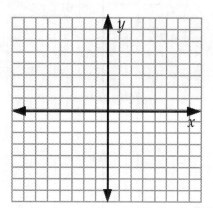

b._____

1.17 $\begin{cases} y = 2x - 3 \\ x + y = 3 \end{cases}$

a._____

b._____

1.18 $\begin{cases} x + y = 6 \\ y = 3 - x \end{cases}$

a._____

b._____

1.19 $\begin{cases} x + y - 4 = 0 \\ x - y = 0 \end{cases}$

a._____

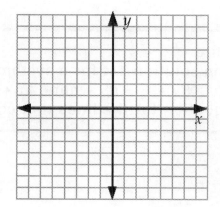

b._____

12

1.20
$$\begin{cases} y = -x + 4 \\ 2x + 2y = 8 \end{cases}$$

a._____

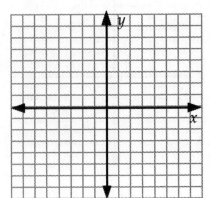

b._____

1.21
$$\begin{cases} 2x + y = 2 \\ x - y = 1 \end{cases}$$

a._____

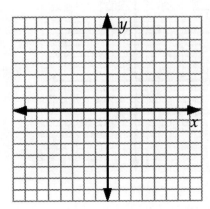

b._____

1.22
$$\begin{cases} x + y = 2 \\ x = 1 \end{cases}$$

a._____

b._____

1.23
$$\begin{cases} y - 4 = 0 \\ 2x - y - 2 = 0 \end{cases}$$

a._____

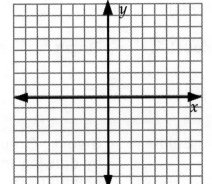

b._____

1.24 $\begin{cases} x = -5 \\ y = -6 \end{cases}$

1.25 $\begin{cases} x + y = 0 \\ x - y + 2 = 0 \end{cases}$

a._____

a._____

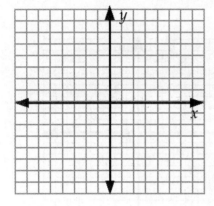

b._____

b._____

INEQUALITIES

Systems made up of two (or more) linear inequalities can also be solved graphically by sketching the graphs on the same number-place grid. Study the following models carefully.

Model 1:   Graph $\begin{cases} x \geq -2 \\ y < 3. \end{cases}$

Solution: Step 1. Graph $x \geq -2$ by drawing the solid boundary ($x = -2$) and shading the half-plane to its right.

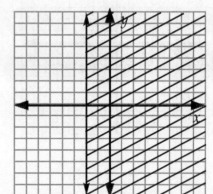

Step 2. Graph $y < 3$ by drawing the dashed boundary ($y = 3$) and shading the half-plane below it.

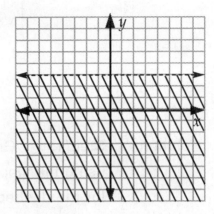

Step 3. Locate all points that are common to both inequalities — the cross-shaded region.

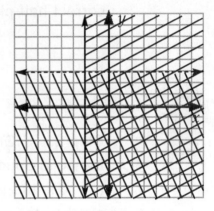

Step 4. Erase the shading of all noncommon points. (Note: The point of intersection of the two boundary lines is indicated by a small circle in this case since it is not included in $y < 3$.)

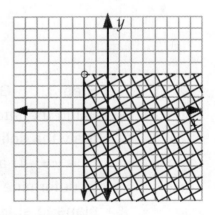

Model 2:   Graph $y < \frac{1}{2}x + 2$
                               $x \leq 0$
            $x + y \geq -4.$

Solution: Step 1.   Graph $y < \frac{1}{2}x + 2$ by
             using the slope, y-intercept form
             for the dashed boundary
             $(y = \frac{1}{2}x + 2)$ and by testing
             points to determine the
             correct half-plane to shade.

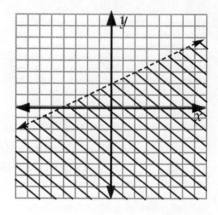

             Step 2.   Graph $x \leq 0$ by drawing
             the solid boundary
             $(x = 0$ is the y-axis) and
             shading the correct half-plane.

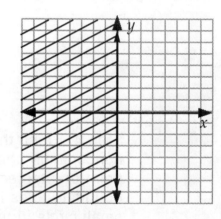

             Step 3.   Graph $x + y \geq -4$ by
             using the intercept method to
             draw the solid boundary
             $(x + y = -4)$ and by testing points
             to determine the correct half-
             plane to shade.

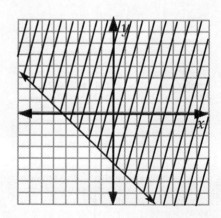

Step 4.   Find the common points and erase the shading of all noncommon points.
(Note: One of the points of intersection of the boundary lines is common; the other two are not.)

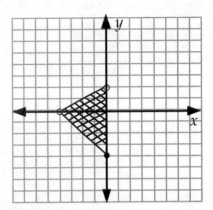

 Graph the solution for each of the following linear inequality systems. Show only the final result for each system.

1.26 $\begin{array}{l} y > x \\ y < -x \end{array}$

1.27 $\begin{array}{l} y > 5 \\ y \geq x \end{array}$

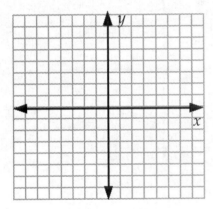

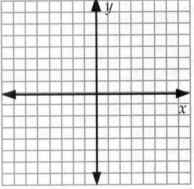

1.28 $\begin{array}{l} y < 2x \\ 2x + y < -5 \end{array}$

1.29 $\begin{array}{l} x + y \geq 6 \\ x \geq 4 \end{array}$

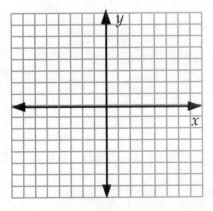

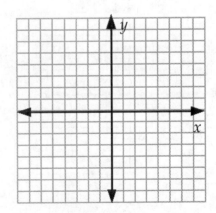

17

1.30
$$\begin{cases} y < 8 \\ y \geq 3 \end{cases}$$

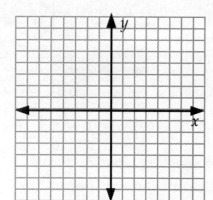

1.31
$$\begin{cases} y \geq 2x - 4 \\ 2x - y \geq -4 \end{cases}$$

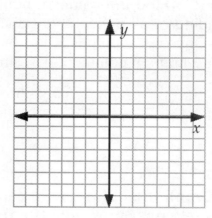

1.32
$$\begin{cases} x + y > 0 \\ x + y + 5 < 0 \end{cases}$$

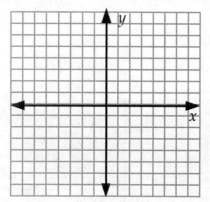

1.33
$$\begin{cases} x + 3 \leq 0 \\ x - 2 \geq 0 \end{cases}$$

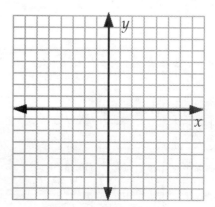

1.34
$$\begin{cases} y \geq 0 \\ y < x \\ x + y < 6 \end{cases}$$

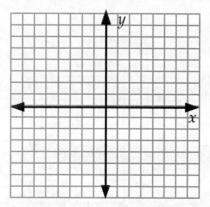

18

1.35
$$x \geq 0$$
$$y \geq 0$$
$$x + y - 10 \leq 0$$

Hint: Let each grid interval equal two units rather than one unit.

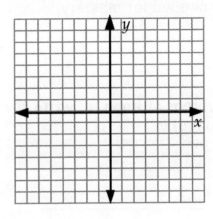

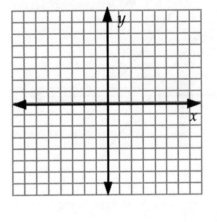

1.36
$$x \geq -2$$
$$x \leq 3$$
$$y \leq 3$$
$$y \geq -2$$

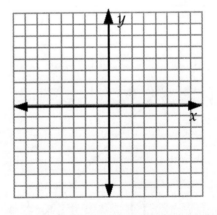

1.37
$$x + 5 \geq 0$$
$$y - 4 \leq 0$$
$$y + 4 \geq 0$$
$$x + y \leq 7$$

Hint: Let each grid interval equal two units rather than one unit.

Review the material in this section in preparation for the Self Test. The Self Test will check your mastery of this particular section. The items missed on this Self Test will indicate specific areas where restudy is needed for mastery.

SELF TEST 1

For each system of lines, a. write the type and b. find the solution set (each answer, 2 points).

1.01   a._____

       b._____

1.02   a._____

       b._____

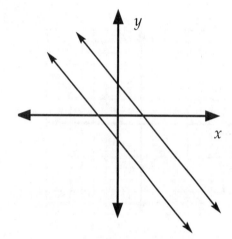

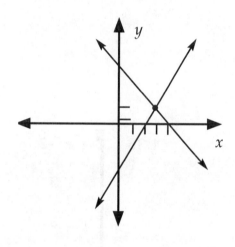

1.03   a._____

       b._____

1.04   a._____

       b._____.

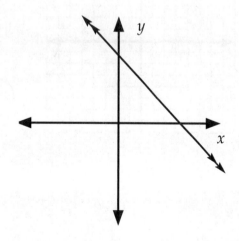

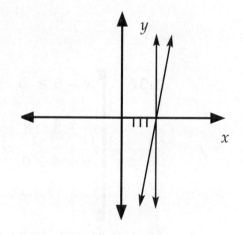

1.05   a._____   1.06   a._____

       b._____   b._____

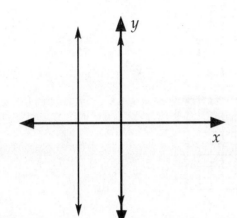

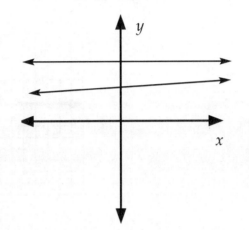

Find the solution set by graphing (each graph, 4 points).

1.07 $\begin{cases} x - y = 4 \\ x + y = 2 \end{cases}$ 1.08 $\begin{cases} y = 2x \\ x + 2y = 2 \end{cases}$

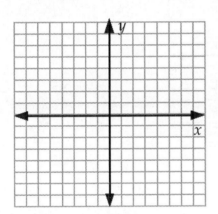

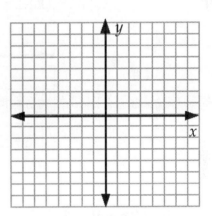

1.09 $\begin{cases} 2x + 3y - 6 = 0 \\ x - y = 0 \end{cases}$ 1.010 $\begin{cases} y = -3 \\ x - y = 8 \end{cases}$

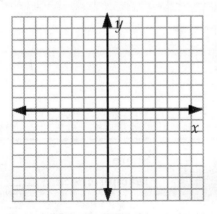

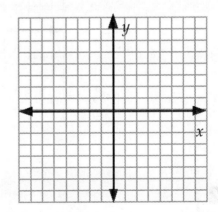

Graph the solution for each of the following pairs of inequalities. Show only the final result for each system (each graph, 4 points).

1.011
$$\begin{cases} y \le x \\ x + y \ge 1 \end{cases}$$

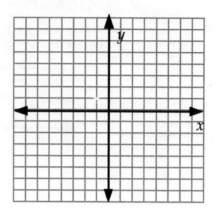

1.012
$$\begin{cases} x + y > 3 \\ x + y < \text{-}4 \end{cases}$$

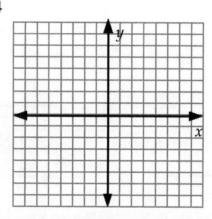

1.013
$$\begin{cases} 2x + y < 1 \\ y \ge \text{-}4 - 2x \end{cases}$$

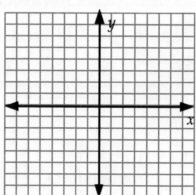

42 / 52

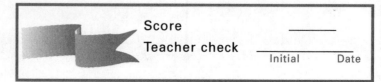

Score _____

Teacher check _____

Initial   Date

22

SECTION OBJECTIVE

Review these objectives. When you have completed this section, you should be able to:

3. Solve systems of linear equations by the methods of opposite-coefficients, comparison, substitution, and (OPTIONAL) determinants.

The graphical methods for solving systems of two consistent linear equations is often inconvenient or inaccurate or both. In this section, you will learn several nongraphical methods for solving linear systems. The goal in the first three methods is to convert two equations to a single equation by temporarily eliminating one of the variables. In the fourth (optional) method, you can solve for both variables directly after learning to use determinants.

OPPOSITE-COEFFICIENTS METHOD

One way of eliminating a variable from a system is to combine like terms of the equations when the coefficients of one of the variables are opposites. Two properties of equality are used in this method; they will be indicated by number as they are applied in the following models.

PROPERTIES:

(1) If $M = 0$ and $N = 0$, then $M + N = 0$.
(2) If $M = 0$, then $k \cdot M = 0$ for any number k.

Model: Solve $\quad\begin{cases} x + 2y - 7 = 0 \\ x - 2y + 1 = 0. \end{cases}$

Solution: Like terms are aligned in columns. The coefficients of y are opposites (2 and -2). Thus, combining the like terms will result in a single equation having only the variable x.

$$
\begin{array}{ll}
x + 2y - 7 = 0 & [M = 0] \\
\underline{x - 2y + 1 = 0} & [N = 0] \\
2x + 0y - 6 = 0 & [M + N = 0 \text{ by (1)}] \\
2x - 6 = 0 & \\
2x = 6 & \\
x = \frac{6}{2} \text{ or } 3 &
\end{array}
$$

The coefficients of x in the original equations are both 1; to make them opposites, multiply the terms of one equation by -1. Then, combining the like terms will result in a single equation having only the variable y.

$$
\begin{array}{l}
x + 2y - 7 = 0 \xrightarrow{k\,=\,\text{-}1} -x - 2y + 7 = 0 \; [k \cdot M = 0 \text{ by (2)}] \\
\qquad\qquad\qquad\quad \underline{x - 2y + 1 = 0} \\
\qquad\qquad\qquad\quad 0x - 4y + 8 = 0 \; [\text{ by (1)}] \\
\qquad\qquad\qquad\qquad\quad -4y + 8 = 0 \\
\qquad\qquad\qquad\qquad\quad -4y = -8 \\
\qquad\qquad\qquad\qquad\quad y = \frac{-8}{-4} \text{ or } 2
\end{array}
$$

As in the graphing method, the solution should be written as an ordered pair (x, y) — in this case (3, 2). You should always verify that the x-value and the y-value actually satisfy both equations of the original system.

Checks:

$x + 2y - 7 = 0$	$x - 2y + 1 = 0$
$3 + 2 \cdot 2 - 7 \;?\; 0$	$3 - 2 \cdot 2 + 1 \;?\; 0$
$3 + 4 - 7 \;?\; 0$	$3 - 4 + 1 \;?\; 0$
$7 - 7 \;?\; 0$	$-1 + 1 \;?\; 0$
$0 = 0 \;\checkmark$	$0 = 0 \;\checkmark$

$\therefore$ The solution set for this system is $\{(3, 2)\}$.

Model 1:   Solve $\begin{cases} 2x + 6y + 3 = 0 \\ x - 4y - 9 = 0. \end{cases}$

Solution: To eliminate y, first determine that the LCM of the coefficients 6 and -4 is 12. Then multiply the terms of each equation by the appropriate number to make opposite coefficients for y. Finally, combine the like terms as before.

$$2x + 6y + 3 = 0 \xrightarrow{\quad 2 \quad} 4x + 12y + 6 = 0 \quad \text{[by (2)]}$$
$$x - 4y - 9 = 0 \xrightarrow{\quad 3 \quad} 3x - 12y - 27 = 0 \quad \text{[by (2)]}$$
$$\overline{ 7x - 21 = 0} \quad \text{[by (1)]}$$
$$7x = 21$$
$$x = 3$$

To eliminate x, first determine that the LCM of the coefficients 2 and 1 is 2. Then multiply the terms of each equation by the appropriate number to make opposite coefficients for x. Finally, combine the like terms as before.

$$2x + 6y + 3 = 0 \xrightarrow{\quad 1 \quad} 2x + 6y + 3 = 0 \quad \text{[by (2)]}$$
$$x - 4y - 9 = 0 \xrightarrow{\quad -2 \quad} -2x + 8y + 18 = 0 \quad \text{[by (2)]}$$
$$\overline{ 14y + 21 = 0}$$
$$14y = -21$$
$$y = \frac{-21}{14} \text{ or } -\frac{3}{2}$$

Checks: $2x + 6y + 3 = 0$ $\qquad x - 4y - 9 = 0$

$2 \cdot 3 + 6(-\frac{3}{2}) + 3 \ ? \ 0$ $\qquad 3 - 4(-\frac{3}{2}) - 9 \ ? \ 0$

$6 - 9 + 3 \ ? \ 0$ $\qquad 3 + 6 - 9 \ ? \ 0$

$-3 + 3 \ ? \ 0$ $\qquad\qquad 9 - 9 \ ? \ 0$

$0 = 0 \ \sqrt{}$ $\qquad\qquad 0 = 0 \ \sqrt{}$

$\therefore$ The solution set is $\{(3, -\frac{3}{2})\}$.

You will probably wish to write all equations in the $M = 0$ form with integral coefficients before using this method.

Model 2: Solve

$$\begin{cases} -8x + 5y = 1 \\ y = \dfrac{4}{7}x - 5. \end{cases}$$

Solution: Rewrite each equation:

$-8x + 5y = 1$	$y = \dfrac{4}{7}x - 5$
$-8x + 5y - 1 = 0$	$7y = 4x - 35$
	$-4x + 7y + 35 = 0$

Now solve the system

$$\begin{cases} -8x + 5y - 1 = 0 \\ -4x + 7y + 35 = 0. \end{cases}$$

To eliminate y:

The LCM of 5 and 7 is 35.

$$
\begin{array}{lll}
-8x + 5y - 1 = 0 \xrightarrow{7} & -56x + 35y - 7 = 0 & \text{[by (2)]} \\
-4x + 7y + 35 = 0 \xrightarrow{-5} & \underline{20x - 35y - 175 = 0} & \text{[by (2)]} \\
& -36x - 182 = 0 & \text{[by (1)]} \\
& -36x = 182 & \\
& x = \dfrac{182}{-36} \text{ or } -5.0\overline{5} &
\end{array}
$$

To eliminate x:

The LCM of -8 and -4 is 8.

$$
\begin{array}{lll}
-8x + 5y - 1 = 0 \xrightarrow{1} & -8x + 5y - 1 = 0 & \text{[by (2)]} \\
-4x + 7y + 35 = 0 \xrightarrow{-2} & \underline{8x - 14y - 70 = 0} & \text{[by (2)]} \\
& -9y - 71 = 0 & \text{[by (1)]} \\
& -9y = 71 & \\
& y = \dfrac{71}{-9} \text{ or } -7.\overline{8} &
\end{array}
$$

Checks: (You may use a calculator if one is available.)

$-8x + 5y = 1$	$y = \dfrac{4}{7}x - 5$
$-8(-5.0\overline{5}) + 5(-7.\overline{8}) \, ? \, 1$	$-7.\overline{8} \, ? \, \dfrac{4}{7}(-5.0\overline{5}) - 5$
$40.\overline{4} - 39.\overline{4} \, ? \, 1$	$-7.\overline{8} \, ? \, -2.\overline{8} - 5$
$1 = 1 \; \checkmark$	$-7.\overline{8} = -7.\overline{8} \quad \checkmark$

$\therefore$ The solution set is $\{(-5.0\overline{5}, -7.\overline{8})\}$.

Solve each system by the opposite-coefficients method. Check your work.

2.1
$$\begin{cases} x + y - 6 = 0 \\ x - y - 8 = 0 \end{cases}$$

2.2
$$\begin{cases} x - y - 10 = 0 \\ x + y - 12 = 0 \end{cases}$$

2.3
$$\begin{cases} 2x + y - 4 = 0 \\ 2x - y - 4 = 0 \end{cases}$$

2.4
$$\begin{cases} 2x + 3y - 10 = 0 \\ 4x - 3y - 2 = 0 \end{cases}$$

2.5
$$\begin{cases} x - 4y - 6 = 0 \\ x + 4y - 8 = 0 \end{cases}$$

2.6
$$\begin{cases} -2x + y + 6 = 0 \\ 2x + y - 8 = 0 \end{cases}$$

2.7
$$\begin{cases} x + y - 7 = 0 \\ 3x + 2y - 11 = 0 \end{cases}$$

2.8
$$\begin{cases} 3x - 2y - 7 = 0 \\ 5x + y - 3 = 0 \end{cases}$$

2.9
$$\begin{cases} 3a + 5b - 7 = 0 \\ a - 2b - 4 = 0 \end{cases}$$

2.10
$$\begin{cases} 2x - 3y - 1 = 0 \\ 3x - 4y - 7 = 0 \end{cases}$$

2.11
$$\begin{cases} R - 9S = 2 \\ 3R - 3S = -10 \end{cases}$$

2.12
$$\begin{cases} 10p + 15q = 3 \\ 6p + 9q - 4 = 0 \end{cases}$$

2.13
$$\begin{cases} x - 3y = 0 \\ 3y - 6 = 2x \end{cases}$$

2.14
$$\begin{cases} 2a + 3b = 6 \\ 5a + 2b - 4 = 0 \end{cases}$$

2.15
$$\begin{cases} 7x - 3y = 4 \\ 2x - 4y = 1 \end{cases}$$

COMPARISON METHOD

Another way to eliminate a variable from a system is to solve for that variable in each equation. Then form an equation by setting these two results equal to each other. The property of equality used in this method will be indicated by number as it is applied in the following models.

PROPERTY:

(3) If $M = N$ and $M = P$, then $N = P$.

Model 1:   Solve $\begin{cases} x + 2y - 7 = 0 \\ x - 2y + 1 = 0. \end{cases}$

Solution: Solve each equation for x:

$x + 2y - 7 = 0$	$x - 2y + 1 = 0$
$x = -2y + 7$	$x = 2y - 1$
$[M = N]$	$[M = P]$

Write a single equation of the results and find the value of y:

$$-2y + 7 = 2y - 1 \quad [N = P \text{ by } (3)]$$
$$-4y + 7 = -1$$
$$-4y = -8$$
$$y = \frac{-8}{-4} \text{ or } 2$$

Now solve each equation for y:

$x + 2y - 7 = 0$	$x - 2y + 1 = 0$
$2y = -x + 7$	$-2y = -x - 1$
$y = \frac{-x + 7}{2}$	$y = \frac{-x - 1}{-2}$

Write a single equation of the results and find the value of x:

$$\frac{-x + 7}{2} = \frac{-x - 1}{-2} \qquad \text{[by (3)]}$$
$$2x - 14 = -2x - 2 \qquad \text{[by cross-multiplication]}$$
$$4x - 14 = -2$$
$$4x = 12$$
$$x = \frac{12}{4} \text{ or } 3$$

(The checks are as before on page 24.)

∴ The solution set is {(3, 2)}.

Model 2:   Solve $\begin{cases} 2x + 6y + 3 = 0 \\ x - 4y - 9 = 0. \end{cases}$

Solution: Solve each equation for y:

$2x + 6y + 3 = 0$

$6y = -2x - 3$

$y = \dfrac{-2x - 3}{6}$

$x - 4y - 9 = 0$

$-4y = -x + 9$

$y = \dfrac{-x + 9}{-4}$

Write a single equation of the results and find the value of x:

$\dfrac{-2x - 3}{6} = \dfrac{-x + 9}{-4}$ [by (3)]

$8x + 12 = -6x + 54$

$14x + 12 = 54$

$14x = 42$

$x = \dfrac{42}{14}$ or 3

Now solve each equation for x:

$2x + 6y + 3 = 0$

$2x = -6y - 3$

$x = \dfrac{-6y - 3}{2}$

$x - 4y - 9 = 0$

$x = 4y + 9$

Write a single equation of the results and find the value of y:

$\dfrac{-6y - 3}{2} = 4y + 9$ [by (3)]

$\dfrac{-6y - 3}{2} = \dfrac{4y + 9}{1}$

$-6y - 3 = 8y + 18$

$-14y - 3 = 18$

$-14y = 21$

$y = \dfrac{21}{-14}$ or $-\dfrac{3}{2}$

(The checks are as before on page 25.)

$\therefore$ The solution set is $\{(3, -\dfrac{3}{2})\}$.

Solve each system by the comparison method. Check your work.

2.16
$$\begin{cases} x + 2y = 6 \\ x - 4y = 8 \end{cases}$$

2.17
$$\begin{cases} 3x + y = 8 \\ y = 2x - 5 \end{cases}$$

2.18
$$\begin{cases} x - 4y - 1 = 0 \\ x + 5y - 4 = 0 \end{cases}$$

2.19
$$\begin{cases} x + y = 5 \\ 2x + y = 7 \end{cases}$$

2.20
$$\begin{cases} 2x + y = -2 \\ x + y = 5 \end{cases}$$

2.21
$$\begin{cases} 2x + y = 3 \\ x = 2y - 1 \end{cases}$$

2.22
$$\begin{cases} 3a + 5b - 78 = 0 \\ 2a - b = 0 \end{cases}$$

2.23
$$\begin{cases} 2p + q = 1 \\ 9p + 3q + 3 = 0 \end{cases}$$

MATHEMATICS

909

LIFEPAC TEST

$$\frac{34}{42}$$

Name _____

Date _____

Score _____

MATHEMATIC 909: LIFEPAC TEST

For each of the following pairs of lines, a. identify the type and b. give the solution set of the system (each answer, 2 points).

1. a._____

    b._____

2. a._____

    b._____

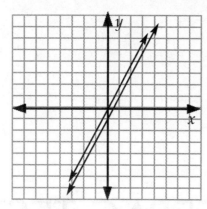

Solve by graphing (each graph, 4 points).

3. $\begin{cases} 2x + 3y = 6 \\ x + 2y = 4 \end{cases}$

4. $\begin{cases} x + y < 0 \\ x - y \geq 2 \end{cases}$

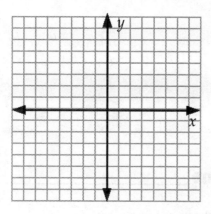

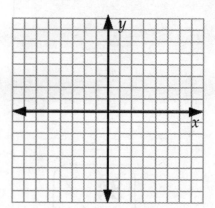

1

Solve each system algebraically. Check your work (each answer, 4 points).

5. $\begin{cases} 2x + y - 10 = 0 \\ x - y - 4 = 0 \end{cases}$

6. $\begin{cases} 5x + 2y = 10 \\ 3x + 2y = 6 \end{cases}$

7. $\begin{cases} 4x - 5y = 3 \\ x = 3 - \dfrac{1}{2}y \end{cases}$

8. $\begin{cases} 3x - 2y - 1 = 0 \\ y = 5x + 4 \end{cases}$

Solve algebraically using two equations. Check your work (each problem, 5 points).

9. One number is 7 more than twice another. If their difference is 22, find the numbers.

10.   In a certain clothing store 6 shirts and 3 ties cost $79.50, and 3 shirts and 2 ties cost $41. Find the cost each shirt and each tie.

2.24 $\begin{cases} 3x + 2y - 5 = 0 \\ x = y + 10 \end{cases}$ 2.25 $\begin{cases} a = 3b \\ 3b - 6 - 2a = 0 \end{cases}$

--- **SUBSTITUTION METHOD** ---

A third way to eliminate a variable from a system is to solve for that variable in one equation and use the result in place of that variable in the other equation. The property used in this method will be indicated by number as it is applied in the following models.

PROPERTY:

(4) If $M = N$, then N may replace M in an algebraic expression.

Model 1:   Solve $\begin{cases} 2x + 6y + 3 = 0 \\ x - 4y - 9 = 0. \end{cases}$

Solution: You may begin by solving for either variable in either equation. However, since the coefficient of x is 1 in the second equation, this variable will be the best choice to start with.

Solve the second equation for x:

$$x - 4y - 9 = 0$$
$$x = 4y + 9 \qquad [M = N]$$

Substitute this result, $(4y + 9)$, in the first equation in place of x and find the value of y:

$$2x + 6y + 3 = 0$$
$$2(4y + 9) + 6y + 3 = 0 \qquad \text{[by (4)]}$$
$$8y + 18 + 6y + 3 = 0$$
$$14y + 21 = 0$$
$$14y = -21$$
$$y = \frac{-21}{14} \text{ or } \frac{-3}{2}$$

Now substitute this value of y in either of the original equations to find the value of x:

$$x - 4y - 9 = 0$$
$$x - 4(-\frac{3}{2}) - 9 = 0 \quad \text{[by (4)]}$$
$$x + 6 - 9 = 0$$
$$x - 3 = 0$$
$$x = 3$$

(The checks are as before on page 25.)

$\therefore$ The solution set is $\{(3, -\frac{3}{2})\}$.

Model 2:   Solve $\begin{cases} -8x + 5y = 1 \\ y = \frac{4}{7}x - 5. \end{cases}$

Solution: Since the second equation is already solved for y, substitute this result, $(\frac{4}{7}x - 5)$, in the first equation in place of y and find the value of x:

$$-8x + 5y = 1$$
$$-8x + 5(\frac{4}{7}x - 5) = 1 \quad \text{[by(4)]}$$
$$-8x + \frac{20}{7}x - 25 = 1$$
$$\frac{-56}{7}x + \frac{20}{7}x = 26$$
$$\frac{-36}{7}x = 26$$
$$x = -\frac{7}{36} \cdot 26$$
$$x = -5.0\overline{5}$$

Now substitute this value of x in either of the original equations to find the value of y:

$$y = \frac{4}{7}x - 5$$

$$y = \frac{4}{7}(-5.0\overline{5}) - 5 \quad \text{[by (4)]}$$

$$y = -2.\overline{8} - 5$$

$$y = -7.\overline{8}$$

(The checks are as before on page 26.)

∴ The solution set is $\{(-5.0\overline{5}, -7.\overline{8})\}$.

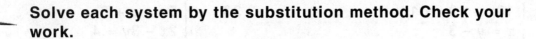

Solve each system by the substitution method. Check your work.

2.26 $\begin{array}{l} 2x + y = 6 \\ y = 3x + 4 \end{array}$

2.27 $\begin{array}{l} 3x + y = 1 \\ y + 4 = 5x \end{array}$

2.28 $\begin{array}{l} x + 5y - 10 = 0 \\ x = 2y - 8 \end{array}$

2.29 $\begin{array}{l} 3x + 2y = 7 \\ x - y + 3 = 0 \end{array}$

35

2.30 $\begin{cases} 2x + y = 7 \\ y - x = 1 \end{cases}$

2.31 $\begin{cases} x - y = 0 \\ x - y - 2 = 0 \end{cases}$

2.32 $\begin{cases} 10x + 10y = 1 \\ x = y - 3 \end{cases}$

2.33 $\begin{cases} 5x = y + 6 \\ 2x - 3y = 4 \end{cases}$

2.34 $\begin{cases} x = b - y \\ y = x + a \end{cases}$

2.35 $\begin{cases} 8x = 2y + 5 \\ 3x = y + 7 \end{cases}$

(NOTE: THE FOLLOWING LESSON AND ACTIVITY SETS ARE OPTIONAL; IF YOU ARE NOT TO SOLVE SYSTEMS BY THIS METHOD, THEN GO AHEAD TO SELF TEST 2 AT THIS TIME.)

—————— (OPTIONAL) DETERMINANTS METHOD ——————

A method for solving linear systems also exists that does not require the temporary elimination of one variable. Instead, the value of each variable is found directly from the coefficients and the constants of the system. First you need to learn about determinants.

DEFINITION:

A 2 x 2 *determinant* is a number indicated by $\begin{bmatrix} Q & R \\ S & T \end{bmatrix}$ and having the value $QT - RS$.

Model 1: $\begin{bmatrix} 4 & 2 \\ 3 & 7 \end{bmatrix}$ = 4 • 7 − 2 • 3 = 28 − 6 = 22

Model 2: $\begin{bmatrix} -1 & 3 \\ 5 & 0 \end{bmatrix}$ = -1 • 0 − 3 • 5 = 0 − 15 = -15

Model 3: $\begin{bmatrix} 5 & -2 \\ 3 & 8 \end{bmatrix}$ = 5 • 8 − (-2)3 = 40 + 6 = 46

Model 4: $\begin{bmatrix} 3 & -10 \\ -4 & -3 \end{bmatrix}$ = 3(-3) − (-10)(-4) = -9 − 40 = -49

Find the value for each of the following determinants. Show your steps as in the preceding models.

2.36 $\begin{bmatrix} 2 & 3 \\ 1 & 4 \end{bmatrix}$ = _____

2.37 $\begin{bmatrix} 2 & 4 \\ 3 & 9 \end{bmatrix}$ = _____

2.38 $\begin{bmatrix} 1 & -2 \\ 3 & 4 \end{bmatrix}$ = _____

37

2.39 $\begin{bmatrix} 5 & -4 \\ 8 & 2 \end{bmatrix} =$ _____

2.40 $\begin{bmatrix} 3 & 5 \\ -2 & 4 \end{bmatrix} =$ _____

2.41 $\begin{bmatrix} 9 & 6 \\ -3 & -1 \end{bmatrix} =$ _____

2.42 $\begin{bmatrix} -3 & -4 \\ -1 & -2 \end{bmatrix} =$ _____

2.43 $\begin{bmatrix} 10 & -4 \\ -9 & -3 \end{bmatrix} =$ _____

2.44 $\begin{bmatrix} x & 2 \\ 3 & x \end{bmatrix} =$ _____

2.45 $\begin{bmatrix} 3x & 2 \\ 4x & 1 \end{bmatrix} =$ _____

2.46 $\begin{bmatrix} x & 2 \\ y & 3 \end{bmatrix} =$ _____

2.47 $\begin{bmatrix} 2x & 6 \\ 3y & 8 \end{bmatrix} =$ _____

2.48 $\begin{bmatrix} x & 3 \\ \pi & 4 \end{bmatrix} =$ _____

2.49 $\begin{bmatrix} x & -4 \\ \pi & 3 \end{bmatrix} =$ _____

2.50 $\begin{bmatrix} (a+b) & 3 \\ (a-b) & 7 \end{bmatrix} =$ _____

To solve a linear system using determinants, the equations are written in a special form. Three determinant values are then found from the equations. Let us look again at the system $\begin{cases} x + 2y - 7 = 0 \\ x - 2y + 1 = 0 \end{cases}$ in terms of the following definitions and property.

The system $\begin{cases} x + 2y - 7 = 0 \\ x - 2y + 1 = 0 \end{cases}$ would be
written in determinant form as $\begin{cases} x + 2y = 7 \\ x - 2y = -1. \end{cases}$

For the system $\begin{cases} x + 2y = 7 \\ x - 2y = -1, \end{cases}$ $d = \begin{bmatrix} 1 & 2 \\ 1 & -2 \end{bmatrix} = -4.$

For the system $\begin{cases} x + 2y = 7 \\ x - 2y = -1, \end{cases}$ $d_x = \begin{bmatrix} 7 & 2 \\ -1 & -2 \end{bmatrix} = -12.$

For the system $\quad \begin{vmatrix} x + 2y = 7 \\ x - 2y = -1 \end{vmatrix}$, $d_y = \begin{bmatrix} 1 & 7 \\ 1 & -1 \end{bmatrix} = -8.$

PROPERTY:

The solution values of x and y for a system of linear equations are found from the ratios

$$x = \frac{d_x}{d} \text{ and } y = \frac{d_y}{d}.$$

Thus, for the systems $\quad \begin{vmatrix} x + 2y = 7 \\ x - 2y = -1 \end{vmatrix}$ the value of x is $\frac{d_x}{d} = \frac{-12}{-4}$

or 3 and the value of y is $\frac{d_y}{d}$ or $\frac{-8}{-4}$ or 2. The checks are done as

before on page 24 and the solution set is again {(3,2)}.

Once you become familiar with these definitions, this method will be the quickest and most direct way for solving many linear systems. Work through the solutions of the following models before trying the activities.

Model 1:   Solve $\quad \begin{vmatrix} 2x + 6y + 3 = 0 \\ x - 4y - 9 = 0. \end{vmatrix}$

Solution: In determinant form the system is

$$\begin{vmatrix} 2x + 6y = -3 \\ x - 4y = 9. \end{vmatrix}$$

The system determinant is $d = \begin{bmatrix} 2 & 6 \\ 1 & -4 \end{bmatrix} = -14.$

The x-determinant is $d_x = \begin{bmatrix} -3 & 6 \\ 9 & -4 \end{bmatrix} = -42.$

The y-determinant is $d_y = \begin{bmatrix} 2 & -3 \\ 1 & 9 \end{bmatrix} = 21.$

40

Thus, $x = \dfrac{d_x}{d} = \dfrac{-42}{-14} = 3$,

and $y = \dfrac{d_y}{d} = \dfrac{21}{-14} = -\dfrac{3}{2}$.

(The checks are as before on page 25.)

∴ The solution set is $\{(3, -\dfrac{3}{2})\}$.

Model 2:   Solve $\begin{cases} -8x + 5y = 1 \\ y = \dfrac{4}{7}x - 5. \end{cases}$

Solution: Rewrite the second equation in determinant form:

$$y = \dfrac{4}{7}x - 5$$

$$7y = 4x - 35$$

$$-4x + 7y = -35$$

The system is $\begin{cases} -8x + 5y = 1 \\ -4x + 7y = -35. \end{cases}$

$$x = \dfrac{d_x}{d} = \dfrac{\begin{bmatrix} 1 & 5 \\ -35 & 7 \end{bmatrix}}{\begin{bmatrix} -8 & 5 \\ -4 & 7 \end{bmatrix}} = \dfrac{182}{-36} \text{ or } -5.0\overline{5}$$

$$y = \dfrac{d_y}{d} = \dfrac{\begin{bmatrix} -8 & 1 \\ -4 & -35 \end{bmatrix}}{\begin{bmatrix} -8 & 5 \\ -4 & 7 \end{bmatrix}} = \dfrac{284}{-36} \text{ or } -7.\overline{8}$$

(The checks are as before on page 26.)

∴ The solution set is $\{(-5.0\overline{5}, -7.\overline{8})\}$.

Solve each system by the determinants method.

2.51 $\begin{cases} x + y = 8 \\ x - y = 10 \end{cases}$

2.52 $\begin{cases} 3x + y - 10 = 0 \\ 4x - y - 4 = 0 \end{cases}$

2.53 $\begin{cases} y = 3 - \dfrac{1}{2}x \\ 3x + 4y = 1 \end{cases}$

2.54 $\begin{cases} 5x - 4y = 7 \\ x = 5 - \dfrac{3}{2}y \end{cases}$

2.55 $\begin{cases} 3x - 2y + 10 = 0 \\ 5y = 4x + 8 \end{cases}$

2.56 $\begin{cases} \dfrac{x}{y} = \dfrac{3}{7} \\ 10x + 14y = 11 \end{cases}$

 Review the material in this section in preparation for the Self Test. This Self Test will check your mastery of this particular section as well as your knowledge of the previous section.

SELF TEST 2

**For each of the following pairs of lines, a. identify by type and b. write the
solution set** (each answer, 2 points).

2.01   a._____

         b._____

2.02   a._____

         b._____

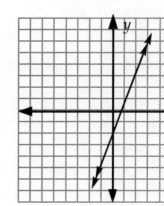

2.03   a._____

         b._____

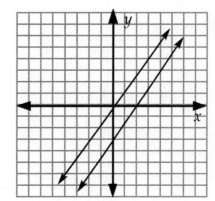

Find the solution by graphing (each graph, 4 points).

2.04 $\begin{cases} 2x + y = 4 \\ 3x - y = 6 \end{cases}$

2.05 $\begin{cases} x + y \geq 2 \\ 2x - y < 1 \end{cases}$

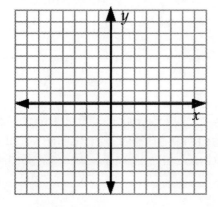

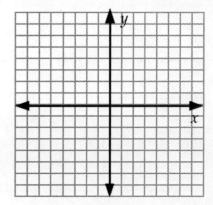

Solve each of the following systems by the most convenient nongraphical method. Check your work (each answer, 4 points).

2.06
$$\begin{cases} 3x + y = 6 \\ x - y = 6 \end{cases}$$

2.07
$$\begin{cases} 3x + y = 1 \\ y = 6 - 4x \end{cases}$$

2.08
$$\begin{cases} 5x - 3y - 10 = 0 \\ x + y - 7 = 0 \end{cases}$$

2.09
$$\begin{cases} 6x + y = 4 \\ 5x + y - 7 = 0 \end{cases}$$

2.010
$$\begin{cases} 3x + 2y = 1 \\ y = \dfrac{6x + 2}{3} \end{cases}$$

2.011
$$\begin{cases} y = 2x + 3 \\ y = 4x + 6 \end{cases}$$

44

2.012　$\begin{cases} y + 3 = 2x \\ y + 4 = 3x \end{cases}$

2.013　$\begin{cases} x = 3 - \dfrac{3}{2}y \\ x + 2y - 4 = 0 \end{cases}$

2.014　$\begin{cases} x + y = 5 \\ x - y = 3 \end{cases}$

2.015　$\begin{cases} 3x + y = 6 \\ y - 4 - x = 0 \end{cases}$

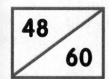

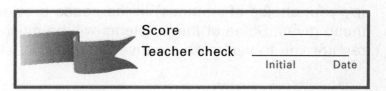

Score _____

Teacher check _____

　　　　　Initial　　　Date

45

This section consists of various types of verbal problems for which you are to set up and solve systems of linear equations using two variables. You must remember to write two equations for each problem. Then you may use any of the algebraic-solution methods learned in the preceding section to solve the resulting system. Try to choose the easiest method for each pair of equations.

Although the solution to a system is written as an ordered pair of numbers, the answer(s) to any word problem should be written in a verbal form. Answers should also include any units with each result, such as seven *years old*, fifteen *quarters*, eight and one-half *inches*, and so on.

Study carefully the setup of the system for each model; then solve that system (by your choice of methods) in the space provided and compare your answers to those given. Some of the problems will be much like the models, but others will require you to use more creative thought.

Number problems usually involve finding two numbers. Facts may be given about the sum or difference of the numbers or about some other relationship between the numbers.

Model: The sum of two numbers is twenty-three, and the larger number is five more than the smaller number. Find these numbers.

Solution: Let l be the larger number, and let s be the smaller number.

THE SUM IS TWENTY-THREE
$$l + s \quad = \quad 23$$

THE LARGER IS FIVE MORE THAN THE SMALLER
$$l \quad = \quad s + 5$$

Solve the system
$$\begin{cases} l + s = 23 \\ l = s + 5 \end{cases}$$

by an algebraic method of your choice in the space provided.

∴ The larger number is fourteen and the smaller number is nine.

 **Solve these problems using an algebraic method of your choice. Check your work.**

3.1   The sum of two numbers is 44, and the larger number is 2 more than the smaller number. Find the numbers.

3.2   The sum of two numbers is 95. If the larger is increased by twice the smaller, the result is 120. Find the numbers.

3.3   The sum of two numbers is 80, and their difference is 50. Find the numbers.

3.4   Find two numbers such that twice the larger increased by the smaller is 2 and the larger decreased by twice the smaller is 11.

3.5   Find two numbers such that one number is 5 times another and their difference is 20.

Age problems require you to find the ages of two people based on facts given about the relationship of the ages. The dimension of time also plays a part in age problems.

Model: The difference between a girl's age and her brother's age is seven years, and a year ago the girl was twice as old as her brother was. Find their current ages.

Solution:

	Now	1 year ago
Girl	g	$g - 1$
Boy	b	$b - 1$

THE DIFFERENCE IS SEVEN
$$g - b = 7$$

THE GIRL WAS TWICE AS OLD AS THE BOY
$$g - 1 = 2(b - 1)$$

Solve the system
$$\begin{cases} g - b = 7 \\ g - 1 = 2b - 2 \end{cases}$$

by an algebraic method of your choice in the space provided.

∴ The girl is now fifteen years old, and her brother is now eight years old.

Solve these problems using an algebraic method of your choice. Check your work.

3.6   John is twice as old as Mary. The sum of their ages is 21. How old are John and Mary?

3.7   The sum of Pete's and Sam's ages is 30. Five years ago Pete was 3 times as old as Sam. Find their ages now.

3.8   Dick is 5 years older than Jane. In 10 years twice Dick's age decreased by Jane's age will be 35. Find their ages now.

3.9   Six years ago Jim was 5 times as old as Henry and in 6 years Jim's age will be 3 times Henry's. Find their ages now.

3.10   Sue's age is 6 years more than twice Ann's, and the difference of their ages is 8. Find their ages.

Coin problems involve identifying the value and quantity of coins that make up a certain sum of money. Any limitations on the value of coins involved are mentioned in each problem. Other items with a specific value, such as stamps or tickets, can also be used in coin-type word problems.

Model: A person has thirteen coins, all nickels and dimes, worth one dollar and five cents. How many of each type of coin are included?

Solution:

	Quantity	Value	Total
Nickels	n	5¢	$5n$
Dimes	d	10¢	$10d$
Together	13		105¢

Solve the system
$$\begin{cases} n + d = 13 \\ 5n + 10d = 105 \end{cases}$$

by an algebraic method of your choice in the space provided.

∴ The person has five nickels and eight dimes.

Solve these problems using an algebraic method of your choice. Check your work.

3.11   A person has 20 coins, all nickels and dimes, worth one dollar and 40 cents. How many of each type of coin are included?

3.12   A bank contains $5.45 in dimes and quarters. If the bank contains 29 coins, how many of each type are in the bank?

3.13   Change for $5 is made with 44 coins, all nickels and quarters. How many of each kind are given?

3.14   A person has 70 stamps, some worth 15¢ and some worth 12¢. If their value is $9.60, how many of each kind does the person have?

3.15   A class sold 480 tickets to their play. The adult tickets cost $2.00, and the children's tickets cost $1.50 each. How many tickets of each type were sold if $820 was collected?

Digit problems are somewhat like number problems. You must find the digits of one number from facts about the relationships of the digits to one another.

Model: The sum of the two digits of a number is twelve. When the digits are reversed, the new number is fifteen more than twice the original number. Find the original number and its reversal.

Solution: A two-digit number such as 74 means $10 \cdot 7 + 4$.
A two digit number such as $\underline{tu}$ means $10t + u$.

The reversal of 74 is 47 or $10 \cdot 4 + 7$.
The reversal of $\underline{tu}$ is $\underline{ut}$ or $10u + t$.

The sum of the digits of 74 is $7 + 4$.
The sum of the digits of $\underline{tu}$ is $t + u$.

Let $\underline{tu}$ be the original number,
and let $\underline{ut}$ be its reversal.

THE SUM OF THE DIGITS IS TWELVE
$$t + u = 12$$

THE REVERSAL IS FIFTEEN MORE THAN TWICE THE ORIGINAL
$$\underline{ut} = 2(\underline{tu}) + 15$$
or
$$10u + t = 2(10t + u) + 15$$

Solve the system $\begin{cases} t + u = 12 \\ 10u + t = 20t + 2u + 15 \end{cases}$

by an algebraic method of your choice in the space provided.

∴ The original number is thirty-nine and its reversal is ninety-three.

 **Solve these problems using an algebraic method of your choice. Check your work.**

3.16   The sum of the two digits of a number is 9. If the tens' digit is one-half the units' digit, find the number.

3.17   The sum of the two digits of a number is 16. The number formed by reversing the digits is 18 more than the original number. Find the original number and its reversal.

3.18   The sum of the digits of a two-digit number is 9, and their difference is 7. Find the number.

3.19   The tens' digit of a two-digit number is 1 more than twice the units' digit. If the difference of the digits is 3, find the number.

3.20   The units' digit of a two-digit number is 2 more than 3 times the tens' digit. When the digits are reversed, the new tens' digit is 4 times the new units' digit. Find the number and its reversal.

Fraction problems are also similar to number problems. The numbers you are looking for in fraction problems are the numerator and denominator of some fraction.

Model: If the denominator of a certain fraction is increased by seven, the fraction becomes one-half. If the numerator of the original fraction is decreased by one, the fraction becomes two-thirds. What is the original fraction?

Solution: Let $\frac{n}{d}$ be the original fraction.

INCREASE THE DENOMINATOR BY SEVEN: $\frac{n}{d+7} = \frac{1}{2}$

DECREASE THE NUMERATOR BY ONE: $\frac{n-1}{d} = \frac{2}{3}$

Use cross-multiplication on each equation to obtain

$$\begin{cases} 2n = d + 7 \\ 3n - 3 = 2d. \end{cases}$$

Solve this system by an algebraic method of your choice in the space provided.

∴ The original fraction is eleven-fifteenths.

 **Solve these problems using an algebraic method of your choice. Check your work.**

3.21   The ratio of the numerator to the denominator of a fraction is 2 to 3. If both the numerator and denominator are increased by 2, the fraction becomes $\frac{3}{4}$. Find the original numerator and denominator.

3.22   If the numerator of a fraction is increased by 3, the fraction becomes $\frac{3}{4}$. If the denominator is decreased by 7, the fraction becomes 1. Find the original fraction.

3.23   The ration of the numerator to the denominator of a fraction is 1 to 3. If the numerator is increased by 4 and the denominator is decreased by 3, the fraction becomes $\frac{1}{2}$. Find the original fraction.

3.24   If the numerator of a fraction is increased by 7, the fraction becomes 2. If
the denominator of the fraction is increased by 5, the fraction becomes 1.
Find the original fraction.

3.25   The denominator of a certain fraction is three times the numerator. If the sum
of the numerator and the denominator is 32, find the original fraction.

Many other application problems can be solved by a two-variable system of linear equations. Some of these types of problems include motion problems, investment problems, mixture problems, perimeter problems, and combination problems. A sampling of these types of problems is included in the following activities. See if you are able to analyze these problems and to set up and solve a correct system for each type.

 Solve these problems using an algebraic method of your choice. Check your work.

3.26   In a certain clothing store 3 shirts and 5 ties cost $60, and 2 shirts and 3 ties cost $39. What is the cost of each shirt and each tie?

3.27   In a certain candy store 3 pounds of candy and 2 pounds of mints cost $10.80, and 1 pound of candy and 3 pounds of mints cost $5.35. Find the cost per pound of candy and of mints.

3.28   The sum of $10,000 is invested, part at 12% interest and part at 9% interest. The combined incomes from the two investments is $1,005. How much money is invested at each rate?

3.29   The sum of $12,000 is invested, part at 12% interest and part at 8% interest. Twice as much money was invested at 8% as at 12%. How much money was invested at each rate?

3.30   A boat can travel 10 miles down stream in 70 minutes. The return trip upstream requires 2 hours. Find the rate of the boat and the rate of the current.

3.31   Flying with the wind, a jet can travel 2,800 miles in 4 hours. Flying against the wind, the same distance takes 6 hours. Find the rate of the jet and of the wind.

3.32   Tickets to a class play cost $1.50 and 75 cents. If 520 tickets were sold for $555, how many of each kind were sold?

3.33   A certain mathematics class has 32 students. If the class has 6 more boys than girls, how many boys are in the class?

3.34   A rectangle is three times as long as it is wide. If the perimeter is 340 feet, what are the length and width of the rectangle?

3.35   Half the perimeter of a building is 100 feet. The length of the building is 20 feet more than the width. Find the dimensions of the building.

Before you take this last Self Test, you may want to do one or more of these self checks.

1. Read the objectives. Check to see if you can do them.
2. Restudy the material related to any objective that you cannot do.
3. Use the SQ3R study procedure to review the material.
4. Review activities, Self Tests, and LIFEPAC Glossary.
5. Restudy areas of weakness indicated by the last Self Test.

Identify each system of lines by type (each answer, 2 points).

3.01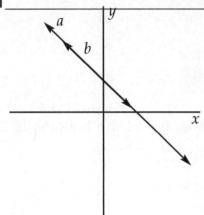

3.02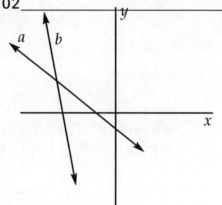

3.03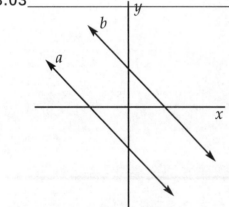

3.04 $\begin{cases} 2x + y = 6 \\ 2x + y = 7 \end{cases}$ _____

3.05 $\begin{cases} y = 2x + 3 \\ y = 4x + 6 \end{cases}$ _____

3.06 $\begin{cases} x = \dfrac{y + 3}{2} \\ 4x - 2y = 6 \end{cases}$ _____

Find the solution by graphing (each graph, 4 points).

3.07 $\begin{cases} x + 2y = 8 \\ x - y + 1 = 0 \end{cases}$ 3.08 $\begin{cases} y \geq x \\ x + y < 3 \end{cases}$

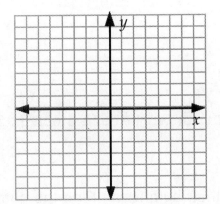 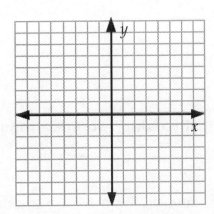

Solve each system algebraically. Check your work (each answer, 4 points).

3.09 $\begin{cases} x + y = 12 \\ x - y = 10 \end{cases}$ 3.010 $\begin{cases} 2x - y - 4 = 0 \\ 3x + y - 9 = 0 \end{cases}$

3.011 $\begin{cases} 5x + 2y = 8 \\ x + y = 4 \end{cases}$ 3.012 $\begin{cases} 5x + 2y = 7 \\ y = x + 1 \end{cases}$

3.013 $\begin{cases} 2y = x + 3 \\ 5y = x - 7 \end{cases}$ 3.014 $\begin{cases} 2x + y - 8 = 0 \\ y = \dfrac{x + 2}{3} \end{cases}$

3.015 $\begin{cases} 7x - 2y = 4 \\ 5y + 3x = 10 \end{cases}$ 3.016 $\begin{cases} 9x + 2y = 5 \\ y - 2x + 3 = 0 \end{cases}$

Solve algebraically using two equations. Check your work (each problem, 5 points).

3.017   One number is 4 more than another and their sum is 60. Find the numbers.

3.018   The sum of the digits of a two-digit number is 12. The number formed by interchanging the digits is 54 more than the original number. Find the original number and its reversal.

3.019   The length of a rectangle is 2 more than 3 times the width. If the perimeter is 100, find the length and width of the rectangle.

3.020   Dad is 4 times as old as his son Jim. In 10 years Dad's age will be 20 years more than twice Jim's age. Find their ages now.

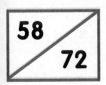

58 / 72

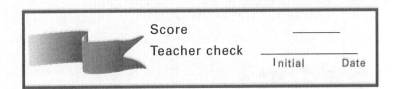

Score   _____

Teacher check   _____

                  Initial   Date

      Before taking the LIFEPAC Test, you may want to do one or more of these self checks.

1. _____ Read the objectives. Check to see if you can do them.

2. _____ Restudy the material related to any objective that you cannot do.

3. _____ Use the SQ3R study procedures to review the material.

4. _____ Review activities, Self Tests, and LIFEPAC Glossary.

5. _____ Restudy areas of weakness indicated by the last Self Test.

GLOSSARY

coincident lines — Lines having all (infinitely many) points in common.

consistent equations — System equations having a common solution.

determinant — A 2 x 2 determinant is a number indicated by $\begin{bmatrix} Q & R \\ S & T \end{bmatrix}$ and having the value $QT - RS$.

equivalent equations — System equations having all common solutions.

inconsistent equations — System equations having no common solution.

intersecting lines — Lines having one common point.

least common multiple (*LCM*) — The smallest positive number into which each of a group of numbers will divide exactly.

parallel lines — Lines having no common point.

system — In this LIFEPAC a group of open sentences solved to find any common solution(s).

MATHEMATICS 910
QUADRATIC EQUATIONS
AND A REVIEW OF ALGEBRA

CONTENTS

I.   **QUADRATIC EQUATIONS**   2
   Identifying Quadratic Equations   2
   Methods of Solving Quadratic Equations   5
   Verbal problems 21

II. **A REVIEW OF ALGEBRA: PART I** 29
   Variables and Numbers 29
   Solving Equations and Inequalities. 30
   Problem Analysis and Solution 32
   Polynomials 34
   Factors 37

III. **A REVIEW OF ALGEBRA: PART II** 43
   Algebraic Fractions 43
   Radical Expressions 46
   Graphing 49
   Systems 52
   Quadratic Equations 57

Author: **Arthur C. Landrey, M.A.Ed.**
Editor-in-Chief: Richard W. Wheeler, M.A.Ed.
Editor: Stephany L. Sykes
Consulting Editor: Robert L. Zenor, M.A., M.S.
Revision Editor: Alan Christopherson, M.S.

Alpha Omega Publications®

804 N. 2nd Ave. E., Rock Rapids, IA 51246-1759

QUADRATIC EQUATIONS AND A REVIEW OF ALGEBRA

This LIFEPAC® is the final LIFEPAC in the first-year study of the mathematical system known as algebra. In this LIFEPAC you will learn how to solve equations that involve second-degree polynomials; these equations are called *quadratic equations*. Then you will review some representative exercises and problems from each of the LIFEPACs in this course of study.

OBJECTIVES

Read these objectives. These objectives tell you what you will be able to do when you have successfully completed this LIFEPAC.

When you have finished this LIFEPAC, you should be able to:

1. Identify quadratic equations.

2. Write quadratic equations in general form.

3. Solve quadratic equations by completing the square, by the quadratic formula, and by factoring.

4. Work representative problems of the first-year algebra course.

Survey the LIFEPAC. Ask yourself some questions about this study. Write your questions here.

_____

_____

_____

_____

_____

_____

_____

I. QUADRATIC EQUATIONS

In this section you will need to apply many skills that you have acquired in previous LIFEPACs, while you learn about a new type of equation. After an introduction to quadratic equations, you will learn three methods for solving them. Finally, you will learn to solve verbal problems that require the use of quadratic equations.

❋ ❋ IDENTIFYING QUADRATIC EQUATIONS ❋ ❋ ❋ ❋ ❋ ❋ ❋ ❋

First you must be able to recognize quadratic equations. Learn these two basic definitions.

DEFINITIONS

A *quadratic equation* is an equation that can be written as
$Ax^2 + Bx + C = 0$, where A is not zero.

In this LIFEPAC, you will consider an equation to be in *general form* when A is positive and when $A, B,$ and C are integers whose greatest common factor is 1.

Model 1: $2x^2 + 3x - 4 = 0$ is a quadratic equation in general form, where A is 2, B is 3, and C is -4.

Model 2: $x^2 + 7 = 0$ is a quadratic equation in general form, where A is 1, B is 0, and C is 7.

Model 3: $-5x^2 + x = 0$ is a quadratic equation. Its general form can be found by multiplying both sides of the equation by negative one.

$$-1[-5x^2 + x] = -1[0]$$
$$5x^2 - x = 0$$

Then A is 5, B is -1, and C is 0.

Model 4: $3x - 11 = 0$ is not a quadratic equation since it does not contain a second-degree term.

Model 5: $x^3 - 2x^2 + 1 = 0$ is not a quadratic equation since it contains a third-degree term.

Model 6: $\frac{1}{3}(x + 2)(x - 7) = 5$ is a quadratic equation that can be rewritten.

$$3[\frac{1}{3}(x + 2)(x - 7)] = 3[5]$$
$$(x + 2)(x - 7) = 15$$
$$x^2 - 5x - 14 = 15$$
$$x^2 - 5x - 29 = 0$$

Then A is 1, B is -5, and C is -29.

Model 7: $0.7x^2 = 1$ is a quadratic equation. Its general form can be found by multiplying both sides of the equation by 10.

$$10[0.7x^2] = 10[1]$$
$$7x^2 = 10$$
$$7x^2 - 10 = 0$$

Then A is 7, B is 0, and C is -10.

Model 8: $2x^2 - 4x + 6 = 0$ is a quadratic equation. Its general form can be found by dividing all the terms by 2.

$$\frac{2x^2}{2} - \frac{4x}{2} + \frac{6}{2} = \frac{0}{2}$$
$$x^2 - 2x + 3 = 0$$

Then A is 1, B is -2, and C is 3.

Indicate (by *yes* or *no*) whether each of the following equations is quadratic. If so, give the values of *A*, *B*, and *C* from each equation's general form; if not, tell why.

1.1 $3x^2 + 5x - 7 = 0$ _____

1.2 $2x - 1 = 0$ _____

1.3 $2x^2 - 1 = 0$ _____

1.4 $-4x^2 + 2x - 1 = 0$ _____

1.5 $5x^2 + 15x = 0$ _____

1.6 $(x - 3)^2 = 0$ _____

1.7 $\frac{1}{4}x^2 + 5 = 0$ _____

1.8 $2x^3 - x = 0$ _____

1.9 $(x + 1)(2x + 3) = 4$ _____

1.10 $\frac{2}{3}(x - 4)(x + 5) = 1$ _____

1.11 $6x - 1 = 4x + 7$ _____

1.12 $6x^2 - 1 = 4x + 7$ _____

1.13 $6x^3 - 1 = 4x + 7$ _____

1.14 $1.3x^2 + 2.5x - 1 = 0$ _____

1.15 $(4x - 1)(3x + 5) = 0$ _____

1.16 $-2x^2 - 3x = 5$ _____

1.17 $(5 + x)(5 - x) = 7$ _____

1.18 $\frac{x^2}{2} = 7x$ _____

1.19 $\frac{1}{5}x = \frac{2}{3}x^2 - 2$ _____

1.20 $x(x + 1)(x + 2) = 3$ _____

4

METHODS OF SOLVING QUADRATIC EQUATIONS

We shall now look at three ways to solve quadratic equations. The first two methods may be used with any quadratic equation. The third method may be used only with quadratic equations that have factorable polynomials.

COMPLETING THE SQUARE

Let us begin by considering the equation $x^2 = 16$. You know that 4^2 and $(-4)^2$ equal 16; therefore, 4 or -4 are the two roots for this quadratic equation. These roots can be written in a *solution set* as {4, -4}.

Now consider the equation $x^2 = 17$. Since $(\sqrt{17})^2$ and $(-\sqrt{17})^2$ equal 17, the solution set for this quadratic equation is $\{\sqrt{17}, -\sqrt{17}\}$. Similarly, the equation $x^2 = 18$ is satisfied by $\sqrt{18}$ or $-\sqrt{18}$. These radicals can be simplified to $\sqrt{9}\sqrt{2}$ or $3\sqrt{2}$, and $-\sqrt{9}\sqrt{2}$ or $-3\sqrt{2}$. Therefore, the solution set for this quadratic equation is $\{3\sqrt{2}, -3\sqrt{2}\}$.

The equation $x^2 = -18$ has no real roots since no real number exists whose square is negative.

In general, to solve equations that contain squares of binomials, we use the following property.

PROPERTY
If $X^2 = N$ and N is not negative, then $X = \sqrt{N}$ or $X = -\sqrt{N}$. This property is called the *Square Root Property of Equations*.

Study these models to see how this property can be applied to solve equations that contain squares of binomials.

Model 1:
$$(x + 1)^2 = 16$$

4^2 is 16, so	$(-4)^2$ is 16, so
$x + 1 = 4$	$x + 1 = -4$
$x = 3$	$x = -5$

The solution set is {3, -5}

Model 2: $(x - 1)^2 = 17$

$(\sqrt{17})^2$ is 17, so $(-\sqrt{17})^2$ is 17, so
      $x - 1 = \sqrt{17}$ $x - 1 = -\sqrt{17}$
      $x = 1 + \sqrt{17}$ $x = 1 - \sqrt{17}$

The solution set is $\{1 + \sqrt{17}, 1 - \sqrt{17}\}$

Model 3: $(3x + 2)^2 = 18$

$(\sqrt{18})^2$ is 18, so $(-\sqrt{18})^2$ is 18, so

$3x + 2 = \sqrt{18}$ $3x + 2 = -\sqrt{18}$

$3x = -2 + \sqrt{18}$ $3x = -2 - \sqrt{18}$

$x = \dfrac{-2 + \sqrt{18}}{3}$ $x = \dfrac{-2 - \sqrt{18}}{3}$

$x = \dfrac{-2 + 3\sqrt{2}}{3}$ $x = \dfrac{-2 - 3\sqrt{2}}{3}$

The solution set is $\{ \dfrac{-2 + 3\sqrt{2}}{3}, \dfrac{-2 - 3\sqrt{2}}{3} \}$.

 **Apply the Square Root Property of Equations to find the solution set for each of the following equations.**

1.21 $x^2 = 25$ 1.22 $x^2 = 26$

1.23 $x^2 = 27$ 1.24 $x^2 - 80 = 0$

6

1.25 $x^2 + 80 = 0$

1.26 $(x + 2)^2 = 36$

1.27 $(2x - 5)^2 = 11$

1.28 $(x - 4)^2 = 12$

1.29 $(3x + 1)^2 - 100 = 0$

1.30 $(4x - 3)^2 - 50 = 0$

You should know how to find the root for quadratic equations that are written in the form $X^2 = N$. In some instances you may be able to write an equation in this form immediately by factoring $Ax^2 + Bx + C$ to the square of a binomial.

Model:
$$x^2 + 6x + 9 = 0$$
$$(x + 3)(x + 3) = 0$$
$$(x + 3)^2 = 0$$
$$0^2 = 0$$
$$\text{Therefore, } x + 3 = 0$$
$$x = -3$$

The solution set is {-3}.

Note: This quadratic equation has only one root since 0 is the only number whose square is 0.

When $Ax^2 + Bx + C$ does not factor to the square of a binomial, a procedure known as *completing the square* may be used to write a quadratic equation in the form $X^2 = N$. The following steps can be used to accomplish this goal.

1. Write the quadratic equation in general form and identify A and B.

2. Multiply the terms of the equation by $4A$.

3. Isolate the constant term on the right side of the equation.

4. Add B^2 to each side of the equation.

5. Factor the left side of the equation to the square of a binomial.

These steps will be indicated by number in the solutions to the next three models.

Model 1: Solve $x^2 + 7x + 12 = 0$ by completing the square.

1. A is 1 and B is 7.

2. $4A$ is 4: $4[x^2 + 7x + 12] = 4[0]$
$$4x^2 + 28x + 48 = 0$$

3. $$4x^2 + 28x = -48$$

4. B^2 is 49: $[4x^2 + 28x] + 49 = [-48] + 49$
$$4x^2 + 28x + 49 = 1$$

5. $$(2x + 7)(2x + 7) = 1$$
$$(2x + 7)^2 = 1$$

Now solve:

1^2 is 1, so	$(-1)^2$ is 1, so
$2x + 7 = 1$	$2x + 7 = -1$
$2x = -6$	$2x = -8$
$x = -3$	$x = -4$

The solution set is $\{-3, -4\}$.

Model 2: Solve $5x^2 = 3x$ by completing the square.

1. $5x^2 - 3x = 0$; A is 5 and B is -3.

2. $4A$ is 20: $20[5x^2 - 3x] = 20[0]$
$$100x^2 - 60x = 0$$

3. The equation contains no constant term.

4. B^2 is 9: $[100x^2 - 60x] + 9 = [0] + 9$
$$100x^2 - 60x + 9 = 9$$

5. $$(10x - 3)(10x - 3) = 9$$
$$(10x - 3)^2 = 9$$

Now solve:

3^2 is 9, so	$(-3)^2$ is 9, so
$10x - 3 = 3$	$10x - 3 = -3$
$10x = 6$	$10x = 0$
$x = 0.6$	$x = 0$

The solution set is $\{0.6, 0\}$.

Model 3: Solve $4x(x - 3) = 2$ by completing the square.

1. $$4x^2 - 12x = 2$$
$$4x^2 - 12x - 2 = 0$$
$$2x^2 - 6x - 1 = 0;\ A \text{ is 2 and } B \text{ is -6.}$$

2. $4A$ is 8: $8[2x^2 - 6x - 1] = 8[0]$
$$16x^2 - 48x - 8 = 0$$

3. $$16x^2 - 48x = 8$$

4. B^2 is 36: $[16x^2 - 48x] + 36 = [8] + 36$
$$16x^2 - 48x + 36 = 44$$

5.
$$(4x - 6)(4x - 6) = 44$$
$$(4x - 6)^2 = 44$$

Now solve: $(\sqrt{44})^2$ is 44 and $(-\sqrt{44})^2$ is 44, so

$$4x - 6 = \pm \sqrt{44}$$
$$4x = 6 \pm \sqrt{44}$$
$$4x = 6 \pm 2\sqrt{11}$$
$$x = \frac{6 \pm 2\sqrt{11}}{4}$$

The solution set is $\{ \frac{3 + \sqrt{11}}{2}, \frac{3 - \sqrt{11}}{2} \}$.

Note: The $\pm$ symbol is read "plus or minus."

Solve each quadratic equation by completing the square.

1.31 $x^2 + 9x + 8 = 0$ 1.32 $x^2 - 4x - 7 = 0$

1.33 $2x^2 = 7x$ 1.34 $3x^2 + x = 0$

1.35 $x(x + 5) = 3$

1.36 $2x(x - 2) + 2 = 0$

1.37 $7x - 5x^2 = 2$

1.38 $(2x + 5)(x - 1) = 1$

1.39 $\frac{1}{2}x^2 + \frac{2}{3}x - \frac{5}{6} = 0$

1.40 $0.4x^2 + 1.1x = 2$

THE QUADRATIC FORMULA

Another method for solving a quadratic equation is derived from using the completing-the-square procedure on the general equation $Ax^2 + Bx + C = 0$. Study the following steps carefully.

DERIVATION

$$Ax^2 + Bx + C = 0$$

Multiply by $4A$:
$$4A[Ax^2 + Bx + C] = 4A[0]$$
$$4A^2x^2 + 4ABx + 4AC = 0$$

Isolate the constant:
$$4A^2x^2 + 4ABx = -4AC$$

Add B^2:
$$4A^2x^2 + 4ABx + B^2 = -4AC + B^2$$

Factor:
$$(2Ax + B)(2Ax + B) = -4AC + B^2$$
$$(2Ax + B)^2 = -4AC + B^2$$

Solve for x:
$$2Ax + B = \pm \sqrt{-4AC + B^2}$$
$$2Ax = -B \pm \sqrt{-4AC + B^2}$$
$$x = \frac{-B \pm \sqrt{-4AC + B^2}}{2A}$$

The result is known as the *quadratic formula* and is usually written as

$$x = \frac{-B \pm \sqrt{B^2 - 4AC}}{2A} \ .$$

Note: $-B$ is read " the opposite of B."

Notice that <u>two possible values</u> of x are indicated by the quadratic formula – one value is $\frac{-B + \sqrt{B^2 - 4AC}}{2A}$ and the other value is $\frac{-B - \sqrt{B^2 - 4AC}}{2A}$. You should memorize this formula, since it will be used often. To use the formula, replace A, B, and C by their numerical values in the equation to be solved and simplify.

Model 1: Solve $x^2 + 7x + 12 = 0$ by using the quadratic formula.

A is 1, B is 7, and C is 12.

$$x = \frac{-B \pm \sqrt{B^2 - 4AC}}{2A}$$

$$x = \frac{-7 \pm \sqrt{7^2 - 4 \cdot 1 \cdot 12}}{2 \cdot 1}$$

$$x = \frac{-7 \pm \sqrt{49 - 48}}{2}$$

$$x = \frac{-7 \pm \sqrt{1}}{2} \text{, and since } \pm \sqrt{1} = \pm 1,$$

$$x = \frac{-7 + 1}{2} \qquad x = \frac{-7 - 1}{2}$$

$$x = \frac{-6}{2} \qquad x = \frac{-8}{2}$$

$$x = -3 \qquad x = -4$$

The solution set is {-3, -4}.

Model 2: Solve $4x^2 = 2x + 1$ by using the quadratic formula.

The equation rewritten in general form is $4x^2 - 2x - 1 = 0$;
A is 4, B is -2, and C is -1.

$$x = \frac{-B \pm \sqrt{B^2 - 4AC}}{2A}$$

$$x = \frac{-(-2) \pm \sqrt{(-2)^2 - 4 \cdot 4(-1)}}{2 \cdot 4}$$

$$x = \frac{2 \pm \sqrt{4 + 16}}{8}$$

$$x = \frac{2 \pm \sqrt{20}}{8} \text{, and since } \pm \sqrt{20} = \pm 2\sqrt{5},$$

$$x = \frac{2 \pm 2\sqrt{5}}{8}$$

$$x = \frac{\cancel{2}(1 \pm \sqrt{5})}{\cancel{2} \cdot 4}$$

The solution set is $\{\frac{1 + \sqrt{5}}{4}, \frac{1 - \sqrt{5}}{4}\}$.

These values in the solution set are the exact irrational values of x. You can also find approximate rational values of x by using a decimal representation for $\sqrt{5}$ and then rounding to the desired accuracy.

$$\frac{1 + 2.236}{4} \qquad \Bigg| \qquad \frac{1 - 2.236}{4}$$

$$\frac{3.236}{4} \qquad \Bigg| \qquad \frac{-1.236}{4}$$

The values of the solution set rounded to the nearest tenth are {0.8, − 0.3}.

Solve each quadratic equation by using the quadratic formula. If the roots are irrational, give both the exact value and the rational approximation to the nearest tenth.

1.41 $x^2 + 5x + 4 = 0$ 1.42 $x^2 + 5x - 4 = 0$

1.43 $2x^2 - 3x - 1 = 0$ 1.44 $6x^2 - 5x - 6 = 0$

1.45 $2x^2 = 8x - 3$

1.46 $\dfrac{x^2}{3} + \dfrac{7}{12}x + \dfrac{1}{4} = 0$

1.47 $2x(x + 5) = 4$

1.48 $\dfrac{5x}{3} = x^2 + \dfrac{1}{2}$

1.49 $x(x + 8) = 9$

1.50 $\dfrac{x^2}{6} = \dfrac{x}{2}$

A quadratic equation can also be solved using another method when $Ax^2 + Bx + C$ is factorable. This method requires the use of a simple, yet important property.

PROPERTY

$M \bullet N = 0$ means that $M = 0$ or $N = 0$ (or both).
This property is called the *Zero-Product Property*.

Model 1: $x(x - 2) = 0$ means that the first factor x equals 0, or the second factor $x - 2$ equals 0, or both factors equal zero.

$x = 0$ $\quad x - 2 = 0$

$\qquad\qquad x = 2$

The solution set is {0, 2}.

Model 2: $(x + 1)(2x + 3) = 0$ means that
$x + 1 = 0 \quad\mid\quad 2x + 3 = 0$
$\quad x = -1 \quad\mid\quad\quad 2x = -3$
$\qquad\qquad\mid\qquad\quad x = -1.5$

The solution set is {-1, -1.5}.

The following steps can be used to solve a quadratic equation by the factoring method.

1. Write the quadratic equation in general form.
2. Find the factors of $Ax^2 + Bx + C$.
3. Apply the Zero-Product Property.
4. Solve for x.

These steps will be indicated by number in the solutions to the next three models.

16

Model 1: Solve $11x = 4 - 3x^2$ by factoring.

1. $3x^2 + 11x - 4 = 0$

2. $(3x - 1)(x + 4) = 0$

3. $3x - 1 = 0 \quad | \quad x + 4 = 0$

4. $3x = 1 \quad | \quad x = -4$

$\quad x = \dfrac{1}{3}$

The solution set is $\{\dfrac{1}{3}, -4\}$.

Model 2: Solve $5x^2 - 20 = 0$ by factoring.

1. $\dfrac{5x^2}{5} - \dfrac{20}{5} = \dfrac{0}{5}$

$\quad x^2 - 4 = 0$

2. $(x + 2)(x - 2) = 0$

3. $x + 2 = 0 \quad | \quad x - 2 = 0$

4. $x = -2 \quad | \quad x = 2$

The solution set is $\{-2, 2\}$.

Model 3: Solve $(x + 4)(x + 5) = 8$ by factoring.

1. $x^2 + 9x + 20 = 8$

$\ x^2 + 9x + 12 = 0$

2. The trinomial $x^2 + 9x + 12$ is prime, so you cannot use the factoring method.

Find the value of x by using the quadratic formula, where A is 1, B is 9, and C is 12.

$$x = \frac{-9 \pm \sqrt{9^2 - 4 \cdot 1 \cdot 12}}{2 \cdot 1}$$

$$x = \frac{-9 \pm \sqrt{81 - 48}}{2}$$

$$x = \frac{-9 \pm \sqrt{33}}{2}$$

The exact roots are $\dfrac{-9 + \sqrt{33}}{2}$, $\dfrac{-9 - \sqrt{33}}{2}$.

The roots to the nearest hundredth are -1.63, -7.37.

Note: You could also have used the completing-the square method to solve $x^2 + 9x + 12 = 0$.

✸ ✳ ✳ Solve each quadratic equation by factoring.

1.51 $x^2 + 3x - 4 = 0$

1.52 $2x^2 + x = 0$

1.53 $4x^2 - 11x + 6 = 0$

1.54 $7x^2 - 63 = 0$

1.55 $6x^2 = 13x + 5$

1.56 $9x^2 = 7x$

1.57　　$\dfrac{4}{5}x^2 = 2x - \dfrac{4}{5}$　　　　　　　　　　　1.58　　$(x + 4)(x - 3) = 8$

1.59　　$4x^2 - 25 = 0$　　　　　　　　　　　1.60　　$(x + 5)(x + 3) = 3$

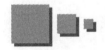 **Solve each quadratic equation. Factor when possible; otherwise complete the square or use the quadratic formula. For irrational roots give both the exact forms and the rational approximations to the nearest hundredth.**

1.61　　$3x^2 + 5x - 2 = 0$　　　　　　　　　　　1.62　　$3x^2 - 5x - 2 = 0$

1.63 $3x^2 - 5x + 2 = 0$

1.64 $x^2 - 49 = 0$

1.65 $x^2 - 50 = 0$

1.66 $2x^2 + 7x + 4 = 0$

1.67 $2x^2 + 7x - 4 = 0$

1.68 $\dfrac{x^2}{4} - \dfrac{x}{3} = \dfrac{1}{2}$

1.69 $\quad \dfrac{x^2}{4} - \dfrac{x}{3} = 0$ $\qquad\qquad$ 1.70 $\quad (2x + 1)(3x + 2) = 1$

✦ ✦ ✦ ✦ ✦ ✦ **VERBAL PROBLEMS** ✦ ✦ ✦ ✦ ✦ ✦

Several types of verbal problems can be solved using quadratic equations. Study the set-ups and solutions of the following models carefully. Be sure that each result is reasonable for the conditions of the original problem before you give the final answer(s).

Model 1: $\qquad$ The sum of the squares of two consecutive negative integers is eighty-five. Find the numbers.

Let n and $n + 1$ be the consecutive negative integers.

Number	Square	Sum
n	n^2	
$n + 1$	$(n + 1)^2$ or $n^2 + 2n + 1$	$n^2 + n^2 + 2n + 1$

Thus, the quadratic equation for this problem is

$2n^2 + 2n + 1 = 85$.

Solve: $\quad 2n^2 + 2n - 84 = 0$

$\qquad \dfrac{2n^2}{2} + \dfrac{2n}{2} - \dfrac{84}{2} = 0$

$\qquad\qquad n^2 + n - 42 = 0$

$\qquad\qquad (n + 7)(n - 6) = 0$

$n + 7 = 0$	$n - 6 = 0$
$n = \text{-}7$	$n = 6$
and $n + 1 = \text{-}6$	and $n + 1 = 7$

21

Since the conditions of the problem indicate that the integers are to be negative, we must reject the pair of numbers 6 and 7.

∴ The desired integers are -7 and -6.

Model 2: The length of a rectangle is two centimeters more than four times its width, and its area is one hundred ten square centimeters. Find the dimensions of this rectangle.

w | Area is 110 sq. cm

$4w + 2$

Since the area of a rectangle is found by multiplying its width by its length, the quadratic equation for this problem is $w(4w + 2) = 110$.

Solve:
$$4w^2 + 2w = 110$$
$$\frac{4w^2}{2} + \frac{2w}{2} = \frac{110}{2}$$
$$2w^2 + w = 55$$
$$2w^2 + w - 55 = 0$$
$$(2w + 11)(w - 5) = 0$$

$2w + 11 = 0$	$w - 5 = 0$
$2w = -11$	$w = 5$
$w = -\frac{11}{2}$	and $4w + 2 = 22$
and $4w + 2 = -20$	

Since the length and width of a rectangle must be positive, we must reject the dimensions $-\frac{11}{2}$ by -20.

∴ The dimensions are 5 cm by 22 cm.

 Solve each verbal problem with a quadratic equation using your choice of methods for solving each equation.

1.71   The sum of the squares of two consecutive negative integers is forty- one. Find the numbers.

1.72   The sum of the squares of three consecutive positive even integers is one hundred sixteen. Find the numbers.

1.73   The square of a number is equal to seven times that number less ten. Find the number. (Hint: Two numbers will satisfy this condition; include both numbers in your final answer.)

1.74   The square of a number exceeds that number by twelve. Find the number (two answers).

1.75   The length of a rectangle is three inches more than twice its width, and its area is sixty-five square inches. Find the dimensions.

w | A = 65 sq. in.

$2w + 3$

1.76   The width of a rectangle is two-thirds of its length, and its area is two hundred sixteen square meters. Find the dimensions.

$\frac{2}{3}l$ | $A = 216 \ m^2$

l

1.77   The width and length of a rectangle are consecutive odd integers. If the length is increased by five feet, the area of the resulting rectangle is sixty square feet. Find the dimensions and the area of the original rectangle.

1.78   Find two negative factors of ninety-six such that one factor is four less than the other.

1.79   Find two factors of negative thirty-six such that one factor is eleven less than half of the other factor. (Hint: You should have two pairs of factors.)

1.80   The square of a certain positive irrational number is equal to two more than half of that number. Find the exact value of the number and find the value of its approximation to the nearest thousandth.

Review the material in this section in preparation for the Self Test. The Self Test will check your mastery of this particular section. The items you missed on this test will indicate where restudy is needed for mastery.

SELF TEST 1

Indicate (by *yes* **or** *no***) whether each of the following equations is quadratic. If so, give the values of** A**,** B**, and** C **from the general form of each equation; if not, tell why** (each part, 3 points).

1.01 $2x^2 - 4x + 1 = 0$ _____ ; _____

1.02 $x(x^2 + 1) = 0$ _____ ; _____

1.03 $5(4x + 2) = 3$ _____ ; _____

1.04 $(x + 3)(x + 4) = 5$ _____ ; _____

1.05 $-\frac{3}{4}x^2 + 2 = 0$ _____ ; _____

Apply the Square Roots Property of Equations to find each solution set (each answer, 3 points).

1.06 $x^2 = 9$ 1.07 $(3x - 1)^2 = 5$

1.08 $x^2 + 5x + 1 = 0$ 1.09 $2x(x - 1) = 3$

Solve each quadratic equation by using the quadratic formula. If the roots are irrational, give both the exact value and the rational approximations to the nearest tenth (each problem, 4 points).

1.010 $3x^2 + 4x - 2 = 0$ 1.011 $\dfrac{x^2}{3} + \dfrac{1}{2} = \dfrac{5}{6}x$

Solve each quadratic equation by factoring (each answer, 3 points).

1.012 $7x^2 + 3x = 0$ 1.013 $(x - 2)(x - 3) = 2$

Solve each verbal problem with a quadratic equation using your choice of methods for solving the equation (each answer, 5 points).

1.014   The square of a certain negative number is equal to five more than one-half of that number. Find the number.

1.015   The width and the length of a rectangle are consecutive even integers. If the width is decreased by three inches, then the area of the resulting rectangle is twenty four square inches. Find the dimensions of the original rectangle.

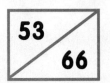

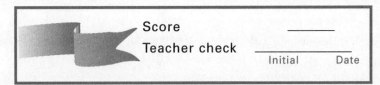

Score _____

Teacher check _____

Initial   Date

28

II. A REVIEW OF ALGEBRA: PART I

OBJECTIVES

When you have completed this section, you should be able to:

4. Work representatives problem of the first-year algebra course.

This section is a review of the first five mathematics LIFEPACs dealing with algebra. Ten representative samples have been selected from the self tests of each LIFEPAC. The corresponding self test numbers are given in parentheses to help you locate the section of the LIFEPAC where each concept was presented. Be certain to restudy any section for which you have trouble doing a review activity.

VARIABLES AND NUMBERS

(Mathematics LIFEPAC 901)

You will often use the distributive property to change a product to a sum (or difference). Sometimes you can simplify the result by combining like terms. An exponent indicates the number of times that the base is to be used as a factor.

Work the following problems.

2.1 (1.03) Multiply $8(3 - 2x)$. _____

2.2 (1.06) Simplify $6(x + 2) + 7$. _____

2.3 (1.013) Evaluate $(3 + 4)^2$. _____

2.4 (1.016) Evaluate $N^2 + 2N + 1$ for $N = 5$. _____

2.5 (1.018) Write this phrase in algebraic form: The difference of 3 squared and 5 times a number.

_____

To evaluate an expression, replace any variable (letter) with the value assigned to it. Then add, subtract, multiply, or divide to find the final answer. Remember to evaluate terms with exponents first. Then multiply or divide, and then add or subtract.

Evaluate each expression for $A = 5$, $B = -2$, $C = 4$, **and** $D = -6$.

2.6   (2.026) $C + D - B$ _____

2.7   (2.021) $5B^2$ _____

2.8   (2.027) $\dfrac{A \bullet C \bullet D}{B}$ _____

Changing a product to a sum is the reversal of changing a sum to a product. When you change a sum to a product, place the common factors outside the parentheses and the remaining factor inside the parentheses. Then simplify the expression if possible.

 Change the following expressions as indicated.

2.9   (2.045) Change to a sum: $5(-8 + P)$.   _____

2.10   (2.048) Change to a product: $5R - 2R$.   _____

 **SOLVING EQUATIONS AND INEQUALITIES**

(Mathematics LIFEPAC 902)

You probably remember that the absolute value of any number is always nonnegative. Conditional, or open, sentences are algebraic sentences that may be true or false depending on the value of the variable. To solve an equation, use the distributive property to remove any parentheses, and then solve for the variable.

Sentences that use the equal sign are called equations. Sentences that use the less than symbol (<) or the greater than symbol (>) are called inequalities.

 Work the following problems. Work in the space below each problem and circle your answers.

2.11   (1.06) Evaluate $5\,|7 - 9| - 2$.

2.12   (1.021) Solve $3x - 1 = 20$.

2.13   (1.028)   Solve $\frac{1}{4}x + \frac{3}{4} = 1$.

2.14   (2.015)   Solve $\frac{-x}{8} = -5$.

2.15   (2.017b)   Evaluate $I = prt$ for $p = 3{,}000$, $r = 0.07$, and $t = 3$.

2.16   (2.038)   Solve $5(2x - 6) + 3(2x - 8) = 0$.

2.17   (2.040)   Solve $P = 2l + 2w$ for l.

2.18   (3.025)   Solve $3(x + 2) > x$.

2.19   (3.029)   Graph the solution of $|x| = 2$.

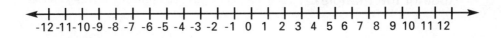

2.20   (3.035)   Graph the solution of $|x| + 3 > 7$.

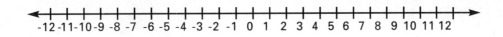

To translate phrases into mathematical symbols, look for clue words such as *sum, difference, product, quotient, more than, increased by, diminished by, twice, divided by, cube of,* and *is equal to.* These words indicate the operation or operations that will be used to solve the word problem.

 Write this word expression in mathematical symbols.

2.21   (1.012) "The quotient of y and 6 increased by 4."

_____

To solve word problems, or verbal problems, use the four-steps system:

1.   Identify the unknown number; choose a variable for it.
2.   Write an equation or inequality.
3.   Solve the equation or inequality.
4.   Identify your answer, label it, and check it for conditions stated in the problem.

 Use the four steps to solve each problem.

2.22   (2.011) The quotient of a number and 3 is the same as the difference of the number doubled and five. What is the number?

_____

2.23   (2.016) A triangle has an area of 144 sq. in. and a base of 2 ft. What is the altitude of the triangle?

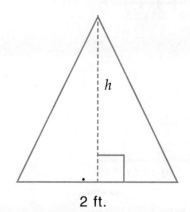

2 ft.

MATHEMATICS

9 1 0

LIFEPAC TEST

$$\frac{61}{76}$$

Name _____

Date _____

Score _____

MATHEMATICS 910: LIFEPAC TEST

Work the following problems (each answer, 3 points).

1.   Multiply $9(3 - 2x)$.   _____

2.   Evaluate the expression $2A - B^2 + 3C$ for $A = -3$, $B = 4$, and $C = 6$.

        _____

3.   Write this word expression in mathematical symbols: the quotient of b and 4 increased by 3.

        _____

4.   In which quadrant is the point (2, -4) located?

        _____

5.   Solve this equation by completing the square: $x^2 + 5x - 5 = 0$.

        _____

6.   Solve this equation by using the quadratic formula: $2x^2 + x = 15$.

        _____

1

7.   Solve this equation by factoring: $6x^2 - 24 = 0$.

Indicate by *yes* or *no* whether this equation is quadratic. If so, give the values of A, B, and C from the general form of the equation; if not, tell why (each part, 3 points).

8. $y(y + 4) - y = 6.$ _____ ; _____

Work the following problems as indicated (each answer, 4 points).

9.   Solve $4(3y - 2) + 5(y + 8) = 0$.

        _____

10.   Mentally find the quotient of $(36j^3 - 24j^2 - 18j) \div 6j$.

        _____

11. $\dfrac{d - 3}{6d} + \dfrac{d^2 + 4d + 2}{18d^2} =$ _____

12.   Simplify $\dfrac{4 - \sqrt{3}}{\sqrt{15}}$.   _____

13.   Solve $\sqrt{3x + 1} - 2 = 3$.   _____

14.   Solve this system by the most convenient algebraic method: $x = -2y + 6$
                                                                    $3x = 4y + 8$

2

Complete these activities as indicated (each numbered item, 5 points).

15.   Factor $4n^2 - 21n - 18$. _____

16.   Graph the solution of $|x| - 8 > 2$.

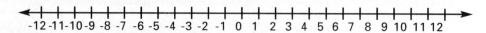

17.   Graph the solution of $x > |y + 2|$.

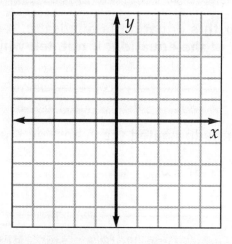

Solve these verbal problems; check your work (each problem, 5 points).

18.   The area of a triangle is one-half times the base times the height. If the area of a triangle is 54 sq. in. and its height is 12 in., what is the base?

_____

19.   The sum of the digits of a two-digit number is 9. The number formed by interchanging the digits is 27 less than the original number. Find the original number and its reversal.

a. original number _____

b. reversal _____

3

2.24   (2.018)   A boy has a total of $0.93 in pennies, nickels, dimes, and quarters. He has two more quarters than dimes. If he has as many nickels as dimes and if he has as many pennies as quarters, how many of each coin does he have?

_____

2.25   (3.010)   Joe's age is 4 years less than twice the age of his brother Tom. The sum of their ages of 41. Find the age of each one.

a. Joe's age _____

b. Tom's age _____

2.26   (3.012)   Sharon and Ken drove to the service station at 60 km per hour. They returned home by bicycle at 15 km per hour. The entire trip took 4 hours. How far was the round trip?

_____

2.27   (3.017)   Marvin can exert a force of 180 lbs. How heavy a rock can he lift if he uses a crowbar that is 5 ft. long and if he places the fulcrum so that it is 6 in. from the rock?

_____

2.28   (4.01)   If 18 is decreased by 6 times the sum of 4 and twice a number, the result is 15 more than three times the sum of the number and 5. Find the number.

_____

2.29   (4.07)   A sum of $3,500 is invested in two parts. One part brings a return of 5% and the other brings a return of 8%. The total annual return is $250. Find the amount invested at each rate.

_____

2.30   (4.08)   How many pounds of seed worth 60 cents a pound must be mixed with 300 pounds of seed worth 35 cents a pound to produce a mixture worth 50 cents a pound?

_____

POLYNOMIALS

(MATHEMATICS LIFEPAC 904)

The terms of a polynomial arranged in ascending powers are arranged so that the exponents of a particular variable increase in size. The terms of a polynomial arranged in descending powers are arranged so that the exponents of a particular variable decrease in size.

To add or subtract polynomials make sure that terms are like terms and then add or subtract. To find the product of a monomial and a polynomial, multiply the monomial by each term in the polynomial. Be careful with the sign of each term in the answer. To find the product of polynomials, use the distributive property.

$$x^2 \quad 2a^3$$
$$y$$
$$3a^2 + a - 2$$
$$a$$

Use the appropriate properties for powers to find the product of terms with exponents. Property 1 is $A^M \bullet A^N = A^{M+N}$; if the bases are the same, then the product is found by keeping that base and adding the exponents. Property 2 is $(AB)^M = A^M \bullet B^M$; if a product is raised to a power, then each factor is raised to that power. Property 3 is $(A^M)^N = A^{MN}$; if a power is itself raised to a power, then the result is found by keeping the same base and multiplying the exponents.

To divide polynomials, use Property 4. Property 4 is $A^M \div A^N = A^{M-N}$; if the bases are the same, then the quotient is found by keeping the base and subtracting the exponents

Monomials are divided by finding the quotient of their numerical factors and the quotient of their literal factors.

To divide a polynomial by a monomial, divide each term of the polynomial by the monomial. Be careful with the sign of each term in your answer.

To divide a polynomial by another polynomial, be sure that both the divisor and the dividend are written in descending powers of a variable. If the dividend has a missing power, you may want to insert a zero term or leave a space in its position. Then divide by the step-by-step procedure similar to long division in arithmetic.

 **Work the following problems.**

2.31   (1.011)   Write $4x^2 + x^4 + 3x^3 + 2x$ in descending powers of x.

_____

2.32   (1.014)   Mentally find the sum of the polynomials $ax + by + c$, $2ax - 3by + c$, and $by - c$.

_____

2.33   (2.03)   Mentally find the difference of $11y^3 - (-5y^3)$.

_____

2.34   (2.010)   Find $-x^2 + 10$ less than 0.

_____

2.35   (2.014)   Using the polynomials $Q = 3x^2 + 5x - 2$, $R = 2 - x^2$,
                    and $S = 2x + 5$, find $Q - (R + S)$.

_____

2.36   (3.011)   Simplify $b(a + b) - a(a - b)$.

_____

2.37   (3.012)   Mentally find the product of $(y^2)^5 \bullet y^8$.

_____

2.38   (3.017)   Mentally find the product of $(2p + 7)(3p - 9)$.

_____

2.39   (4.016)   Mentally find the quotient of $(35n^3 - 30n^2 + 25n) \div (-5n)$.

_____

2.40   (4.017)   Find the quotient of $(10b^2 + b - 1) \div (2b + 3)$ by long division.

_____

(MATHEMATICS LIFEPAC 905)

The greatest common factor (GCF) of two or more expressions is the largest value that will divide each expression exactly. The GCF for numerical terms, literal terms, and polynomials may be found by listing all the factors or by prime factorization. If no common factor exists, then the GCF is 1.

Binomials can be multiplied by the use of *FOIL* (mentally multiply the *first* terms together, the *outer* terms together, the *inner* terms together, and the *last* terms together). Only the final product should be written. The reversal of this procedure gives a method for factoring trinomials. To find the correct factors, choose factors so that the sum of the outer product and the inner product equals the middle term of the trinomial.

Sometimes the product of two binomials is not a trinomial, as in $y^2 - 9$. This kind of binomial is called a difference of two squares. In general, $A^2 - B^2 = (A + B)(A - B)$. Therefore, $y^2 - 9$ factored is $(y + 3)(y - 3)$.

 Work the following problems about factors or factoring.

2.41   (1.01)   List all the factors (positive integral divisors) of 48.

_____

2.42   (1.06)   Find the greatest common factor of $8a^3b^2$ and $12ab^4$.

_____

2.43   (1.09)   Factor $3a^3 + 7a^5$.

_____

2.44   (2.06)   Factor $n^2 + 7n - 44$.

_____

2.45   (2.010)   Factor $8n^2 - 26n + 15$.

_____

2.46   (2.014)   Factor $49t^6 - k^8$.

_____

2.47   (3.012)   Factor the four-term polynomial $mn - 15 + 3m - 5n$.

_____

2.48   (3.016)   Factor $2ay^2 + 5ay - 3a$.

_____

2.49   (3.019)   Factor $-2y^4 + 8y^2 + 90$.

_____

2.50   (3.020)   Factor $75n + 3n^3$.

_____

Review the material in this section in preparation for the Self Test. This Self Test will check your mastery of this particular section as well as your knowledge of the previous section.

SELF TEST 2

Work the following problems as indicated (each problem, 3 points).

2.01   Simplify $8(x - 3) + 14$.

_____

2.02   Evaluate $\dfrac{P \bullet Q}{2R}$ for $P = 4$, $Q = -2$, and $R = 2$.

_____

2.03   Evaluate $V = lwh$ for $l = 6$, $w = 4$, and $h = 3.5$.

_____

2.04   If a triangle has sides of x, $2x$, and $3x - 1$, what is the perimeter?

_____

2.05   Write this polynomial in ascending powers of r: $4r^2 + r^3 - 5r + 3$.

_____

2.06   Solve this equation by completing the square: $3x(x + 4) = 5$. Circle your answer.

2.07   Solve this equation by using the quadratic formula: $x^2 + 4x - 11 = 10$. Circle your answer.

_____

2.08   Solve this equation by factoring: $(x - 4)(x - 6) = 1$. Circle your answer.

Indicate by _yes_ **or** _no_ **whether each of the following equations is quadratic. If so, give the values of** $A, B,$ **and** C **from the general form of each equation; if not tell why** (each part, 3 points).

yes or _no_

2.09 $(x + 3)(x - 4) = 8$ _____ ; _____

2.010 $x^3 + 7 = 0$ _____ ; _____

Work these problems (each answer, 4 points).

2.011   Evaluate $5 |16 - 20| + 3$.

_____

2.012   Find the product of $m^2 \cdot (m^3)^4$.

_____

2.013   Find the quotient of $(3g^2 + 14g + 8) \div (g + 4)$ by long division.

Solve these items as indicated (each item, 5 points).

2.014   Write this word expression in mathematical symbols: The product of two and the square of a number added to seven.

_____

2.015   Graph the solution of $|x| - 4 < 5$.

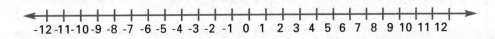

2.016   Solve this problem. Amy is 4 years older than her brother Steve. In 5 years Steve will be four-fifths as old as Amy. What are their ages now?

_____

2.017   Factor $6a^4 + 18a^3 + 12a^2$.

_____

2.018   Factor $64y^2 - 9$.

_____

2.019   Find the greatest common factor (GCF) of $4c^2d^4 + 12c^3d$.

_____

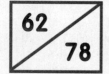

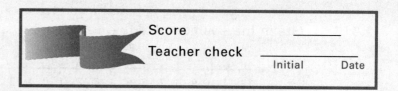

Score _____

Teacher check _____
                Initial   Date

III. A REVIEW OF ALGEBRA: PART II

OBJECTIVES

When you have completed this section, you should be able to:

4. Work representative problems of the first-year algebra course.

In this section you will review the last five mathematics LIFEPACs dealing with algebra. Ten representative samples have been chosen from the self test of each LIFEPAC, with the corresponding self test numbers given for each problem. Again, work carefully and restudy any section with which you have trouble.

 **ALGEBRAIC FRACTIONS**

(MATHEMATICS LIFEPAC 906)

The excluded value(s) of a fraction are the value(s) that would result in zero for the denominator. Since a fraction indicates division and division by zero is undefined, the denominator cannot be zero.

To reduce a fraction to lowest terms, find the greatest common factor of the numerator and the denominator. Remember that when you are reducing fractions that contain variables with exponents, you must subtract the exponents.

 Work the following problems.

3.1   (1.02)   Give the excluded value(s) for the fraction

$$\frac{y + 5}{y^2 + 4y - 32} .$$

3.2   (1.04)   Reduce the fraction $\frac{6a^2b^3}{8ab^4}$ to lowest terms.

The procedure for adding or subtracting algebraic fractions is done in these five steps:

1.   Determine the LCD from the prime factorization of the denominator of each fraction.

2. Change each fraction to an equivalent one having the LCD for its denominator.

3. Find all numerator products.

4. Write a single fraction made up of the combined numerators over the LCD.

5. Reduce, if possible.

The procedure for multiplying or dividing algebraic fractions is the same as for multiplying or dividing arithmetic fractions. Reduce the result to lowest terms. Polynomials, however, must be factored before any reducing is done.

To solve an equation or inequality that contains fractions, first eliminate the fractions by multiplying both sides of the open sentence by the LCD of all the fractions. Then solve the open sentence by the procedure you learned before. The main difference between solving equations and solving inequalities is that the inequality sign is reversed when both sides are multiplied or divided by a negative number.

A formula is written by solving for the desired subject; use the properties of equations as usual.

To solve any verbal problem, organize the given information into an equation that fits the problem. Then solve the problem.

 **Perform the indicated operations.**

3.3   (1.08) $\dfrac{d + 3}{8d} - \dfrac{2d + 1}{10d^2}$

_____

3.4   (1.012) $\dfrac{k + 5}{k^2 + 3k - 10} \div \dfrac{7k + 14}{4 - k^2}$

_____

3.5   (2.08)   Solve $\dfrac{x}{5} - \dfrac{x}{6} = \dfrac{1}{3}$.

_____

3.6   (2.012)   Solve $\dfrac{y}{4} - \dfrac{y - 1}{2} \geq 3$.

_____

3.7 (2.015) Rewrite the formula $V = \frac{Bh}{3}$ with h as the subject.

_____

■ ■ ■ **Solve these verbal problems. Show your work and circle your answer.**

3.8 (3.010) Two people together can do a certain job in twenty minutes. If one of them can do the job alone in forty-five minutes, how long will the other person take to do the job alone?

_____

3.9 (3.013) Find two consecutive even numbers such that the difference of one-half the larger number and two-fifths the smaller number is equal to five.

_____

3.10 (3.017) A mixture contains five quarts of acid and water and is forty per cent acid. If the mixture is to be weakened to thirty per cent, how much water must be added?

_____

RADICAL EXPRESSIONS

(MATHEMATICS LIFEPAC 907)

Fractions can be converted to decimals by dividing the numerator by the denominator. Repeating decimals can be converted to fractions by letting a variable equal the decimal. Then multiply the decimal by 10^1 if the period is 1, by 10^2 if the period is 2, by 10^3 if the period is 3, and so on. Subtract the original decimal from the multiplied decimal. Solve for the variable and reduce the fraction to lowest terms.

Radical expressions are in the form $\sqrt[N]{A}$, read "the Nth root of A," where N is the index, A is the radicand, and $\sqrt{}$ is the radical sign. Be careful if the index is even (square roots, fourth roots, and so on) because the radicand cannot be negative. For example, $\sqrt{-25}$ is undefined for real numbers since no real number exists whose square is -25 (or any other negative number). Irrational numbers are graphed by graphing their approximations on a number line.

Radical expressions can be added or subtracted only when they are like radicals; the radicals must have the same root index and the same radicand.

The three requirements for simplified radical expressions are these:

1. No square factor other than 1 can be in a radicand.

2. No fraction can be within a radical sign.

3. No radical can be in a denominator.

When a fraction has a radical in the numerator and the denominator or in the denominator only, the procedure used to simplify the fraction is called rationalizing the denominator. To do this procedure, multiply the numerator and the denominator by a radical that will eliminate the radical from the denominator.

To find a rational approximation for an irrational root, find the infinite nonrepeating decimal, perform any indicated operations, and round the resulting decimal to the desired accuracy.

Go by the following steps to solve a radical equation:

1. Isolate the radical expression containing the variable on one side of the equation.

2. Square both sides of the equation to eliminate the radical.

3. Solve for the variable.

4. Check the root in the original equation.

 Work the following problems.

3.11   (1.03)   Convert $\frac{19}{16}$ to its equivalent decimal form.

_____

3.12   (1.05)   Convert $0.\overline{72}$ to its equivalent (reduced) fraction form.

_____

3.13   (1.020)   Draw the graph of $|h| \geq \sqrt{13}$.

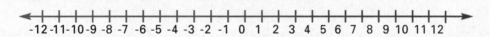

3.14   (2.08)   Find $\sqrt{36a^{10}b^2}$.

_____

3.15   (2.011)   Simplify $-\frac{2}{3}\sqrt{63x^3}$.

_____

3.16   (2.016)   Simplify $\sqrt{45} + \sqrt{20} - \sqrt{5}$.

_____

3.17   (2.025)   Simplify $\dfrac{8 + \sqrt{6}}{\sqrt{2}}$.

_____

3.18   (3.011)   Solve $\frac{M}{2} - \sqrt{5} = 3$ for its exact irrational root and its rational approximation to the nearest hundredth.

3.19   (3.014)   Solve $\sqrt{2y - 1} - 1 = 2$.

3.20   (3.017)   Solve $a + 1 = \sqrt{b + 1}$ for b.

The real-number plane is made up of two reference lines, called axes, that meet at a common zero point called the origin. These two axes, the x-axis and the y-axis, divide the plane into four quadrants. The quadrants are labeled starting with Quadrant I on the upper right, moving counterclockwise to Quadrant II, Quadrant III, and Quadrant IV. The x-axis (the horizontal line) is numbered with negative numbers to the left of the origin and positive numbers to the right of the origin.

The y-axis (the vertical line) is numbered with negative numbers below the origin and positive numbers above the origin.

The x-intercept of a line is the x-value of the point where the line crosses the x-axis. The y-intercept of a line is the y-value of the point where the line crosses the y-axis. The x- or y- intercept is found by letting the other variable have a value of 0.

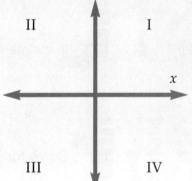

The slope of a line is found by first locating two points on the line. Then find the difference of the y-values (Δy) and the difference of the x-values (Δx). The slope of the line $= \frac{\Delta y}{\Delta x} = \frac{\text{rise (or drop)}}{\text{run}} = \frac{\text{vertical change}}{\text{horizontal change}}$. This fraction should always be simplified.

When you graph an equation of a line with one variable, find at least three points, even though two points determine a line, so that you can check to see if the points are collinear (all on the same line). Then plot the points and draw a line through them with a straightedge. Graphing an inequality is the same as graphing an equation, except for the following three steps:

1. Replace <, >, ≤, or ≥ by = to find the boundary.

2. Make the line dashed when < or > and make the line solid when ≤ or ≥ .

3. Shade the half-plane whose points satisfy the original inequality.

Remember that the absolute value, | |, of a number is always nonnegative. When you work with open sentences with two variables, look for a V-graph. If the open sentence is an inequality, test points "inside" and "outside" the dashed or solid V-graph to determine which region to shade.

To write the equation of a line through two points, find the slope of the line first. Choose another point (x, y) on the line and find the slope between point (x, y) and one of the other two known points. Since the slope of a line is constant, the slopes will be equal. Cross-multiply and write the resulting equation in general form ($Ax + By + C = 0$, where A, B, and C are integers and A is positive).

When a line is vertical, the slope is undefined. The equation of a vertical line is $x - K = 0$, where K is the abscissa of any point on the line. When a line is horizontal, the slope is zero. The equation of a horizontal line is $y - K = 0$, where K is the ordinate of any point on the line.

▶ ▶ ▶ **Solve the following problems.**

3.21   (1.02)   In which quadrant is the point (-3, 5) located?

_____

3.22   (1.012)   Translate the sentence, "The abscissa less the ordinate is one," to an equation.

_____

3.23   (1.016)   Solve for y: $2x + 3y = 10$.

_____

3.24   (2.020)   Find the x-intercept and the y-intercept of the line corresponding to the equation $5x - 2y = 10$.

a. x-intercept _____

b. y-intercept _____

3.25   (2.018)   Find the slope of the line corresponding to the equation $5x + 2y + 1 = 0$.

slope _____

50

3.26   (2.028)   Graph $x - 2y = 4$.

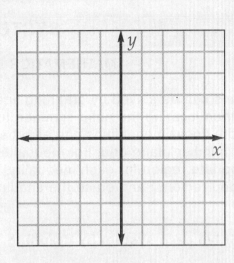

3.27   (2.029)   Graph $x + y \leq 1$.

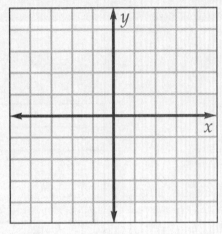

3.28   (2.035)   Graph $y \leq |x + 2|$.

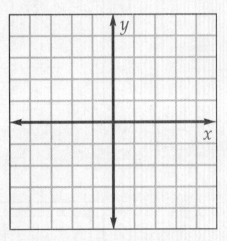

3.29   (3.01)   Write the equation of the line through (3, 2) and (-4, 5).

_____

3.30   (3.08)   Write the equation of the vertical line through (6, 1).

_____

51

SYSTEMS

(MATHEMATICS LIFEPAC 909)

Systems can be solved by graphing linear equations on the same number-plane grid and then locating the point common to each equation. Systems made up of two or more linear inequalities can also be solved by graphing each inequality on the same number-plane grid. For inequalities, use dashed or solid lines and shade the appropriate region for each inequality. Then find the common points (the common shaded regions) and erase the shading of the noncommon points.

 **Solve each system by graphing.**

3.31 (1.07) $x - y = 4$
$x + y = 2$

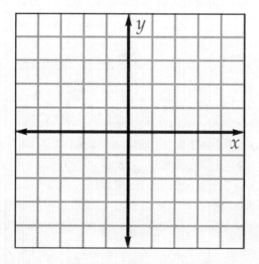

3.32 (1.010) $y = -3$
$x - y = 8$

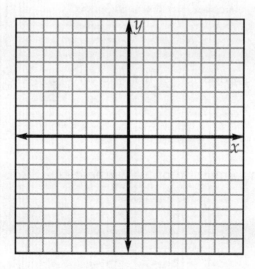

3.33　(1.013)　　$2x + y < 1$
$$y > -4 - 2x$$

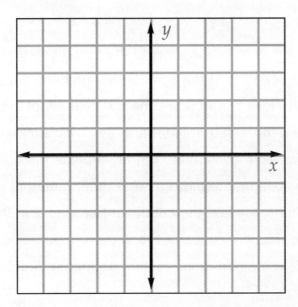

Since solving systems by graphing is often inconvenient, inaccurate, or both, we use other methods to solve systems. One way to eliminate (temporarily) one variable from a system is by the opposite-coefficients method. In this method you combine like terms of the equations when the coefficients of one of the variables are opposites. If the coefficients of one of the variables are the same, subtract one equation from the other; or find the least common multiple (LCM) of the coefficients of one variable and multiply the terms in each equation by the number that will make opposite coefficients. For all methods of solving systems, as in graphing, the solution should be written as an ordered pair (x, y) and should be checked in the original equations to make sure the x- and y-values satisfy both equations.

Another way to eliminate a variable from a system is by the comparison method. In this method you solve for that variable in each equation and form an equality of the results.

A third way to eliminate a variable from a system is by the substitution method. In this method you solve for that variable in one equation and use the result in place of that variable in the other equation.

Another method of solving linear systems is the determinants method. This method is optional; therefore, if you have not solved systems by this method, go ahead to the activities.

To solve a system using determinants, write the equations in determinant form ($Qx + Ry = F$ and $Sx + Ty = G$). Find the system determinant, which is $d = \begin{bmatrix} Q & R \\ S & T \end{bmatrix} = QT - RS$ where Q and S are the coefficients of x and R and T are the coefficients of y. Then find the x-determinant and the y-determinant. The x-determinant is $d_x = \begin{bmatrix} F & R \\ G & T \end{bmatrix}$ where the constants F and G replace the coefficients Q and S in the x-column of the system determinant. The y- determinant is $d_y = \begin{bmatrix} Q & F \\ S & G \end{bmatrix}$ where the constants F and G replace the coefficients R and T in the y-column of the system determinant. The solution values of x and y are found from the ratios $x = \frac{d_x}{d}$ and $y = \frac{d_y}{d}$. This method is the fastest and most direct way for solving many linear equations.

 **Solve each system algebraically by the most convenient method.**

3.34   (2.06) $3x + y = 6$
$x - y = 6$

3.35   (2.011) $y = 2x + 3$
                         $y = 4x + 6$

3.36   (2.013) $2x + 3y = 6$
                           $x + 2y = 4$

3.37   (3.015) $7x - 2y = 4$
                           $3x + 5y = 10$

Some verbal problems can be solved by using systems of two linear equations with two variables. Each system can then be solved by any of the algebraic-solution methods you have learned. Try to choose the easiest method for each pair of equations.

Write the answer in a verbal form (instead of an ordered pair) and include any units for each result, such as fourteen *years old*, nine *inches*, and so on. The types of verbal problems, or word problems, are number, age, coin, digit, fraction, and miscellaneous problems (such as motion, investment, mixture, perimeter, and combination problems).

Solve the following word problems. Check your work.

3.38　　(3.018)　　The sum of the digits of a two-digit number is 12. The number formed by interchanging the digits is 54 more than the original number. Find the original number and its reversal.

　　　　　　　　　　　　　　　a. original number　　　_____

　　　　　　　　　　　　　　　b. reversal　　　_____

3.39　　(3.019)　　The length of a rectangle is 2 more than 3 times the width. If the perimeter is 100, find the length and width of the rectangle.

　　　　　　　　　　　　　　　a. length　　　_____

　　　　　　　　　　　　　　　b. width　　　_____

3.40   (3.020)   Dad is 4 times as old as his son Jim. In 10 years Dad's age will be 20 years more than twice Jim's age. Find their ages now.

a. Dad's age   _____

b. Jim's age   _____

♣ ♥ ♣ ♥ ♣ ♥ ♣ QUADRATIC EQUATIONS ♥ ♣ ♥ ♣ ♥ ♣ ♥

(MATHEMATICS LIFEPAC 910)

A quadratic equation is an equation that can be written as $Ax^2 + Bx + C = 0$, where A is not zero. In this LIFEPAC we are considering an equation to be in general form when A is positive and when A, B, and C are integers whose greatest common factor is 1.

 **Indicate by _yes_ or _no_ whether each equation is quadratic. If so, give the values of A, B, and C from the general form of the equation; if not, tell why.**

yes or _no_

3.41   (1.01) $2x^2 - 4x + 1 = 0$ _____ ; _____

3.42   (1.02) $x(x^2 + 1) = 0$ _____ ; _____

3.43   (1.03) $5(4x + 2) = 0$ _____ ; _____

Quadratic equations can be solved by three methods–by completing the square, by using the quadratic formula, or by factoring. These methods are explained in this LIFEPAC. Quadratic equations can also be used to solve verbal problems.

Solve each quadratic equation. When the roots are irrational, give only the exact values (in simplified radical form).

3.44   (1.06) $x^2 = 9$

3.45   (1.09) $2x(x - 1) = 3$

3.46   (1.010) $3x^2 + 4x - 2 = 0$

3.47   (1.011) $\dfrac{x^2}{3} + \dfrac{1}{2} = \dfrac{5}{6}x$

3.48   (1.012) $7x^2 + 3x = 0$

3.49   (1.013) $(x - 2)(x - 3) = 2$

 **Solve this word problem.**

3.50   (1.014)   The square of a certain negative number is equal to five more than half of the number. Find the number.

_____

   Before you take this last Self Test, you may want to do one or more of these self checks.
1. _____ Read the objectives. Determine if you can do them.
2. _____ Restudy the material related to any objectives that you cannot do.
3. _____ Use the SQ3R study procedure to review the material:
   a. **S**can the sections.
   b. **Q**uestion yourself again (review the questions you wrote initially).
   c. **R**ead to answer your questions.
   d. **R**ecite the answers to yourself.
   e. **R**eview areas you didn't understand.
4. _____ Review all activities, and Self Tests, writing a correct answer for each wrong answer.

SELF TEST 3

Work the following problems as indicated (each item, 3 points).

3.01   Evaluate $(5 + 1)^2$.   _____

3.02   Change to a product: $8s + 2s$.   _____

3.03   Give the excluded value(s) for $\dfrac{v^2 + 1}{v^2 - v - 6}$.

_____

3.04   Convert $\dfrac{7}{16}$ to its equivalent decimal form.

_____

3.05   Write the equation of the line that passes through the points (-4, 2) and (6, 8).

_____

3.06   Solve the equation $x^2 + 3x + 1 = 0$ by completing the square.

_____

3.07   Solve the equation $2x^2 - 7x + 4 = 0$ by using the quadratic formula.

_____

3.08   Solve the equation $4x^2 + 3x - 10 = 0$ by factoring.

Indicate by *yes* **or** *no* **whether each equation is quadratic. If so, give the values of** *A,* *B,* **and** *C* **from the general form of the equation; if not, tell why** (each part, 3 points).

3.09 $(x - 2)(x + 5) = 0$ _____ ; _____

3.010 $x(x^2 + 4) = 0$ _____ ; _____

Work the following problems. Circle your answer (each problem, 4 points).

3.011   Solve $\frac{4}{7}y + \frac{2}{7} = 6$.

3.012   Solve $A = \pi r^2$ for π.

3.013   Using the polynomials $J = 5x^2 + 3x - 2$, $K = 2x^2 + x - 4$, and $L = x^2 - 7x + 8$, find $J + K - L$.

3.014   Simplify $\sqrt{3} - \sqrt{12} + \sqrt{27}$.

3.015   Solve the system $\begin{array}{l} 4x + y = 9 \\ x - 3y = -1 \end{array}$ by the most convenient algebraic method. Check your work.

Complete these activities (each answer, 5 points).

3.016   A girl has $0.78 in pennies, nickels, dimes, and quarters. She has as many quarters as dimes, one less nickel than dimes, and one more penny than dimes. How many of each does she have?

_____

3.017   List all the factors (positive integral divisors) of 64.

_____

3.018   Factor the four-term polynomial $pq - 24 + 6p - 4q$.

_____

3.019   Find two consecutive even numbers such that the sum of one-sixth the larger number and one-fourth the smaller number is two less than one-half the smaller number.

_____

3.020   Graph the equation $2x - y = 6$.

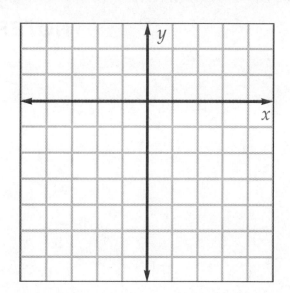

3.021   One-fifth the perimeter of a building is 50 feet. The length of the building is 30 feet longer than the width. Find the dimensions of the building.

_____

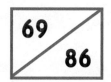

69 / 86

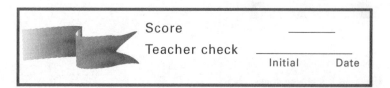

Score _____

Teacher check _____
                Initial   Date

   Before taking the LIFEPAC Test, you may want to do one or more of these self checks.

1. _____ Read the objectives. Check to see if you can do them.
2. _____ Restudy the material related to any objectives that you cannot do.
3. _____ Use the SQ3R study procedure to review the material.
4. _____ Review activities, Self Tests, and LIFEPAC Glossary.
5. _____ Restudy areas of weakness indicated by the last Self Test.

NOTES